Young Israel of Woodmere
51st Annual Dinner

Honoring

Rabbi Dr. Aaron and Margie Glatt
GUESTS OF HONOR

Alan and Gloria Stern
AMUD CHESED AWARD

David and Aviva Weber
AMUD AVODAH AWARD

Moishe and Erica Dachs
NEW LEADERSHIP AWARD

May 8, 2011 ⌒ Iyar 4, 5771

⌒ *Dedicated by* ⌒

Bini and Adam Dachs	*Melanie and Yehuda Konig*
Rachel and Ari Ellenberg	*Rachel and Jonathan Marks*
Dana and Jeremy Frenkel	*Tami and Ben-Zion Radinsky*
Estee and Noam Greenberg	*Devora and Nathaniel Rogoff*
Lisa and Elie Hecht	*Bonnie and Kenny Sicklick*

Tamar and Andrew Sicklick

דרוש דרש יוסף

Discourses *of*
Rav Yosef Dov Halevi Soloveitchik
on the Weekly Parashah

RABBI AVISHAI C. DAVID

Preface by
RABBI MENACHEM GENACK

OUPRESS

URIM PUBLICATIONS

YESHIVA
TORAT
SHRAGA

JERUSALEM · NEW YORK

Printed in Israel
First Edition
ISBN 978-965-524-046-7
Typeset by Ariel Walden

Urim Publications
P.O.Box 52287
Jerusalem 91521
Israel

Lambda Publishers Inc.
3709 13th Avenue
Brooklyn, New York 11218 U.S.A.
Tel: 718-972-5449, Fax: 718-972-6307
mh@ejudaica.com

Orthodox Union Press
11 Broadway, New York
NY 10004
www.ou.org

Yeshiva Torat Shraga
40 Baruch Duvdevani
Bayit Vegan, Jerusalem
Israel 96428

www.UrimPublications.com

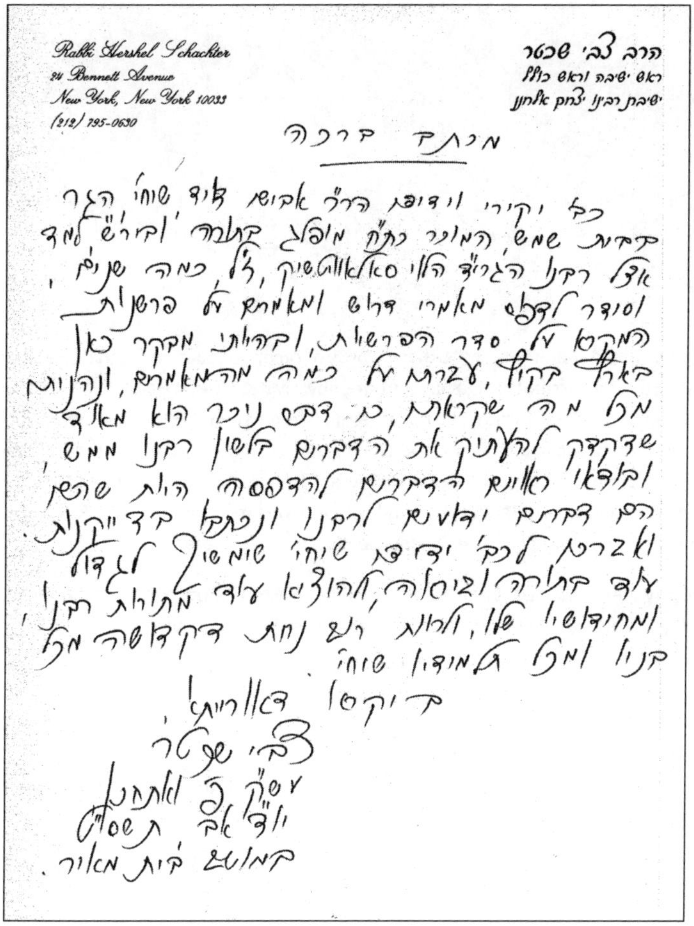

Rabbi Hershel Schachter
24 Bennett Avenue
New York, New York 10033
(212) 795-0630

בהא ג' שבט
ראו שמ"ש ואו מברכ מלב
שיבת רבני צהק אטון

אבני קודש

[Handwritten Hebrew letter]

M Y DEAR AND HONORABLE FRIEND, Harav AVISHAI DAVID who lives in Beit Shemesh is known as an outstanding Torah scholar and God fearing person. He learned under the tutelage of Rav YOSEF DOV HALEVI SOLOVEITCHIK z"l for a number of years and has compiled for publication essays of a homiletic, philosophical and exegetical nature on each of the Parshiyot of the Torah that he heard from the Rav (Rav YOSEF DOV HALEVI SOLOVEITCHIK). In the course of a summer visit to Eretz Yisroel, I reviewed a number of these essays and I enjoyed all that I read. It is patently clear that the author was exceedingly careful to transmit the content utilizing the precise terminology of our Rebi. Certainly, the ideas are eminently worthy of publication since they represent the well-known positions of our Rebi and were written with great precision. I would like to bless my friend the author that he should continue to grow in Torah and in the fear of God and to publish more from the Torah of our Rebi and from his own novellae, and to reap an abundance of nachat of sanctity from all of his children and students.

With the honor of the Torah
(Rabbi) TZVI (HERSHEL) SCHACHTER
Erev Shabbat Kodesh
Parshat Va'Etchanan
10th day of Av 5769
Moshav Beit Meir, Israel

Rabbi Hershel Reichman
Yeshivat Rabbenu Yitzchak Elchanan

It is with awe and trepidation that I write these words of recommendation for the compilation of Divrei Torat Harav ztz"l on the Parshiot Hashavua, authored by my dear friend Harav Avishai David Shlit"a. Awe, for the magnificent Divrei Torah recorded herein. Trepidation, for the Rav's words and ideas are words and ideas fit for a Malach Hashem, and we, his mortal students, shake with fearful emotion, lest they fall on our oftentimes deaf ears. The Rav's Divrei Torah are both profound and inspirational. They command us to respond with a deeper faith and with a stronger commitment to Torah. May the Almighty help us to respond fully to that charge so eloquently delivered.

May the Almighty bless Rabbi David for his remarkable rendition of our Rebbe the Rav's insights into the Parshiot. We thank him for sharing with us this immensely important contribution to Torah scholarship and Hashem Yisborach's service.

Respectfully,

Hershel Reichman

Hershel Reichman

Rosh Yeshiva, Yeshivat Rabbenu Yitzchak Elchanan

With great pride,
I dedicate this sefer by my Rav,
in loving memory of my first and greatest teacher,
my father,

יצחק טוביה בן נפתלי הערץ

He instilled in me a love for learning and respect for all the
values associated with עשה לך רב,
both of which Rabbi David helps me fulfill
through my association with him
and his בית כנסת - בית מדרש תורני לאומי
in בית שמש.

Mimi & Geoffrey Rochwarger

מוקדש לעילוי נשמתו של

שלום משה (מייקל) בן אברהם
סלסני ז"ל

(ל' ניסן תש"ל - ג' שבט תש"ס)

אהבת ה' בערה בלבו
בתורה התמיד בכל מאודו
נפטר בצעירותו
לאחר העלייה לארץ עם משפחתו
יהי זכרו ברוך

המשפחה
אותה כל כך אהב

In Memory of
Zev (Velvel) Citron
זאב בן משה אהרן ז"ל

Zev (Velvel) Citron was a sincere and pious Jew- a "pashut yid" in the most beautiful sense of the term. His life was dedicated to his community and to klal yisrael. He did whatever he could for his kehilla- he was the gabai, was constantly being mevaker cholim, ran the chevra kadisha, and on the yamim noraim he inspired everyone with his sweet melodious voice. He loved his fellow Jew and brought a smile to everyone's face through his friendly demeanor, and his uncanny ability to recall a story or joke that fit the particular situation.

In Memory of
Baruch (Benny) Javasky
ברוך בן יעקב הכהן ז"ל

Baruch (Benny) Javasky grew up in a small town in Poland in a home where learning Torah was not just the focus- it was everything. His father, a shochet, was a shas yid, and he himself was blessed with a sharp mind and excellent memory. Like many holocaust survivors he did not often talk about the past, but when he did, it was invariably about his joy in learning with his father, his being accepted to Yeshivas Kesser Torah in Cracow at a very young age, or about the constant hasmada in the yeshiva.

In memory of our fathers and mother
of blessed memory

Rabbi Joseph Schapiro
הרב יוסף שלמה בן הרב יעקב ע"ה

Mrs. Rosalee Schapiro
מרת שושנה לאה בת ר' שלמה צבי ע"ה

Mr. Aron Steinberg
הרב אהרן בן ר' שלמה הלוי ע"ה

May the Torah learned by those using this sefer
be a merit to their souls

Contents

CONTENTS

≈   SEFER SHEMOT

≈   SEFER VAYIKRA

SEFER BAMIDBAR

CONTENTS

Preface

THE OU PRESS is proud to be the publisher, together with Urim Publications and Yeshiva Torat Shraga, of *Darosh Darash Yosef: Discourses of Rav Yosef Dov Halevi Soloveitchik on the Weekly Parashah*, Rabbi Avishai David's collection of *shiurim* on Chumash delivered by the Rav *zt"l*.

Aside from imparting powerful insights into the *parshah*, the Rav was keen on providing tools to his students so that they should be equipped to approach the Torah on their own. As Rabbi David writes in *parashat Noach*, the Rav urged his listeners to read between the lines. We should understand what is implicit in the text as much as what is spelled out.

A remarkable expression of this idea was an insight the Rav had on the initial portion of Sefer Bamidbar culminating in the two *psukim* in *parashat Be'haalotcha*, bracketed before and after by an inverted letter *nun*, "*Vayehi bi'nesoa ha'aron . . .*" Rabbi Yitzchak Twersky, *zt"l*, the Rav's son-in-law, told me that the Rav's view of the structure of Sefer Bamidbar and the transitions in the narrative leading up to these two *psukim* represented what was perhaps the Rav's favorite insight in all of Chumash. In looking at the curious phenomenon of these two *psukim* bracketed by inverted *nun*s, the Rav focused on the statement by Chazal that these two *psukim* constitute a *sefer bifnei atzmo*, an independent book of the Torah, so that the Torah could be seen as having seven, rather than five books. Instead of

Sefer Bamidbar comprising one book of the Torah, in effect it comprised three – the portion before the two *psukim* of *"vayehi bi'nesoa ha'aron,"* the two *psukim* of *"vayehi bi'nesoa ha'aron"* bracketed by the inverted *nuns*, and the portion of Sefer Bamidbar after the two *psukim* (see *Shabbos* 137a).

In trying to understand the significance of Chazal's statement that these two *psukim* constitute a *sefer bifnei atzmo*, the Rav saw a unified theme being played out in *Parashat Beha'alotecha* instead of what appears on the surface to be a disjointed series of unrelated events. The Rav explained that, after receiving the Torah at Har Sinai, the Jewish people were seized by a great sense of anticipation and excitement. Reading the beginning of *Be'haalotcha*, one can sense the optimism, the accelerating tempo, the quickening tension and expectancy. We read of the clouds of glory that guide the nation on its inexorable forward path, the *chatzotzrot*, the trumpets that rally the people to action, the tribes' order of march. Confident that the final destination is at hand, Moshe invites his father-in-law Yitro to accompany them. *Bnei Yisrael* are mobilized for the journey; the sense of momentum is palpable. On the threshold of deliverance and final redemption, they are ready to enter the promised land. They could have merited *kefitzat haderech*, and God could have hurried them into Eretz Yisrael within three days. Triumphantly leading the people into the Land of Israel, Moshe would have been the *mashiach*, and he would have built a *Beit Hamikdash* that, through his participation, would have never been destroyed. Never would we have been thrust into exile; our inheritance of the land would have been permanent, our redemption everlasting, our glorious future secure. But all this was not to be. At that critical moment in our national destiny, the Jewish people suffered a failure of *emunah*, a lack of faith and self-discipline. They fell into a miasma of complaints, bickering, hedonism, which occupies the text of *Be'haalotcha* after the two *psukim* of *"vayhei bi'nesoa ha'aron."* The precious opportunity was lost. Entrance into the land was delayed for forty years, and Moshe was not permitted to lead the people into the land. The course of our history was irretrievably changed.

The two verses in *Parshat Be'haalotcha* represent the decisive point when our *emunah* failed and tragedy overtook us. The two inverted *nuns* symbolize the reversal of our fortunes – history was turned on its head. Instead of anticipation and triumph, there was only sadness and decline. Explaining the dictum of Chazal, the Rav said that the two verses constitute a *sefer* by itself because these were the first and last *psukim* in the *sefer* that Moshe *would have written* had history not taken the long and tragic turn that it did.

I later felt a proof for this point is the *halacha* cited in *Shabbos* (116a) that a worn out *sefer Torah*, a ספר תורה שבלה as long as it has 85 letters, retains the *kedusha* of a *sefer Torah*. The source for this *halacha* is this brief *parshah*, which contains 85 letters. It is considered a complete *sefer*, but it is also considered the *remnant* of a *sefer* – a *sefer* in which only the first and last *psukim* are present.

The book of the Torah represented by the two verses in *Parashat Be'haalotcha* is the "book of potential." It is the *sefer* of glorious triumphs that could have been written but wasn't, a mute testimony to the *geulah* that was in our grasp if only we had the courage and faith to reach for it. It remains for us to see that the book is written, to make explicit that which is implicit. In order to do this, one must first be sensitive to the unwritten text. As was noted above, in studying Chumash, it is important to "read between the lines," as often more is left unsaid than said. One needs great skill to bring into clear focus that which is only hinted at. Rabbi Avishai David is possessed of this skill, and with his talent, Rabbi David is helping to write the unwritten *sefer* described by the Rav. An exceptional educator and a close disciple of the Rav, he is the Rosh Yeshiva (head) of Yeshiva Torat Shraga in Yerushalayim. In *Darosh Darash Yosef*, he has skillfully culled together lectures and shiurim of the Rav as well as other material so that he provides us with teachings from the Rav on every *parsha* of the Chumash. His presentation of the Rav's profound thinking on Chumash is clear yet sophisticated. Rabbi David has done us all a great service in making available to a wider audience the the Rav's insight, creativity, and wisdom.

— MENACHEM GENACK
General Editor, OU Press

Introduction

THE *SHIURIM* OF my revered *rebbi*, Maran ha-Rav Yosef Dov ha-Levi Soloveitchik *zt"l*, were the most captivating *shiurim* that I was privileged to hear in my life. The excitement and heightened expectations that he engendered, together with his scintillating analysis, left one riveted and transfixed. In the course of his *shiurim,* we were catapulted to rhapsodic heights of *kedushah*. When my family lived in Providence, Rhode Island and in St. Louis, Missouri, in the late 1970s and early 1980s, I would drive to New York and back to hear the Rav's *yahrzeit* shiurim and *Teshuvah derashot*. I remember commenting to my wife on the way back that I felt as if I were soaring on the wings of eagles, having been wafted on a magic carpet of sorts. (See Exodus 19:4 and the commentary of the Targum Yonatan ben Uziel on that verse.)

I merited hearing the Rav's daily *shiurim* in the yeshiva for several years during the early and mid-1970s, and I was a staunch attendee of the *shiurim* in Congregation Moriah in Manhattan for over a decade. In the course of our peregrinations, we lived in Providence, Rhode Island, and for five years, between 1977 and 1982, I attended the Rav's *Humash shiurim* on *motza'ei Shabbat* in Boston, as well as many of the summer *shiurim* that he presented on various topics. The *Humash shiurim* published here are an amalgam of all of the aforementioned venues, but were drawn primarily from the shiurim in Boston on *motza'ei Shabbat*.

Those *shiurim* were delivered from after Sukkot until Pesah. I adapted the chapters of the other parshiyot from other *shiurim* that I heard or, in a small number of cases, that other students transcribed. The goal of this book is to make the major ideas of Rav Soloveitchik's *divrei Torah* on *Humash* accessible to readers with a range of Judaic backgrounds. I have not made an attempt to recreate the shiurim precisely as they were delivered, though I have tried my best to convey the flavor of the Rav's language and dramatic presentation.

Tosafot on BT *Hagigah* 15a cites a story from the Talmud Yerushalmi that relates that Abuya, the father of the sage Elisha, was one of the great Talmudic luminaries of Jerusalem. On the day of his son's circumcision, he summoned all the great scholars of Jerusalem and placed them in one house and Rabbi Eliezer and Rabbi Yehoshua in another location. As the guests ate and drank, sang, clapped and danced, Rabbi Eliezer and Rabbi Yehoshua said to each other: While the other group is doing as they like, let us occupy ourselves with words of Torah. A fire descended from heaven and encompassed them. Abuya asked them, "Did you come to start a fire and burn my house down?!" They answered, "God forbid! We were sitting and reviewing words of Torah, and we went from Torah to Nevi'im and from Nevi'im to Ketuvim, and the words were so joyous, as if we were at Sinai. Wasn't the Torah at Sinai given in fire?" One who attended a *shiur* of the Rav felt as if he were at Mount Sinai with the Torah descending in a ball of fire. The experience was joyous, uplifting and exhilarating, and left a powerful impression that we hope remains etched in our souls for eternity. I recall that during the *shiur*, I felt that an act of *beniyah*, building, was materializing before us as brick joined to brick and the towering edifice began to emerge in front of us.

My entire upbringing was founded upon the doctrine of *hakarat ha-tov* – gratitude. Although my parents, Netanel and Tzippora (Faige Rivka) David, *z"l*, never received a Torah education, they were steeped in Torah and possessed exemplary character traits of impeccable honesty and piety. They were practitioners of *hesed* par excellence. Their davening and tremendous care in the performance of mitzvot were models for all to emulate. I owe them a profound debt of gratitude for all that God has helped me to accomplish.

My in-laws, Avraham Yitzchak and Henna Cousin, *z"l*, were individuals whose *emunah* and *bitahon* in Hashem never faltered. Even though they experienced a great deal of adversity in their lives, their unwavering commitment to God and his Torah, and to the *kedushah* of Shabbat, were their shield.

For the past eight years, I have merited being the Rosh Yeshiva of Yeshivat Torat Shraga in Jerusalem. With great *siyata di-shmaya,* this yeshiva has achieved tremendous success. Its strength lies in its devoted *hanhalah* and outstanding *rebbeim,* whose love for their *talmidim* and commitment to their continued overall growth and spiritual prowess are legendary. It is a source of tremendous *nahat* for me to watch budding *bnei Torah* mature in their learning and *menschlichkeit* as well, and go on to become productive members of the Jewish community. I very much appreciate the fact that Yeshivat Torat Shraga is publishing this *sefer* jointly with Urim Publications and the OU Press under the dedicated stewardship of Rabbi Menachem Genack.

Simultaneously, I am blessed to be the rav of a *shul* in Beit Shemesh, Beit Midrash Torani Leumi, and have watched it blossom. The shul is primarily constituted of *olim* whose ideals prompted them to make aliyah. They are an outstanding cadre of *baalei batim,* exemplary role models, whose genuine *hesed* for their fellow Jews, indefatigable commitment to the study of Torah and earnestness and sincerity in *tefillah* have created a wonderful environment in which a rav may be a teacher, friend, guide and mentor. May they continue to be successful in all their endeavors and have much *nahat* from their wonderful families.

I would like to express my *hakarat ha-tov* to my beloved daughter, Ahuva Bracha, who spent countless hours typing this manuscript and who devoted herself to this project tirelessly for many years. Simultaneously, I am very grateful to one of my wonderful *talmidim,* Raphael Shorser, an alumnus of Yeshivat Torat Shraga, who invested untold hours of his time inserting the Hebrew text and correcting numerous typographical errors. His elaborate and precise comments reflect an incredible kindness on his part. All of the aforementioned labor was done with his usual *sever panim yafot* (friendly and amiable personality).

My heartfelt thanks are also extended to a wonderful friend, Geoff Rochwarger, who carefully proofread the entire text, combing it for typographical errors and enhancing it considerably with his own writing flair. His devotion to this project was distinctive, and I am very grateful to him for his outstanding efforts.

Above all, I would like to thank Rabbi Dr. Joshua Lipsitz, who volunteered to edit the work. He invested gargantuan efforts and many hours to make the work "reader- and user-friendly." His facility with language and felicity of expression are *sui generis*. He himself is a very fine *talmid hacham*, blessed with a keen mind. His advice, counsel and talent have proven to be a major boon to this work. His prodding and personal investment of time and energy helped bring this work to completion, and I thank him from the depths of my heart.

I would also like to thank my brothers, Menachem, Hillel, and Aaron, and my sister, Pearlie, for their support. I owe profound gratitude to my brother, Aaron, who has been a personal bulwark to me and a model for our entire family.

Simultaneously, I would like to honorably mention my wife's brother and sisters and their spouses.

Aharon aharon haviv, I am indebted to my wife, Chaya Leah, who has created a home where the warmth and light of Torah shine out from every corner and whose resoluteness and competence have enabled me to be successful as a rav, a *rosh yeshiva* and a *mehanech*. I am very proud of my children, Simcha Rafael and Brocha David, Dovid and Devora Rochel Greenwald, Yehuda Leib, Tzvi Dov and Bracha David, Ahuva Bracha, Eli and Esther Malka Rimler, Nechama Tova and Avraham Yitzchak, who, each in their own way, have blazed their own trails even as they followed in their illustrious forbears' footsteps. It is my prayer that we shall all merit many more years of success and nahat from our wonderful children and grandchildren.

I am profoundly grateful to Hashem Yitbarach for guiding me in my life. When I look back at the last several decades, I am absolutely amazed and thunderstruck at the incredible *hashgachah* of the Almighty and his kindness to our family. May we all continue to be the recipients of His wonderful beneficence, and may we be *zocheh* to witness the coming of *Mashiah,* speedily in our days.

— Avishai David

ॐ Sefer Bereshit

Bereshit: Aspects of Creation as Moral-Religious Imperatives

Often, we focus our attention exclusively on the text of the Torah, and do not sufficiently heed the spiritual message that it conveys. The Torah possesses a charisma of its own. It is not concerned only with the physical pragmatic performance of *mitzvot* but also with *Hovot ha-levavot*, the duties of the heart; our thoughts and feelings. The Rav explained how four specific features of creation, as described in Parashat Bereshit, convey a moral or religious lesson that we are challenged to internalize.

~ I Creatio Ex Nihilo

The first article of faith in the Rambam's *Mishneh Torah* is the principle of *yesh me-ayin* (creatio ex nihilo).[1] The Torah's position conflicts with that of Greek philosophy and modern science. There is no room for a reconciliation between these two diametrically opposed positions. Aristotle posited that matter is coexistent and coeternal with God. We contend that אדון עולם אשר מלך בטרם כל יציר נברא – God's existence was

---

1   See Rambam, Hilchot Yesodei ha-Torah, 1:1.

and is eternal, infinite, and boundless, and that he reigned before the creation of the universe.

The Torah uses various verbs to describe creation. *Bara* implies creation *ex nihilo,* while *yatzar* connotes *yesh mi-yesh,* an artist fashioning from existing raw material. The *Midrash Rabbah* cites the opinion of a philosopher who denied *creatio ex nihilo,* arguing that God utilized raw materials in the process of creation. Rabban Gamliel responded that God was responsible for creating those raw materials.[2] Scientists will always say that matter is coterminous with God, but science actually has nothing to say on these matters. This is a metaphysical issue, not a scientific one, and therefore my opinion is as good as Albert Einstein's.

We disagree with Mendelssohn's assertion in his work, *Jerusalem, Or On Religious Power and Judaism,* in which he contended that Jews should emphasize deeds rather than thoughts. There are cardinal principles in Judaism which are not merely theoretical, but are also moral precepts and norms that translate into practical deeds. One example is prophecy. Our belief is that God communicates directly with human beings. This is a basic tenet of Jewish faith that neither the pagan nor Christian world understands. No matter how transcendent God is, the ultimate telos of human beings is to make themselves worthy of prophecy. God communicates at the prophetic level only with those who have prepared themselves morally and ethically.[3]

So, too, the idea of *creatio ex nihilo* has moral implications. The Torah distinguishes between the first two chapters of Genesis in several ways. The first chapter uses the name *Elohim* to highlight God's omnipotence and His role as Architect and Maker of the universe. In the second chapter, the *Shem Havaya* (*hayah, hoveh ve-yihyeh*) emerges, emphasizing the

---

2 *Genesis Rabbah* 1:9 – פילוסופוס אחד שאל את רבן גמליאל אמר לו ציר גדול היה אלהיכם אלא מצא לו סימנים טובים שסייעוהו, אמר לו מה אינון, אמר ליה תהו ובהו וחשך ומים ורוח ותהומות, אמר ליה תיפח רוחיה דההוא גברא, כולם כת' בהם בריאה.

3 Mishneh Torah, Hilchot Yesodei ha-Torah 7:1.

fact that God not only created the world, but also carries and sustains it. The world exists because of God, and shares in His existence.

৵ II God as Mamtzi – Perpetual Sustainer

In the beginning of *Hilchot Yesodei ha-Torah,* the Rambam formulates a fundamental article of our faith:

לידע שיש שם מצוי ראשון, והוא ממציא כל נמצא, וכל הנמצאים משמים וארץ ומה שביניהם לא נמצאו אלא מאמתת המצאו.

> To know there is a Creator who creates all beings, and all of his created beings from the heavens and the earth, and that which is between them, only exist from the truth of his existence.[4]

The Rambam uses not the terminology of *bara* but rather *matza,* which implies not a single incident of creation but a continuous bestowing of existence. The Rambam interprets the divine name *Ehyeh Asher Ehyeh* as existence par excellence.[5] The *Shem Havayah* presupposes continuous creation. Man's ideal is to be attached to God. The entire universe clings to Him and finds itself in His embrace. *Elohim* was responsible for creating the world but the *Shem Havayah* sustains it and carries it like a nursing mother who protects her baby. The world was formless and inchoate until God fashioned it and he continues to constantly sustain it.

תסתיר פניך יבהלון תסף רוחם יגועון ואל עפרם ישובון.

> When You hide Your face, they are dismayed. When You retrieve their spirit, they perish, and to their dust they return.[6]

---

4 Rambam, Hilchot Yesodei ha-Torah 1:1.
5 Rambam, Guide for the Perplexed I:63. See Treasury of Tradition, Confrontation, 59.
6 Psalms 104:29.

Is there a source in Genesis for the notion that God is not merely a creator, but also sustains the world? Rabbenu Yona Ibn Ganach interprets the verse אשר ברא א־לֹהים לעשות[7] in the following way. If two Hebrew verbs appear consecutively, the first is a verb and the second is the infinitive. It is as if it were written "*asher bara Elohim ve-asah*" – that God created and (then) did. This means that the all important work of *ve-asah* began only after *bara* was completed.[8]

The verse that epitomizes this notion of sustaining the *beriyah* is the verse וירא א־לֹהים את כל אשר עשה והנה טוב מאד – "Elohim saw his handiwork and behold, it was very good,"[9] which indicates Divine approval of his creation. Approval indicates that God continues His active involvement in the world. Disapproval, on the other hand, would have resulted in *hester panim,* and then the world would have been subject to calamity.

וחרה אפי בו ביום ההוא ועזבתים והסתרתי פני מהם והיה לאכל ומצאהו רעות
רבות וצרות . . . ואנכי הסתר אסתיר פני ביום ההוא . . .

My anger will flare against it on that day. I will forsake them and I will conceal my face from them. They will become prey and many evils and troubles will befall them ... But I will surely have concealed my face on that day ...[10]

Divine justice is beyond our ken. As the *paytan* noted, גזרה היא מלפני קבלוה משעשעי דת יומים – "This is My decree. Accept it, you who delight in the two-thousand-year-old law."[11]

The Rambam maintains that we are obliged not only to have *emunah*

---

7 Genesis 2:3.
8 Similarly, the Torah with reference to Yom Kippur states: כי ביום הזה יכפר עליכם לטהר אתכם – "For on this day he will atone for you to purify you." Here we encounter a similar phenomenon of two consecutive verbs and it's as if it were written: "Ki ba-yom ha-zeh yechaper alechem ve-yitaher etchem" (For on this day he will atone for you and purify you).
9 Genesis 1:31.
10 Deuteronomy 31:17–18.
11 Piyut of the Ten Martyrs, from the Yom Kippur mussaf service, based on Proverbs 8:30.

in God, but to know him.[12] Knowing involves not only an intellectual awareness but also experiencing and feeling the presence of God. While most young children are taught to perform *mitzvot maasiot*, they do not have enough experience to appreciate davening or *Shabbat* or the exaltation and grandeur of Yom ha-Kippurim, which is predicated upon feeling God's presence. Young people are not lonely, even though they don't like to be alone. Middle-aged people are lonelier, and this sense of loneliness can be alleviated only by God's companionship. People mistakenly saw the Rav's grandfather, Rav Chaim Soloveitchik, as coldly brilliant, having brains and no heart. This was an egregious error, since Rav Chaim was possessed of a profound religious sensitivity. When Rav Chaim recited the Avodah service on Yom Kippur and reached the phrase *"Ve-ha-kohanim ve-ha-am,"* he saw himself in the *azarah* of the Beit ha-Mikdash. He was totally transformed by a deep longing and clear vision of what once was and now, unfortunately, is no longer.

III The Concept of Adnut

There is another idea embedded in Genesis over and above the notions of God as a creator and sustainer of the world. It is a legal category – God as Master and Lord of the world, a major theme of Judaism. לה' הארץ ומלואה תבל וישבי בה – "The earth and all that is in it belong to God,"[13] קנה שמים וארץ – "Maker of heaven and earth."[14] Halachically, God is the Craftsman who acquires ownership of the vessel he creates by virtue of his artisanship and innovative talent – אומן קונה בשבח כלי – "The artisan acquires the vessel by dint of his creative talent embedded in the vessel."[15] The divine name Elohim symbolizes creation, while Havayah is the idea of God as perpetual Sustainer – but Adon implies mastery. Avraham

---

12 Rambam, *Sefer ha-Mitzvot*, Mitzvat Aseh 1.
13 Psalms 24:1.
14 Genesis 14:19.
15 BT *Bava Kamma* 98b.

Avinu was the first to identify this attribute of God.[16] Adam ha-Rishon lacked understanding of this quality. Had he absorbed the doctrine of God's mastery over the universe, he could not have eaten from the *etz ha-da'at.* The offense was one of theft, for Adam had been placed in Gan Eden only in order לעבדה ולשמרה – "to cultivate it and to guard it."[17]

The Torah identifies the *dor ha-mabul* with the transgression of *hamas.* The generation of Nineveh was plagued with the same evil – ומן החמס אשר בכפיהם[18] – "and from the robbery that is in their hands." Our sages defined *hamas* as *gezel.*[19] Why is this crime so heinous that the Torah deems it *hashhatah* (corruption)?[20] In the *Neilah* service, the *paytan* refers to *oshek* as being the root of all sin that Yom Kippur is intended to cleanse.[21] Why is that sin singled out? The answer is that all sins are categorized under *oshek* because not only does the material world belong to God, but so does the entirety of our physical being – our bodies, nerves, energy, and knowledge. When a Jew commits a sin with one of his limbs, that limb loses the right to exist.[22] God gives human beings tenancy in their bodies. Once a limb deviates from its function

---

16 BT *Berachot* 7b. See Divrei Hashkafah of Rav Soloveitchik, "Adon kol ha-ma'asim," 11–19.
17 Genesis 2:15.
18 Jonah 3:8.
19 BT *Taanit* 16a, Targum on verse, as well as Rashi and Targum on Genesis 6:11.
20 Genesis 6:11.
21 Confession Liturgy of the Neilah Service, Yom Kippur.
אתה נותן יד לפושעים וימינך פשוטה לקבל שבים ותלמדנו ה' א-להינו להתודות לפניך על כל עונותינו למען נחדל מעשק ידינו ... אתה הבדלת אנוש מראש ותכירהו לעמוד לפניך כי מי יאמר לך מה תפעל ואם יצדק מה יתן לך ותתן לנו ה' א-להינו באהבה את יום הכפרים הזה קץ מחילה וסליחה על כל עונותינו למען נחדל מעשק ידינו ...
You stretch out a hand to willful sinners and Your right hand is extended to accept penitents. You taught us, Hashem our God, to confess before You regarding all our sins so that we may withdraw our hands from oppression ... You set man apart from the beginning and You considered him worthy to stand before you, for who can tell You what to do, and if he is righteous what can he give You? Now You gave us, Hashem our God, with love, this Day of Atonement, a deadline, pardon and forgiveness for all our iniquities, so that we may withdraw our hands from oppression ...
22 Ramban, Leviticus 1:9.

and a Jew sins, he forfeits that right of tenancy. This is termed *oshek*. Therefore, the concept of *oshek* is the foundation of all transgression.[23]

The three aforementioned principles: *creatio ex nihilo,* God as the perpetual Sustainer of the universe, and God as *Adon* – Master – are some of the fundamental moral mandates that we learn from Genesis. The midrashic and kabbalistic writings mention a fourth moral lesson, which complements and builds upon the three mentioned above: rebuilding from the ruins.

✣ IV Rebuilding from the Ruins

There is a possibility that the initial words, *"Bereshit bara Elohim,"* reveal that the theme of the verse is not a mere chronology of Creation. Rather, it hints at the idea that other worlds preceded this one. The author of the *Tiferet Yisrael* advances this theory in a commentary entitled *Or ha-Hayyim* at the end of Tractate *Sanhedrin.* It is based on a midrashic doctrine that this fourth world was preceded by three others.[24] Kabbalistically, this concept, which is called *shevirat ha-kelim,* is alluded to in the *parashah* at the end of *Vayishlah*:

ואלה המלכים אשר מלכו בארץ אדום לפני מלך מלך לבני ישראל.

Now these are the kings who reigned in the land of Edom before a king reigned over the children of Israel.[25]

This is also the intent of Rabbi Abahu: that God created worlds and destroyed them.

However, there is a fundamental problem with this *midrash*. A human being floats an idea and constantly toys with it and experiments until he

---

23 See *Reflections of the Rav,* "The Three Biblical Names of God," vol. I, 20.
24 Genesis Rabbah 3:7.
אר"י בר סימון יהי ערב אין כתיב כאן, אלא ויהי ערב, מכאן שהיה סדר זמנים קודם לכן, א"ר אבהו מלמד שהיה בורא עולמות ומחריבן, עד שברא את אלו, אמר דין הניין לי, יתהון לא הניין לי.
25 Genesis 36:31.

finds the correct model. Then, he manufactures it and then begins to disseminate it. But why does God, Who is omnipotent and omniscient, have any need to engage in any kind of experimentation?

The Ramban explains that the process of creation is a profound mystery that cannot be understood from the biblical text alone.[26] The whole story of creation mandates and speaks to the doctrine of *imitatio dei – "Ma hu, af ata."*[27] Just as the Almighty is compassionate, so must you be compassionate. Just as the Almighty is a creator, so must you be a creator.[28] We are creators via the mitzvah of פרו ורבו – procreation.[29] We are also bidden to combat evil and to heal maladies ורפא ירפא – "he shall provide for healing."[30] This directive also operates in the spiritual realm. A teacher who takes an ignorant and undisciplined child and provides him with direction and instills into him form and content is also engaged in the act of creating a full-fledged *yetzirah.*[31]

Parashat Bereshit challenges man to be a creator, but that isn't so difficult. To start a business from scratch and succeed is one challenge. But to go bankrupt and confront frustration and despair and then to pick oneself up and start anew – that is a formidable task of reconstruction. That is the secret of the greatness of Jewish history. Rabbi Akiva taught Torah to twenty-four thousand students, shaped their *weltanschaaung* and succeeded in producing a group of great scholars. Yet they perished within a short time.

The Talmud describes that state of affairs as והיה העולם שמם – "the world was in shambles and desolate."[32] Any ordinary person would have been crushed. But Rabbi Akiva persevered and prevailed until he

---

26 Ramban, Genesis 1:1.
27 BT *Sotah* 14a.
28 See *Halachic Man*, Joseph B. Soloveitchik.
29 Genesis 1:28.
30 Exodus 21:19.
31 See introduction to Menachem Genack, *Birkat Yitzchak*, for a discussion of the principle of "*Uman koneh be-shevah keli*" as it applies to a teacher-student relationship.
32 BT *Yevamot* 62b.

restored the glory of Torah to its former splendor. How did he do it? We don't know, but ultimately he engaged in *imitatio dei* – emulating God, who created worlds and destroyed them. Jewish history is replete with worlds that were created and then destroyed – Jewish communities and Torah scholars in Babylonia, the Byzantine Empire, Spain, Poland and Germany. Following the destruction of one world, a new world is born. Our survival, our ability to persevere in the face of hardship and to rebuild, are founded upon this midrashic principle of Rav Abahu, "He created worlds and destroyed them."[33] That is the saga of Jewish history as told in Parashat Bereshit.

33 Op. cit.

נח

Noah

THE RAV BEGAN the discussion of the parashah with a general statement relating to *parshanut ha-mikra,* specifically that of the Ramban. The modern methodology of conceptualization and classification in the realm of Halacha was introduced by the Rav's grandfather, Rav Chaim Soloveitchik. This methodology entails an appreciation that each word is an idea that must be properly defined and formulated. Rabbi Akiva Eiger, whose children testify about him, also foreshadowed the methodology of Rav Chaim. Rav Chaim, like Rabbi Akiva Eiger, was neither dismayed by the question nor elated at the answer. Most important for him was the proper formulation of the problem.

Rav Chaim wrote no commentary on Humash and Tanach. It is unfortunate that when we read Tanach, we do not try to read between the lines of the text, as we ought to do. We should try to gain insight into the world of the Humash and see the image that the sages projected. The best commentator for this is the Ramban, whose spiritual perceptions are extraordinary. The Ramban formulated a *weltanschaaung* in his commentary on the Torah even more than the Rambam did. The Rambam, who was highly educated and a scholar of philosophy, uses the philosophic concepts and jargon of his generation, which often obscures his unique and distinctive spiritual insights from us. On the other hand, the Ramban used more intuition than logic and was as a result very original and creative. Therefore, one must study the Ramban's commentary on the Humash in the same way that one studies the *Ketzot ha-Hoshen* and the *Netivot ha-Mishpat* on *Hoshen Mishpat*.

✌ The Migration of Terah

At the conclusion of Parashat Noah, the Torah describes Terah's departure from Ur Kasdim.

ויקח תרח את אברם בנו ואת לוט בן הרן בן בנו ואת שרי כלתו אשת אברם בנו ויצאו אתם מאור כשדים ללכת ארצה כנען ויבאו עד חרן וישבו שם.

Terah took his son Abram and Lot the son of Haran his grandson and his daughter in law Sarai, the wife of Abram his son, and departed with them from Ur Kasdim to go to the land of Canaan. They arrived at Haran and settled there.[1]

The relationship of this description of Terah's departure and God's command to Abraham to leave his homeland at the beginning of Parashat Lech Lecha several verses later is the source of a striking *mahloket* (argument) between Rashi and Ibn Ezra. In Lech Lecha, God commands Abraham to leave his land and his birthplace.[2] However, from the verses quoted above, it would seem that Abraham already left his birthplace, Ur Kasdim, at the end of Parashat Noah.

Rashi resolves the difficulty by reinterpreting the verse.

והלא כבר יצא משם עם אביו ובא עד לחרן, אלא כך אמר לו התרחק עוד משם וצא מבית אביך.

But had he not already departed from there and reached

---

1   Genesis 11:31.
2   Genesis 12:1.

Haran? Yet God told him: Separate yourself from there even more and leave your father's home [in Haran].[3]

According to Rashi's reconstruction of the verse, it reads "Go for yourself from your father's house, from your land and from your relatives." According to Rashi, the initial migration of Terah and his family from Chaldea to Haran was a voluntary decision that preceded the mitzvah of Lech Lecha chronologically.

The Ibn Ezra disagrees with Rashi. He rearranges not the verses, but the chronology, in line with the principle *"Ein mukdam u-meuhar ba-Torah."* The Ramban cites the Ibn Ezra as follows:

וכבר אמר ה' אל אברם לך לך מארצך, כי הדבור הזה היה בעודנו באור כשדים,
ושם צוהו לעזוב ארצו ומולדתו ובית אביו אשר שם.

God had already said to Abram: Depart from your land, since this command came to him when he was still in Ur Kasdim and it was there that he commanded him to leave his country, his birthplace and his father's house.[4]

According to the Ibn Ezra, the instructions to Abraham to leave Ur Kasdim (in Lech Lecha) were in fact revealed to him prior to Terah's migration to Haran. According to the Ibn Ezra, Parshat Lech Lecha begins with the verse:

וילך אברם כאשר דבר אליו ה' וילך אתו לוט ואברם בן חמש שנים ושבעים שנה
בצאתו מחרן.

So Abram departed, as God had commanded him, and Lot went with him. Abram was seventy-five years old when he left Haran.[5]

---

3 Rashi on Genesis 12:2.
4 Ramban on Genesis 12:1.
5 Genesis 12:4.

Thus, according to the Ibn Ezra, Terah's initial departure (in Parashat Noah) was actually according to God's command to Abraham (in Parashat Lech Lecha).

The Ramban is troubled by Ibn Ezra's explanation. If the departure followed the commandment of Lech Lecha, then Ibn Ezra would understand that Abraham, rather than Terah, was the major figure in the migration from Ur Kasdim. If this is so, however, why would the verse read: ויקח תרח את אברם בנו – "And Terah took Abram his son"?[6] The verse teaches us that Abram followed his father and that it was by his counsel that Abram left Ur Kasdim for Canaan. Wouldn't it be more accurate to give Abram full credit for initiating the move? For this reason, the Ramban rejects Ibn Ezra's approach.[7]

ꙮ The Spiritual Transformation of Terah

The Ibn Ezra can be understood if we first consider another mysterious aspect of Terah's life. Rashi, later in Parashat Lech Lecha, cites Hazal on the verse:

ואתה תבוא אל אבתיך בשלום תקבר בשיבה טובה.

As for you, you shall come to your ancestors in peace; you shall be buried at a good old age.[8]

Rashi seems astounded by the fact that Terah, Abram's father, is an idolater and God promises Abram that he will come to his ancestors in peace. According to Rashi, this meant that Terah would one day do *teshuvah*. Yet the verse in Sefer Yehoshua states:

ויאמר יהושע אל כל העם כה אמר ה' א־להי ישראל בעבר הנהר ישבו אבותיכם
מעולם תרח אבי אברהם ואבי נחור ויעבדו א־להים אחרים.

---

6 Genesis 11:31.
7 Ramban on Genesis 12:1.
8 Genesis 15:15.

Joshua said to the entire nation, "Thus says the Lord, the God of Israel: Your forefathers – Terah, the father of Abraham and the father of Nahor – always dwelt beyond the the river and served other gods."[9]

How are we to understand Terah's repentance in light of his relationship with Abraham? After all, prior to his change, his relationship with Abraham had been hostile. According to the sages, Terah had conspired with the local tyrant to destroy Abram both physically and spiritually.[10] He informed the king of Abram's "blasphemous behavior" and wanted Abram executed. If God had not intervened, he would have succeeded.

When a father's antipathy toward a son reaches the level of enmity, it is often psychopathological. While enmity towards a stranger is not always a sign of a sick mind or mental aberration, this kind of hostility between father and son is due to a "sick soul" and a personality permeated with hatred and insanity. Hazal therefore tell us the story of Terah's hostility towards Abram, for he saw his son destroying everything that he, Terah, had worked to accomplish. Then, suddenly, we hear that Terah repented. When did this wondrous transformation occur?

This change occurred precisely at the point when Terah decided to abandon Ur Kasdim and migrate to Haran. The decision to move was strange indeed, for Terah was a prominent citizen of Ur Kasdim. According to one aggadah, he was a member of the royal council, yet chose to depart suddenly.[11] We know through documentary evidence that Chaldean society was technologically sophisticated and highly developed and disciplined. A decision to emigrate from there to Haran, which was a primitive, pastoral, agriculturally undeveloped society, is surprising. One usually migrates from a lower civilization to a higher

---

9 Joshua 24:2.
10 Rambam, *Hilchot Avodat Kochavim,* Chapter 1; see *Genesis Rabbah* 38:28 (in some versions, 38:13).
11 See *Yalkut Me-Am Loez* on Genesis 11:28, section 11.

one. What motivated Terah to abandon the luxury of his origins and become a wanderer, a straying Chaldean?

The answer is *hirhurei teshuvah* – stirrings of repentance. Here, the patron of the idolaters, a well-known manufacturer of idols, revered and respected by everyone, suddenly abandons everything. Apparently, he realized that all he stood for was absurd and that his son Abram was correct, and Abram's ideas reflected the divine truth. He then reappears as a *baal teshuvah,* one who has repented, and is responsible for the move to Haran, towards Eretz Yisrael, to begin his life anew.

According to Ibn Ezra, the divine decree of Lech Lecha coincided with the transformation of Terah's personality. This was not coincidental. When the proper moment arrived, Terah was ready to uproot himself. God appeared to Abram and told him to set out. The Torah did not reveal to us how much Terah knew of Abraham's rendezvous with God, or whether he knew about it at all. In general, the Torah does not provide information that is irrelevant to the development of Knesset Yisrael.[12] What is significant is that when Abraham began his journey, he discovered that his father's bags were already packed. This dramatic moment sees the father and son, who formerly were locked in combat, now starting together on the march to Canaan.

Ramban's difficulty with the Ibn Ezra is now easily explained. Even though the order is rearranged and the mitzvah of Lech Lecha was given earlier (to Abraham), it still makes sense that Terah is described as the central protagonist at the end of Parashat Noah. This is because the Torah has a primary interest in the metamorphosis of Terah over and above Abraham's obedience to God's command. Therefore, the text

---

12 The Rav noted parenthetically that the Torah contains no information about Abraham's physiognomy. It reveals some physical characteristics of King David, King Saul, Rachel, Joseph and Sarah, where these details are pertinent to the story. Rarely does the Torah digress from its account of the development of the covenantal community. For example, in Joseph's search for his brothers, the Torah interrupts the encounter with the appearance of a mysterious person, but this digression is directly related to the realization of the covenant in which we and our descendants are participants.

emphasizes Terah's initiative even though God's command (to Abraham) of Lech Lecha preceded the family's migration. Abraham had only limited success with other individuals, such as Nahor and Lot. However, his success with his father was enduring – and extraordinary.

A great teacher must be capable of inspiring and convincing his own family. Abraham had a great vision to transmit. When he succeeded in converting his father, he receded momentarily into the background. The Rambam says that the obligation to honor one's parents applies even to a father who is wicked.[13] Although Terah had been wicked for much of his life, he became a great *baal teshuvah,* and Abraham was obligated to show him respect in any case. Terah, who initiated the move to Haran, is the hero at this point. His departure to Canaan is a heroic act. For now, Abraham stays in the shadows.

13 Rambam, *Hilchot Mamrim* 6:11.

לֶךְ לְךָ

Lech Lecha: The Magnetism of Kedusha

I N THE BEGINNING of *Parashat Lech Lecha,* the *Torah* states:

ויאמר ה' אל אברם לך לך מארצך וממולדתך ומבית אביך אל הארץ אשר אראך.

God said to Abram: Go for yourself from your land, from your relatives and from your father's house to the land that I will show you.[1]

Rashi notes that God did not show Eretz Yisrael to Abraham immediately in order to make it dear to him and to give him a reward for each utterance. The Rav pointed out that we find a similar phenomenon regarding another mission, *akedat Yitzhak.* First, God says, קח נא את בנך את יחידך אשר אהבת את יצחק – "Take your son, your only one, whom you love, Isaac,"[2] and then, in assigning the location, God says: והעלהו שם לעלה על אחד ההרים אשר אמר אליך – "and offer him as a burnt offering on one of the mountains that I will tell you."[3]

However, these two missions differ. In the context of the Akedah, Abraham knew the ultimate destination, the land of Moriah. Only the

---

1   Genesis 12:1.
2   Genesis 22:2.
3   Ibid.

identity of the mountain was not revealed to him. However, here in Lech Lecha, he was not given specific information. How, then, was he to know where to go?

In his commentary, the Ramban states as follows:[4]

היה נודד והולך מגוי אל גוי וממלכה אל עם אחר, עד שבא אל ארץ כנען ואמר לו לזרעך אתן את הארץ הזאת, אז נתקיים "אל הארץ אשר אראך," ואז נתעכב וישב בה. ומה שאמר ויצאו ללכת ארצה כנען, לא להתישב בה, כי עדיין לא ידע כי על הארץ ההיא נצטוה, אלא שאחז צדיק דרכו דרך ארץ כנען, כי כן היה בדעתו ובדעת אביו גם מתחלה בצאתם מאור כשדים. ומפני זה אמר ויהי כאשר התעו אותי א‑להים מבית אבי כי היה "תועה כשה אובד."

He [Abraham] wandered from nation to nation, from one kingdom to another people until he came to the land of Canaan, where he said to him, "To your seed will I give this land." Then the promise contained in [the verse] "to the land that I will show you" was fulfilled, "and Abraham tarried and settled there." The verse "They went forth to go to the land of Canaan" does not mean that they intended to settle there, since he did not yet know that he had been commanded concerning this particular land. Rather, the righteous one set out for the land of Canaan, for that was his intention as well as his father's when they originally departed from Ur Kasdim. This is the reason why Abraham later said, "And it came to pass, when God caused me to wander from my father's house, he was indeed gone astray like a lost sheep."[5]

Clearly, the Ramban was troubled by the fact that Abraham was not given a specific destination and was therefore left confused and perplexed. Why would God wish to bewilder and mystify him? God wanted Abraham to discover the Promised Land intuitively. It was essential that

---

4 Ramban on Genesis 12:1.
5 Psalms 119:176.

Abraham feel the pull of Eretz Yisrael. God wanted Abraham to be fascinated by the land and migrate to it, just as some species of fish migrate instinctively. God wanted Abraham to be guided not by the logic of his mind but by his intuition. In this way, God challenged Abraham to nurture his spiritual antennae, his ability to distinguish between *kodesh* and *hol*. Had Abraham erred at this juncture in his selection of the land, all would have been lost.

In our daily prayers, we say:

אתה הוא ה' הא־להים אשר בחרת באברם והוצאתו מאור כשדים ושמת שמו
אברהם ומצאת את לבבו נאמן לפניך וכרות עמו הברית לתת את ארץ הכנעני ...
לתת לזרעו ותקם את דבריך כי צדיק אתה.

You are God, who chose Abram and took him out of Ur Kasdim and conferred upon him the name Abraham and found his heart to be faithful to you. And you made a covenant with him to give him the land of Canaan ... to give to his descendants, and You kept Your word, for You are righteous.[6]

The sequence here is somewhat difficult as it suggests that God chose Abraham before he left Ur Kasdim. However, the verses convey the idea that the exodus from Ur Kasdim and the charge to discover the land would be the test that determined whether Abraham was indeed worthy of Divine attention and whether he would reach the heights of אב המון גוים – "The father of a multitude of nations."[7] In what sense, then, did God choose Abraham before he left Ur Kasdim?

Perhaps God also singled out Abraham before he left Ur Kasdim – in the charge of Lech Lecha itself. Apparently, Abraham guessed correctly and his spiritual compass directed him to the land of Canaan long before

---

6   From the daily *Tefillat Shaharit* service.
7   Genesis 17:4.

God appeared to him and said, לזרעך אתן את הארץ הזאת – "To your descendants I will give this land."[8]

What indeed was the element responsible for Abraham gravitating to Eretz Canaan? In response to what stimuli did he act? The answer is the most central theme in Judaism: *kedusha*. This was the profound discovery of Abraham. The notion of *kedushah* contrasted sharply with the existing value systems of the times, as embodied by *dor ha-mabul* and *dor ha-palagah* (the generations of the Flood and of the Tower of Babel, respectively).

Competing Value Systems

Major decisions in people's lives are often not a function of rational calculations but based on impulse and intuition.[9] People respond to stimuli and to powerful challenges. Adam and Eve were activated by the esthetic draw of the *etz ha-da'at*. ותרא האשה כי טוב העץ למאכל וכי תאוה הוא לעינים – "The woman saw that the tree was good for eating and that it was a delight to the eyes."[10] The generation of the flood, which was also goaded by the allure of beauty, saw the esthetic challenge as the major goal of humanity.

> ויהי כי החל האדם לרב על פני האדמה ובנות ילדו להם. ויראו בני הא־להים את בנות האדם כי טבת הנה ויקחו להם נשים מכל אשר בחרו.

> It came to pass when man began to multiply upon the earth and daughters were born to them, the sons of the rulers saw that the daughters of man were good and they took themselves wives from whomever they chose.[11]

Modern man is still a captive of beauty, not just symmetry. There is an

---

8 Genesis 12:7.
9 See *Reflections of the Rav*, vol. I. "Mt. Sinai – Their Finest Hour," 91–93.
10 Genesis 3:6. See *Guide of the Perplexed*, section I, chapter 2.
11 Genesis 6:1, 2.

entire world view revolving around man seeking only enjoyment in life, exploiting all of its opportunities and availing himself of all the various esthetic pleasures. This view gained expression in the campus revolts of the 1960s. These were marked by individuals who wanted to enjoy life without restraints or controls. The only moment that is considered meaningful is the fleeting present, not the jaded past or the unapproachable future.

The generation known as the *dor ha-palagah* also held a particular philosophy. Its members believed that human beings' great challenge is the attainment of power as reflected in technological achievement and ingenuity. Humanity, which controls its environment, should be worshipped. That generation was a technologically highly organized unit. Yet if a brick fell from the scaffolding, they grieved and lamented its disappearance, while remaining indifferent to the loss of human life. For them, human dignity was secondary to technological growth.[12]

Communist societies, which worship technological man as the being who orbited the earth and reached out for the infinite, are the quintessence of this philosophy. It holds that human beings want to triumph and become heroes, and hate defeat. Opposing it is Western society and culture, which is classic *dor ha-mabul,* bent on the pursuit of enjoyment, which is merely transient. To a certain degree, Western society celebrates the collapse of order and moral restraints.

ᴈ A World Order of Kedushah

Abraham proclaimed a new world order of *kedushah,* which is fascinating beyond the attraction of power or the allure of beauty. Abraham understood that humankind's deepest hopes and yearnings are not for power or esthetic enjoyment, but rather to find God and cling to Him.

---

12 See *Yalkut Shimoni, Parashat Noah,* 62:44 for a midrash that also indicates the underlying lack of unity and human sensitivity.

In this pursuit, personal success is not a *sine qua non,* and one may even endure defeat.

The impact of *kedushah* is complex. *Kedushah* is a dialectical process, an antithetical experience, that frightens people. Its nature is daunting even as its pull is magnetic. People who are not thinkers are frightened by it because they live in a world of clichés and platitudes. *Kedushah* presupposes and demands sacrifice and self-defeat. On the other hand, people with powerful imaginations and depth of thought and character are swept up by *kedushah* and drawn to their Creator instinctively and automatically. It was this innate sensitivity that God sought to sharpen and solidify within Abraham by challenging him to discover the *kedushah* of Eretz Yisrael and align himself with it using the navigational powers of his own heart.

In Psalms, King David pines for the Almighty: כאיל תערג על אפיקי מים כן נפשי תערג אליך א־להים – "As the deer longs for brooks of water, so my soul longs for you, O God."[13] Why did David choose the metaphor of the deer or gazelle? How does an animal in the thickets of the African jungle make its way towards a stream several miles away? Like the migratory pattern of birds and fish, the deer or gazelle is driven by an inexplicable instinct that does not pass until it reaches the brook. So, too, man is impelled instinctively and mechanically to reach out to his Creator, a quest that is both ineluctable and inevitable. Such was the drive of Abraham as he succeeded in finding the *Ribbono shel Olam* in the spring of *kedushah* that is Eretz Canaan.

---

13 Psalms 42:2.

Vayera I:
From Lech Lecha to Vayera:
Transcendence to Immanence

THE TORAH STATES in the beginning of Vayera:

וירא אליו ה' באלני ממרא והוא ישב פתח האהל כחם היום.

God appeared to him [Abraham] at the Terebinth of
Mamre as he sat at the entrance of his tent in the heat of
the day.[1]

Rashi comments that God came in order to fulfill the mitzvah of visiting a sick person. Rashi cites the Midrash: אמר רבי חמא בר חנינא יום שלישי
למילתו היה, ובא הקב"ה ושאל בשלומו – "Rav Hana ben Hanina says that it was
the third day after the circumcision, and God came to ask how Abraham
was feeling."[2] Rashi was troubled by the Torah's use of the pronoun *elav*
– "to him" – as opposed to אל אברהם – "to Abraham." The use of the
pronoun rather than the proper name implies that we are engaged in a
continuation of the previous subject. In this case, the previous subject

---

1 Genesis 18:1.
2 Rashi on Genesis 18:1.

45

was *brit milah* – Abraham's circumcision, which was described at the end of Parashat Lech Lecha.

What does the use of אליו intend to highlight? The Torah seeks to focus our attention on the contrast between the nature of the relationship with God in Lech Lecha and this relationship in Vayera. The previous parasha, which focuses on Abraham's circumcision, uses the name Elohim. After the circumcision, the name of God is shifted to the Shem Havayah. These various names of God in Lech Lecha, as opposed to the ones in Vayera, reflect a fundamental shift in the relationship between humanity and God, which was precipitated by the act of *brit milah*.

Different usages of the names of God imply different relationships. In Parashat Bereshit, the name Elohim appears in the context of the Creation. Elohim refers to God as immutable lawgiver, who introduced the fundamental laws of nature. *Shem Havayah,* on the other hand, emphasizes the unique nature of the relationship between God and humanity.

The journey of human beings to God through the name Elohim is longer and more circuitous than their journey to God via the Shem Havayah. With the *Shem Havayah,* man enjoys a privilege of intimacy and closeness with God. Elohim is God as the בעל הכחות כלם – Master of Power.[3] The cosmos exists because Elohim is the source of all physical existence. Organic matter follows natural law fashioned by Elohim, who caused the universe to function.

The quality of Elohim is embedded in the liturgy of Rosh ha-Shannah. We say:

כי אתה א־להים אמת ודברך מלכנו אמת וקיים לעד.

You are the true God and your words, our King, are truthful and exist forever.[4]

---

3 *Shulhan Aruch,* Orah Hayyim 5:1.
4 Rambam's order of prayers for Rosh ha-Shannah and the *nusah* used by Ha-Rav Soloveitchik.

46

Rosh ha-Shannah, the anniversary of the creation of the world, connotes permanent existence. Rosh ha-Shannah is the experience of the numinous; קדוש אתה ונורא שמך – "You are holy and your name is awe-inspiring."[5] *Shem Havayah* is different. It tells humankind, particularly Jews, to be like God and to be close to Him. Yom ha-Kippurim presents God not as King but as our Father in Heaven.

Consider the description of the revelation in Parashat Lech Lecha in the context of the *berit bein ha-betarim.* In Lech Lecha, the language and tone indicate fear and awe.

ויהי השמש לבוא ותרדמה נפלה על אברם והנה אימה חשכה גדלה נפלת עליו.

And it happened as the sun was about to set, a deep sleep fell upon Abram, and behold – a dread, great darkness fell upon him.[6]

The description of the revelation in Lech Lecha is also somewhat verbose compared to the succinct description in the beginning of Parshat Va-yera, וירא אליו ה' באלני ממרא – "God appeared to him in the plains of Mamre."[7] In Lech Lecha, the rendezvous with God obligates human beings to lose their own independent identity and self-awareness. In the presence of Elohim, human beings are frightened. They are overwhelmed with humility and a sense of their insignificance.

In Va-yera, God appears to Abraham as an intimate friend. On the verse והוא ישב פתח האהל כחם היום – "While he was sitting at the entrance to the tent in the heat of the day,"[8] Rashi comments:

ישב כתיב, בקש לעמוד, אמר לו הקב"ה שב ואני אעמוד, ואתה סימן לבניך, שעתיד אני להתיצב בעדת הדיינין והן יושבין, שנאמר א-להים נצב בעדת א-ל.

It is spelled without a *vav,* as if it read *yashav* – "sat." This

---

5 From the Rosh ha-Shannah liturgy.
6 Genesis 15:12.
7 Genesis 18:1.
8 Genesis 18:1.

teaches us that Abraham wanted to stand out of respect for the Divine presence. The Holy One, Blessed be He, said to him, "Sit and I will stand. You are a sign to your posterity, while I am destined to stand in the assembly of judges who sit, as it is written: 'God stands in the Divine assembly.'"[9]

The dialogue reflects a conversation that might occur between two intimate friends.[10]

✥ The Power of the Brit

What engendered the shift between Parashat Lech Lecha and Parashat Va-yera? Apparently, *brit mila,* the covenant between God and Abraham, signified a new relationship between them. Before, Abraham had been a great human being, but not yet a member of the covenantal community. Upon his circumcision, he became a member of the covenantal community, from within which he engages in dialogue with the Almighty. The Ramban on Genesis 48:15 encapsulates this friendship in his commentary on the verse:

ויברך את יוסף ויאמר הא־להים אשר התהלכו אבתי לפניו אברהם ויצחק הא־להים הרעה אתי מעודי עד היום הזה.

He blessed Joseph and said, "O God, before Whom my forefathers Abraham and Isaac walked, God Who has shepherded me my whole life to this very day . . ."[11]

---

9 Rashi on Genesis 18:1.
10 The beginning of Parashat Va-era (Exodus 6:3) reads as follows: וארא אל אברהם אל יצחק ואל יעקב בא־ל ש־די ושמי יהוה לא נודעתי להם – "I appeared to Abraham, Isaac and Jacob as El Shaddai [Almighty God], but I did not show myself to them as the Lord" [the Tetragrammaton]. Why did God reveal himself to Moshe, but not to the Patriarchs, by this name? The answer is that the Patriarchs believed and trusted in God with no need for proofs or assurances.
11 Genesis 48:15.

Ramban maintains that the word *ha-roeh* ("who shepherds") refers to "the God who befriended me at a young age."

According to the Kabbalists and hasidic masters, the *het ha-kadmon* (primordial sin of Adam and Eve) caused the immanent God to become transcendent and remote. The world was created to provide God with a "main residence," but the first human couple's transgression drove a wedge between God and His universe. A synopsis of this banishment appears in the verse

וישמעו את קול ה' א־להים מתהלך בגן לרוח היום.

They heard the sound of the Lord God manifesting Itself in the garden toward evening.[12]

The intimate relationship had been fractured. The goal of the covenant is to restore that intimacy.

Only owing to this covenant does tefillah (prayer) become comprehensible. Tefillah is founded on a dialogue and intimate conversation between ourselves and God. Abraham was the one who enacted tefillah. Our prayer services lack formal ceremony. Liberal Judaism had a tendency to introduce a cultic aspect to prayer via the introduction of the organ and highlighting the role of the rabbi or *hazan* to formalize the prayer service. In Catholic prayer services, the priest's role is indispensable. To us, ceremony is secondary – indeed, almost unnecessary. Two friends, confidants who know each other, can approach each other directly without fanfare or without having recourse to intermediaries. Prayer is not a drama or performance. Its only requirement is a pure and contrite heart.

This is the reason for bridging Lech Lecha with Va-yera with the pronoun אליו – to emphasize the transition from Elohim to Havayah, from transcendence to immanence. God told Abraham, in effect: You are indeed on a higher level than you were before. Instead of being

---

12 Genesis 3:8.

49

simply overwhelmed and humbled by the presence of Elohim, Abraham would now become God's partner and collaborator. This role would be continued by Abraham's children and all subsequent generations of the Jewish people.

This partnership is also the foundation of Jewish morality. The concept of *imitatio dei* – imitating God, which presumes a collegial rather than a merely subservient relationship – is the philosophy of behavior and moral code that serves as a supreme guide for our actions. Just as God clothes the naked, so should we. Just as God buries the dead, so should we. Just as God visits the sick and inquires into their welfare, as he did with Abraham, so should we.[13]

---

13 BT *Sotah* 14a.

⋟ וירא ⋞
Vayera II

⋟ Abraham's Reluctance regarding Brit Milah

ACCORDING TO RASHI, Mamre was the one who advised Abraham regarding *brit milah*. Why was it necessary for Abraham to get advice? Apparently, Abraham was somewhat reluctant to undergo *brit milah*. Why? His reluctance is also evident from the verses themselves. In the beginning of Chapter 17, the Torah states:

ויהי אברם בן תשעים שנה ותשע שנים וירא ה' אל אברם ויאמר אליו אני א־ל ש־די.

Abram was ninety-nine years old when God appeared to him and said, "*Ani El Shaddai* – I am God, the Almighty."[1]

Then, in verse 17, the text reads, ויפל אברהם על פניו ויצחק – "Abraham fell on his face and rejoiced."[2] When God revealed Himself to Abraham at other times – for example, when He told him to leave his homeland and at the *akedah* – there was neither dialogue nor delay. Abraham obeyed

---

1 Genesis 17:1.
2 Genesis 17:17.

immediately. Yet here, regarding the *brit milah,* Abraham questions God and engages Him in dialogue:

ויאמר בלבו הלבן מאה שנה יולד ואם שרה הבת תשעים שנה תלד. ויאמר אברהם אל הא־להים לו ישמעאל יחיה לפניך. ויאמר א־להים אבל שרה אשתך ילדת לך בן וקראת את שמו יצחק והקמתי את בריתי אתו לברית עולם לזרעו אחריו.

He thought: Shall a child be born to a hundred-year-old man? And shall Sarah, a woman of ninety, give birth? Abraham said to God, "If only Ishmael might live before you!" God said, "Nevertheless, your wife Sarah will bear you a son, and you shall name him Isaac. I will fulfill my covenant with him as an everlasting covenant for his offspring after him."[3]

✌ The Risk of Alienation

We can suggest the following explanation. The Midrash raises the following important issue:

אמר עד שלא מלתי היו באים ומזדווגים לי ... אמר לו הקב"ה אברהם דייך שאני א־לוהך.

He [Abraham] said: "Prior to my circumcision, they would come and join me ..." The Holy One, blessed be He, said to him, "It is sufficient for you that I am your God."[4]

Prior to his circumcision, Abraham was happily extroverted in his behavior. He mingled with others and gathered many adherents, with whom he communicated openly.[5] When God commanded him to become circumcised, Abraham became frightened that as a result, his extroverted nature would quickly erode. Circumcision would place an

---

3 Genesis 17:17–19.
4 Genesis Rabbah 46:3.
5 See Rashi on Genesis 12:5.

insurmountable barrier between him and his neighbors. He would be ostracized and a militant opposition would emerge, making him isolated and lonely – which could well undermine his mission to spread monotheism throughout the world.

The Midrash continues: רבי נתן ורבי אחא ורבי ברכיה בשם רבי יצחק אני א״ל ש״די God said to Abraham, אני א״ל ש״די התהלך לפני והיה תמים – "I am El Shaddai; walk before me and be perfect."[6] Rashi comments:

אני הוא שיש די בא־להותי לכל בריה, לפיכך התהלך לפני ואהיה לך לא־לוה ולפטרון.

I am He of whose Divinity there is enough for every creature. Therefore, walk before me and I will be your God and Patron.[7]

God assured Abraham by explaining that if one has a relationship with God, then one needs no one else in order to obtain fulfillment. In other words, God said to Abraham, "You may lose others, but you will never lose Me." The name Shaddai is a composite term and contains the word *dai,* enough, limiting the expansion that would have otherwise continued.[8]

The text in the beginning of *Va-yera* hints that Abraham's worries may have been justified. In the past, people had flocked to him. Now, after his circumcision, people seemed to be deserting him. This is evidenced by the fact that Abraham set up a chair outside his tent in order to watch for wayfarers.

Abraham was actually not reluctant to perform the mitzvah of circumcision. He simply wanted to understand the goal and the reason. At first, he thought that his mandate was to convert the entire world, and that his mission was primarily a universal one as *av hamon goyim,*[9] the father of a multitude of nations. Abraham traveled through large

---

6 Genesis 17:1.
7 Rashi on Genesis 17:1.
8 BT *Hagigah* 12a.
9 Genesis 17:4.

segments of the civilized world in order to spread monotheism. He thought he would complete the process in his lifetime, but the Almighty told him that his plan was to develop a nation, small in numbers but powerful in faith, an *am segulah* that would be a covenantal community that taught the unity of God. If there was a *mitzvah* throughout the millennia that set the Jewish people apart from the gentile world, it is the mitzvah of *brit milah*.

Essentially, God said: I want you to be different. They (the gentiles) write from left to right. We write from right to left. They calculate time using the sun as their calendar, while our calendar is based primarily upon the moon. Our mourning customs differ from theirs. We observe modesty and practice kindness differently as well. In effect, God told Abraham that it is not necessary to be respected or beloved. Ultimately, it is the friendship of God that is the *festung* of man.

✂ חיי שרה ✂

Hayyei Sarah I

✂ Abraham's interaction with Bnei Het

IT IS STRIKING that the Torah describes Abraham's discussion with *Bnei Het* in great detail while in general, it uses only sparse language in other places. Several important principles may be derived from the expansiveness of the text.

✂ Stages of mourning

The death of Sarah is described in the following terms:

ותמת שרה בקרית ארבע הוא חברון בארץ כנען ויבא אברהם לספד לשרה ולבכתה. ויקם אברהם מעל פני מתו וידבר אל בני חת לאמר.

Sarah died in Kiryat Arba – that is, Hebron – in the land of Canaan. Abraham came to eulogize Sarah and to bewail her. Abraham rose up from the presence of his dead and spoke to the children of Heth, saying . . .[1]

The expression "rose up from the presence of his dead" is not

---

1 Genesis 23:2–3.

superfluous. It teaches the halakhic etiquette of mourning. First Abraham mourned and wept, and only afterward did he rise in a controlled fashion to attend to the burial. When one has not yet asserted control over one's emotions, the Torah uses the expression ויפל – "to fall." ויפל יוסף – על פני אביו ויבך עליו וישק לו – "Then Joseph fell upon his father's face; he wept over him and kissed him."[2] ויקם – "to rise up" – implies the end of this most intense stage of mourning. In the Lecha Dodi prayer of Friday night, we encounter a similar phrase, התנערי מעפר קומי – "Shake off the dust! Arise"[3] – arise from mourning. *Avelut,* or mourning, is characterized by the inability to stand erect. Here, despite his distress, Abraham demonstrated his distinctiveness as a human being in two areas. The first was in his speech. The second was in his ability to rise up, stand erect and regain his dignity.

This reflects a transition from one confronted directly with death, who loses his dignity and is wont to ask, "Am I no different from a beast?" The sages equate *avelut* with silence. This is why the festivals, which are times of great joy, cancel public mourning. Here, the text emphasizes the act of Abraham's rising. Even in the Yiddish language, we have the expression *"tzu aufshtein fun avelus"* – to get up from mourning. The Mishnah in *Berachot*[4] teaches that if the dead is before you, you are exempt from the performance of mitzvot because when one is bereft of one's human dignity he is exempt from responsibility. A dignified being is a responsible being.

Another aspect of Jewish mourning is alluded to in the earlier words, ויבא אברהם – "and Abraham came."[5] Abraham, who was not with Sarah when she died, was undoubtedly devastated when he received the news of her death upon his return from the *akedah*. When the Torah states

---

2 Genesis 50:1.
3 This refers to Isaiah 52:2, in which the prophet laments the fact that Jerusalem is wallowing in the dust and bids her rise up.
4 Mishnah *Berachot* 3:1.
5 Genesis 23:2.

ויבא אברהם לספד לשרה ולבכתה – "Abraham came to eulogize Sarah and to bewail her"[6] – the phrase "He came" signifies withdrawal from the public to the private domain. Abraham mourned for Sarah privately. However, when the time came to negotiate for the burial plot, he composed himself and "arose" so that he would be able to negotiate with the *Bnei Het* in a state of emotional calm.

❧ Ger ve-Toshav

Abraham told the *bnei Het*, גר ותושב אנכי עמכם – "I am an alien and resident among you."[7] According to the Rav, the translation contains a fundamental dilemma – the nature of Abraham's relationship with his interlocutors. Is Abraham a citizen of their society or does his value system clash with theirs, resulting in an identity that is distinctive and autonomous? That the *Bnei Het* respected Abraham is evident because of the profound reverence that they displayed towards him. But a tensile balance pervades the entire dialogue. This is conveyed by three distinct segments in the dialogue between Abraham and the *Bnei Het*.

The first segment is Abraham's declaration and request:

גר ותושב אנכי עמכם תנו לי אחזת קבר עמכם ואקברה מתי מלפני.

I am an alien and a resident among you; grant me a holding for a grave with you that I may bury my dead from before me.[8]

The second segment is the response of the *Bnei Het* to Abraham's request:

שמענו אדני נשיא א־להים אתה בתוכנו במבחר קברינו קבר את מתך איש ממנו
את קברו לא יכלה ממך מקבר מתך.

---

6 Genesis 23:2.
7 Genesis 23:4. See Soloveitchik, Joseph B. *A Treasury of Tradition*, "Confrontation," 74–77, for a discussion of the balance between *ger* and *toshav*.
8 Genesis 23:4.

Hear us, my lord! You are a prince of God in our midst. In the choicest of our burial places bury your dead. None of us will withhold his burial place from you, from burying your dead.[9]

The third and last segment concludes with Abraham's response.

וידבר אתם לאמר אם יש את נפשכם לקבר את מתי מלפני שמעוני ופגעו לי בעפרון בן צחר. ויתן לי את מערת המכפלה אשר לו אשר בקצה שדהו בכסף מלא יתננה לי בתוככם לאחזת קבר.

He spoke to them, saying: If it is truly your will to bury my dead from before me, hear me and intercede for me with Ephron, son of Zohar. Let him grant me the cave of Machpelah which belongs to him, on the edge of his field. Let him give it to me for its full price, in your midst, as a burial plot.[10]

Initially, when Abraham made his request, the *Bnei Het* told him unconditionally that they would give him any of their sepulchers, even the choicest of them. This was surely a magnanimous gesture. Moreover, they treated Abraham with reverence, addressing him as a נשיא א־להים – a prince of God. However, there was also an implicit condition attached to their offer: נשיא א־להים אתה בתוכנו (amongst *us*), and במבחר קברינו "In the choicest of *our* burial places." Their language suggested that Abraham would have to give up his right to keep himself apart from them, saying, in effect: Abraham, you are part of our society, and as one of us, you must bury your dead in a burial site that belongs to us.

Abraham had already articulated Judaism's doctrine regarding interaction with other peoples by his first statement – גר ותושב אנכי עמכם. The message was: In certain ways, I am part of you (*toshav*) through my participation in industry and commerce, my payment of taxes, and so on. Yet in other ways, I am and will always remain totally separate from you (*ger*), demarcated in my relationship to God as reflected in my worship.

---

9 Genesis 23:6.
10 Genesis 23:8–9.

58

When the *Bnei Het* failed to understand this, Abraham responded in unmistakable terms. וידבר אתם לאמר – "He spoke to them, saying."[11] The word *dibbur* indicates sternness and precision. Abraham was telling them, in effect: Your offer is generous, but I cannot accept it. Instead, he asks for a grave that is located at the edge of the field, apart from the other graves, one that will be legally his own. Here, Abraham asserts the fundamental doctrine of *kever Yisrael* (burial in a Jewish cemetery).

✌ Ahuzat Kever

A final struggle ensues between Abraham and Efron over the nature of the transfer of ownership of the burial property. The *Bnei Het* had no understanding of the concept of *ahuzat kever* – ownership that brooks no compromise. Efron pressed Abraham to accept the property unconditionally as a gift. Centuries later, King Solomon stated: ושונא מתנת יחיה – "One who accepts no gifts will live long."[12] The teacher of Maimonides contended that the legal hold upon a gift is inferior to the legal hold upon an item that is purchased. It is said that no one should be buried in a grave that does not belong to him. The only thing that a person really owns and that cannot be taken from him is the four cubits of his grave. No compromise may be allowed on this issue.

By recording the conversation between Abraham and Efron in detail, the Torah teaches several principles related to mourning and burial. In addition, the dialogue between Abraham and the *Bnei Het* reflects the tense balance that exists for Jews who interact with the world at large while preserving their distinctive spiritual identities as members of the covenantal faith community.[13]

---

11 Genesis 23:8.
12 Proverbs 15:27, Rambam, *Hilchot Zechiyyah u-Matanah* 12:17.
13 See *A Treasury of Tradition*, 55–77, in which Rav Soloveitchik addresses this dialectic directly, and the addendum, 78–80, regarding interfaith relationships.

Hayyei Sarah II: The Search for a New Matriarch

THE DEATH OF Sarah, which followed the *akedah,* precipitated the search for a wife for Isaac. The *akedah* was the last great incident that involved Abraham. Afterward, we find no recorded conversation between God and Abraham. Eliezer's mission was to find a woman who would replace the mother of the covenantal community.

⁊ The Centrality of *Hesed*

Our sages made reference to אפרו של יצחק נראה לפני צבור ומונח על המזבח – "the ashes of Isaac appear before me, placed upon the altar."[1] Psychologically and spiritually, a dramatic event occurred at the *akedah.* When Abraham journeyed to Mount Moriah, he did so together with Isaac, as the Torah tells us: וילכו שניהם יחדו – "The two of them traveled together."[2] After the *akedah,* the Torah records: וישב אברהם אל נעריו – "Abraham returned to his servants."[3] Where was Isaac? Before the *akedah,* both Abraham and Isaac were operating jointly with the quality of *midat ha-hesed,*

---

1   Rashi on Leviticus 26:42.
2   Genesis 22:6.
3   Genesis 22:19.

lovingkindness. After the *akedah,* Isaac became the personification of *gevurah,* withdrawal and self-limitation. His task was now different from that of his father Abraham, who had been given the task of teaching morality to mankind. Isaac, the quintessence of *gevurah* or *kedushah,* was not permitted to leave the Land of Israel.[4] Thus, Abraham and Isaac could not return together after the *akedah.* Abraham returned alone to Beer Sheba, the symbol of the hostel which, in its unlimited *hesed,* reaches out to everyone,[5] while Isaac remained in his tent, secluded in holiness.

Abraham was a sensitive, courageous, dignified and imaginative man who was not afraid to sacrifice his life. Therefore, he was chosen to be the father of the covenantal community. Since he carried a certain genetic code, he insisted that Eliezer choose only a wife from his family.[6] In this search, Eliezer was guided by only one criterion: *hesed.*

ჯ Two Types of *Hesed: Hesed* and *Arichut Apayim*

There are two genres of *hesed:* rational and irrational. While rational *hesed* is ubiquitous and common, *hesed* that is performed without bounds is rare. This quality is endemic to Abraham's household. When Moshe heard God proclaim the Thirteen Attributes of Mercy, he prostrated himself. However, there are two views as to exactly when Moshe bowed down. One view is that he prostrated himself when he heard the phrase *rav hesed* (abundant in lovingkindness). Another maintains that he did so at the phrase *erech apayim* (forbearing and patient). The quality known as *arichut apayim* (the noun form of the adjective *erech apayim*) reflects the irrational side of *hesed,* the ability to respond with kindness

---

4 See Rashi on Genesis 26:2.
5 See Rashi on Genesis 21:33.
6 See *Derashot ha-Ran,* fifth derasha, for an explanation of why Abraham wished to choose a wife from his own family, who were not monotheists, instead of searching for a bride in the land where he was currently living.

even in the face of improper behavior from the potential recipient of that kindness.

If someone approaches me and asks for a favor, I don't mind complying. This is a natural response of *hesed*. But if that person is arrogant and insolent in his approach, that calls for *arichut apayim*. Eliezer, Abraham's servant, wished to determine whether Rebecca possessed not only the attribute of *hesed* but also that of *arichut apayim*. Therefore, he approached her in a tactless manner, literally asking to be spoon-fed. He did not approach her in a gentlemanly fashion. When he saw her *arichut apayim* – her great patience and eagerness to practice *hesed* – he realized immediately that she was fit to be a partner in the Abrahamic community.

ᢌ The Source of Rebecca's Greatness

Rebecca exemplified extraordinary qualities: her modesty and diligence, and her outstanding performance of *hesed*. Although Rebecca had been reared in a pagan home, in a licentious society, she demonstrated such outstanding personal qualities that the moment she entered Sarah's tent, she became the image of Sarah.[7] How are we to understand this?

Apparently there was an underground movement that disseminated the morality and teachings of Abraham. Even though Rebecca grew up in a pagan home, she absorbed these qualities osmotically. But from whom? The Torah mentions that when Rebecca was sent to Isaac, her nurse accompanied her.[8] Why was it necessary to convey this bit of information? After all, it was common for aristocratic families to employ a nurse for a child. In *Parashat Va-yishlah*, the nurse is mentioned once more and identified by name – this time in the context of her death.

---

7 See Rashi on Genesis 24:67.
8 Genesis 24:59.

ותמת דברה מינקת רבקה ותקבר מתחת לבית אל תחת האלון ויקרא שמו אלון
בכות.

Deborah, the wet-nurse of Rebecca, died and was buried below Beth-el beneath the oak tree, which he named Allon-bakhut [the oak of weeping].[9]

Why is it so significant to record the death of Deborah, Rebecca's wet-nurse, together with the tree or the bottom of the plain where she was buried, when the Torah does not tell us when Rebecca herself died? According to Rashi, Rebecca had promised Jacob that she would send someone to recall him at the proper time, and Deborah was the one whom she sent.[10]

Deborah was Rebecca's teacher, the one responsible for Rebecca's superior character and outlook. She taught Rebecca the values that made her worthy of becoming the mother of the covenantal community. Therefore, the Torah mentions her death. Jacob takes note of it and proclaims mourning over her loss. Deborah had a critical role in shaping Rebecca's personality, which was pure and good even though she had grown up in a home that seemed to be the opposite of the virtues that she embodied.

---

9   Genesis 35:8.
10 Rashi on Genesis 35:8.

תולדות ✺ תולדות ✺

Toldot I: Isaac as the Personification of *Gevurah*

ואלה תולדת יצחק בן אברהם אברהם הוליד את יצחק.

These are the offspring of Isaac the son of Abraham: Abraham begot Isaac.[1]

THE TORAH ENVELOPS Isaac, a cryptic figure, in an aura of mystery. It does not reveal much of his personality except for two episodes: his brief stay in the land of Gerar and his role in the confrontation between Jacob and Esau in their competition for his blessing. The Torah assigned three *parshiyyot* to Abraham and many more to Jacob, but only one to Isaac. Why is this so?

The kabbalists provide the answer. Each of the patriarchs personified one of God's own attributes. Abraham epitomized *hesed* (lovingkindness), Jacob exemplified *emet* or *tiferet,* and Isaac was the quintessence of *gevurah. Hesed* expresses itself in *hitpashtut* or *hitgalut,* expansion or revelation. When a person practices *hesed,* he lets other people share in his actions and in his existence, leading to communication and dialogue. *Gevurah* connotes retreat or withdrawal into one's private world. It is a

---

1 Genesis 25:19.

joining with the Almighty. *Kedushah,* holiness, is also characterized by privacy and solitude.[2]

The verse at the end of *Parashat Bamidbar* states, ולא יבאו לראות כבלע את הקדש ומתו – "But they shall not come and look as the holy objects are placed inside, lest they die."[3] The *aron ha-kodesh,* as the symbol of holiness, may not be exposed. It must be covered by a curtain.[4] The story of the *aron ha-kodesh* in Beit Shemesh illustrates this basic principle.[5] Chabad hasidism refers to this as *hitkasut* (concealment). This is the reason why Judaism eschews nudity: the human body, which it deems a holy vessel, represents a microcosm of the Temple, perhaps even more sacred than the one built of wood and stone in Jerusalem. The human body should be covered because it was created *be-tzelem Elohim* – in God's image. This is also inherent in the idea of the the curtain that separates the the outer sanctuary from the the inner sanctuary, or Holy of Holies.

Therefore, *gevurah* is associated with *kedushah,* and Isaac is the personification of these qualities. Isaac was the actual *korban* (sacrifice), while the ram was his substitute. Thus, Isaac is wrapped in a mantle of mystery. This is the reason that the Torah provides so little information about him. It is Isaac's nature to be hidden and to defy description. It is also true that such a hidden personality is more difficult to fathom and appreciate. Not everyone is capable of understanding Isaac's personality. He was a monastic figure, separated from society.

Throughout Jewish history there were two types of *gedolei Yisrael.* One type was extroverted and gregarious, mingling with the people and teaching them. Their hallmark was *hesed* writ large, encouraging the downtrodden and practicing lovingkindness and charity. The *Baal Shem Tov* is an example of that group. The other type of *gedolim* is characterized

---

2 See Hayyei Sarah II for further explication of this idea.
3 Numbers 4:20.
4 See Ramban on Numbers 4:20.
5 See 1 Samuel 6:19.

by *gevurah*. One example was the Vilna Gaon, who studied alone in his room, far from the public eye. Both types of *gedolei Torah* are intrinsic to the survival of the mesorah. However, the *gadol* characterized by *gevurah* is often enigmatic. His contribution is quieter and more elusive. In our daily prayers, we recite: תתן אמת ליעקב, חסד לאברהם – "Give truth to Jacob, kindness to Abraham"[6] – but there is no mention of Isaac. Even in this daily reflection, we must acknowledge that Isaac remains a mystery.

Understanding Isaac as the personification of *gevurah* provides insight into another curious piece of Isaac's life, his delay in marrying. The Torah tells us that Isaac's marriage to Rebecca did not take place until he reached the age of forty.[7] Why? The answer is that prior to the *akedah,* Isaac had no right to marry because *kodshei kodashim* (sacrifices that carry the highest degree of sanctity) are consecrated totally to God, as was Isaac. Marriage is a function of *hesed* – expansion and extension of oneself to another person – and companionship. These qualities, which corresponded to the personalities of Abraham and Jacob, conflicted with the *gevurah* of Isaac. Our sages opine that Isaac's ashes rest upon the altar.[8] Therefore, the verse emphasizes the fact that he was forty years old because he had not been allowed to marry until then. As the personification of *gevurah,* Isaac had mostly withdrawn from the world.

---

6 From the section of the morning prayers that begins "U-va le-tzion go'el."
7 Genesis 25:20.
8 See Rashi on Leviticus 26:42.

תולדות

Toldot II: Spiritual Growth through Adversity

I N THE BEGINNING of Toldot, the Torah seems to focus unduly on Rebecca's family background and genealogy.

ויהי יצחק בן ארבעים שנה בקחתו את רבקה בת בתואל הארמי מפדן ארם אחות
לבן הארמי לו לאשה.

Isaac was forty years old when he took Rebecca, daughter of Bethuel the Aramean of Paddan Aram, sister of Laban the Aramean, as a wife for himself.[1]

Clearly the purpose of this elaboration is to teach us a basic lesson. The meaning of the focus on Rebecca's family can be understood in light of a comment of the *Targum Yonatan ben Uziel* on the Torah's depiction of the Jewish people in Egypt. On the verse ויאמר אנכי הא־ל א־להי אביך אל תירא מרדה מצרימה כי לגוי גדול אשימך שם – "He said: I am God, the God of your father. Have no fear of descending to Egypt, for I shall establish you as a great nation there"[2] – the Targum comments: There God will make us into a great nation. Furthermore, the *Baal Haggadah* exegetically derives

---

1   Genesis 25:20.
2   Genesis 46:3.

from the verse: ויהי שם לגוי גדול – "There they became a great nation"[3] –
that שם – מלמד שהיו ישראל מצינים שם – "This teaches that the Jews there became
distinguished and distinctive."

This implies that only in the midst of Egypt were the descendants
of Abraham able to develop into a great nation. In another context, we
would not have become a great nation. In order to develop the qualities
that characterize our nation – mercy, modesty and lovingkindness[4] – we
had to be thrust into the vortex of power, might and brutal force and
experience the antithesis of our ethos. Only through exposure to these
adverse character traits could we achieve our true essence as a people.
Similarly, Joseph had to be sold to an executioner, for otherwise he
would not have been able to appreciate Jacob's greatness.

The verse in Songs of Songs notes כשושנה בין החוחים כן רעיתי בין הבנות
– "As a rose among the thorns, so is my beloved among the young
women."[5] The rose, a soft-petaled flower, flourishes specifically in an
environment of thorns. It is the very pain and suffering that confers
upon the rose its beauty. The Jewish nation's greatness was a function
of its suffering in Egypt and the recognition that its moral heritage was
of an entirely different nature. Therefore, the Torah felt constrained to
emphasize Rebecca's genealogical background. Only by growing up in
such an adverse environment could she truly appreciate the greatness of
the world of Abraham.

---

3 Deuteronomy 26:5.
4 BT *Yevamot* 79a and Rambam, *Hilchot Issurei Biah* 19:17.
5 Song of Songs 2:2.

Toldot III: *Holid vs. Yoldah: Toldot Yitzchak* as a Model of Jewish Parenting

WE SHOULD NOTE the difference between the language that the Torah uses regarding Isaac and the language that it uses for Ishmael. This substantial difference sheds light on two different educational and moral approaches to raising children.

At the beginning of Parashat Toldot, the Torah tell us, ואלה תולדת יצחק בן אברהם אברהם הוליד את יצחק – "These are the offspring of Isaac son of Abraham: Abraham begot Isaac."[1] Prior to this presentation, juxtaposed to it at the end of Parashat Hayyei Sarah, we read ואלה תלדת ישמעאל בן אברהם אשר ילדה הגר המצרית שפחת שרה לאברהם – "These are the descendants of Ishmael, Abraham's son, whom Hagar the Egyptian, Sarah's maidservant, bore to Abraham."[2] The formulation is almost identical but the contrast of verbal forms הוליד – *holid* – versus ילדה – *yolda* – is clear and provocative.

The progeny of Ishmael multiply numerically and exponentially, occupy large swathes of territory and are dispersed geographically. It appears that they accomplished their growth and territorial expansion by military might. There appear to be no *akedot* in the lifetime of Ishmael.

---

1 Genesis 25:19.
2 Genesis 25:12.

He grows freely, unencumbered by tension, struggles or internecine quarrels.

The story of Isaac's family is the opposite. Isaac and Rebecca had only two children, whose births were complicated and painful. Their lives were riddled with conflict. Jacob was compelled to leave his paternal home to wander from place to place and was never able to establish himself in any one location for long. The covenantal community must pay a steep price for its accomplishments.

People often criticize Sarah's banishment of Ishmael from the household, for it shows a strong lack of kindness. In reality Sarah was making a critical assertion about membership in the covenantal community. She prevented Ishmael from becoming part of the history of the covenant because his nature would not have allowed him to live the kind of sacrificial life that the people of the covenant must live.

Abraham suggested that Ishmael be included in the covenant: ויאמר אברהם אל האֵ־להים לו ישמעאל יחיה לפניך – "Abraham said to God, 'O that Ishmael might live before You!'"[3] But God Himself sanctioned Sarah's decision.

ויאמר אֵ־להים אבל שרה אשתך ילדת לך בן וקראת את שמו יצחק והקמתי את בריתי אתו לברית עולם לזרעו אחריו.

> God said: "Indeed, your wife Sarah will bear you a son, and you shall name him Isaac. I will fulfill my covenant with him as an everlasting covenant for his offspring after him."[4]

In effect, Ishmael is not ready to live a life of heroism and self-sacrifice, which includes readiness for possible martyrdom. Therefore, he cannot be part of the covenantal community.

All of the above is embedded in the two contrasting verbal forms for giving birth. The Hebrew word *yolda,* as applied to Ishmael, denotes a

---

3 Genesis 17:18.
4 Genesis 17:19.

biological process of continuity. The Hebrew word *holid,* as applied to Isaac, implies a multi-generational educational process with an eternal effect.[5] The words differ in that the word *holid* includes the letter *heh.* In order to understand the significance of this additional letter, we must consider other places in the Torah where it is added.

On the verse ויוצא אתו החוצה ויאמר הבט נא השמימה וספר הכוכבים אם תוכל לספר אתם ויאמר לו כה יהיה זרעך – "He took him outside and said: 'Look at the heavens and count the stars if you can.' He said to him: 'So numerous shall your offspring be.'"[6] Rashi comments: צא מאצטגנינות שלך שראית במזלות שאינך עתיד להעמיד בן, אברם אין לו בן, אבל אברהם יש לו בן – "abandon your astrology, through which you have seen in the signs of the zodiac that you are not destined to bear a son. Abram will not father a son, but Abraham will."[7] Why was the change of name from Abram to Abraham so important? What additional dimension does the letter *heh* indicate, and why is it connected to Abraham's becoming the father of Isaac?

✌ A Spiritual Revolution in the Parent–Child Bond

Before the addition of the letter *heh,* fatherhood and motherhood were natural institutions, impelled entirely by biological, mechanical drives, common to the animal kingdom as well. The addition of the letter *heh* caused a dramatic change, since it introduced an element of teaching to fatherhood. This spiritual revolution was so novel that the sages said of it, כל המלמד בן חבירו תורה מעלה עליו הכתוב כאילו ילדו – "One who teaches Torah to his friend's child is considered as having given birth to him."[8] The Torah considers children as gifts that God bestows out of grace.

---

5   The Rav cited Ibn Ezra, who refers to the verse in Genesis 50:23: "Joseph saw three generations through Ephraim. Even the sons of Machir, the son of Manasseh, were raised on Joseph's knees." According to Ibn Ezra, the implication in these two contexts is educational, didactic, and spiritual.

6   Genesis 15:5.

7   Rashi on Genesis 15:5.

8   BT *Sanhedrin* 19b.

However, the strongest *kinyan* (legal hold of an object) applies to an item that is purchased rather than an item that is given as a gift.[9] Abraham refused to accept the Cave of Machpelah as a gift and paid the full price for it. King David bought the plot of land upon which the Temple was built. The city of Shechem was also purchased. All three sites played, and continue to play, a pivotal role in Jewish history. Our ownership of them must be beyond all legal question. So too, in a manner of speaking, parents must carry out a "*kinyan*," a process of acquisition, in order to "reacquire" the child whom God first gave to them as a gift.

Abraham placed his son Isaac on the altar, displaying the ultimate in *mesirut nefesh,* so that he could reacquire his child. As we educate, shape and guide our children, we, too, reacquire them.

The sages derived this idea exegetically from a verse in Genesis: אלה תולדות השמים והארץ בהבראם ביום עשות ה' א‑להים ארץ ושמים – "These are the products of the heavens and the earth when they were created."[10] The exegesis is בהבראם: בה' בראם – "He created them with the letter *heh*."[11] A rearrangement of the letters results in the name Abraham. God's message, therefore, is that Abraham can become a creator by teaching and then be transformed into the father of all mankind. Also, according to Jewish law, Abraham, as *av hamon goyim* (father of the multitude of nations), is also considered the father of all prospective converts.[12]

Thus, the usage, "Abraham *holid* (begot) Isaac" demonstrates that this was much more than a mere biological link. The new and radical philosophy of parenthood that Abraham espoused was essential for the creation of the covenantal community.

---

9 See Hayyei Sarah I, Ahuzat Kever.
10 Genesis 2:4.
11 Rashi, op. cit.
12 See Rambam, *Hilchot Bikkurim* 4:3.

❧ ויצא ❧

Vayetze: A Difficult Departure

ויצא יעקב מבאר שבע וילך חרנה.

Jacob departed from Beer-Sheba and went toward Haran.[1]

R ASHI CITES A famous *Midrash Rabbah* that relates to the question why does the Torah mention the departure from Beer Sheba? The *Midrash*, as cited by Rashi, reports as follows:

שיציאת צדיק מן העיר עושה רושם שבזמן שהצדיק בעיר הוא הודה הוא זיוה הוא הדרה יצא משם פנה הודה פנה זיוה פנה הדרה וכן ותצא מן המקום האמור בנעמי ורות.

The departure of a righteous person from a place makes an impression, for when a righteous person is in a city, he constitutes its magnificence, its splendor and its grandeur. Once he leaves, its magnificence, splendor and grandeur vanish. Similarly, this is implied by the verse in Megillat Ruth: "She [Naomi] departed from the place [where she was]," which is said in the story of Naomi and Ruth.[2]

---

1 Genesis 28:10.
2 *Midrash Rabbah* on Genesis 68:6.

73

On what basis does the *Midrash* derive this interpretation about the departure? What specific part of the phrase ויצא יעקב מבאר שבע suggests that Beer Sheba was a beautiful city before Jacob left it, and that his departure rendered it desolate?

The word *va-yetze* appears in the Torah in several different contexts, each with its own connotation. When Pharaoh asked Moshe to pray for him at the end of Parashat Va-era it states ויאמר אליו משה כצאתי את העיר אפרש את כפי אל ה' – "Moshe said to him: When I leave the city, I will spread out my hands to the Lord."[3] Here, the Torah uses the term את. The Torah describes Moshe leaving the city to pray to God, but the word את denotes departure from a person, in this case from Pharaoh.[4]

In Parashat Vayakhel we find a different usage of the word *va-yetze*. ויצאו כל עדת בני ישראל מלפני משה – "The entire assembly of the Jewish people left the presence of Moshe."[5] The term מלפני (from before) implies a temporary departure in order to attend to the business at hand of amassing the material for the Mishkan and subsequently returning to Moshe.

In Parashat Bo, we read ויצא מעם פרעה בחרי אף – "Moshe went out from Pharaoh in great anger."[6] Here the term מעם appears. The words מן or מעם imply disengagement and severing. This implies a permanent dislocation, as in the verse ויצא מבת ציון כל הדרה – "Gone from the daughter of Zion is all her splendor."[7] All the beauty departed from Zion.

Similarly, ויצא יעקב מבאר שבע denotes that Jacob was severed somehow from Beer Sheba. Jacob was uprooted by forces beyond his control, compelled to leave a place he loved. It is in light of the phrase ויצא יעקב מבאר שבע, that the Midrash and Rashi conclude that Jacob left a place to which he had become bonded. Jacob and Beer Sheba had merged into one symbiotic entity, and now Jacob had to leave Beer Sheba and wander.

---

3 Exodus 9:29.
4 See Exodus 9:33 and Ramban on Exodus 9:29.
5 Exodus 35:20.
6 Exodus 11:8.
7 Lamentations 1:6.

How, then, are we to understand the symbiotic relationship between Jacob and Beer Sheba? In order to gain insight into this connection, we must consider Beer Sheba's special significance in Jacob's life.

The Torah uses a dramatic expression regarding Beer Sheba that it does not use anywhere else: "ויטע אשל בבאר שבע ויקרא שם בשם ה' א-ל עולם" – "He (Abraham) planted an "eshel" in Beer Sheba and there he proclaimed the name of the Lord, God of the universe."[8] Elsewhere, Abraham employs the expression 'ויקרא שם אברם בשם ה' – "He invoked God by name."[9] Beer Sheba deserved this special expression because it was the first home of the covenantal community, the center of spiritual life for the adherents of Abraham's teaching. When Jacob left Beer Sheba, he was pulled away from this spiritual center. Perhaps he was frightened that if he left the home of his father and grandfather and the center of their teaching, he would also lose his role as leader and teacher of the covenantal community.

Beer Sheba was rooted in a wellspring of *kedushah*. It was a fulcrum for offerings to God and a conduit for the Divine Presence. But when Jacob left, Beer Sheba lost its glory. Once Jacob had gone, Beer Sheba resembled Mount Sinai when the shofar was sounded and the sanctity of the mount dissipated.[10] Later on in Jewish history, that *kedushah* found its home in the place that Jacob encountered on his journey from Beer Sheba: the holy city of Jerusalem.

✣ Why leave Eretz Yisrael?

Jacob was also perplexed by the following conundrum: the blessings of Abraham could only be manifest in Eretz Yisrael.[11] When Isaac was faced with famine and wanted to leave Eretz Yisrael, he was barred from

---

8 Genesis 21:33. See Rashi and Ramban on Genesis 21:33.
9 Genesis 13:4.
10 See Exodus 19:13 and Rashi on the verse.
11 See Ramban on Genesis 12:2.

doing so.[12] If leaving the Promised Land was forbidden, then why did God tell Jacob to do so? Was not his mission as an ancestor of the Jewish people also bound up with the land of Israel?

This dilemma accounts for Jacob's plea to God: אשא עיני אל ההרים מאין יבא עזרי – "I raise my eyes to the mountains; whence will come my help?"[13] Jacob was surely asking himself: Can I really succeed in building a community in Haran? Why should I leave behind the myriads of adherents whom Abraham and Isaac trained? Apparently, it was God's will that that Jacob begin anew with a community of twelve souls and, ultimately, כל הנפש לבית יעקב הבאה מצרימה שבעים – "All the people of Jacob's household who came to Egypt – seventy."[14] Jacob's departure from the city of Beer Sheba temporarily detached him from the spiritual destiny of the Jewish people. Perhaps this is implied in the statement, "Once he leaves, its magnificence, spendor and grandeur vanish."

✄ A Model for Spiritual Survival in Exile

What message could there be in this surprising move of separating Jacob from the land of his spiritual destiny? The explanation is as follows: Despite the centrality of Eretz Yisrael, Judaism and its tenets have universal applicability and must endure even outside its borders. Eretz Yisrael is not a condition *sine qua non* for Jewish observance. God wanted to teach Jacob – and, through him, the Jewish people – that even if we suffer displacement and destruction, we can rebuild.[15]

While both Jacob and Joseph had to experience *galut* (exile), their experiences of exile were different. Jacob experienced the *galut* of poverty and hard work. Joseph experienced the *galut* of poverty as well, followed by that of great material success. Each of these was necessary

---

12 Genesis 26:2.
13 Psalms 121:1 and *Genesis Rabbah* 68:2.
14 Genesis 46:27.
15 See *Reflections of the Rav*, volume 1, 23–29. "Imitating God: The Basis of Jewish Morality."

in order to provide models of how a Jew should deal with each type of *galut*. Throughout history, Jews often suffered terrible poverty and oppression. This type of *galut* presents specific challenges to maintaining one's Jewish heritage. On the other hand, Jews in many places today find themselves in *galut* in which they enjoy great material success. This presents a different kind of challenge, for which the model of Joseph provides inspiration.

✌ *Va-yisa Yaakov Raglav*

The *Midrash* comments on the verse ויפגע במקום – "He encountered the place"[16] by noting that for Jacob, the world was like a wall that he bumped into.[17] He was now destined to wander aimlessly. Our sages interpreted the verse אשא עיני אל ההרים מאין יבוא עזרי – "I raise my eyes to the mountains; whence will come my help?"[18] as referring to Jacob.[19] All this transpired when he left Beer Sheba for Haran.

After Jacob tarried there for the night, in the morning he was elated and rejuvenated because of his encounter with God and his assurance of divine assistance. On the verse וישא יעקב רגליו וילך ארצה בני קדם – "So Jacob lifted his feet and went toward the land of the easterners,"[20] Rashi comments:

משנתבשר בשורה טובה שהובטח בשמירה, נשא לבו את רגליו ונעשה קל ללכת.

Once he had been given good tidings that he was assured of protection, his heart lifted his feet and it became easy to walk.

There was another reason for Jacob's joy. Abraham was the founder of the covenantal community. While his covenant with God carried

---

16 Genesis 28:11.
17 *Midrash Rabbah*, Genesis 68:10.
18 Psalms 121:1.
19 *Midrash Rabbah* on Genesis 68:2.
20 Genesis 29:1.

mutual obligations for both parties, its main stipulation was that Abraham transmit his heritage to his children. Any member of the covenantal community leaves a dual will to his descendants: to distribute his material possessions and to transmit his heritage and tradition to his children.

This second mandate is mentioned in the verse:

כי ידעתיו למען אשר יצוה את בניו ואת ביתו אחריו ושמרו דרך ה' לעשות צדקה
ומשפט למען הביא ה' על אברהם את אשר דבר עליו.

I have cherished him because he commands his children and his household after him that they keep the way of God, doing charity and justice, in order that God may bring upon Abraham that which he had spoken of him.[21]

This second overriding obligation to transmit the mesorah is a sine qua non for God to comply with his part of the agreement. According to the Rambam, the term ki yetzaveh (because he commands) is not a mere commandment but a statement of the divine will, a spiritual property and moral code, a last will and testament that must be transmitted as a legacy. It is a mitzvah *she'beal peh*.[22] Once reassured of God's ongoing protection, Jacob is confident that he will be able to fulfill God's mandate to transmit the mesorah.

---

21 Genesis 18:19.
22 See Rambam in his preamble to *Mishneh Torah*: "All the commandments given to Moshe at Sinai were given with the oral commentary, as it is written: 'I will give you the tablets of stone and the Torah and the *mitzvah*.' 'Torah' refers to the written law. '*Mitzvah*' refers to the Oral Law. We are duty-bound to keep the Torah based on the mitzvah. This *mitzvah* is termed *Torah she'beal peh* [the Oral Law]."

וישא ❦

Vaeyetze II

❦ **Jacob's Dual Inheritance**

I N PARASHAT VAYETZE, Jacob is charged with his inheritance as leader and teacher in the covenantal community for the first time. This is the message of the second set of blessings that Isaac gives Jacob before he leaves home.

> ואל שׁדי יברך אתך ויפרך וירבך והיית לקהל עמים. ויתן לך את ברכת אברהם
> לך ולזרעך אתך לרשתך את ארץ מגריך אשר נתן אלהים לאברהם.

May El Shaddai bless you, make you fruitful and numerous, and may you become a congregation of peoples. May he grant you the blessing of Abraham, to you and to your offspring with you, that you possess the land of your sojourns which God gave to Abraham.[1]

These blessings, deemed the *Birchat Abraham* (blessings of Abraham), were designated exclusively for Jacob. They are inexorably bound up with the mandate of the trusteeship of the covenantal community.

---

1 Genesis 28:3–4.

ויתן לך הא־להים מטל השמים ומשמני הארץ ורב דגן ותירש.

May God give you of the dew of the heavens and the fatness
of the earth and abundant grain and wine.[2]

These earlier blessings that were intended for Esau focus on material riches and prosperity. There, the name of *Elokim* appears, while the
name of *El Shaddai* is employed for the *birkat Avraham* (Blessings of
Abraham), similar to its use in the *brit milah*.[3]

What is the meaning of this chain of inheritance embedded in the
birkat Avraham? The Rav noted that Abraham was the first teacher par
excellence who transmitted his legacy to tens of thousands of adherents.[4] His relationship with them was that of both teacher and father.
Abraham succeeded in developing a community of students and even
a nation that "loved its God."[5] Abraham's responsibility was not only
to establish the covenantal community, but to establish it for posterity
that would perpetuate its eternal existence. The transfer of leadership to
Isaac was the next important step.

How do we know that Abraham was successful? God reveals himself
to Isaac and says:

גור בארץ הזאת ואהיה עמך ואברכך כי לך ולזרעך אתן את כל הארצת האל
והקמתי את השבעה אשר נשבעתי לאברהם אביך ... עקב אשר שמע אברהם
בקלי ...

Sojourn in this land and I will be with you and bless you, for
to you and your offspring will I give all these lands, and I will
keep the oath that I swore to Abraham your father . . . because
Abraham obeyed my voice . . . .[6]

---

2 Genesis 27:28.
3 Genesis 17:1.
4 See Rambam, Hilchot Avodat Kochavim 1:1.
5 See Rambam, Hilchot Avodat Kochavim 1:3.
6 Genesis 26:3, 5.

This is clear confirmation of that leadership that Abraham success-fully transferred to Isaac. Later, the Torah links Isaac's status with his connection to Abraham once more:

ויעל משם באר שבע. וירא אליו ה' בלילה ההוא ויאמר אנכי א׳להי אברהם אביך
אל תירא כי אתך אנכי וברכתיך והרביתי את זרעך בעבור אברהם עבדי. ויבן שם
מזבח ויקרא בשם ה'.

He (Isaac) went up from there to Beer Sheba. God appeared to him that night and said, I am the God of your father Abraham. Fear not, for I am with you. I will bless you and increase your offspring because of Abraham my servant. He built an altar there and invoked God by name.[7]

Just as the symbol for Abraham's teaching was the altar,[8] Isaac, his heir, builds an altar as well. Even the king of Gerar, Abimelech, recognizes Isaac's greatness and comes to sign a treaty with him.

ויאמרו ראו ראינו כי היה ה' עמך ונאמר תהי נא אלה בינותינו ביננו ובינך ונכרתה
ברית עמך.

They said, "We have indeed seen that God is with you, so we said: Let there be an oath between ourselves, between us and you, and let us make a covenant with you."[9]

One cannot help but see the parallel to the statement of Avimelech's earlier namesake and his treaty with Abraham.

ויהי בעת ההוא ויאמר אבימלך ופיכל שר צבאו אל אברהם לאמר אלקים עמך
בכל אשר אתה עשה...ויכרתו שניהם ברית...

At that time, Abimelech and Phicol, the general of his army,

---

7 Genesis 26:23–25.
8 See Ramban on Genesis 12:8. He sees the altar as a kind of podium from which the glory of God is disseminated.
9 Genesis 26:28.

said to Abraham: God is with you in all that you do . . .They
made a covenant at Beer Sheba . . .[10]

In every way, the Torah emphasizes the link between Isaac and
Abraham. Thus, in receiving the second set of blessings from Isaac, Jacob
was being charged by his father Isaac to become the next leader – the
next link in the chain of the covenantal community.

---

10 Genesis 21:22, 27.

ויצא

Vayetze III

~ The Significance of Tefilat Maariv

IN PARASHAT VAYETZE, the Torah tells us ויפגע במקום – "He encountered the place."[1] It was there that he prayed to God. The expression ויפגע במקום implies that he interceded with God. If one's heart is completely absorbed in prayer, the distance to God is shortened. If the prayer is less intense, the distance is greater. Moshe, in the intensity of his prayer, entreating God's forgiveness after the sin of the Golden Calf, was so involved in his prayer that the Talmud compared it to "seizing God's garment."[2] Moshe's passion transcended the distance between himself and God. So too, the *Ba-makom* of Jacob was very close. This *paga* was *naga* (meeting was touching). Connected with this experience, our sages taught that Jacob instituted *tefillat maariv* (the evening prayer).[3]

Let us explore the conceptual and philosophical distinctions between the three *tefillot* of *shaharit, minha* and *maariv*. The differences between them are not based solely on the passage of time but are primarily conceptual in nature. One may not eat or engage in any other enter-

---

1 Genesis 28:11.
2 BT *Berachot* 32a.
3 BT *Berachot* 26b.

prise before reciting the morning prayer.[4] Before *davening,* the world does not belong to us. It is only through *tefillah* that we reacquire our existence, in a manner of speaking. *Minha,* which occurs *in medias res,* in the midst of my frenzied activities throughout the day, is an interruption. I must interrupt my daily routine and withdraw from it for several minutes, turning my attention to God. It is a difficult task, but our sages tell us that the prayers of the prophet Elijah were answered specifically at *minha* time.[5] *Tefillat Maariv,* the evening prayer, symbolizes the later stages in human life, when our insecurity rises to the fore.

The *maariv* prayer includes *Hashkivenu,* which focuses on the frightening experience of entrusting one's soul to God – akin to death – and then revival. In effect, during *maariv,* we pray to God for survival. It is therefore appropriate that Jacob introduced *maariv* at the place (במקום). He prayed for survival from his conflicts with his enemies. We, the descendants of Jacob who were and continue to be exposed to numerous attempts to destroy us, follow in his footsteps and continue to recite the *maariv* prayer, asking God for our survival.

---

4   BT *Berachot* 14a.
5   BT *Berachot* 6b.

✦ וישלח ✦

Vayishlah

✦ The Challenge of a Dual Existence

JACOB'S CONFRONTATION WITH Esau provides tremendous insight into current events. This is our most seminal source of knowledge in dealing with Esau and his descendants, and Jews must understand it well before interacting with non-Jews.

וישלח יעקב מלאכים לפניו אל עשו אחיו ארצה שעיר שדה אדום.

Jacob sent *malachim* before him to Esau his brother, to the land of Seir, the fields of Edom.[1]

✦ True Angels

Rashi comments at the beginning: מלאכים ממש – "Actual angels" –metaphysical, heavenly beings. It is important to understand why Rashi chose this interpretation as opposed to the word's other meaning: "human messengers."

---

1   Genesis 32:4.

85

It's noteworthy that one must first understand Jacob's encounter with angels several verses earlier. At the end of Parashat Vayetze, Jacob encountered angels of God:

ויעקב הלך לדרכו ויפגעו בו מלאכי א־להים. ויאמר יעקב כאשר ראם מחנה
א־להים זה ויקרא שם המקום ההוא מחנים.

Jacob went on his way and angels of God encountered him.
Jacob said, upon seeing them, "This is a Godly camp!" So he
named the place Mahanayim [two camps].[2]

Jacob, who sensed intuitively that these were no ordinary beings, identified them clearly as angels. Such discernment indicates a high spiritual level. The wife of Manoah, the mother of Shimshon, also had this ability. She realized that the man who had come to speak to her was an angel, even as her husband did not.[3]

The term Mahanayim was more than a name. It was a personal state-ment by Jacob as he returned to Eretz Yisrael from *hutz la-aretz* that he would now be leading a double life of sorts. The angels came to show Jacob that his life henceforth would not be on one plane exclusively, as it had been with Laban. In Eretz Yisrael, Jacob would be living on two planes. For some years, his life had been characterized by physicality: עקדים נקדים וברדים – "ringed, speckled and striped"[4] – the constant nego-tiations with his shrewd and clever uncle about the payment he would receive for watching his flocks. Now that Jacob has returned to Eretz Yisrael, he will continue his involvement in the physical world, but will also return to the spiritual level of Avraham Avinu. The term Mahanayim alludes to this duality. Jacob realized that although he would still have to deal with matters on the earthly plane, such as defense treaties and land

---

2 Genesis 32:2–3.
3 Judges 13:6.
4 Genesis 31:10.

purchases, he would also have access to the higher spiritual planes and a closer relationship with the Divine.

To a certain extent, this duality illustrates Jewish life throughout much of history. Jews often lived in poverty in ghettos, with all the deprivation and suffering that such a life entailed. Yet even then, they lived on the highest plane of spirituality, practicing *hesed* (lovingkindness) and *tzedaka* (charity), like true *malachim* (angels), living lives of purity despite the stress and suffering of their daily lives.

In light of the aforementioned analysis, we can interpret the message that Jacob sent, via the *malachim*, to Esau, who asks: Why be different from the world at large? Why must you preach Abrahamic ideas? Jacob answers: While it is true that I must now live on two levels, there is something that you must understand. I am willing to give up a great deal regarding *mi-tal ha-shamayim* – material prosperity. However, I will never be willing to compromise on my religious principles. The only way to drive this message home to a person like Esau is through the agency of מלאכים ממש – actual angels, who represent the uncompromising aspect of spirituality. As Jews, we are willing to compromise regarding one *mahaneh* – material success. But as far as the second *mahaneh*, the spritual plane, is concerned, we will never negotiate. The Rav explained that Jacob's firm statement of principles is precisely what we are saying four thousand years later. Certain things, such as Jerusalem, are not negotiable.

Im Lavan Garti

Where do we find this assertion by Jacob of total commitment to religious principles in his words to Esau? In the charge of the messenger to Esau, the Torah states:

כה תאמרון לאדני לעשו כה אמר עבדך יעקב עם לבן גרתי ואחר עד עתה. ויהי לי שור וחמור צאן ועבד ושפחה ואשלחה להגיד לאדני למצא חן בעיניך.

Thus shall you say: To my lord Esau: Thus says your servant Jacob: *Im Lavan garti* – I sojourned with Laban and have lingered until now. I have acquired oxen and donkeys, flocks, servants and maidservants, and I am sending to tell my lord in order to find favor in your eyes.[5]

What is the meaning of this message? Esau certainly knew all about Jacob's sojourn with Laban, as his intelligence network was certainly up to par. What was Jacob telling him?

The critical word here is *garti* (I sojourned). A *ger* is a temporary resident, the antithesis of *ger ve-toshav* (A stranger and a sojourner, as Abraham said to the *Bnei Het*.)[6] After having spent twenty years in Laban's employ, Jacob said, "I was a stranger all that time." Usually, according to law, a *ger* is not obligated to contribute to the local charity or pay taxes until a period of twelve months elapses and he becomes a citizen, subject to all the laws of permanent residents.[7] Jacob told Esau that he had remained a *ger*, a stranger, for twenty years with Laban in order to make the point that if he were to live with Esau, the same would hold true. Jacob was telling his brother: even if I were to live with you for decades, it would be only in the sense of *garti*. I would remain only a *ger*, a temporary sojourner. This message had to be conveyed by angels so that it would be perfectly clear.

○ Defiance vs. Appeasement

At the time of the Second Temple's destruction, there was a question as to whether the Jews' attitude toward the Romans should be one of defiance or one of appeasement. The Talmud records an intense dispute on this issue between Rav Yohanan ben Zakkai, who favored compromise,

---

5 Genesis 32:5, 6.
6 Genesis 23:4.
7 See BT *Bava Batra* 7b.

and younger, hot-headed men who were willing to take on the Roman Empire at all costs.[8] No one knows what would have happened if Rav Yohanan ben Zakkai had taken the opposite view. Politically, we do not know whether we would have been transformed into a mighty political empire or remained a small, insignificant community dominated by the Moslem world. But the last nineteen hundred years would certainly have been different. It has not been easy for the Jewish nation to survive just with the Torah and without its own territory.

During the Second Commonwealth, the identity of the Jewish nation revolved around Jerusalem and the three annual pilgrimages to the Temple. After the destruction of the *Beit ha-Mikdash,* the Jewish people were so lost and traumatized that they had difficulty with holidays such as Yom Kippur. It was Rabbi Akiva who stated, אשריכם ישראל, לפני מי אתם מטהרין, מי מטהר אתכם אביכם שבשמים – "Happy are you, O Israel! Before whom do you cleanse yourselves, and who cleanses you from your transgressions? Your Father in Heaven."[9] He meant that the Temple was not an end in itself but rather a means to an end. The Temple was a place of ceremony, and Yom Kippur revolved around the service of the High Priest, to which the nations looked for expiation. Then Rav Yohanan ben Zakkai decided that the nation was built around God and his Torah rather than around land. Thus we are prepared to compromise, temporarily, on one *mahaneh* – our physical existence in the land of Israel – in order to preserve the other *mahaneh* – our spiritual existence.

✃ Implications for the State of Israel

As we reflect on the historical significance of the establishment of the state of Israel, we see that Divine Providence, in its inscrutable will, now declared a *volte face* – to build a government and a country. This was a radical departure from the last nineteen hundred years, when we

---

8 BT *Gittin* 56a.
9 BT *Yoma* 85b.

had the Torah without a land. Now we were bidden, as Jacob was, to operate on a dual level: to establish a government while simultaneously maintaining our commitment to God's Torah and mitzvot, which is our primary objective. With the government apparatus at our disposal, it will hopefully facilitate our ability to observe *mitzvot*. The ideal is that the *am segulah* (a people that is outstanding by dint of its actions) shall merge with the *eretz segulah* (the outstanding land) into one great entity.

Returning to the dispute between Rav Yohanan ben Zakkai and the young radicals of his generation, we are bewildered by the position of these young revolutionaries. While Rav Yohanan ben Zakkai saw the Roman Empire as an evil, he believed that its continued existence was a tool of God. Otherwise, it would have vanished. Therefore, he concluded, we must "walk softly with them." The younger radicals disagreed, contending that God, who had wrought miracles in Egypt, would intervene to save the *Beit ha-Mikdash* from destruction and give the Jews victory against the Romans.

There is an additional meaning in the message to Esau about the need for action on Jacob's part. The angels raised, regarding Jacob, the same dilemma that Rav Yonanan ben Zakkai and the radicals faced in response to Roman conquest. In effect, the angels challenged Jacob: Why are you passive in the face of a potential onslaught by Esau? He is powerful and well-organized. Four hundred of his men are marching toward your camp. Your faith is laudable, but don't depend on miracles!

However, Jacob used both approaches. He offered up prayers but he also rolled up his sleeves. True, a single angel could have defeated Esau's army without effort, just as an angel destroyed the Assyrian army of Sanherib, which consisted of 185,000 men, in one night.[10] But it is not guaranteed. These are the principles of *bitahon* and *hishtadlut*. Our

---

10 2 Kings 19:35 and BT *Sanhedrin* 95a.

challenge is to have *emunah*, to offer prayer, but also to be prepared to confront our adversary.[11]

---

11 Extrapolating from the above to the art of healing and medicine, the Rav decried the assertion of Christian Science according to which "God makes a person sick, and therefore only
God heals" (see BT *Bava Kamma* 85a, Rashi רופאים לרפאות ניתנה רשות לרופאים, ד"ה). In medicine, we
must take the initiative. One who becomes ill and does nothing to heal himself is comparable to one who commits *shefichut damim* – bloodshed. This is the essence of Judaism,
which operates on two tracks. On the one hand, one's prayer is not a contradiction of faith,
but reflects the very essence of the principles of faith. On the other hand, when the kings
took Lot prisoner, Abraham could have responded by saying, "Who told him to go and
live in that decadent place?" Instead, on the first night of Passover, he organized an army.
We are talking of Abraham, the prototype of the knight of faith. Why did he resolve to
go to war? He did so because human beings must take action. These two tracks are the
quintessence of the man of faith.

Vayeshev: Internal Conflict
in the House of Jacob

WHAT IS THE connection between Parashat Vayeshev and its *haftarah* from the Book of Amos? The prophecy begins:

כה אמר ה' על שלשה פשעי ישראל ועל ארבעה לא אשיבנו על מכרם בכסף צדיק ואביון בעבור נעלים.

> Thus spoke God: For three transgressions of Israel, but for four I will not pardon them – for selling a righteous man for money, and a poor man for shoes.[1]

According to one midrashic interpretation, the brothers used the proceeds from the sale of Joseph to purchase for each of themselves a pair of shoes.[2] Echoes of this Midrash are also heard in the classic liturgical piece *Eleh Ezkera,* which is recited as part of the *Mussaf* prayer on Yom Kippur in the story of the *asara harugei malchut* (The Ten Martyrs):

> They answered him, "The kidnapper must die." Said he, "Then what of your ancestors who sold their brother, peddling him to a caravan of Ishmaelites in exchange for shoes? Now

---

1 Amos 2:6.
2 *Pirkei de-Rabbi Eliezer* 38; Targum Yonatan ben Uziel on Genesis 37:28.

you must accept the judgment of Heaven upon yourselves, for since your forefathers' times there have been none like you. Were they alive, I would have prosecuted them before you, so you must bear the sin of your ancestors."

The intent is that the execution of the ten sages by the Romans was in expiation for the brothers' sale of Joseph and their purchase of shoes with the proceeds.

However, this exegesis does not correspond to the literal meaning of the text or the context of the entire *haftarah*. The prophet Amos rails against various forms of corruption and injustice, and deplores the exploitation of the poor for selfish ends. The prophet continues:

על בגדים חבלים יטו אצל כל מזבח ויין ענושים ישתו בית אלהיהם ... ואנכי
העליתי אתכם מארץ מצרים ואולך אתכם במדבר ארבעים שנה לרשת את ארץ
האמרי. ואקים מבניכם לנביאים ומבחוריכם לנזרים האף אין זאת בני ישראל נאם
ה'. ותשקו את הנזרים יין ועל הנביאים צויתם לאמר לא תנבאו ... אריה שאג מי
לא יירא א-דני א-להים דבר מי לא ינבא.

They recline on pawned garments beside every altar and drink the wine of victims they penalized in the temple of their gods ... I brought you up from the land of Egypt and I led you through the wilderness for forty years to take possession of the land of the Amorite. I established some of your sons as prophets and some of your young men as Nazirites – is this not also so, O children of Israel? – the word of God. But you gave the Nazirites wine to drink and you commanded the prophets, saying: Do not prophesy .... A lion has roared; who will not fear? The Lord God has spoken; who will not prophesy?[3]

---

3   Amos 2:8, 10–12; 3:8.

Parashat Vayeshev contains three themes: the sale of Joseph, the story of Judah and Tamar, and Joseph in Egypt before his release from prison. What is the common chord of these three themes? Before, Jacob encountered opposition from without – from Esau, Laban, and Shechem – but his own household was at peace. Now, his own sons were fighting each other. Joseph's brothers hated him so deeply that they could not exchange a peaceful word with him. Thus, the theme is one of internal conflict within the house of Jacob.

✣ Joseph's Dreams

What was the nature of the brothers' opposition? What bothered them? Initially, it was Jacob's favoritism toward Joseph. Parents often have preferences. A father may focus on the oldest child who becomes his assistant, while a mother may dote on her youngest child, who remains her baby no matter how old he or she may be. Nevertheless, most parents try to hide their preferences in the interests of good parenting. Jacob not only made no effort to hide his preference for Joseph, but even gave him the coat of many colors in order to show his other sons that he considered Joseph their leader.[4] A visible proof of this proclamation of leadership may be found in the fact that the brothers felt compelled to take the coat from Joseph and damage it – by tearing it and staining it with blood – to the point where it could never be worn again.

The brothers' hatred and envy of Joseph only increased when Joseph revealed his dreams. This is seen from the text that the brothers referred to him not as *baal kutonet ha-pasim* (owner of the many-colored coat) but rather *baal ha-halomot ha-lazeh* (that dreamer).

ויאמרו איש אל אחיו הנה בעל החלמות הלזה בא. ועתה לכו ונהרגהו ונשלכהו באחד הברות ואמרנו חיה רעה אכלתהו ונראה מה יהיו חלמתיו.

---

4   See Seforno on Genesis: 37:3.

And one said to the other: Look! Here comes that dreamer. So now, let us go and kill him and throw him into one of the pits, and say that a wild beast devoured him – and we shall see what will become of his dreams.[5]

Later, upon recognizing them in Egypt, the text records Joseph's immediate, almost reflexive response:

ויזכר יוסף את החלמות אשר חלם להם ויאמר אלהם מרגלים אתם לראות את ערות הארץ באתם.

Joseph, recalling the dreams that he had dreamed about them, said to them, "You are spies! You have come to spy out the land's vulnerabilities!"[6]

It is obvious that the tragedy of the sale of Joseph was ultimately caused by the dreams.

A *baal ha-halomot* is not a dim-witted person, but often a gifted, bright individual – a visionary, leader and innovator. What did the brothers want, then? The answer is that they wanted to squelch Joseph's dreams. Joseph possessed a prophetic spark and a charismatic personality. The brothers attempted to suppress these things, but prophecy is an overwhelming force that breaks through the human personality. In essence, this was the transgression of Joseph's brothers – their attempt to block that visionary power.

This is the organic connection between the *haftarah* and the *parashah* of Vayeshev. Like Joseph's brothers, the contemporaries of the prophet Amos wanted to stifle his prophecies as well. ותשקו את הנזרים יין ועל הנביאים צויתם לאמר לא תנבאו – "But you made the nazirites drink wine and commanded the prophets, saying, 'Do not prophesy.'"[7] Amos tells them that the prophecies of the prophet are inexorable: אריה שאג מי לא

---

5 Genesis 37:19–20.
6 Genesis 42:9.
7 Amos 2:12.

ייא א־דני א־להים דבר מי לא ינבא – "A lion has roared; who will not fear? The Lord God has spoken; who will not prophesy?"[8] The prophet Jeremiah similarly states:

ואמרתי לא אזכרנו ולא אדבר עוד בשמו והיה בלבי כאש בערת עצר בעצמתי ונלאיתי כלכל ולא אוכל.

Yet if I were to say, "I will not mention him or speak in his name anymore," [His word] would be like burning fire in my heart, stored in my bones, and though I might struggle to contain it, I could not.[9]

Joseph's Contribution to Jewish Survival

What contribution does Joseph, the gifted dreamer, make to the survival of the Jewish people? The Rav considered Joseph's gifts in light of the festival of Hanukkah. The miracle of Hanukkah, which took place approximately two hundred years after the canonization of the written law, is bound up inextricably with the Oral Law.

A major motif of Hanukkah is the struggle between Jewish and Greek cultures. Of great importance was our enemies' lack of modesty, particularly in sexual matters. Ancient Greek culture, which regarded the display of the human body as an aesthetic act, regarded nudity as commonplace and rejected what we regard as the most basic standards of modesty. Joseph, by his disciplined response to Potiphar's wife's attempts at seducing him, displayed heroic modesty, which is the very core of Judaism and the character trait that the gentile world wished to destroy.

Even more important, the Rav noted that Joseph provided the model for a Jew to survive in *galut*. In the first commonwealth, the people and the land were indivisible. There were no Jews outside the

---

8 Amos 3:8.
9 Jeremiah 20:9.

land, no Diaspora or *galut*. Joseph was the first Jew to experience the hardships of exile both as a slave and then as viceroy to the Pharaoh of Egypt. He underwent a dual experience of *galut*: from poverty and imprisonment to unimaginable wealth. He showed the way for Jews throughout the millennia to endure the long night of exile without losing faith in God.

❧ מקץ ❧

Miketz: The Mysterious Ish

T HERE IS A fascinating parallel found in the three *parshiyot* that precede and follow the festival of Hanukkah. Vayishlah, Vayeshev and Miketz all have a common denominator: an *ish* (man), a mysterious individual. In Vayishlah, we encounter the *ish* who wrestles with Jacob.[1] In Vayeshev, as Joseph searches for his brothers, he meets an *ish* who tells him where his brothers are.[2] Finally, in Miketz, Joseph himself becomes the mysterious *ish* who confronts his brothers on their arrival in Egypt.[3] In Miketz, the word *ish* appears as many times as to approach absurdity.

There is an important contrast between the *ish* with whom Jacob fights in Vayishlah and the *Ish* of Vayeshev or of Miketz. Jacob knew his enemy, the ministering angel of Esau, and the reason for his brother's hostility. Jacob stood accused of a double crime: of taking the *bechorah*, the special right of the firstborn, and the *berachot* – his father's blessings – and he had to face his adversary. When we know our enemies, however, we can plot a strategy. There are ways to to disengage from them – for example, by offering gifts.

---

1 Genesis 32:25.
2 Genesis 37:15.
3 Genesis 42:30.

In Vayeshev and Miketz, the *ish* was unknown to those to whom he appeared. When an *ish* is unknown, this leads to fear. Is he friend or foe? What does he want? The *ish* whom Joseph encountered is strange and foreboding. Why does the Torah reveal the encounter, and what did Joseph hear about the brothers' location? Had this *ish* not appeared, Joseph might have simply gone back home, and he would not have been sold into slavery. Clearly, it was all part of God's plan. Similarly, in Parashat Miketz, why should this powerful and frightening *ish* ask them all sorts of personal questions about their father and brother? Once again, the answer is that it was all part of the Divine plan, paving the way for the coming of the Messiah.

There are three more illustrations from the first verse of Parashat Miketz that suggest the divine orchestration of events:

(1) The use of the term *ketz*. The Torah begins Parashat Miketz with the following description: ויהי מקץ שנתים ימים ופרעה חלם – "It happened at the end of two years to the day that Pharaoh had a dream."[4] The Hebrew language contains two words both of which signify the notion of ending – *ketz* and *sof*. Why does the Torah use the word *ketz* instead of *sof*? The word *ketz* denotes an ending that has cataclysmic and often messianic overtones, the end of an era, of a particular zeitgeist. In this context, *ketz* signified the end of *galut*, or suffering, for Joseph.[5] The word *sof*, in contrast, implies an act of termination and closure. When a person dies, we use the term *sof* because death carries a sense of finality. When a rainstorm ends, you use the term *sof*, not *ketz*. The word *ketz* applies to a process whose evolution we expect to unfold. It is the end, and the fulfillment, of a particular epoch. In Parashat Noah, after waiting for one hundred and twenty years for the corruption on earth to subside, God finally said to Noah, קץ כל בשר בא לפני – "The end of all flesh has come before me."[6] Here, the word *ketz* signifies the end of an era and

---

4 Genesis 41:1.
5 See Exodus 12:41.
6 Genesis 6:13.

the onset of the flood. In a similar vein, the story of Joseph's life is not a series of coincidental events but rather a tortuous process, planned and designed from above. The end of one of these segments is embedded in the term *Miketz*.[7]

(2) The Torah describes the exact amount of time that leads up to this episode in the phrase שנתים ימים– "two years,"[8] as opposed to the term *shnatayim*, which connotes approximately two years. Here, the precise amount of time is given: two years, not a second more or less. Similarly, the Torah tells us that the redemption from Egypt took place with the same precise timing: "ויהי מקץ שלשים שנה וארבע מאות שנה" – "And it happened at the end of a hundred and thirty years."[9] The process of Joseph's sudden ascent to greatness was ready to begin, similar to the night of the Jewish people's redemption from Egypt. Its consummation had to occur with split-second timing.

(3) Pharaoh's sudden transformation. A further proof of this thesis is the language that the Torah uses: ופרעה חלם – "Pharaoh was dreaming"[10] – in the present tense. *Prima facie,* it should have stated *u-far'o haya holem* (and Pharaoh dreamt), in the past tense. The way the Torah describes the event "is significant"; it is a participle rather than a verb, for it describes not the event (as a verb) but the person (as a participle). The use of the present tense accentuates the remarkable fact that Pharaoh was now a dreamer. His personality underwent a sudden, unexpected change, which occurred precisely when Joseph matured and was ready to be elevated. Had the past tense been used, then Pharaoh would not have appointed Joseph to a royal position of authority, since the fact that he had dreamed would have been perfectly ordinary.

How could Pharaoh distinguish between his magicians' interpretations of his dreams and Joseph's? Why did he accept Joseph's

---

7   See Commentary of the Beit Halevi on the Torah, Parashat Miketz.
8   Genesis 41:1.
9   Exodus 12:41, Rashi, op.cit.
10 Genesis 41:1.

interpretation while rejecting the others? Surely he was not guided by *ruah ha-kodesh.* In order to recognize the authenticity of Joseph's interpretation, Pharaoh had to become a dreamer like Joseph and develop a kinship with him. Only once he, too, became a visionary, could he appreciate Joseph's intellectual genius.

In light of this, we can understand why Pharaoh wanted Joseph's family to immigrate to Egypt. He reasoned that they must all be blessed with genius. Hence the language of *Pharaoh holem*: Pharaoh suddenly became a dreamer and a visionary. When he and Joseph met, they resonated perfectly with each other. How did such a transformation occur, in which a former slave and prisoner rose into royalty, with Pharaoh so awestruck that he declared הנמצא כזה איש אשר רוח א־להים בו – "Could we find another like him – a man in whom is the spirit of God?"[11] How did it happen?

It was Divine providence at work. Pharaoh saw in Joseph two qualifications: *hacham* and *navon*. A *hacham* (wise person) can reason and speculate. He possesses a great and vivid imagination. A *navon,* who possesses profound understanding, can translate plans into action. Joseph was not merely a competent bookkeeper. He had the talent and insight to mastermind the entire economy of the Egyptian empire – and these were the qualities that Pharaoh saw in him.

These elements all illustrate God's careful, precise orchestration of historical events, which were intended to bring about the ultimate redemption of the Jewish people.

---

11 Genesis 41:38.

Vayigash: We Have an Old Father and a Young Child

T HE RAV INTRODUCED his discussion of Parshat Vayigash with a personal reflection and reminiscence. He described himself as "a poor rabbi and a very good teacher." He said that by sheer association, he recalled an experience of his early youth. He grew up in a small town called Chaslovitz in White Russia, where his father, Rav Moshe Soloveitchik, was the rabbi. Like every other Jewish boy in town, the Rav attended the local *heder* (day school). At the time, he questioned the scholarship of his *melamed,* who was a Chabadnik. However, he was grateful to his teacher for his entire life because he taught him something that no one but his mother ever taught him: how a Jew could be imaginative in his practice of Judaism. He addressed himself "to my soul and to my heart." It takes time for an individual to develop breadth and depth. Not many *heder* boys know how to behold a vision. Of his *heder* teacher, the Rav said, "He taught me how to dream and how to feel *Yahadut.*"[1]

The episode that the Rav related took place on an overcast day in January after Hanukkah, in the context of Parashat Vayigash. After

---

1   See "A Tribute to the Rebbetzin of Talne." *Tradition* (Spring 1978).

the holiday atmosphere of Hanukkah had waned for the poor Jews of Chaslovitz – most of whom made a meager living as peddlers – and for the *heder* boys, a long winter lay ahead of them. They would awaken in the dark and return home with lanterns in their hands. On that particular day, all the *heder* boys were depressed, listless and sad. They chanted the first verses of Parashat Vayigash in a dull monotone, in Hebrew and in the Yiddish vernacular.

ויגש אליו יהודה ויאמר בי אדני ידבר נא עבדך דבר באזני אדני ואל יחר אפך בעבדך כי כמוך כפרעה. אדני שאל את עבדיו לאמר היש לכם אב או אח. ונאמר אל אדני יש לנו אב זקן וילד זקנים קטן ואחיו מת ויותר הוא לבדו לאמו ואביו אהבו.

Then Judah approached him and said, If you please, my lord, let your servant speak a word in my lord's ears, and let not your anger flare up against your servant, for you are like Pharaoh. My Lord asked his servants saying: Have you a father or brother? We said to my lord: We have an elderly father and a young child of his old age.[2] His brother is dead. He alone is left to his mother, and his father loves him.[3]

It seemed, as the boys read the question and answer, that the *melamed* was half asleep. Suddenly, he jumped to his feet like a tiger, with a strange, enigmatic gleam in his eyes. His eyes were piercing and searching. The *melamed* motioned to the boy who was reading to stop. Then, he turned to the Rav and said, "*Podravin*" (assistant to the *rebbi*), as he called the Rav whenever he was excited. The *melamed* uttered the word with some sarcasm because, as a Chabadnik, he "could never forgive me for the fact that I was born to a Brisker family" (which represented *hitnagdut* at the highest level). "Of course," the Rav added, "I cannot accept responsibility for that."

---

2   See Targum Yerushalmi, which translates it as "a bright, talented child."
3   Genesis 44:18–20.

The *melamed* asked: What was the nature of the question that Joseph asked his brothers regarding whether they had a father? Of course they had a father, as does every human being except Adam. The Rav tried to answer the *melamed* that Joseph wanted to find out whether his father Jacob was still living. The *melamed* began to talk and didn't address himself to the *heder* children, but gave the impression that he was speaking to a mysterious visitor. Joseph, said the *melamed,* wasn't asking his brothers about *avhut de-itgalun* (revealed fatherhood), but about *avhut de-itkasun* (hidden fatherhood). In our modern idiom, he wasn't asking about biological fatherhood but rather about existential fatherhood. Joseph was eager to know whether the brothers were committed to their origin. *Ha-yesh lachem Av?*[4] Are you rooted in your father as the foundation of your existence, or are you merely a band of rootless, wandering shepherds?

The *melamed* then raised his voice. "Do you acknowledge that the old father represents an ancient tradition? Do you believe that the father is capable of telling you something new and exciting, or are you insolent and arrogant and deny your dependence on your father? – היש לכם אב Have you a father?"[5] The *melamed* pointed to the Rav's study partner,[6] Yitzhak der Schmidt, whose father was a blacksmith, and said, "Do you, Itzik, have a father or not?" He ended by saying that if a Jew admits to the supremacy of his father here, then ipso facto he admits to the supremacy of his universal Father, *Atik Yomin,* the Ancient of Days.

If we use this approach, said the Rav, we can interpret the second question similarly. "Have you a brother?" Joseph was not interested in knowing whether they had another biological brother who had inherited their parents' genetic code. Joseph wanted to know: Does your awareness of time stop at the present moment, or do you consider future

---

4 Genesis 44:19.
5 Op. cit.
6 The Rav commented that his study mate was considered a prodigy, while he himself had the reputation of being a slow child.

generations as well? Do you plan for the world of tomorrow, which is enveloped in the mist of non-being? Do you see a vision? Do you believe in the improbable? The brothers' answer was yes. We have an elderly father, they said – the *Atik Yomin*. We also have a bright, vivacious, talented young child, our younger brother, who represents the world of tomorrow. A young child challenges us to make possible the birth of generations unborn.

The answer that the sons of Jacob gave to Joseph is still true today. God has chosen us and burdened us with many duties. Despite our many faults, we have an "elderly father" and a "young child." We are committed to a great and mysterious past. We had a magnificent physical building, the *Beit ha-Mikdash,* built of stone. It was consumed by fire some one thousand nine hundred years ago, and yet we mourn for it as if it had been destroyed only yesterday.

We still remember Eretz Yisrael. We fight for the possession of the land and continue to sacrifice young lives for each sand dune, for each rocky hill. Why? Here in America, we have freedom and many privileges, and anti-Semitism poses no real threat. Do we expect to be wealthier in Eretz Yisrael? Do we expect to accomplish so much more there? The answer is that about three thousand five hundred years ago, our *av zaken,* Abraham, walked behind his flock on those sandy trails and, by traversing the land, endowed it with *kedushah.*[7] Centuries later, a prophet and king named David played the harp and sang beautiful hymns to God. The hills of our ancient homeland, which echo with ancient melodies and fiery words, are worth the sacrifice of our youth.

Do our collective memory and our loyalty to the *av zaken* justify alienating the world at large? Is it logical or paradoxical? Why can we not break free of the *av zaken* and adapt to the current spirit of the times? The answer is that we cannot because Jews are immensely concerned with the future and with our existence as a spiritual community. No other nation

---

7   See BT *Bava Batra* 100a.

has ever cared as much about survival at the existential-spiritual level as we do. The "young child" challenges us to care for tomorrow.

No other nation emphasizes education as much as the Jews do. Nowhere else do we find norms such as ושננתם לבניך – "You shall teach them thoroughly to your children,"[8] ולמדתם אתם את בניכם לדבר בם – "You shall teach them to your children to discuss them,"[9] והגדת לבנך ביום ההוא – "You shall tell your child on that day,"[10] והיה כי ישאלך בנך מחר – "And it shall be that when your child asks you at some future time,"[11] and so on. Children are the ambassadors of our vision of the future. Because of this, we are oriented toward both the past and the future.

An *av zaken* is addressing you, asking: Why did you come? Who dragged you here? The rabbi? This is an illusion. You came because of the *av zaken* and the *yeled zekunim* – the elderly man and the young child. What does Judaism demand of the Jew? A rendezvous between the *av zaken* and the *yeled zekunim*. That is our tradition: a merger between past tradition and a vision of the future. What does the *av zaken* teach the *yeled zekunim*? What does the patriarch tell him? He tells him the story of his life. The *av zaken* and the *yeled zekunim* understand each other. The second-, third- and fourth-generation American understand the *av zaken*. According to sociologists, Jews should have assimilated into American society long ago, vanishing without a trace. However, they have shown renewed dedication to the 3500-year-old *av zaken*. That splendid old man and the *yeled zekunim* have come to understand and love each other, and therefore are able to maintain and strengthen the heritage of the covenantal community so that it will continue to flourish and prosper far into the future.[12]

---

8 Deuteronomy 6:7.
9 Deuteronomy 11:19.
10 Exodus 13:8.
11 Exodus 13:14.
12 See *Man of Faith in the Modern World: Reflections of the Rav,* vol. 2, Rabbi Abraham Besdin; and *The First Jewish Grandfather* (15–23) for an elaborate explication of this theme.

Vayigash II: The Lessons of the Av Zaken – Principles of Jewish Education

THE *AV ZAKEN* teaches two fundamental lessons. The first is the lesson of divine discipline, and the second is that of divine romance. The first lesson is a normative one. The second lesson is a romantic one.

There are four realms within the divine discipline. The Rav referred to Moshe's farewell address in Deuteronomy: וידעת עם לבבך כי כאשר ייסר איש את בנו ה' א-להיך מיסרך – "You should know in your heart that just as a father will chastise his son, so the Lord your God chastises you."[1] In other words, when you deliver *mussar,* you are articulating the following formula: *mussar* equals ethics, discipline and morality. The Torah teaches Jews to lead disciplined lives that follow specific rules and contain sequence, continuity and orderliness.

~ 1. Discipline in matters of the body

The main distinction between Judaism and paganism lies in the fact that paganism preaches a life of hedonism – orgiastic and hypnotic

---

1 Deuteronomy 8:5.

pleasure. The pagan philosophy is to enjoy life as much as possible for as long as possible. On the other hand, Judaism demands sacrificial action and resignation, the capacity to withdraw from something tempting, attractive and beautiful even as it is within our reach. The great test of human beings, according to Judaism, is the capacity to live a disciplined life rather than a brutish existence. Undisciplined, arrogant behavior leads to the defilement of the human personality, while discipline and modesty lead to *kedushah*. This is what the *av zaken* teaches the young child: the ability to withdraw and engage in disciplined action. Sexual activity demands discipline because while human beings may resemble animals physiologically, we must exercise our physical urges in a disciplined manner. The dignified and modest way in which we satisfy our biological drives for sex and food is the first foundation of Judaism. Even if temptation is overwhelming and orgiastic life is within our reach, we withdraw and resign ourselves.[2]

2. Discipline in interpersonal relationships

A second area of discipline that the *av zaken* teaches is the discipline required in the area of human relationships and interaction. There are hundreds of precepts focused on the category of *bein adam la-havero* (matters between human beings) in the realm of social morality. While disciplined action leads to *kedushah,* disciplined social action leads to *emet* (truthfulness), *hesed* (kindness) and honesty, which command the respect of non-Jews. These are as important as the principles of *bein adam la-makom* (matters between human beings and God). The question of whether I am legally and honestly entitled to a profit that is offered to me is just as important as whether the food that I am about to eat is kosher or not.

---

2   See Ramban, Leviticus 19:2. See also "Catharsis" in *Tradition* (Spring 1978) for an explanation of this basic component of self-discipline.

✍ 3. Discipline in one's inner life

A third important concept that must be taught is a disciplined inner life. The Torah is not limited to the physiological and social elements of a Jew's life, but is also interested in his inner activities, emotional life, feelings and sentiments. The Torah knows that feelings of hatred and envy are destructive and human beings have the ability to rid themselves of them. His father told him that this envy was a character flaw, and he began to train himself until he overcame it successfully. The Rav said: There is no *kinah* (jealousy) in my house, and I rejoice totally in the success of my fellow man. On the other hand, we know of constructive emotions such as love and gratitude that one should strive to cultivate. The Torah therefore obligates us not only to control our physical activities but to discipline our emotional lives – and to teach our children to do so as well.

✍ 4. Discipline in One's Thinking

A fourth area that we must nurture is disciplined thought. Training children in the Oral Law and *Halachah* means much more than giving them a system of rules. It means teaching them a particular system of thought, a unique method of approaching and interpreting the world. *Halachah* is universal and interprets every phenomenon and event with its own indigenous categories, concepts and methods. The Rav noted that he was familiar with the most modern philosophical analysis and, without apologetics, could vouch for the fact that the yeshiva methodology of definition, abstraction and postulating was not only equal to it but better. It is not apologetic to say that our instruments of thought are more precise than those of John Dewey and William James. The *av zaken* teaches the young child far more than Talmud. He teaches him how to think and discipline his thoughts. He gives him a method, a methodology, an approach, conceptual analysis, classification, and techniques of inference. This takes time. The Rav mused that when he studied mathematics, he was taught calculation techniques of multiplication and subtraction. Now, however, because of reforms in education, conceptualization is being taught as part of grade-school mathematics. This is our task in teaching Talmud. The Rav expressed his amazement at the accomplishments of American Jewish children, whom he considered very bright.

⁀ The Lesson of Divine Romance

In addition to the dimensions of discipline on the physical, interpersonal, emotional and intellectual levels, Judaism contains another important aspect: the romantic. Ultimately, we must achieve rapprochement with God, and we must feel and experience our Judaism. The study of the Oral Law and compliance with its precepts is perhaps the most sublime of all pursuits, since the greatest pleasure is to study the Torah in depth. The Jewish way of life is the most exciting and purifying one of all. The *av zaken* also teaches the *yeled zekunim* how to experience Judaism, which is the most formidable of all tasks.

The Rav mentioned that he was a good teacher of Halacha, able to explain and popularize abstract and complex Talmudic topics to his students. Often before Rosh ha-Shannah and Yom Kippur, he would study the laws of those days and search for philosophic concepts that clarified their beauty and structure in contemporary language. Nevertheless, he could not convey to his students how he had felt on those holy days at their age. His experience was fraught with nostalgia and longing. He felt transported to a different time and place when the *sheliah zibbur* sang והכהנים והעם העומדים בעזרה – "And the kohanim and the people who were in the courtyard," etc.[3] It is impossible to transfer experiences, to tell the story of inner restlessness and serenity, of joy and awe, of trepidation and certitude, of ecstasy and mystical outlook in words. Rather, this can only be done through personal contact and modeling, and spirit communing with spirit in silence.

---

3 From the Avodah section of the Yom Kippur *mussaf* service.

Vayehi I

ᴧ Am I in the Place of God?

THE TORAH RECORDS that after Jacob's death and burial,
Joseph's brothers feared that his attitude toward them would
change. Our sages comment that it did.[1] The dialogue in the
Torah is the following:

> ויראו אחי יוסף כי מת אביהם ויאמרו לו ישטמנו יוסף והשב ישיב לנו את כל הרעה
> אשר גמלנו אתו. ויצוו אל יוסף לאמר אביך צוה לפני מותו לאמר. כה תאמרו
> ליוסף אנא שא נא פשע אחיך וחטאתם כי רעה גמלוך ועתה שא נא לפשע עבדי
> אלקי אביך ויבך יוסף בדברם אליו. וילכו גם אחיו ויפלו לפניו ויאמרו הננו לך
> לעבדים. ויאמר אלהם יוסף אל תיראו כי התחת א־להים אני. ואתם חשבתם עלי
> רעה א־להים חשבה לטבה למען עשה כיום הזה להחית עם רב.

When Joseph's brothers saw that their father was dead, they
said, "Perhaps Joseph will nurse hatred against us, and then
he will surely repay us all the evil that we did to him." They

---

1   See Rashi on Genesis 50:15. "What is meant by 'Joseph's brothers saw'? They noticed that
    his death had an effect on Joseph, for they had been accustomed to dine at Joseph's table
    and he was friendly toward them out of respect for his father. But once Jacob died, he was
    not friendly toward them." (Midrash *Tanhuma Yashan*, Exodus 2; *Genesis Rabbah* 100:8).

commanded that Joseph be told, "Your father commanded before his death, saying, 'Thus shall you say to Joseph: Please forgive the spiteful deed of your brothers and their sin, for they did you evil. So now please forgive the spiteful deed of the servants of your father's God.'" Joseph wept when they spoke to him. His brothers themselves also went and fell before him, saying, "We are ready to be your slaves." But Joseph said to them, "Fear not, for am I in the place of God? Although you intended me harm, God intended it for good: in order to accomplish – it is as clear as this day – to keep a large nation alive."[2]

Although Jacob had given no such order, the brothers said that he had for the sake of peace.[3] But the Torah's statement – that they saw that their father was dead – alludes to this shift in attitude and the cooling of their former relationship.

What was the nature of Joseph's response to them – כי התחת א־להים אני – "am I in the place of God?" Jacob used a similar expression earlier in response to Rachel's statement: הבה לי בנים ואם אין מתה אנכי – "Give me children! If not, I am dead."[4] Jacob said, התחת א־להים אנכי אשר מנע ממך פרי בטן – "Am I in the place of God, who has withheld offspring from you?"[5] We can suggest two approaches to understanding this question.

☙ 1. The manner in which one must ask forgiveness

The question "Am I in the place of God?" was not a response to the brothers' petition for forgiveness per se, which was legitimate and justified. It was a response to the manner in which they had made it. There are two domains of transgression: between human beings and God and between

---

2 Genesis 50:15–20.
3 Rashi on Genesis 50:16.
4 Genesis 30:1.
5 Genesis 30:2.

human beings themselves. Each domain requires confession and forgiveness. However, a human being who sins against another must ask for *mehilah* (pardon). The way in which we address and refer to God differs greatly from the way we address and refer to each other. It constitutes two different approaches. When we approach our fellow human beings before Yom Kippur, we do not say "*Ana, selah na*," for such a phrase is appropriate for God only. This is a language of *viddui,* of surrender. When I use it, I state that I am wrong and God is right, and that there are no mitigating circumstances. Jacob's brothers spoke in a manner that is appropriate only for God, and Joseph therefore answered, "Am I in the place of God?" This is an example of Joseph's humility: that despite his great power in Egypt, which deified its rulers, he protested when his brothers addressed him in an idiom reserved only for the divine.

℘ 2. Exact retribution is not in the human domain

A second explanation for Joseph's question, "Am I in the place of God?" can be advanced with more conceptual sophistication. Our sages ruled that the verse עין תחת עין שן תחת שן – "An eye for an eye, a tooth for a tooth"[6] refers to monetary compensation.[7] This is an unequivocal ruling of the sages. The verse may not be interpreted literally. One may then ask: why did the Torah express itself in a way that is open to misinterpretation when it might have said, for example, *kesef tahat ayin* (money for an eye)? If the Torah had used such an expression, then, God forbid, one might, in a moment of uncontrolled anger, destroy a human being's sight and pay damages afterwards.[8]

The Rav referred to an incident in which a psychiatrist advocated institutionalizing a mentally ill child. In a fit of anger, the child's father shot the doctor in the eyes, blinding him. Had the Torah legislated

---

6 Exodus 21:24.
7 BT *Bava Kamma* 83b, 84a.
8 See Ramban on Exodus 21:24.

financial compensation, it would have been a civil matter, not a criminal one. There would be no human dimension. To take away someone's eyesight is subhuman. What sum of money could possibly be considered equivalent to destroying someone's vision? Can one put a price on a human limb or faculty? Thus it is with the language "An eye for an eye." Is any earthly court capable of measuring the pain and suffering involved? Rather, the Torah is saying that the perpetrator deserves to lose his own eye and suffer exactly as his victim suffered, but no human court is capable of carrying out such a punishment.

It follows, then, that the brothers were terrified that Joseph would treat them as they had treated him – and this, in effect, was Joseph's answer: "I was isolated from the family for years. I was imprisoned and subjected to hardships that you deserve to undergo as well. But as a mortal human being, I cannot measure the proper recompense. You will never understand what I went through. Therefore, am I in the place of God? I cannot exact true retribution – *ayin tahat ayin* – for your actions. Only God is entitled to exact retribution on this level. Therefore, no retaliation is feasible or possible, and you need not be concerned."

Vayehi II: Bring My Bones Up with You from Here

AT THE END of Parashat Vayehi, we read the following:

ויאמר יוסף אל אחיו אנכי מת וא-להים פקד יפקד אתכם והעלה אתכם
מן הארץ הזאת אל הארץ אשר נשבע לאברהם ליצחק וליעקב.

Joseph said to his brothers: I am about to die, but God will surely remember you and bring you out of this land to the land that he swore to Abraham, to Isaac and to Jacob.[1]

The expression *pakod yifkod* (God will surely remember you) was a password that Jacob entrusted to Joseph. In turn, Joseph entrusted it to his brothers, who told it to the heads of their families. Joseph said that while he could not identify the precise moment of redemption, it would surely come – and when it did, the Israelites were to carry his bones out of Egypt. In Parashat Beshalaḥ, the Torah recounts that Moshe obeyed Joseph's command.

ויקח משה את עצמות יוסף עמו כי השבע השביע את בני ישראל לאמר פקד יפקד
א-להים אתכם והעליתם את עצמתי מזה אתכם.

---

1   Genesis 50:24.

Moshe took the bones of Joseph with him, for he had firmly adjured the Children of Israel, saying: God will surely remember you, and you shall bring up my bones from here with you.[2]

In Parashat Beshalah, the Torah here adds one word that does not occur in the relevant portion of Parashat Vayehi: אתכם (with you). Why?

Our sages said that the skeletons of all of Jacob's sons were brought out of Egypt during the Israelites' departure. What, then, is the significance of the additional word אתכם? Why did Jacob make Joseph swear an oath that he would not bury him in Egypt? There is a profound bond between a person and the land in which he is buried. The exodus from Egypt would have been affected badly if Jacob had not been buried in Eretz Yisrael when the Jewish people departed.

Joseph was in an uncomfortable position when he asked Pharaoh's permission to bury Jacob in Canaan. As viceroy of Egypt, he had saved the country from famine and rescued its economy. If Egypt was the source of Joseph's power and prosperity, what could possibly be wrong with burying his father there? For this reason, when Joseph asked Pharaoh for permission to bury Jacob in Canaan, he asked through a courtier and not directly.

ויעברו ימי בכיתו וידבר יוסף אל בית פרעה לאמר אם נא מצאתי חן בעיניכם דברו
נא באזני פרעה לאמר. אבי השביעני לאמר הנה אנכי מת בקברי אשר כריתי לי
בארץ כנען שמה תקברני ועתה אעלה נא ואקברה את אבי ואשובה.

When the period of lamentation was over, Joseph spoke to Pharaoh's household, saying: "If it pleases you and if I have found favor in your eyes, speak now to Pharaoh, saying, 'My father adjured me, saying, "Behold, I am about to die. In my tomb, which I dug for myself in the land of Canaan – there

---

2 Exodus 13:19.

you are to bury me." Now, I will go up, if it please you, and bury my father. Then I will return.'"[3]

It seems that despite his high position in the kingdom, Joseph felt that he was treading on thin ice. Essentially, he remained an *Ivri, a Hebrew,* rather than a *Mitzri,* an Egyptian – hence his hesitation in speaking directly to Pharaoh. The Rav related a similar story of Baron Edmond Rothschild, (which was recounted to him by Baron Alain de Rothschild) who died in France in 1948, and stipulated in his will that he be buried in Israel. When years later, he was disinterred and reburied in Israel, Charles de Gaulle commented, "I thought he was a loyal Frenchman. Isn't France good enough for him to be buried here?" Neither Pharaoh nor de Gaulle understood the nature of the Jew and his bond with Israel. This is what Moshe revealed in Exodus when he added the word אתכם (with you). It would have been inappropriate for Joseph, the viceroy of Egypt, to add that word. He would have been buried in a royal tomb befitting his stature. By the use of that one word, אתכם, Moshe showed that despite his high position in Egypt, Joseph was totally committed to the Jewish people and to the land of Israel.

---

3   Genesis 50:4–5.

ॐ Sefer Shemot

שמות

Shemot: A Period of Hester Panim

THE TORAH RECORDS only three incidents from Moshe's early years: his birth, his fight with the Egyptian and resulting flight from Egypt, and his encounter with the Midianite shepherds and subsequent marriage to Jethro's daughter Tzippora. When Moshe later appears before Pharaoh, he is eighty years old. A period of approximately sixty years remains unaccounted for. During this time, Moshe was on the run, a condemned murderer and an outlaw. The Torah does not disclose what happened during that period. We must therefore reconstruct that era despite the Torah's lack of information.

The Rav defined this period as a time of *hester panim,* when God, as it were, concealed his face. It was a tragic period of time when there was no dialogue with God and no encounter with the infinite. The end of Deuteronomy provides a detailed, chilling description of *hester panim.*

ויאמר ה' אל משה הנך שכב עם אבתיך וקם העם הזה וזנה אחרי אלהי נכר הארץ אשר הוא בא שמה בקרבו ועזבני והפר את בריתי אשר כרתי אתו. וחרה אפי בו ביום ההוא ועזבתים והסתרתי פני מהם והיה לאכל ומצאהו רעות רבות וצרות ואמר ביום ההוא הלא על כי אין אלהי בקרבי מצאוני הרעות האלה. ואנכי הסתר אסתיר פני ביום ההוא על כל הרעה אשר עשה כי פנה אל אלהים אחרים.

God said to Moshe: Behold, you will lie down with your forefathers, but this people will rise up and stray after the gods of the foreigners of the land, into whose midst it shall come, and they will forsake me and annul my covenant that I have sealed with them. My anger will flare against them on that day and I will forsake them; and I will conceal my face from them and they will become prey, and many evils and distresses will overtake them. They will say on that day, Is it not because my God is not with me that these evils have come upon me? But I will surely have concealed my face on that day because of all the evil that they did, for they turned to other gods.[1]

Let us now examine more carefully the series of events leading up to the situation of *hester panim*. Moshe, who undoubtedly had heard about his brethren from his parents, wanted to become acquainted with them. To this end, the Torah records: ויהי בימים ההם ויגדל משה ויצא אל אחיו וירא בסבלתם – "It happened in those days that Moshe grew up and went out to his brethren and saw their burdens . . ."[2] After his encounter with the Egyptian who was beating the Hebrew slave and with the two Hebrews who were fighting each other, Moshe reacts: ויירא משה ויאמר אכן נודע הדבר – "Moshe was frightened and he thought: Indeed, the matter has become known."[3]

Rashi[4] cites the Midrashic interpretation that Moshe had been sorely puzzled as to why the Jewish people should be subjected to such hard labor. However, seeing that there were informers among them, Moshe now felt that they deserved it. He felt that a people who could behave in such a way were unworthy of salvation. These words of denunciation – "Indeed the matter has become known" – were a prelude not only to his flight from Egypt, but also to his alienation from his own brethren. Moshe had expected to discover the morality of Abraham, Isaac and Jacob among the Israelites. Instead, he saw a distressing lack of moral commitment.

---

1 Deuteronomy 31:16–18.
2 Exodus 2:11. See Ramban on Exodus 2:23.
3 Exodus 2:14.
4 Rashi on Exodus 2:14.

He then decided to settle in Midian – not as a temporary sojourner similar to Jacob's phrase, עם לבן גרתי – "I have sojourned with Laban"[5] – but rather as a permanent resident. This is to be derived from the double language of the text: ויברח משה מפני פרעה וישב בארץ מדין וישב על הבאר – "So Moshe fled from Pharaoh and settled in the land of Midian, and lived near a well."[6] The double appearance of the word *va-yeshev* implies a sense of permanence. This was indeed a prolonged period of *hester panim* not only between God and the Jewish people, but also between Moshe and his fellow Israelites.

ויהי בימים הרבים ההם וימת מלך מצרים ויאנחו בני ישראל מן העבדה ויזעקו ותעל שועתם אל הא־להים מן העבדה.

And it happened during those many days, the king of Egypt died and the Children of Israel groaned because of the work and they cried out. Their outcry because of the work went up to God.[7]

What is the meaning of the phrase "During those many days"? Those are the days of silence, of *hester panim,* that have not been recorded. People who suffer greatly can lose track of the concept of time: Days, nights, and hours become monotonous and boring. Time becomes abstract and we cease to feel it; sometimes it goes quickly and sometimes slowly. A slave and one who experiences fear or danger have no appreciation of time. It becomes a collection of minutes, hours or days. בימים הרבים ההם – "During those many days," were many days of silence marked by the same humiliation and ridicule. The days in German concentration camps were similar. They merely accumulated without any significance. The Jews who endured Egyptian slavery and the Jews who suffered the Holocaust had this harrowing experience of time in common.[8]

---

5   Genesis 32:5.
6   Exodus 2:15.
7   Exodus 2:23.
8   See Ramban on Exodus 2:23.

The passage continues, וימת מלך מצרים – "the king of Egypt died."[9] Why was it important to note the death of Pharaoh? The new pharaoh's succession portended an even worse time for the Jewish slaves. The Ramban[10] explains that often, when Jews confront hostility, they are inclined to attribute it to a particular ruler or leader. They interpret the hostility as coincidental and hope for the leader to be deposed. There were Jews in Nazi Germany who suffered from this thinking. When Hitler rose to power, they assumed that his anti-Semitism would ultimately wane. They were dreadfully and tragically mistaken. So too, in Egypt, Jews thought that a change in government would result in a new and progressive ruler. Instead, the new pharaoh was much worse. The death of an Egyptian pharaoh meant building an enormous new tomb to house his corpse, a task that the Jewish slaves now had to perform. Their lives became more unbearable than ever.

ויאנחו בני ישראל – "The Children of Israel groaned."[11] What exactly is groaning? It is a bizarre sound, not one of intentional speech, but rather the sound made by an animal in pain. It is a basic defense mechanism of survival that God granted to all creatures. With this groan, the Jewish slaves began to assert their own survival.

Next, ויזעקו – "And they cried out"[12] – engendered another natural reaction – an instinctive question: Why? With this cry of resentment and protest, the Jewish slaves regained their human dignity.

Thus, the Israelite slaves underwent three distinct stages of suffering: (1) Absolute silence, a long night of eerie quiet. (2) Upon Pharaoh's death, they experienced visceral pain and began to groan. (3) "They cried out." Finally, as a result of these three stages, ותעל שועתם אל הא־להים מן העבדה – "Their outcry because of the work went up to God."[13]

---

9 Exodus 2:23.
10 Ramban on Exodus 2:23.
11 Exodus 2:23.
12 Exodus 2:23.
13 Exodus 2:23. See *Tradition* 17/2 (Spring 1978) and *Redemption, Prayer, Talmud Torah*, 55–60, for a further explication of this theme.

✒ Ra'oh ra'iti: I have indeed seen

At this juncture, one would have expected God to intervene. The Torah states, וירא א-להים את בני ישראל וידע א-להים – "God saw the children of Israel and God knew."[14] Of course God saw their plight. What new idea is being introduced here? Suddenly, there is an interruption in the narrative. We are suddenly taken to Midian, where Moshe is grazing his father-in-law's flocks. In a revelation to Moshe, God tells him: ויאמר ה' ראה ראיתי את עני עמי אשר במצרים ואת צעקתם שמעתי מפני נגשיו כי ידעתי את מכאביו – "God said, 'I have indeed seen the affliction of my people in Egypt, and I have heard their outcry because of their taskmasters, for I know their pain.'"[15]

The phrase ראה ראיתי ("I have indeed seen") is an indictment of Moshe by God. It is a direct attack on Moshe's earlier statement, "Indeed it has become known." God says to Moshe: Your perception of the Jewish people was superficial, while mine is much more profound. Your evaluation of them as unworthy is incorrect. Even if they do not display the *hesed* of Abraham, Isaac and Jacob, that is only from a superficial perspective. Deep down, they are certainly worthy. Moshe, it is your task to awaken and teach them. You not only escaped from Pharaoh, but you fled from your brethren as well.

✒ *Va-yeda Elohim*: God Knew

> וישמע א-להים את נאקתם ויזכר א-להים את בריתו את אברהם את יצחק ואת יעקב. וירא א-להים את בני ישראל וידע א-להים.

> God heard their moaning, and God remembered his covenant with Abraham, with Isaac and with Jacob. God saw the children of Israel, and God knew.[16]

---

14 Exodus 2:25.
15 Exodus 3:7.
16 Exodus 2:24–25.

The verb *va-yizkor* means not only to remember but to be concerned and to feel. During our prayers on Rosh ha-Shannah, we recite the verse הבן יקיר לי אפרים אם ילד שעשעים כי מדי דברי בו זכר אזכרנו עוד על כן המו מעי לו רחם ארחמנו נאם ה' – "Is Ephraim my most precious son, a delightful child, that whenever I speak of him I remember him more and more. Therefore, my inner self yearns for him. I will surely take pity on him."[17]

The logical order is to remember and then to articulate the memory. Here, it is reversed. One is led to conclude that in this context, the verb "to remember" refers not to recollection per se, but to nostalgia and longing. Every time I speak of Ephraim, I recollect, empathize and share in his travail. I mention him with a tremor in my heart. Therefore the verb *va-yeda*, which sums up God's response, means that he knew the Israelites' suffering intimately, to the point where he experienced it together with them. Therefore, when he freed the Israelites from slavery, he freed himself together with them.[18]

Moshe's Rapprochement with the Jewish People

However, the entire redemption of the Jewish people hinged on one immutable condition: that Moshe accept the mandate as the nation's leader and become the instrument of its redemption. Years before, he had fled to Midian in order to distance himself from them and their sufferings. Now he had to transform himself into a *shaliah,* a messenger of God. He had to change his opinion of the Israelites in order to become the instrument of their redemption. This is why God spent seven days convincing Moshe to accept the mission. The Divine mandate was not only that Moshe convince Pharaoh to let the Israelites leave, but that he rejoin his people. Only then could he begin his task as their redeemer.

---

17 Jeremiah 31:19.

18 See Hoshanot for Sukkot: כְּהוֹשַׁעְתָּ מַאֲמַר וְהוֹצֵאתִי אֶתְכֶם, נָקוּב וְהוֹצֵאתִי אֶתְכֶם, כֵּן הוֹשַׁעְנָא
As You saved with the declaration "I shall bring you forth," which may be interpreted "I shall be brought forth with you" – so save now.

וארא

Va-era: Free will and the Habitual Sinner

IN PARASHAT VA-ERA, the Torah states:

ואני אקשה את לב פרעה והרביתי את אתתי ואת מופתי בארץ מצרים. ולא ישמע
אלכם פרעה ונתתי את ידי במצרים והוצאתי את צבאתי את עמי בני ישראל
מארץ מצרים בשפטים גדלים.

I shall harden Pharaoh's heart, and I shall multiply my signs
and my wonders in the land of Egypt. Pharaoh will not heed
you, and I shall put my hand on Egypt and I shall take out
my legions, my people, the children of Israel, from the land of
Egypt with great judgments.[1]

Rashi comments that since Pharaoh behaved wickedly, brazenly
opposing God, and also because the nations of the world do not sin-
cerely repent, it was good that Pharaoh's heart should be hardened. In
this way, God's might and miracles would be recognized.[2] Similarly, at
the beginning of Parashat Bo, God says to Moshe:

ויאמר ה' אל משה בא אל פרעה כי אני הכבדתי את לבו ואת לב עבדיו למען שתי
אתתי אלה בקרבו.

---

1 Exodus 7:3–4.
2 Rashi, Exodus 7:3.

God said to Moshe, "Go to Pharaoh, for I have made his heart and the hearts of his servants stubborn, so I shall place these signs of mine in his midst."[3]

One of the fundamental axioms of our belief is the doctrine of *behira hofshit* (freedom of choice). Without it, the foundation of our religion would crumble. In Parashat Nitzavim, this doctrine is clearly articulated:

ראה נתתי לפניך היום את החיים ואת הטוב ואת המות ואת הרע... העידתי בכם היום את השמים ואת הארץ החיים והמות נתתי לפניך הברכה והקללה ובחרת בחיים למען תחיה אתה וזרעך.

See, I have placed before you today life and good, and death and evil ... I call heaven and earth today to bear witness against you; I have placed life and death before you, blessing and curse. Choose life so that you will live, you and your offspring.[4]

In all physical aspects of life, God is the determining factor. However, in the moral realm, God doesn't interfere. Without freedom of choice, a sinner would be able to claim that he could not help himself, and this would be a legitimate grievance. Free choice invalidates the claim of mitigating circumstances. On the other hand, free choice means that a sinner should never despair. The gates of *teshuvah* are always open. Just as sinners can pollute themselves, they can also cleanse themselves thanks to freedom of choice.

Why, then, did God choose to intervene in Pharaoh's case? And once God intervened, how was Pharaoh deserving of punishment? Maimonides states that the entire concept of reward and punishment hinges on freedom of choice.[5] The first verse of Parashat Bo is a difficult

---

3   Exodus 10:1.
4   Deuteronomy 30:15, 19.
5   *Mishneh Torah,* Hilchot Teshuvah, chapters 5 and 6.

one, since in it, God says to Moshe, "Go to Pharaoh, for I have hardened his heart in order to punish him."[6] Where is freedom of choice?

Nahmanides[7] cites the following Midrash Rabbah and comments on it.

א"ר יוחנן מכאן פתחון פה למינין לומר לא היתה ממנו שיעשה תשובה, שנא' כי אני הכבדתי את לבו, א"ל ר"ש בן לקיש יסתם פיהם של מינים אלא (משלי ג) אם ללצים הוא יליץ שהקב"ה מתרה בו באדם פעם ראשונה שניה ושלישית ואינו חוזר בו והוא נועל לבו מן התשובה כדי לפרוע ממנו מה שחטא, אף כך פרעה הרשע כיון ששיגר הקב"ה ה' פעמים ולא השגיח על דבריו אמר לו הקב"ה אתה הקשית ערפך והכבדת את לבך הריני מוסיף לך טומאה על טומאתך.

Rabbi Yohanan said: This verse provides a pretext for the heretics to say that God did not allow Pharaoh to repent, as it states: For I have made his heart stubborn. Rabbi Shimon ben Lakish said, "Let the mouths of the heretics be closed. If it concerns the scorners, he scorns them" (Proverbs 3). When God warns a person on three occasions and he does not repent, he closes the door of repentance before him in order to punish him for his sin. Such was the case with the wicked Pharaoh. After God sent him five warnings and he did not heed his words, God told him: You have stiffened your neck and made your heart stubborn. I will add to your defilement.[8]

Rabbi Yohanan and Rabbi Shimon ben Lakish (also known as Resh Lakish) engaged in a debate. Rabbi Yohanan contended that the sinners cite this text to defend their behavior, for it appears that since God hardened Pharaoh's heart, Pharaoh was unable to repent and therefore should not be blamed. Resh Lakish disagrees, stating his opinion that there are no mitigating circumstances. If the issue relates to the scorn-

---

6   See Exodus 10:1.
7   Ramban, Exodus 7:3.
8   Exodus Rabbah 13:3.

ers, then God scorns them. God warns human beings three times. If they refuse to repent, God then closes the sinner's heart, rendering him unable to do so. Pharaoh, who was warned five times, paid no heed to the warnings, whereupon God took away his freedom of choice. God gives incidental sinners the opportunity to do *teshuvah,* while habitual sinners encounter closed doors. The moment sin becomes entrenched in one's lifestyle, one is barred from *teshuvah.* In modern history, certain European countries took a similar attitude toward criminals. In France, for example, habitual criminals were sentenced to imprisonment in remote locations under harsh conditions.

The above-mentioned Midrash poses a dilemma for Jews who pray on Rosh ha-Shannah and Yom Kippur. According to Jewish belief, a person may repent until the very last moment of his life. The evil Emperor Nero, who wanted to destroy the Holy Temple in Jerusalem, became the ancestor of Rabbi Meir.[9] When Rabbi Hanina ben Teradion's executioner asked for life in the World to Come in return for ending the rabbi's suffering, his wish was granted.[10] God gave human beings wisdom, reason and intellect in order to increase their opportunity for salvation and to protect them from evil. Therefore, human beings always retain the potential to be divine.

The Ibn Ezra divides human beings into two kinds: *adam* and *tzelem Elohim.*[11] Adam is the human being prior to his being endowed with divine charisma. Here, humanity is focused on enjoyment and the pursuit of pleasure. This *adam* is actually not a brute. He can be cultured and sophisticated and even establish moral laws and objectives. However, his humanity exhausts itself in his self-proclaimed goals. His freedom of choice is somewhat limited because he cannot rebel against his own pragmatic interests.

Adam's limitations can be illustrated through examples of modern

---

9   BT *Gittin* 56a.
10   BT Avodah Zarah 18a.
11   See Ibn Ezra on Genesis 1:26.

life. One is the manufacturer who pollutes streams and rivers, threatening the ecological environment. Such a company will fight any effort to oppose them even though they know that they are causing damage. Their activities threaten not only society in general, but ultimately their own children and grandchildren. Nevertheless, their greed is so powerful that they are totally blinded. Similarly, the military establishment explodes nuclear weaponry even as it realizes that the fallout may have global, catastrophic consequences to human beings. Yet its action takes on a compulsive nature and is almost stripped of freedom of choice. All the motivations mentioned above, such as money or pride, are included in the term "Adam."

It often happens that Adam, or natural man, thinks that he is enriching himself, but is actually engaged in self-destruction. The Rav cited the example of capitalism, particularly during the first two decades of the twentieth century. Fledgling capitalists became so intoxicated by the profits they were reaping that they sought to increase them by any means possible. To this end, they forced their employees to work in terrible conditions. In the sweatshops that they created in New York and elsewhere, they paid their workers extremely low wages, forced them to work long hours and even demanded that their workers pay them rent if they lived in the same building in which they worked. Often, the conditions under which their employees had to labor damaged their health and even endangered their lives. Such behavior is detrimental not only to the workers but to the entire capitalist enterprise.

Of course, not all human beings behave this way. Some are guided in their lives and their work by the principle of *tzelem Elohim* – moral and ethical norms derived from divine law. Ironically, this adherence to divine principles is what allows them freedom of choice. Only through *tzelem Elohim* can one reach beyond the compulsive pursuits of Adam.

God's statement, "I will harden Pharaoh's heart," did not mean that God would prevent or actively discourage Pharaoh from letting the Jewish slaves go free, or revoke his freedom of choice. Rather, it meant that he would make the choice very difficult for Pharaoh.

If we examine Egypt's economic situation during the Israelites' period of slavery there, we discover that Egypt was the prime manufacturer of cotton, linen and other products. Slave labor enabled them to become wealthy and prosperous. They built massive storehouses and enjoyed a high standard of living. When Moshe and Aharon appeared and demanded that Pharaoh allow the slaves to leave, Pharaoh was shocked. He knew that his country's prosperity rested on slave labor. Without the slaves, Egypt's economy would collapse and perhaps lead to civil war. Here, God intervened and Adam, the natural man, was frightened. Thus the fear of losing his enslaved workers forced Pharaoh to refuse.

Had God not hardened Pharaoh's heart, he could have somehow informed him that his country could prosper without slave labor. Although the economy would suffer temporarily during the adjustment ultimately the slaves' departure would present an opportunity for even greater growth. This can be compared with the stubbornness of Czarist Russia, where the serfs were subject to the czars' whims. This can be contrasted with the emancipation of the slaves in America during and after the Civil War. Eventually, an economy that did not depend upon slave labor increased America's strength and wealth. The Czars, who were confined to the level of Adam – frightened of losing the labor of their serfs – could not see this potential. The fact that God did not share this information with Pharaoh influenced Pharaoh's decision, hardening his heart. But God never interfered directly with Pharaoh's freedom of choice.

Another example can be adduced in which individuals encountered a difficult choice that they might perceive as a loss of free will, but in which they retained the freedom to choose. In Lithuania, before World War II, it was relatively easy to observe Shabbat and close one's store. Even if the store were to be left open, the storekeeper would not earn anything. On the other hand, American Jews at the turn of the century had a difficult choice. Closing their businesses on Shabbat meant economic suicide. But did this mean that they no longer had freedom of choice? Certainly not. Some Jews, after having lost many jobs in succession on account of Shabbat, eventually gave in. However, others persevered, keeping Shabbat no matter what the cost, and eventually won their fight. In this case, neither group of Jews lost its freedom of choice. Even the most hardened criminals still possess it.

The Rav, referring to the original discussion between Rav Yohanan and Resh Lakish, noted that Rav Yohanan, who had always been religiously observant, had never known the experience of sin and teshuvah. But Rabbi Shimon ben Lakish had spent years as a gladiator. He was fortunate enough to meet Rabbi Yohanan, under whom he began to study Torah, and eventually became a prominent scholar.[12] Rav Yohanan, who had been devout all his life, could not understand Resh Lakish's position. His background was similar to that of people who cannot understand why anyone would choose to drink alcohol or take drugs. Therefore, Resh Lakish declared: Those who scorn are scorners. Everyone gets a warning from his conscience the first time he sins. If he allows his sin to become habitual, *teshuvah* becomes almost impossible for him, though the gates are never completely locked.

Pharaoh's punishment consisted of three parts. The first five plagues – blood, frogs, lice, noxious animals and boils – constituted the first group, which inflicted plain misery. The second group of plagues involved the destruction of livestock, burning hail and locusts that ravaged the fields, destroying the economy. The third group, darkness and the death of the firstborn, wreaked havoc in Egypt. With the second group of plagues, God showed Pharaoh that despite his stubbornness, the economy collapsed. The opulent society that slavery had created for the Egyptians was now in ruin. Pharaoh was thus forced to live with the consequences of his own recalcitrance.

---

12 BT Bava Metzia 84a.

ﺑﺎ Bo

(Hebrew title: בא)

I. THE EXODUS AS EXPRESSED IN
THE COMMANDMENTS

a. Laws Pertaining to Holiness

THE EXODUS FROM Egypt is one of the most significant episodes in Jewish history. Many areas of the Torah are intimately connected with it. During the *minha* service of Yom Kippur, we read the section of the Torah that warns us to keep away from the moral decadence of Egypt. כמעשה ארץ מצרים אשר ישבתם בה לא תעשו – "Do not engage in the practices of the land of Egypt in which you dwelled."[1] Immediately afterward, the Torah sets forth the forbidden sexual relationships. Elsewhere, in the context of the laws of forbidden foods, the Torah states:

אל תשקצו את נפשתיכם בכל השרץ השרץ ולא תטמאו בהם ונטמתם בם . . .
כי אני ה' המעלה אתכם מארץ מצרים להית לכם לאלקים והייתם קדשים כי
קדוש אני.

---

1 Leviticus 18:3.

134

Do not make yourselves abominable by means of any teeming thing. Do not contaminate yourselves through them lest you become contaminated through them ... I am the Lord who elevates you from the land of Egypt to be a God unto you. You shall be holy, for I am holy.[2]

God commands self-discipline and restraint in the areas of food and sexual morality. A disciplined body is capable of retreating from pleasurable actions. The Torah therefore prohibits physical pleasures that will defile us. Maimonides combined both domains in the *Sefer Kedushah* (Laws of the Book of Holiness). To discipline a mind is relatively easy. To discipline our bodies by harnessing our biological functions and drives to serve God is much more difficult.

Maimonides states in *Hilchot De'ot*[3] that one should seek God not only during the Neilah prayer on Yom Kippur, but also in one's dining room and bedroom – in other words, in all aspects of public and private life. In Egypt, pleasure was the highest value. The Egyptians developed a decadent way of life that centered around pleasurable activities. It is against this backdrop that the Torah presents the laws governing forbidden foods and sexual morality.

ᴘ **b. Laws pertaining to Social Justice**

The Rav suggested that there is a second group of mitzvot whose essence also derives from the exodus from Egypt. The Torah states:

לא תטה משפט גר יתום ולא תחבל בגד אלמנה. וזכרת כי עבד היית במצרים ויפדך ה' א-להיך משם על כן אנכי מצוך לעשות את הדבר הזה.

You shall not pervert the judgment of a proselyte or orphan, nor shall you take the garment of a widow as a pledge. You

---

2   Leviticus 11:43, 45.
3   See Rambam, *Hilchot Deot* 3:2.

shall remember that you were a slave in Egypt, and the Lord your God rescued you from there. Therefore, I command you to do this thing.[4]

We must draw on our own experience of slavery in Egypt to institute a legal system that addresses the needs of the less fortunate.

Similarly, the Torah expresses our obligation to show ongoing sensitivity to the needy.

וגר לא תונה ולא תלחצנו כי גרים הייתם בארץ מצרים.

You shall not taunt or oppress a stranger, for you were strangers in the land of Egypt.[5]

This group of *mitzvot,* which encompasses injunctions relating to justice and charity, also derives from our slavery and subsequent exodus from Egypt.

‿‿ c. The Sabbath

Both categories of *mitzvot* – those pertaining to *kedushah* and those pertaining to social justice – embody the entirety of Judaism. Both of these categories were unified in the *mitzvah* of the Sabbath, regarding which the exodus is also invoked. In Deuteronomy, the presentation of the Sabbath highlights the aspect of justice:

שמור את יום השבת לקדשו ... למען ינוח עבדך ואמתך כמוך ... וזכרת כי עבד
היית בארץ מצרים ויצאך ה' א‑להיך משם ביד חזקה ובזרע נטויה על כן צוך ה'
א‑להיך לעשות את יום השבת.

Safeguard the Sabbath day to sanctify it ... So that your male and female slaves will then be able to rest as you do ... Remember that you were a slave in the land of Egypt and

---

4 Deuteronomy 24:17–18.
5 Exodus 22:20.

the Lord your God took you out of there with a strong hand and an outstretched arm. Therefore, the Lord your God has commanded you to observe the Sabbath day.[6]

However, in Genesis[7] and in Exodus,[8] the Torah's presentation of the Sabbath focuses on *kedushah*.

This is the Sabbath through which our inner spirituality is enhanced and exalted. Thus the Sabbath, in recalling the Exodus, encompasses both of the above ideas.

ᔒ d. Commandments That Commemorate the Exodus

There is also a third group of *mitzvot* that serve as commemorations and reminders of the exodus. This group can be subdivided into two. The first is observances that are connected with the celebration of the festivals. On Pesah, the prohibition against eating or possessing leaven, the paschal lamb, and obligation to eat *matzah* are all geared toward reliving the exodus from Egypt. Dwelling in a *sukkah* reminds us of the exodus as well.

---

6   Deuteronomy 5:12–15.

7   Genesis 2:1–3.

ויכלו השמים והארץ וכל צבאם. ויכל א-להים ביום השביעי מלאכתו אשר עשה וישבת ביום השביעי מכל מלאכתו אשר עשה. ויברך א-להים את יום השביעי ויקדש אתו כי בו שבת מכל מלאכתו אשר ברא א-להים לעשות.

Thus the heavens and the earth were finished, and all their array. By the seventh day, God completed His work that He had done, and He abstained on the seventh day from all His work which He had done. God blessed the seventh day and sanctified it because on it He abstained from all His work which God created to make.

8   Exodus 20:8–11.

זכר את יום השבת לקדשו. ששת ימים תעבד ועשית כל מלאכתך. ויום השביעי שבת לה' א-להיך לא תעשה כל מלאכה אתה ובנך ובתך עבדך ואמתך ובהמתך וגרך אשר בשעריך. כי ששת ימים עשה ה' את השמים ואת הארץ את הים ואת כל אשר בם וינח ביום השביעי על כן ברך ה' את יום השבת ויקדשהו.

Remember the Sabbath day to sanctify it. Six days shall you labor and do all your work, but the seventh day is Sabbath to the Lord your God. You shall not do any work – you, your son, your daughter, your slave, your maidservant, your animal, and your convert within your gates – for in six days the Lord made the heavens, the earth, the sea and all that is in them, and He rested on the seventh day. Therefore the Lord blessed the Sabbath day and sanctified it.

The second category includes precepts that commemorate the exodus from Egypt regardless of the time of year. Two examples of this genre are *bechor* (the laws of the firstborn), which relates to both humans and animals, and the laws of *tefillin.* After describing the *mitzvot* of *bechor* and *tefillin,* the Torah states:

והעברת כל פטר רחם ה' וכל פטר שגר בהמה אשר יהיה לך הזכרים ה' ... וכל בכור אדם בבניך תפדה ... והיה כי ישאלך בנך מחר לאמר מה זאת ואמרת אליו בחזק יד הוציאנו מה' ממצרים מבית עבדים. ויהי כי הקשה פרעה לשלחנו ויהרג ה' כל בכור בארץ מצרים מבכר אדם ועד בכור בהמה על כן אני זבח ה' כל פטר רחם הזכרים וכל בכור בני אפדה. והיה לאות על ידכה ולטוטפת בין עיניך כי בחזק יד הוציאנו מה' ממצרים.

Then you shall set apart any livestock which emerges from the womb for the Lord, and of each first calving of livestock that belongs to you the males are the Lord's ... and each firstborn among your sons you shall redeem ... And it shall be when your son will ask you tomorrow, what is this, you shall say to him, with a strong hand Hashem removed us from Egypt from the house of bondage. And it happened when Pharaoh stubbornly refused to send us out, that the Lord killed all the firstborn in the land of Egypt, from the firstborn of man to the firstborn of the beast. Therefore I offer to the Lord each male firstborn of the womb, and I shall redeem all the firstborn of my sons. And it shall be a sign upon your arm and for frontlets between your eyes, for with a strong hand the Lord took us out of Egypt.[9]

The mitzvot of *bechor* and *tefillin,* like the observances of Pesah and Sukkot, provide perpetual reminders of the Exodus.

---

9 Exodus 13:12–16.

II. THE COMMANDMENT OF THE FIRST-BORN

Let us analyze the relationship between the sanctification of the first-born child and the exodus from Egypt. When we try to understand a *mitzvah*, we cannot ask why it was given to us, for God is omnipotent, lacks nothing, desires nothing and encompasses all. A scientist asks questions regarding causal nexus, but we can and must ask only what we can learn from a particular *mitzvah*, what moral lesson we are to derive from it and what we should feel as we perform it.

ॐ a. My Firstborn Son is Israel

To understand the concept of the *bechor* (firstborn), we must investigate the plague in which Egypt's firstborn were slain. Why did God punish the firstborn? Why were they deemed responsible for the slavery of the Jews in Egypt? Let us backtrack to Moshe's encounter with God at the burning bush, where God gave him the task of redeeming the Jewish people from Egypt. After some hesitation, Moshe agreed to undertake the mission and returned to his father-in-law in Midian, requesting permission to leave and return to Egypt. God instructs him to perform the miracles before Pharaoh. Then, out of the blue, the Torah records:

ואמרת אל פרעה כה אמר ה' בני בכרי ישראל. ואמר אליך שלח את בני ויעבדני ותמאן לשלחו הנה אנכי הרג את בנך בכרך.

Tell Pharaoh this: God says: My firstborn son is Israel. I have told you: Let my son go that he may serve me, but you have refused to let him go. Behold, I shall kill your firstborn son.[10]

The transition from "God says: My firstborn son is Israel" to "Behold, I shall kill your firstborn son" is difficult to understand. Furthermore,

---

10 Exodus 4:22–23.

why did God not tell Moshe of this command at their first encounter? Why did he give Moshe this message only after Moshe returned to his father-in-law and received permission to go to Egypt? Immediately afterwards, the Torah records another incident:

ויהי בדרך במלון ויפגשהו ה' ויבקש המיתו.ותקח צפרה צר ותכרת את ערלת בנה
ותגע לרגליו ותאמר כי חתן דמים אתה לי.

When he was on his way at the inn, the Lord encountered him and sought to kill him. So Tzipporah took a sharp stone, cut off her son's foreskin and touched it to his feet, saying, "A bridegroom of blood you are to me."[11]

What is the continuity between this episode and the one that precedes it?

b. The Position of the Firstborn in Egypt

In order to resolve these questions, the Rav explained the significance of God's statement, "My firstborn son is Israel." This statement expresses the philosophy of power in ancient times. In ancient cultures, a family's oldest son was second only to his father. He had authority over his younger siblings. He could often be cruel and prey on the younger children. When he became a teenager, he could use his size to exploit his younger brothers and sisters.

The Rav described American youth gangs, in which young people joined together in order to terrorize adults. The Rav said that in his time, the idea of a child robber or murderer was unheard of. The origin of this phenomenon is the parental home in which the oldest child used threats and violence to discipline his siblings. After a while, an organizational conspiracy developed. Sociologists and historians speak of an ancient patriarchal slave society.

In the patriarchal society of antiquity, the father represented the law

---

11 Exodus 4:24–25.

because he was the strongest. Tyranny reigned supreme. The Israelites were not slaves to Pharaoh only, but were subject to the cruelty of every Egyptian who wielded power. The unifying element of that society was fear. On the night of Passover, God slew the firstborn who exercised brutal authority over others. At the end of Sefer Bamidbar the Torah states:

ומצרים מקברים את אשר הכה ה' בהם כל בכור ובאלהיהם עשה ה' שפטים.

> The Egyptians buried those whom the Lord had struck, every firstborn, and the Lord executed judgments against their gods.[12]

One who would punish a nation must destroy their gods – in other words, their philosophy. The slaying of the firstborn destroyed the Egyptians' ability to use force and inspire fear.

In contrast to the rest of the ancient world, Jewish society combines patriarchy and matriarchy. Both parents teach the children, arousing in them respect, reverence and love. The wish of both father and mother is their children's command – not because the parents use violence to impose their will, but because they inspire love and respect in their children.

✍ c. The Jewish Notion of the *Bechor*

Does Judaism recognize the distinctiveness of the firstborn, or did it abolish the institution of the firstborn? The answer is that while Judaism acknowledges the unique role of the firstborn, it replaced the Egyptian institution of power with the Jewish idea of *kedushah*. A firstborn's distinction comes not from power, but from sanctity.

Jacob wanted the *bechorah* (the privileges of the firstborn) not because he was greedy for power, but rather because it would enable him to inherit the covenantal destiny of the Jewish people. Esau wanted it because he viewed it as a source of power and authority. Rebecca and

---

12 Numbers 33:4.

Sarah fought for the *bechorah* for their sons for covenantal reasons, not because they wanted their sons to become tyrants. The Rav noted with irony that it was no coincidence that the important tasks were given to biblical personalities who were not the oldest, but younger: Abraham, Isaac, Jacob, Judah, Levi, Benjamin, Joseph, Moshe, David and Solomon. While they were chosen as leaders and had great leadership ability, they did not seek power for their own ends. Their greatest concern was the well-being of the Jewish people.

What are the parameters of the *bechorah*? While God rules the world of both organic and inorganic matter, his juridical claim to ownership is stronger regarding living beings, particularly mankind. The dietary laws relate primarily to the animal kingdom, both domesticated and undomesticated species. The prohibitions of blood and forbidden fat apply to the animal world. The vegetable kindgom has far fewer restrictions. We may not mingle species. Even the laws of tithing and restrictions on produce during the first years of a tree's growth are not nearly as numerous as those that apply to the animal kingdom.

There are hardly any laws governing our interaction with the mineral kingdom. (The only requirement is to say a blessing before drinking water.) Why is this so? Only one conclusion may be drawn: the number of prohibitions is proportionate to the claims that God has over the object or being. Regarding blood, the Torah states:

כי נפש הבשר בדם הוא ואני נתתיו לכם על המזבח לכפר על נפשתיכם כי הדם הוא בנפש יכפר. על כן אמרתי לבני ישראל כל נפש מכם לא תאכל דם והגר הגר בתוככם לא יאכל דם.

The soul of the flesh is in the blood. I have assigned it for you upon the altar to provide atonement for your souls, for it is the blood that atones for the soul. Therefore I have said to the Children of Israel: no one among you may eat blood. The proselyte among you may not eat blood either.[13]

---

13 Leviticus 17:11–12.

However, our most precious possessions are our children, who belong exclusively to God. This idea was stated by Hannah, the mother of Samuel the prophet. ותקרא את שמו שמואל כי מה' שאלתיו – "She named him Samuel for, she said, 'I petitioned him from the Lord.'"[14]

וגם אנכי השאלתהו לה' כל הימים אשר היה הוא שאול לה' – "Furthermore, I have dedicated him to the Lord. He shall be dedicated to the Lord all the days of his life."[15] *Akedat Yitzhak* is the embodiment of the idea that children belong to God.

If the birth of every child is a significant event for the mother – perhaps even more so than for the father, then the birth of the first child is the greatest and most cathartic experience for the mother. When we speak of motherhood, we do not refer merely to a biological relationship but to a spiritual one. There is total identification between mother and child. Therefore, one should not terminate a pregnancy except in a case of clear danger to the mother.[16] The firstborn child, while an infant, is a source of boundless pleasure. The joy that parents experience upon the birth of a first child exceeds the joy that they experience at the birth of the following children. Therefore, God's claim is more precise regarding the firstborn because he is the most precious. Whatever belongs to God carries *kedushah*.

וידבר ה' אל משה לאמר. קדש לי כל בכור פטר כל רחם בבני ישראל באדם ובבהמה לי הוא.

God spoke to Moshe, saying: Sanctify to me every firstborn. The first issue of every womb among the Children of Israel, man or beast, is mine.[17]

---

14 1 Samuel 1:20.

15 1 Samuel 1:28.

16 The Rav discussed his particular distress over the fact that abortions were legal in Israel. He said that the destruction of a life and the snuffing out of internal aliyah were beyond his comprehension. The Rav said that one who killed a fetus would in time kill infants as well, God forbid.

17 Exodus 13:1–2.

The result of the above-mentioned idea is that the Egyptian and Jewish conceptions of the firstborn – power and sanctity – are mutually exclusive. On the night of the fifteenth of Nissan, the Jewish conception of the firstborn defeated the Egyptian one for all time.

➳ d. The Distinction between *Peter Rehem* and *Reshit Ono*

The *halachah* of *kedushat bechor* is founded upon the principle of *peter rehem* (the first issue of every womb),[18] while primogeniture, or inheritance, is predicated upon the principle of *reshit ono* (the father's initial vigor).[19] Why is there a distinction between a maternal and a paternal firstborn? Regarding inheritance, the paternal *bechor* is his father's helper, who shoulders part of his father's burden.[20] When a person's home included his extended family and community, people shared in each other's troubles. The firstborn, as the father's helper, was compensated with a double portion.

In a patriarchal society where women were enslaved, paternal authority was transferred to the *bechor,* who used that authority to become a tyrant. In Jewish tradition, however, the *bechor* opens the womb and engenders the spiritual community of his father and mother.

➳ The Firstborn's Role among Other Children

When God said to Moshe, "My first born son is Israel," this implied that he had other children. Every nation is a child of God, for every human being was created in the divine image. At the moment of theophany, when God revealed himself to the Jewish people and gave us the Torah, we were chosen as the *am segulah (a treasured nation),* but God did not

---

18 Exodus 13:2.
19 Deuteronomy 21:17.
20 The Rav noted that he was already a responsible person when his brother was still a child. His father would have him accompany his brother in order to assist him.

abandon the rest of the world. We are God's firstborn – and a critical task of a firstborn child is to be a role model and an effective teacher for the other children. This is accomplished not only through learning but by setting an example in our daily lives of sanctifying the divine name: behaving honestly and treating others with dignity. A Jew who commits a crime violates the teaching of "My first born son is Israel."

This is what God had in mind when he gave Moshe the task of redeeming the Israelites from slavery. As long as he refused to let them go, Pharaoh prevented the firstborn nation from carrying out its task of redeeming humanity – and prevented God from adopting the other nations as his children as well. Therefore, Pharaoh sinned not only against the Jewish people, but also against his own people, the Egyptians, and against the entire world. His stubbornness ultimately led to the death of the Egyptian firstborn.

Now we can understand why the Torah tells us about Moshe's failure to circumcise his son before he appears before Pharaoh. Moshe could not persuade Pharaoh to let God's firstborn go until he had fulfilled his obligation toward his own firstborn. The ultimate goal of the impending struggle with Pharaoh and with Egypt was to introduce the Jewish conception of the *bechor*, which is based on sanctity and communal responsibility – to the world. Moshe could not become the instrument of this transformation until he had done his duty toward his own son. This is the message of קדש לי כל בכור – "Sanctify to me every firstborn."[21]

---

21 Exodus 13:2.

בשלח

Beshalah: Hallel over the Miraculous and the Ordinary

THE CONCEPT OF *shirah* (song), which appears frequently in the Tanach, is a fundamental principle in *Halachah*. *Kiddush, havdalah,* and *birkat ha-mazon,* which are all recited over a cup of wine, all contain an element of *shirah.* Indeed, the Talmud says that *shirah* must be recited over a cup of wine.[1] So, too, *birkot erusin, birkot nissuin* (the *blessings recited over* betrothal and marriage) and *birkat she-hehiyyanu on festivals and birkat asher kidesh* at a circumcision, are all arranged around a cup of wine because of this element of *shirah.* Elements of *shirah* may even be found where no wine is used. Some examples are the recitation of Hallel on festivals, the Hallel that is recited over the slaughter of the paschal lamb and the *kedushah* that is recited in *shemoneh esreh.*[2]

There are two kinds of *shirah.* The first is recited over miraculous and supernatural events in which the Divine Will transcends the laws of nature. The *Ibn Ezra* comments that the name of *Shaddai* connotes God as *shoded ma'archot ha-shamayim,* a kind of robber baron, *le-havdil,* who transcends the laws of nature for the sake of an individual or a

---

1   BT *Berachot* 35a.
2   See Tosafot, BT *Berachot* 35a; שאין אומרים שירה.

multitude.[3] This was the *shirah* recited over the exodus from Egypt in Parashat Beshalah, which the sages termed *hallel ha-Mitzri*.[4] This *shirah* is recited on each of the *shalosh regalim* in order to commemorate the miracles associated with them.

The exodus from Egypt was filled with miracles. In this type of *shirah*, there is no difference between Moshe Rabbenu and a servant girl, both of whom witnessed the splitting of the Red Sea.

בצאת ישראל ממצרים בית יעקב מעם לעז. היתה יהודה לקדשו ישראל ממשלותיו. הים ראה וינס הירדן יסב לאחור. ההרים רקדו כאילים גבעות כבני צאן.

When Israel went out of Egypt, Jacob's household from a people of alien tongue, Judah became his sanctuary, Israel his dominion. The sea saw and fled; the Jordan turned backward. The mountains skipped like rams, the hills like young lambs.[5]

The entire Jewish nation attained the level of *ruah ha-kodesh* (a heightened sensitivity to *kedushah*).

On the other hand, there is a *shirah* that is recited over nature's cyclical patterns. This is *shirah* over sunrise and sunset, over natural processes such as photosynthesis, over green summer landscapes and frozen tundras. This *shirah* does not relate to transcendence over the forces of nature, but rather to its regularity and flow. King David excels in this kind of *shirah* over nature and its beauty. An example of it is Psalm 104, which celebrates the wonders of nature.

ברכי נפשי את ה'. ה' א-להי גדלת מאד הוד והדר לבשת. עטה אור כשלמה נוטה שמים כיריעה . . . המשלח מעינים בנחלים בין הרים יהלכון. ישקו כל חיתו שדי ישברו פראים צמאם. עליהם עוף השמים ישכון מבין עפאים יתנו קול. משקה הרים מעליותיו מפרי מעשיך תשבע הארץ.

---

3   Quoted by Ramban, Exodus 6:2 and Genesis 17:1.
4   See Rashi on BT *Berachot* 56a.
5   Psalms 114:1–4.

Bless the Lord, my soul. Lord, my God, you are very great. You have donned majesty and splendor, cloaked in light as with a garment, stretching out the heavens like a curtain ... He sends the springs into the streams; they flow between the mountains. They water every beast of the field; they quench the wild creatures' thirst. Near them dwell the birds of the sky; from among the branches they give forth song. He waters the mountains from the upper chambers; from the fruit of your works the earth is sated.[6]

This second genre of *shira* is best reflected in the daily *pesukei de-zimra*. The Talmud in Tractate *Shabbat*[7] *poses a famous contradiction.* On the one hand, the sages said, "Whoever recites Hallel daily is guilty of blasphemy." On the other hand, Rav Yosi says, "Let my share be with those who recite Hallel daily." The Talmud resolves the contradiction. To recite the festival Hallel, which is known as *Hallel ha-Mitzri,* every day would be a travesty and an act of blasphemy, since we would be asking God to destroy the natural processes that were built into creation. However, the recital of *pesukei de-zimrah* every day is ideal, for by doing so we thank God for his daily sustaining of the natural world.[8]

ᴪ The Primacy of Hallel over the Ordinary

Which of the two approaches is better? Prima facie, one might have argued that the miraculous, supernatural mode is preferable, for here God demonstrates his ability to transcend nature. Even Torah scholars might have suggested such an approach. Yet this notion should be rejected, as

---

6 Psalms 104:1–3.
7 BT *Shabbat* 118b.
8 Although *pesukei de-zimrah* also includes *shirat ha-yam,* which describes the splitting of the Red Sea, the section's central theme is uttering song over the miracles of everyday natural life. See the sefer *Nefesh ha-rav* by Rabbi Herschel Schachter (110–111) with reference to the status of *shirat ha-yam* according to the Rambam.

the religious experience cannot be based solely on the miraculous. The Rav cited three reasons for this.

First, one sees evidence of God's work much more in daily occurrences and in the growth of the natural world than in miraculous occurrences such as the Ten Plagues and the splitting of the Red Sea. The seemingly ordinary existence of nature as we know it is much greater than the occasional suspension of its laws. The Ramban at the conclusion of Parashat Bo, states this idea clearly and emphatically:

ומן הנסים הגדולים המפורסמים אדם מודה בנסים הנסתרים שהם יסוד התורה כלה, שאין לאדם חלק בתורת משה רבינו עד שנאמין בכל דברינו ומקרינו שכלם נסים אין בהם טבע ומנהגו של עולם . . . הכל בגזרת עליון . . . ויתפרסמו הנסים הנסתרים.

From the great public miracles one acknowledges the hidden miracles that are the foundation of the entire Torah. One does not have a share in the Torah of Moshe Rabbenu until one believes that every event is miraculous; there are no natural occurrences . . . everything is determined from on high . . . and the hidden miracles will be therefore publicized.[9]

Second, the Divine Will has been crystallized in the world order – an order that does not countenance radical alterations.

עד כל ימי הארץ זרע וקציר וקר וחם וקיץ וחרף ויום ולילה לא ישבתו.

Continuously all the days of the earth, seed time and harvest, cold and heat, summer and winter, day and night shall not cease.[10]

The routine of nature is not meant to be broken. If God has recourse to a miracle, it is the fault of human beings, for they have sunk so low that God must break the laws of nature to save them. It is for this reason that the *Midrash Rabbah* describes God's descent into Egypt to save

---

9 Ramban, Shemot 13:16.
10 Genesis 8:22.

us as a *yerida le-tzorech aliyah* (a descent for the purpose of ultimately ascending), for involvement with miracles is actually a move downward for God, so to speak.

וארד להצילו מיד מצרים ולהעלתו מן הארץ ההוא אל ארץ טובה ורחבה אל ארץ
זבת חלב ודבש . . .

I shall descend to rescue it from the land of Egypt and to bring it up from that land to a good and spacious land to a land flowing with milk and honey . . .[11]

אמר רבי שמעון גדולה חיבתן של ישראל שנגלה הקב"ה במקום עבודת כוכבים
ובמקום טנופת ובמקום טומאה בשביל לגאלן, משל לכהן שנפלה תרומתו לבית
הקברות אומר מה אעשה, לטמא את עצמי אי אפשר, ולהניח תרומתי א"א, מוטב
לי לטמא את עצמי פעם אחת וחוזר ומטהר ולא אאבד את תרומתי, כך אבותינו
היו תרומתו של הקב"ה שנאמר קדש ישראל לה' וגו' היו בין הקברות שנאמר כי
אין בית אשר אין שם מת ואומר ומצרים מקברים אמר הקב"ה היאך אני גואלן
להניחן א"א מוטב לירד ולהצילן שנאמר וארד להצילו מיד מצרים.

Rabbi Shimon said: Great is the love of the Jewish people. God revealed himself to them in a place of idolatry, in a place of refuse, in a place of defilement, in order to redeem them. This can be compared to a *kohen* whose *terumah* falls into a cemetery. He says: What can I do? I can neither defile myself nor leave my *terumah*. Better I should defile myself on a one-time basis and purify myself afterward rather than lose my *terumah*. So, too, our forefathers were the *terumah* of God, as it says: The Jewish people are sanctified to the Lord . . . They were in a cemetery, as it says: "There was no house without a corpse," and it says, "The Egyptians were burying . . ." God said: How could I redeem them? I cannot leave them. Better I

---

11 Exodus 3:8.

should descend in order to save them, as it says: "I descended to save them from Egypt."

This excerpt of *Midrash Rabbah*[12] draws an analogy to the *terumah* of a *kohen* that fell into a cemetery. The *kohen* finds himself in a quandary. On the one hand, he may not enter a cemetery. On the other hand, he wants to retrieve the *terumah,* so he enters the cemetery on a one-time basis in order to bring it out. Similarly, God descended into Egypt on a one-time basis in order to save the Jewish people, who are referred to as the *terumah* – God's own first fruits. קדש ישראל לה' ראשית תבואתה כל אכליו יאשמו רעה תבא אליהם נאם ה' – "Israel is holy to God, the first of his crop. All who devour it will be held guilty. Evil shall come upon them – the word of God."[13]

Finally, the Hallel over the ordinary is more central because a religion that is based on supernatural phenomena cannot survive. All of human experience is founded upon natural phenomena. It is only through connection and response to natural phenomena that human spirituality can endure in this natural world. The tragedy of modern humanity is that it confuses metaphysical and natural phenomena. Judaism can only be grounded upon the Hallel of *pesukei de-zimrah* and not upon the *Hallel ha-Mitzri.*

∿ Moshe vs. Abraham

The Rav mused many times over the following question. Both Moshe Rabbenu and Avraham Avinu were exemplary Jews. Who was greater? On the one hand, Moshe surpassed everyone in prophecy, as the verse states: ולא קם נביא עוד בישראל כמשה – "Never again did a prophet like Moshe arise in Israel."[14] The Rambam established as one of the thirteen cardinal principles that Moshe's prophecy transcended that of all other prophets who preceded and followed him.[15] On the other hand, God

---

12 Exodus Rabbah 15:5.
13 Jeremiah 2:3.
14 Deuteronomy 34:10.
15 The seventh of Rambam's Thirteen Principles of Faith.

scolded Moshe Rabbenu and bemoaned the death of the Avot. In the language of Rashi, God said:

הרהרת על מדותי, לא כאברהם שאמרתי לו כי ביצחק יקרא לך זרע ואחר כך
אמרתי לו העלהו לעולה, ולא הרהר אחרי מדותי ...

You questioned my practices, unlike Abraham, to whom I said, "Through Isaac shall your seed be called," and afterwards I told him, "Offer him as a burnt offering," yet he did not question my practices . . .[16]

Furthermore, the name of Elohim is distinctively associated with the Avot, as we recite in the *shemoneh esreh*: *Elohei Avraham, Elohei Yitzhak,* and *Elohei Yaakov.* Yet Moshe was the human being par excellence and the greatest of all the prophets. Why the unique association with the Avot?

The Rav pointed out that *Elohei Avraham* reflects the relationship of *kinyan* (acquisition). "*Beit avi*" means "the house that belongs to my father." Similarly, *Elohei Avraham* is the God who belongs to Abraham; meaning that the *ba'al ha-bayit* is Abraham and God became his *kinyan* (acquisition). Abraham acquired God. How? He did this through a long and difficult search that began at the age of either three or forty.[17] Yet God did not reveal himself to Abraham until he had reached the age of seventy-five. Abraham fulfilled the verse:

ובקשתם משם את ה' א־להיך ומצאת כי תדרשנו בכל לבבך ובכל נפשך.

From there you will seek the Lord your God, and you will find him if you search for him with all your heart and with all your soul.[18]

Abraham discovered God in the constellations above Mesopotamia – not through the miracle-filled *Hallel ha-Mitzri,* but through the *Hallel*

---

16 Rashi on Exodus 6:1.
17 See Rambam, *Hilchot Avodah Zarah,* Chapter 1, and Raavad there.
18 Deuteronomy 4:29.

of *pesukei de-zimrah,* of nature. Abraham's life does not contain overt miracles such as that of the manna, the quail, the pillars of cloud and fire, and so on. Abraham discovered God in the sun and stars. When Abraham found God, God became *Elohei Avraham* – Abraham's acquisition.

Moshe did not seek out God. He did not struggle with questions. The first time, God revealed himself to Moshe at the burning bush, Moshe realized that it was God. He did not search. On the contrary: God found Moshe and summoned him. Therefore, Moshe's relationship with God was far different from Abraham's. Abraham acquired God, while God acquired Moshe, who became the *eved Hashem* (servant of God) par excellence. Unlike Abraham, whose encounter with God was through the medium of the Hallel of *pesukei de-zimrah,* Moshe's encounter came about through *Hallel ha-Mitzri* – the supernatural. Moshe's lifespan is filled with miracles and the Divine Providence that watched over the Jewish people under his leadership.

Only after the sin of the Golden Calf did Moshe realize the necessity to seek God out rather than merely respond to him. When he asked God to forgive the Israelites, God did not agree to do so immediately. Moshe persisted, challenging God boldly on behalf of his beloved nation. The Rav added that when a Jew approaches a rabbi and asks him about the essence of Judaism, Hillel's answer – דעלך סני לחברך לא תעביד – "That which is hateful to you, do not do to your fellow human being,"[19] is not sufficient. Every individual must acquire his connection with God on his own, as Abraham did.

✃ The Hallel of *Pesukei de-Zimrah* as the Key to Jewish Survival

In the long run, Judaism operates with the Hallel of *pesukei de-zimrah* and not with *Hallel ha-Mitzri.* There are no quick fixes or quantum leaps of faith in becoming a Jew. The nations of the world can easily meet God

---

19 BT *Shabbat* 31a.

in a one-time sensational religious experience. Our religion is the most difficult and demanding, with paradoxes that Christianity and Islam do not possess. A Jew who wants to observe Shabbat in America, where he is socially and economically integrated into the land, must make a sacrifice by closing his business on one of the week's best shopping days. A worker must leave earlier on Friday afternoons and not work at all on Saturday. A student enrolled in a university where exams are administered on Shabbat must either forfeit the course or inconvenience himself. The observance of *mitzvot* is a direct function of the Hallel of *pesukei de-zimrah,* of self-sacrifice and ongoing devotion.

In this sense, the most challenging issue of all is the commitment to an intensive Jewish education. In Catholic schools, pupils are required to recite the catechism. But a Jewish day school, with its Hebrew language requirement and the demands to master complicated Jewish texts, is much more challenging. Talmud study is neither easy nor smooth. The surface of the Talmud appears dry and cold until one enters deeply into its waters. Only after long study does one discover a warm and lively world full of feeling and passion. It is a long trek, which we begin to demand of our charges at a young age.

How can we demand that our students master two different intellectual worlds? The Rav quoted from the *haftarah* about Elkana and Chana.

ויהי איש אחד מן הרמתים צופים מהר אפרים ושמו אלקנה.

There was a certain man from Ramathaim Zophim from the
hill country of Ephraim whose name was Elkana . . .[20]

The Gemara comments[21] that there are two mountains that face each other. Between them is an abyss. In order to live on both mountains, one needs a bridge to travel from one to the other. One must live in

---

20 I Samuel 1:1.
21 See BT *Megillah* 14a.

two worlds that interact with one other. When I close my Gemara, I can travel to the world of physics and mathematics and understand it as well. Ultimately, the telos is to see the "beauty of Yefet in the tents of Shem."[22] Many people have fallen into the chasm between the two mountains, while others failed to build a bridge between them. But – what can we do? Do we have another choice in the matter?

---

22 BT *Megillah* 9b.

⤳ יתרו ⤳

Yitro: The Many Facets of Jewish Leadership

⤳ Yitro's Challenge to Moshe

YITRO ASKED:

וירא חתן משה את כל אשר הוא עשה לעם ויאמר מה הדבר הזה אשר אתה עשה לעם מדוע אתה יושב לבדך וכל העם נצב עליך מן בקר עד ערב.

The father-in-law of Moshe saw everything that he was doing to the people and he said: "What is this thing you are doing to the people? Why do you sit alone with all the people standing over you from morning until evening?"[1]

Note that the language of the text – "you are doing to the people" – uses the dative case and seems to be superfluous. When I do something to a person, it is either good or bad. It is clear that Moshe meant no harm in the way that he judged the people. Why not simply ask, "What are you doing?"

From the language, we see that Moshe had a mesmerizing influence over the people. He had a mysterious quality that fascinated them, so that they enjoyed being in his presence and did not leave him alone.

---

1 Exodus 18:14.

156

Yitro realized that Moshe was the central cohesive force. Elsewhere, when Moshe delayed in his return from Mount Sinai, we also see his influence. That delay caused one of the greatest tragedies in our history, the sin of the Golden Calf. Yitro was not trying to reproach Moshe. He wanted to discover the secret of Moshe's popularity and influence.

We find elsewhere in Tanach that Delilah asked Samson: במה כחך גדול – "What is the secret of your strength?"[2] After many attempts at evasion, Samson revealed the secret and lost his strength, his eyesight and, ultimately, his life. Moshe simply responded to Yitro by outlining his daily routine. כי יבא אלי העם לדרש א־להים – "The people come to me to inquire of God."[3] The Targum Onkelos translates the phrase as "They come to inquire," while Rashi translates it as "They come to ask for instructions from God." In this way, Moshe sets forth the role of a leader.

✥ Moshe as *Posek* (Halachic Arbitrator)

What is it that Moshe described? In effect, he said: My job is to render halachic decisions – "*tsu pasken shailos*," as it is described in Yiddish. Moshe decided matters such as the inheritance of Zelafhad's daughters,[4] or how those who had been ritually impure during Passover should make the festival offering and eat the ritual meal.[5] A rabbi is asked endless questions about every conceivable aspect of life. In our electronic age, the questions have become even more complex. There is no area or item that falls outside the halachic purview. Therefore, a rabbi must be a scientist, an engineer, a philosopher and a physician, not in the literal sense but in terms of the requisite knowledge he must bring to bear in a multitude of areas.

Judaism places great importance on specifics. If we stand at a distance from a painting, we see the general outline. If Sabbath observance were

---

2 Judges 16:6.
3 Exodus 18:15.
4 Numbers 27:1–11.
5 Numbers 9:6–14.

merely cultic in nature, we could attend shul whenever we wished without conforming to any schedule, and we could carry a handkerchief wherever we pleased. Such details are trivial to the overall concept of Shabbat. But we know that the essence of Shabbat observance is in the details. Thus, the task of Moshe and the leaders is to inform the people of those details when it is necessary.

What qualities does one need to teach others? The Rav suggested that knowledge must be combined with great humility. Often, when many people ask for information from a particular person, this person may begin to feel pride and and a sense of superiority. People from all walks of life, rich and poor alike, approached Moshe with their questions, and Moshe treated them equally. A great person treats the one who asks an absurd question with the same respect as the one who asks an important question.

As the Romans were taking Rabbi Yishmael the High Priest to his execution, he burst into tears. Rabban Gamliel asked him, "Why do you weep? Are you afraid of death?" Rabbi Yishmael answered, "I weep not because I am about to suffer martyrdom, but because we are being taken to the executioner like common robbers and murderers." He could not understand what he had done to deserve the death penalty. Rabban Gamliel answered, "Don't you remember that once in your career, you arrived home exhausted and lay down to rest? While you were resting, a poor woman came to your house to ask a question about ritual law. Your servant asked her to wait until you awakened. She waited, but for an instant, a fleeting thought undoubtedly passed through her mind: *Had I been a rich neighbor, he would have answered me right away.* A tear dropped onto her cheek, but she shook off these thoughts at once." Rabban Gamliel continued, "The Torah warns: 'Do not afflict a widow or an orphan.' If you do, God will punish you with the sword. It does not matter how you afflict them. It is for this reason that you were condemned to death."[6]

---

6   BT *Semahot,* Chapter 8.

Humility is the ability to step back and view events with detachment. Moshe had this ability. Because of it, he judged the cases of the daughters of Zelafhad and of people who were ritually impure. The Rav related that his mother told him a story about his grandfather, Rav Chaim Soloveitchik. Once, while he was in an important meeting with distinguished people, a distraught woman burst into the room, shouting, "Help me. I had a strange dream that my son was insane" (which he actually was). Rav Chaim arose, excused himself, proceeded to go to an adjoining room with the woman and listen to her. Then he returned to the conference. We must learn to emulate the patience of God, *arichut apayim*. When we feel that people are wasting our time with foolish questions, we have lost the capacity to judge.

℘ The Heroism of a Judge

A judge or *posek* must possess not only knowledge and compassion, but also heroic qualities. Not only must he defend the poor and forgotten, but he must also be willing to defy public opinion. The Rav recounted several anecdotes that illustrate the risks involved in doing so.

At one time, a rav had to render a decision as to whether a cow that was a farmer's sole possession was kosher or not. After slaughter, it had been inspected and found to be not kosher. This *pesak* caused the farmer to incur a loss of perhaps a hundred dollars, the sum total of all the material goods that he possessed. Yet he accepted the decision with the same grace as if his cow had been declared kosher.

In contrast, a case that involved one dollar so angered the person against whom the rav ruled that he became his sworn enemy.

Of far greater consequence was the case of a young woman who had converted to Judaism and became fully observant. Later on, she met a young Jewish man who came from a non-observant family. As their relationship grew stronger, the young woman strove to bring her boyfriend closer to Judaism. After they became engaged, the boy's father suggested that the boy go to his grandfather's grave in order to tell him that he was engaged to be married, for his grandfather had loved him very much.

Upon arrival at the cemetery, the young man noticed a strange emblem engraved on the memorial stone: a pair of joined hands. This meant that the young man's grandfather had been a *kohen*. The young man then realized that he, too, was a *kohen*. The case was brought to the Rav, who ruled that the couple could not marry because Jewish law forbade a *kohen* to marry a convert. This decision took heroism because it involved enormous pain to the parties. Nevertheless, they accepted the decision and remained friends.

Similarly, Moshe embodied heroism or *gevurah,* not merely strength.

✌ Moshe as Compassionate Caretaker

The Ramban highlights another facet of Moshe's leadership by interpreting the above-mentioned verses differently. He suggests that the phrase "When the people come to me to inquire about God" refers to the custom of *bikkur holim* (visiting the sick).[7] According to the Ramban, the people came to Moshe to ask him to pray to God on their behalf. Moshe devoted much of his day to praying for the sick. The Hasidic movement devoted much of its time and effort to prayer for the sick and to providing sustenance for the poor. These practices continue to this day.

In order to pray for the sick, one must do three things. He must visit in person and provide him with whatever assistance he can, and he must shore up his spirits by telling him, "You must get well because we need you and depend upon you." The Talmud[8] relates that when a certain student contracted a contagious disease and everyone stayed away from him, Rabbi Akiva, his rebbi, visited him, swept his room and nursed him back to health. By caring for those who are ill, we restore their faith and fill them with confidence and optimism. The third and most significant component is prayer for the sick, which must come from the depths of

---

7 Ramban on Exodus 18:15.
8 BT *Nedarim* 40a.

our hearts.[9] A hastily pronounced *mi she-berach* without inner conviction has little value. We must share in the pain of the sick person. Only then do we have the right to pray. If one is in a position to pray for his fellow human being and fails to do so, Jewish tradition considers him guilty. We should do our best to emulate the compassion of people like Moshe and Rabbi Akiva.

৵ Moshe's Greatest Role – That of Teacher

Moshe's greatest accomplishment was his teaching. In order to teach well, one must embody the quality of *hesed*. What is the difference between *hesed* (kindness) and *rahamim* (mercy)? *Rahamim* is not really mercy, as it is widely translated, but love. The Hebrew word *rahamim,* which is derived from the word *rehem,* "womb," describes a mother's love for her child.

I can be full of *hesed* toward someone, but I always know who I am and who he is. I try to help him, I feel his pain and anguish and I have compassion for him, but we are two different people, not one. Similarly, parents and children constitute a single unit when the children are small, a relationship founded upon *rahamim*. As they grow older and want to break away, this unity is sometimes lost. At that point, the relationship is based not on love or on *rahamim,* but on *hesed*. When people practice *hesed* in their dealings with each other, their existence again becomes one of community, and not necessarily one of *rahamim*.

In order to teach, one must practice *hesed*. Teaching does not end with the act of passing on information. There is no true teaching as well without *rahamim*. To teach is an act of emanation – of spilling over. כוסי רויה "My cup overflows,"[10] so to speak. Maimonides states that one who possesses an abundance of knowledge is compelled to address himself to

---

9 Ramban, Torat ha-Adam, and Shulhan Aruch, Yoreh Deah 335, Hilchot Bikkur Holim, Rama, paragraph 4.
10 Psalms 23:5.

his fellow human being.[11] The prophet Zechariah did not stop teaching until he was murdered. Jeremiah could not refrain from teaching even though the people despised him and his message. Moshe also taught the community and suffered on their behalf. God told him to gather the seventy men:

וירדתי ודברתי עמך שם ואצלתי מן הרוח אשר עליך ושמתי עליהם ...

And I will come down and take the spirit from you and place it on them.[12]

This spirit refers to Moshe's great qualities as a judge and teacher.

Yitro wished to understand the secret of Moshe's connection with the Jewish people. Moshe did not answer Yitro's question directly. Instead, he provided him with a sketch of his handiwork. Parashat Mishpatim follows Parashat Yitro to emphasize the importance of Moshe's role as a judge to render halachic rulings. Thus, Yitro received the answer to his question when he witnessed Moshe's multi-faceted role among the Israelites.

---

11 Guide for the Perplexed, part 2, chapter 37.
12 Numbers 11:17.

✦ משפטים ✦

Mishpatim: The Parashah
of *Torah She'beal Peh*

FOR THE LAST several hundred years in Eastern Europe, the Shabbat of Parashat Mishpatim was the designated Shabbat of the *hevra Shas* (the organization devoted to learning Shas). This organization felt a kinship with Parashat Mishpatim because more than any other *parashah*, it epitomizes the *Torah she'beal peh*. The *hevra Shas* held their annual dinner on this Shabbat. They read the *Torah she-bi-chtav* on Shabbat morning and devoted Shabbat afternoon to the study of *Torah she'beal peh*. After *Minha*, they recited Sefer Tehillim based on the tradition that Moshe died on a Shabbat afternoon. The *Shulhan Aruch* states that when a *hacham* passes away, the *Beit Midrash* is rendered nonfunctional, and those who would ordinarily study, recite *Tehillim*.[1]

✦ The Tradition of Studying Seder Nezikin

There was a tradition for young boys to be taught the tractates of *Seder Nezikin.* Tractate *Bava Batra* teaches us that one who wishes to become wise should delve into *Nezikin,* for there is no greater enterprise in Torah

---

1   Shulhan Aruch, Orah Hayyim 292:2, Mishnah Berurah 6.

than *Seder Nezikin.*[2] The Rav said as a boy, he studied the chapters of *Elu metziot, Shenayim ohazim* and *Meruba. Nezikin,* he said, is saturated with a certain strength that inspires the child, helps him develop his intuition and sharpens his intellect. It creates emotional and intellectual inspiration, thereby making it the strongest *seder* imbued with special qualities.

The sages developed this strength further with the outstanding works that they wrote about *Nezikin,* specifically *Ketzot ha-hoshen* and *Netivot ha-mishpat.* The author of *Ketzot ha-hoshen* was a *melamed* whom the well-to-do townspeople considered a ne'er-do-well. During the winter months, he was compelled to study Torah in bed, under his blankets, because he had no money for fuel. Yet the *Ketzot* revolutionized the *seder* of *Nezikin.* The author of the acclaimed *Netivot ha-mishpat* on *Nezikin* was a wealthy man who was the Rav of the city of Lisa. Rav Chaim Brisker saw his strengths in a number of areas: *shtarot (Nezikin), tumat met* and *oholot (tumah* and *taharah).*

✣ Interruption of the Divine Revelation and Covenant

Is there a deeper rationale for the importance of *Seder Nezikin?* Upon the heels of the *Aseret ha-dibrot* (The Ten Commandments) at the close of Parashat Yitro, the Torah states:

> וכל העם ראים את הקולת ואת הלפידם ואת קול השפר ואת ההר עשן וירא העם
> וינעו ויעמדו מרחק. ויאמרו אל משה דבר אתה עמנו ונשמעה ואל ידבר עמנו א-
> להים פן נמות . . . לא תעשון אתי אלהי כסף ואלהי זהב לא תעשו לכם מזבח
> אדמה תעשה לי וזבחת עליו את עלתיך ואת שלמיך את צאנך ואת בקרך בכל
> המקום אשר אזכיר את שמי אבוא אליך וברכתיך. ואם מזבח אבנים תעשה לי
> לא תבנה אתהן גזית כי חרבך הנפת עליה ותחללה. ולא תעלה במעלת על מזבחי
> אשר לא תגלה ערותך עליו.

---

2   BT *Bava Batra* 175b.

The entire people saw the thunder and the flames, the sound of the shofar and the smoking mountain; the people saw and trembled and stood from a distance. They said to Moshe: You speak to us and we shall listen. Let God not speak to us, lest we die . . . You shall not make images of what is with me; do not make for yourselves gods of silver and gods of gold. An altar of earth you shall make for me and you shall slaughter near it your *olot* and *shelamim*, your flock and your herd; wherever I permit my name to be mentioned I shall come to you and bless you. And when you make for me an altar of stones, do not hew them for you will have raised your sword over it and desecrated it. You shall not ascend my altar on steps, so that your nakedness may not be uncovered upon it.[3]

Following the *giving of the Ten Commandments,* the Torah should have proceeded immediately with Chapter 24 of Parashat Mishpatim, in which God tells Moshe to seal the covenant with the people. Instead, there is an interruption between these two chapters. Parashat Mishpatim, with its many detailed laws of *Nezikin,* seems to depart from the context.

What follows immediately after Parashat Mishpatim is the construction of the *Mishkan* in *Parshiyot Terumah* and *Tetzaveh.* Only after this do we return to the story of the revelation, with the episode of the Golden Calf. The construction of the *Mishkan* is a required step toward the fulfillment of the Divine promise בהוציאך את העם ממצרים תעבדון את האֱ-להים על ההר הזה – "When you take the people out of Egypt, you will serve God upon this mountain."[4] This verse encompasses two commandments: the Revelation at Mount Sinai and the construction of the *Mishkan.* Only Parashat Mishpatim represents a dramatic departure from the logical sequence. Why was it given such preference?

---

3 Exodus 20:15–16, 20–23.
4 Exodus 3:12.

✥ Religious Meaning in Civil Law

Apparently, Parashat Mishpatim is an interpretation of the Ten Commandments. Without Parashat Mishpatim, there can be no ממלכת כהנים וגוי קדוש – "kingdom of priests and holy nation."[5] Almost all the fundamental principles of the *mitzvot* may be found here. While we also see them in Kedoshim and Ki Teze, these two *Torah readings* focus primarily on the crime. *Mishpatim* focuses on both the crime and its punishment.

Parashat Mishpatim is not only a description of laws between human beings and a moral code. It lays out an entire framework of civil relationships. Why should the Torah address the question of financial commitments? Why should the Torah care about the situation of a paid or unpaid watchman? In Parashat Kedoshim, in which the Torah forbids talebearing and theft, the theme is primarily moral in nature. Parashat Mishpatim discusses issues of *kinyanim* (acquisitions), *hazakot* (presumptions of ownership) and *shtar* (the transfer of promissory notes). These monetary issues have no place in a moral code. The conclusion, then, is that civil laws carry religious significance. Destruction of property and trespassing are not merely violations of civil law but moral transgressions.

If one studies the law of the *Avodah* on Yom Kippur or the laws of *shofar* on Rosh ha-Shannah, there is a fulfillment of studying *inyanei de-yoma* (passages relevant to the themes and the sanctity of these days). But no less exalting is the study of *perek hezkat ha-batim* (the laws concerning squatters' rights) on Yom Kippur or the study of *shenyaim ohazim be-tallit* (two people seizing a garment) on Rosh ha-Shannah. Even though such study may not constitute *inyanei de-yoma,* it fulfills the *mitzvah* of Torah study. Parashat Mishpatim was introduced at this

---

5 Exodus 19:6.

particular point in the Torah not only because of the importance of the civil code alone. The Torah sought to show that these civil laws are, in fact, religious laws.

The Rav told the story of a Gerer hasid in Warsaw, Rav Moshe Polevsky, who was a great admirer of his grandfather, Rav Chaim Soloveitchik. Rav Polevsky told the Rav that once he was building his *sukkah* with great enthusiasm, singing and dancing, when a bystander asked him, "Why are you getting all excited over putting evergreen branches as *schach* on the roof of the *sukkah*?" He said that he answered that this act excited him so much because it was more than a simple act of construction. The Rav said: So it is with *Seder Nezikin* or *Parashat* Mishpatim with their precise detail. These details provide a technical structure that is infused with meaning and moral stature.

✑ A Kingdom of Priests and a Holy Nation

In its preamble to the Ten Commandments, the Torah states:

ועתה אם שמוע תשמעו בקלי ושמרתם את בריתי והייתם לי סגלה מכל העמים
כי לי כל הארץ. ואתם תהיו לי ממלכת כהנים וגוי קדוש . . .

And now, if you listen well to Me and keep My covenant, you shall be to Me the most beloved treasure of all peoples, for the entire world is Mine. You shall be to Me a kingdom of priests and a holy nation . . .[6]

What did God promise us? He promised us Divine Revelation by miraculous means. However, the concept of *havdalah* (differentiation) between ourselves and the nations of the world was not yet fully spelled out.

The Magid of Kelm said that Gog and Magog were rich with Yiddish homiletic significance. *"Gog iz a ganev un a gazlan. Magog is mere a*

---

6   Exodus 19:5–6.

ganev un mere a gazlan." – "Gog is a ganev [thief] and a gazlan [bandit]. Magog is more a ganev and more a gazlan."

The Rav taught that there were two disparate promises. The first was a universal divine revelation of כי לי הארץ – "the entire world is Mine."[7] Maimonides speaks of *hasidei ummot ha-olam* (the devout pious individuals of the world).[8] The divine revelation of Parashat Bereshit was given to non-Jews as well.

The second promise was a divine revelation for the Jewish people alone, as described by the phrase ואתם תהיו לי ממלכת כהנים וגוי קדוש – "You shall be to me a kingdom of priests and a holy nation."[9] That second promise is an apocalyptic divine revelation for which we were chosen from among all the nations. Ramban writes that the history of the Jews is not guided by the zodiac, but directed by God himself.[10] The recurring warnings in Parashat Yitro against going beyond a certain point reflect the universal revelation with its fences and boundaries. The majestic description of the revelation at the climax of Parashat Mishpatim reflects not the universal revelation, but rather God's personal relationship with the Jewish people.

ויעל משה ואהרן נדב ואביהוא ושבעים מזקני ישראל. ויראו את א־להי ישראל ותחת רגליו כמעשה לבנת הספיר וכעצם השמים לטהר. ואל אצילי בני ישראל לא שלח ידו ויחזו את הא־להים ויאכלו וישתו.

Moshe, Aharon, Nadav and Avihu and seventy of the elders of Israel ascended. They saw the God of Israel. Beneath his feet was the likeness of sapphire brickwork, and it was like the essence of heaven in purity. Against the great men of Israel he

---

7 Leviticus 25:23.
8 Rambam, *Hilchot Melachim* 8:11.
9 Exodus 19:6.
10 Ramban, Genesis 17:1.

did not stretch out his hand – they gazed at God, yet they ate and drank.[11]

In God's revelation to the Jewish people, the boundaries are abolished, and one can reach out to infinity.

There is an argument in the *Mechilta* as to whether the covenant that was made at the end of Mishpatim took place before or after the giving of the Torah.[12] This is also the subject of a controversy between Rashi and the Ramban.[13] Apparently, the need for two kinds of divine revelation, one in Yitro and one in Mishpatim, reflect this dual revelation: the one in Yitro is for Jews and all the nations, while the one in Mishpatim is for the Jewish people alone.

The idea of a kingdom of priests and a holy nation is the forerunner of the notion that every Jew should strive to be a prophet. The Jew's ideal is prophecy, and through *nevuah,* the prophetic spirit, one may merit the apocalyptic revelation that is meant for the Jewish people alone.

We will experience the second kind of divine revelation in the Messianic era. This supernatural *gilui shechinah* is the goal of Parashat Mishpatim, with its detailed monetary laws. Our care in obeying these laws will one day lead to the *gilui shechinah* and a covenant with the prophetic spirit, together with our fulfillment of God's commandment to become a kingdom of priests and a holy nation where all borders between ourselves and God will disappear.

---

11 Exodus 24:9–11.
12 *Mechilta,* Mishpatim 19:10.
13 Ramban, Exodus 24:1.

ּתְרוּמָה

Parashat Terumah

THE COMMANDMENT IN Parashat Terumah, וְעָשׂוּ לִי מִקְדָּשׁ וְשָׁכַנְתִּי בְּתוֹכָם – "You shall make a sanctuary for me and I will dwell among them,"[1] is actually a twofold *mitzvah*. First, we are commanded to build a *Mikdash* that will function as a sanctuary. Second, we are ordered to establish a *beit ha-behira* – a permanent, irreplaceable, and exclusive abode for God.

The Rambam says in the beginning of *Hilchot Beit ha-Behira* (Laws of the Sanctuary) that the reason we were given the *mitzvah* of building the *Mikdash* was so that we could offer sacrifices to God and to create a place for the fulfillment of the *mitzvah* of *aliya la-regel* (the thrice-annual pilgrimage to Jerusalem).[2] The Rambam cites a list of temporary *batei mikdash* but then says that once Jerusalem had been chosen, it superseded all the other sites. The Torah does not tell us when the shift from a temporary structure to a permanent one will occur. It simply states:

וְהָיָה הַמָּקוֹם אֲשֶׁר יִבְחַר ה' אֱ־לֹהֵיכֶם בּוֹ לְשַׁכֵּן שְׁמוֹ שָׁם שָׁמָּה תָבִיאוּ אֵת כָּל אֲשֶׁר אָנֹכִי מְצַוֶּה אֶתְכֶם . . .

---

1 Exodus 25:8.
2 Rambam, Hilchot Beit ha-Behirah, 1:1.

It shall be that the place where the Lord your God will choose to place his name. There you shall bring all that I command you . . .[3]

At both levels of the *mitzvah,* we are confronted with a question already posed by King Solomon at the inauguration of the *Beit ha-Mikdash.*

כי האמנם ישב א־להים על הארץ הנה השמים ושמי השמים לא יכלכלוך אף כי הבית הזה אשר בניתי.

Would God truly dwell on earth? Behold, the heavens and the highest heavens cannot contain you, and surely not this Temple that I have built.[4]

How can infinity be encompassed in a "world of finitude"? The *Midrash*[5] comments that Moshe was also confounded by the question of how an abode could be built to accommodate the infinite God. But God told Moshe, "Your thinking is not my thinking."[6] God has the capacity to circumscribe the Shechinah by using *tzimtzum,* the kabbalistic idea of self-contraction. This process is incomprehensible to a mortal human being.

King Solomon continues:

ופנית אל תפלת עבדך ואל תחנתו ה' א־להי לשמוע אל הרנה ואל התפלה אשר עבדך מתפלל לפניך היום. להיות עינך פתחות אל הבית הזה לילה ויום אל המקום אשר אמרת יהיה שמי שם לשמוע אל התפלה אשר יתפלל עבדך אל המקום הזה.

But may you turn to the prayer of your servant and to his supplication, O Lord my God, to hear the cry and prayer that your servant prays before you today; that your eyes be open towards this Temple night and day to the place of which you

---

3 Deuteronomy 12:11.
4 1 Kings 8:27.
5 Shemot Rabbah 34:1.
6 Shemot Rabbah 34:1.

said: "My name shall be there," to hear the prayer that your servant shall pray toward this place.[7]

King Solomon provides no answer the above-mentioned dilemma, but instead prays that God will be responsive to our prayers. He describes several types of situations, such as war, that warrant heartfelt prayer:

בהנגף עמך ישראל לפני אויב אשר יחטאו לך ושבו אליך והודו את שמך והתפללו והתחננו אליך בבית הזה. ואתה תשמע השמים וסלחת לחטאת עמך ישראל והשבתם אל האדמה אשר נתת לאבותם.

If your people are defeated by an enemy because they sinned against you, and then they return to you and praise your name and pray and supplicate to you in this Temple, may you hear from heaven and forgive the sin of your people Israel and return them to the land that you gave their forefathers.[8]

In a situation of drought:

בהעצר שמים ולא יהיה מטר כי יחטאו לך והתפללו אל המקום הזה והודו את שמך ומחטאתם ישובון כי תענם.

If the heavens are restrained and there is no rain because they sinned against you, they will pray toward this place, praise your name and repent their sin so that you may respond to them.[9]

In a situation of famine:

רעב כי יהיה בארץ דבר כי יהיה שדפון ירקון ארבה חסיל כי יהיה כי יצר לו איבו בארץ שעריו כל נגע כל מחלה כל תפלה כל תחנה אשר תהיה לכל האדם לכל עמך ישראל אשר ידעון איש נגע לבבו ופרש כפיו אל הבית הזה.

---

7 I Kings 8:28–29.
8 I Kings 8:33–34.
9 I Kings 8:35.

If there be a famine in the land, if there be a plague, if there be windblast or withering, locust or grasshopper, or if Israel's enemy oppresses it in the land of their cities – any plague, any disease – for any prayer and any supplication that any person of your entire people Israel may have, each person knowing the affliction of his heart – let him spread out his hands towards the Temple.[10]

The conclusion to King Solomon's question was that God is always responsive to our prayers, which are warranted under all circumstances. A person who is suffering should not be embarrassed to call out to God. Even if one's prayer should be for extraordinary wealth or the status of royalty, God will grant the prayer if he finds it reasonable. God will not indict a human being for asking for something that appears to be foolish.

There is a well-known disagreement between the Rambam and the Ramban as to whether the obligation to pray originates in the Torah or in later rabbinic writings. The Rambam contends that prayer is of Torah origin,[11] while the Ramban argues that it is only of Torah origin during a time of distress.[12] According to the Ramban, the definition of distress is a cataclysmic, physical event. However, the Rambam teaches that our very existence and ability to function generates a Torah obligation to pray.[13] Finite, mortal human beings must turn to the infinite God for their sustenance.

In brief, no one can answer the question of how infinitude may be encompassed in a finite world. It is a mystery, similar to the impossibility of understanding God's essence. According to the *Midrash*,[14] King Solomon was also upset by his inability to understand the secret of the red heifer. This question posed a dilemma for Moshe as well. If neither

---

10 1 Kings 8:37–38.
11 Rambam, Hilchot Tefillah 1:1.
12 Ramban's commentary on Rambam's *Sefer ha-Mitzvot,* Mitzvat Aseh 5.
13 See Besdin, *Reflections of the Rav,* vol. 1, 79–82.
14 Bamidbar Rabbah 19:3.

King Solomon nor Moshe could penetrate God's secrets, we must accept that we cannot understand how infinity can be contained in a world of a finite nature.

The Rav mentioned a story he heard from Rav Simcha Zelig Reguer, the Dayan of Brisk. Rav Simcha Zelig once accompanied Rav Chaim Soloveitchik to a town in Latvia on the Baltic Sea to visit a second cousin of Rav Chaim who was a follower of Chabad. The Rav said that Rav Chaim was very accommodating by nature and sensitive to Rav Shneur Zalman of Liadi, the author of the Tanya and the founder of the Chabad movement. When they arrived, his cousin was not at home. They noticed a *sefer* entitled *Magen Avot* on his bookshelf. This was the work that had popularized the Chabad movement.

In his preamble, the author cites a famous disagreement between the Jewish sages regarding the reason for creation. Some claimed that God had created the world in order to enhance his glory. Others contended that the creation was a function of God, who, as the supreme practitioner of *hesed,* wanted to share it with others. By definition, a *baal hesed* is driven to share his wealth with others. (The words and writings of Rabbi Yitzhak Luria, the Ari ha-Kadosh, and his student, Rav Chaim Vital, reflect this second position.) Rav Simcha Zelig told the Rav that Rav Chaim immediately reacted to these two positions, saying that even though both are correct, the ultimate telos is unknown and the world was created "because of his will and desire." The purpose of creation was to carry out God's will, whatever it may be. Rav Chaim cited a proof from the text of *Kaddish*, in which we recite, יתגדל ויתקדש שמה רבא בעלמא, "די ברא כרעותה" – "Praised and magnified is his great name in the world that was created according to his will."[15]

In the same way, we cannot answer King Solomon's question about housing God's infiniteness within the finite world. The only answer we can proffer is that the Temple was built in order to fulfill God's will. The

---

15 From the *Kaddish*. See Soloveitchik, Joseph B., *Halakhic Man*, translated by Lawrence Kaplan, The Jewish Publication Society of America, pp. 52–3.

less we understand, the greater the necessity to comply with the will of God.

❧ The *Beit ha-Mikdash* as a Locus of Prayer

The *Beit ha-Mikdash* as a locus for prayer is one of Judaism's central themes. Even though the Talmud tells us that *tefillah* corresponds to *korbanot*,[16] there is a fundamental distinction between the two. *Korbanot* may be offered through a proxy, while *tefillah* may not.[17] The difference lies in the fact that the efficacy of a sacrifice is a function of compliance with its halachic norms. If *Halachah* is followed, God will accept the sacrifice. On the other hand, *tefillah* must include a personal experience of closeness to God. This experience cannot be fulfilled by proxy. Since Judaism defines *tefillah* as standing in the presence of the king, prayer presupposes closeness to God.

In the eighth chapter of Kings I, King Solomon offers a prayer upon the dedication of the *Beit ha-Mikdash*. In this *tefilla*, Solomon repeats the phrase, ואתה תשמע השמים – "You will hear in Heaven."[18] This phrase depicts the true character of *tefillah* as an intimate, face-to-face conversation with God. In this sense, God lives, so to speak, at 12 Har ha-Bayit, while I live at 13 Har ha-Bayit, and we are on excellent terms.

The verse in Tehillim states, שמע תפלה עדיך כל בשר יבאו – "O You who hear prayer, all flesh shall come to you."[19] Here the word *adecha* is used instead of the more typical *elecha*. What is the difference? The word *elecha* implies, "I am moving toward you," while *adecha* means, "I have

---

16 BT *Berachot* 26b.
17 The Mishnah in BT *Berachot* 34b applies the principle of שלוחו של אדם כמותו – "a man's proxy is akin to himself" to prayer. Although the *sheliah zibbur* acts as a proxy to some degree, this is only for the verbal repetition of the prayers, and requires the presence and participation of each individual. See the Ran, page 11b, in the pages of the Rif, and the Gra, in the second comment in Imrei Noam on Tractate *Berachot*, that the concept of *shomea ke-oneh* does not apply to prayer.
18 1 Kings 8:30, 32, 34, 36, 39, 43, 45, 49.
19 Psalms 65:3.

reached you."[20] There is, so to speak, a collision between God and myself. Human beings should come so close to God that they should touch one another. For this reason, God engaged in the process of *tzimtzum* in order to make the *Beit ha-Mikdash* into his earthly abode. He did this so that we could feel "at home" with him. King Solomon illustrated this by stating, "You will hear in Heaven," meaning that *tefillah* refers to intimate conversation with God while standing in his presence.

---

20 See BT *Yoma* 86a – "Great is repentance, which reaches the celestial throne, as it is written: 'Return, O Israel, to your God.'"

✥ תצוה ✥

Tetzaveh I: The Importance of the Esthetic Form in the *Beit ha-Mikdash*

P ARASHAT TETZAVEH USUALLY coincides with Parashat Zachor, and its *haftarah* describes Shmuel's mission to Shaul. However, in a leap year, we read the *haftarah* from the book of Yehezkel. The Rav discussed the connection of this *haftarah* to Parashat Tetzaveh, mentioning how its terminology illuminates certain statements of the sages.

✥ Yehezkel's Emphasis on *Tzurah* (Form)

The *haftarah* focuses on the Third Temple, which will be built by the Messiah:

אתה בן אדם הגד את בית ישראל את הבית ויכלמו מעונותיהם ומדדו את תכנית. ואם נכלמו מכל אשר עשו צורת הבית ותכונתו ומוצאיו ומובאיו וכל צורתו ואת כל חקתיו וכל צורתיו וכל תורתיו הודע אותם וכתב לעיניהם וישמרו את כל צורתו ואת כל חקתיו ועשו אותם.

Son of man, tell the house of Israel about the Temple so that they will be ashamed of their sins and measure the design. And if they are ashamed of all they did, the *form* of the Temple and its design; its exits and entrances with all its *forms*; all its decrees with all its *forms*; and make all its regulations known to them and write them down before their eyes, that they remember all its *form* and all its decrees and perform them.[1]

The term *tzurah* (form), which appears four times in this verse, is clearly being emphasized. Why?

✦ Moshe's Difficulty in Building the Mishkan

The Rav raised another question from a seemingly difficult statement of the sages on a verse in Parashat Terumah: וראה ועשה בתבניתם אשר אתה מראה בהר – "See and construct according to their form that you are shown on the mountain."[2] Rashi quotes the Talmud's explanation:

מגיד שנתקשה משה במעשה המנורה עד שהראה לו הקב"ה מנורה של אש.

This shows us that Moshe had great difficulty with the construction of the *menorah*. God then showed him a *menorah* of fire.[3]

What was the nature of the great difficulty that Moshe encountered in building the *Mishkan*?

When a person explores the possibility of purchasing a home, two main things will occupy his attention: the home's measurements, dimensions and cost, and its appearance. Similarly, the prophet Yehezkel pointed out that there are two crucial factors, one of which is the *tzurah*. The term *hukotav* (its decrees) refers to physical measurements, and the term *tzurotav* (its form) refers to the home's architecture, its ability to elevate the spirit and create a sense of harmony. The Rav felt that architecture was eighty percent taste and twenty percent mathematics.

---

1 Ezekiel 43:10–11.
2 Shemot 25:40.
3 BT *Menahot* 29a.

ᴣ Judging Others: The Architectural Fallacy

When we judge people incorrectly, it's usually a result of our having used aesthetic criteria while lacking a complete perspective. The *yetzer ha-ra* represents desire, which is governed largely by aesthetics. We often make decisions based on our perception of beauty and harmony. However, such criteria often keep us from understanding the entire picture. If someone travels to Jerusalem and promises his friend he will send back reports of all that which he has seen and experienced, and the friend who stayed home studies all the reports carefully, can we honestly say that the friend knows Jerusalem? Of course not. Even though the friend has absorbed all the facts individually, he cannot experience the city as a holistic unit. Similarly, I may know all the facts about a person, but I do not see him in the totality of his experience. Therefore, I do not truly know him, and I cannot judge him based on aesthetic evaluation. The sages were referring to this when they said, "One cannot compare hearing to seeing."[4]

ᴣ The Dual Requirement of the *Beit ha-Mikdash*

The *Beit ha-Mikdash* had to meet two criteria. It had to include precise mathematical measurements of the varying utensils of the *Mishkan*, including the table, altar and panels. It also had to be an inspiring and impressive structure. It is analogous to placing a satellite, as opposed to a human being, on the moon. From a logical and technological perspective, there is no difference. However, there is a great deal of difference on the level of human experience. When several astronauts circled the moon and expressed their wonder, or when we observed pictures via satellite, this was admiration from afar. When a human being lands

---

4 *Mechilta* 19:9.

on the moon, it is an entirely different experience. The actions of the astronaut in space show *gevurah,* and the entire enterprise becomes filled with excitement and meaning.

God wanted Moshe to build a *Mishkan,* with its quantitative measurements and physical form, mainly because he wanted a home. He wanted people to understand that the *Beit ha-Mikdash* has a certain mysterious, ethereal quality in addition to its architectural and mathematical blueprint. It is this quality that will inspire people to rejoice even while reminding them that they are capable of accomplishing much more.

God wanted a *Mishkan* that would attract and inspire the Jewish people. This could not be accomplished by means of *hukotav* (its decrees), but primarily through *tzurotav* (its form). The *Mishkan* had to radiate an aura of inspiration, beckoning the individual to reach out to new horizons. This is the real *tzurah* of the *Mishkan.*

It is this second element of *tzurah* (form) that Moshe found difficult. In effect, he said to God, "Once you have shown me the image of the *Mishkan* and the *menorah,* how shall I convey their inner essence to the people?"

A similar observation could be made regarding the *menorah.* It was not a mere combination of oil, knobs and other decorations, but rather embedded in it was the spark of the Godly personality and of the *Shechinah.* The phrase להעלת נר תמיד – "to kindle a lamp continually"[5] is not a mere oil-fueled light but rather the reflection of a transcendental world. The phrase וירא א־להים את האור כי טוב – "God saw that the light was good"[6] – implies a light that was too good for sinful humanity to enjoy.

The Torah states regarding Betzalel – who, together with Oholiav, was chosen as the architect of the *Mishkan* – as follows:

וימלא אתו רוח א־להים בחכמה בתבונה ובדעת ובכל מלאכה.

---

5   Exodus 27:20.
6   Genesis 1:4.

He filled him with Godly spirit, wisdom, insight and knowledge and with every craft.[7]

The *menorah* and the *Mishkan* thus become imbued with a quality that raises humanity to a higher reality, a metaphysical world, a world of prophecy and prophets. Moshe was able not only to construct the *Mishkan* according to its physical specifications, but also to imbue it with the spirit of the divine.

---

7 Exodus 35:31–32.

✥ תצוה ✥

Tetzaveh II: The Omission of the Name of Moshe

P ARASHAT TETZAVEH IS the first *parashah* since Moshe's first appearance in the Torah in which his name is not mentioned. The seventh day of the month of Adar, which is Moshe's yahrzeit, usually coincides with the reading of Parashat Tetzaveh. One explanation for the fact that Moshe's name does not appear in this *parashah* is that he himself requested it:

ועתה אם תשא חטאתם ואם אין מחני נא מספרך אשר כתבת.

And now, if You will, forgive their sin – but if not, erase me now from the book that You have written.[1]

According to Jewish tradition, the prayers of a *tzaddik* are always granted in some way. That is the reason why Moshe's name does not appear in this *parashah*.

But why does this happen in Parashat Tetzaveh? The reason is because it was here that God told Moshe for the first time that he would not serve as high priest.

---

1 Exodus 32:32.

ואתה הקרב אליך את אהרן אחיך ואת בניו אתו מתוך בני ישראל לכהנו לי אהרן
נדב ואביהוא אלעזר ואיתמר בני אהרן.

Bring near to yourself Aharon your brother and his sons with him, from among the Children of Israel, to minister to me: Aharon, Nadav and Avihu, Elazar and Itamar, the sons of Aharon.[2]

Earlier, in Egypt, when God commanded Moshe to redeem the Jewish people from bondage, Moshe answered, ויאמר בי ה' שלח נא ביד תשלח – "He replied, 'Please, my Lord, send whomever you wish to send.'"[3] God answered him angrily, הלא אהרן אחיך הלוי – "Is there not Aharon your brother, the Levite?"[4] In his commentary on this verse, Rashi cites the sages' statement that God had originally chosen Moshe as high priest. As a result of Moshe's repeated attempts to avoid the mission that God wished to give him, God took the priesthood from him and gave it to Aharon.

In Parashat Tetzaveh, Moshe is told of this indirectly when God appoints Aharon to the priesthood. This is Moshe's first defeat. His last and worst defeat is God's refusal to permit him to enter Eretz Yisrael. Although Moshe had served as high priest during the week-long consecration of the *Mishkan*, it was only as a preparation for Aharon's induction into the priesthood. Therefore, the name of Moshe was specifically left out of Parashat Tetzaveh.

✣ Why Does Moshe Not Wear the Garments of the High Priest?

The Talmud[5] tells us that during the consecration, Moshe did not wear the High Priest's vestments, but rather a white robe. Why did God not

---

2 Exodus 28:1.
3 Exodus 4:13.
4 Exodus 4:14.
5 BT *Taanit* 11b, see Rashi there.

tell Moshe to put on the eight garments of the High Priest? The Rav suggested the following explanation. Certain appointments, such as kingship, are conferred upon individuals. Once the king has ascended to the throne, he develops a certain existential quality that is manifest in his authority and in his ability to inspire awe. The sages say, מלך – שתהא אימתו עליך – "Let the awe of a king be upon you."[6] Although a high priest is anointed, he must also have the approval of the public.

The eight garments that the High Priest must wear confer his priestly status upon him. In Judaism, clothing is a reflection of one's personality. A human being's most significant aspect is his dignity. The Talmud tells us that Rav Yohanan[7] deemed his clothing as his honor and dignity. Once people undress, nothing differentiates one person from another. Therefore, clothing completes and enhances an individual's personality. Dignity is something that must be cultivated. We recognize a person of special status by his clothing. The Talmud states that priests function as such only when they are wearing their vestments.[8] The community, we are told,[9] must elevate the High Priest, setting him apart from everyone else. Here, again, the community's consent is essential.

Our history includes well-known commentators and scholars who were not in the mainstream of halachic thinking because they did not have the consensus of the community. The king and the high priest require that consensus as well, and the priestly vestments facilitate a kohen's transformation into a serving, functioning priest.

Moshe required neither the priestly vestments nor the community's approval because he had been chosen by God himself. Yet even if Moshe had become the High Priest for the long term, he still would not have

---

6   BT *Sanhedrin* 22a.
7   BT *Shabbat* 113b.
8   BT *Zevahim* 17b and *Sanhedrin* 83b.
9   BT *Yoma* 18a.

required the eight vestments in order to perform his function. This is because he had all the qualities that an appointed official requires. Moshe, a priestly representative *in a class by himself,* wore a white frock to emphasize the clarity of his character. He was so exalted that by his very nature, he was considered a Kohen Gadol.

כי תשא

Ki Tisa I: Moshe as Prophet and Rebbi

I. Moshe as Prophet and *Rebbi*

UNLIKE PARASHAT TETZAVEH, Parashat Ki Tisa features the name of Moshe Rabbenu prominently, emphasizing two different aspects of his character. The first is the special quality of Moshe's prophecy. Parashat Ki Tisa contains the idea that Moshe's prophecy was genuine, authentic, and beyond the ken of any other prophet before or since. Also, Parashat Ki Tisa introduces a different aspect of Moshe's leadership. It is there that Moshe becomes the *rebbi* – a caring teacher of the Jewish people.

The Prayers of a Prophet

Moshe's role as a prophet contains a certain irony. On the one hand, his prophecy was superior to that of all other prophets, and his stature as a prophet was distinct and special. On the other hand, he was denied a privilege that was granted to many lesser prophets. While their prayers were often answered, many of his were not.

In Parashat Vayera, God appeared to Avimelech in a dream and told him:

ועתה השב אשת האיש כי נביא הוא ויתפלל בעדך וחיה ואם אינך משיב דע כי
מות תמות אתה וכל אשר לך.

But now, return the man's wife, for he is a prophet. He will
pray for you and you shall live. But if you do not return her, be
aware that you and all that is yours shall surely die.[1]

It is clear from this passage that a prophet's prayers are particularly
effective. To some degree, this follows the logic that the prayer of any
inspired person is likely to be accepted. One example is King Hizkiyahu's
prayer as he lay ill.[2] Another is Eliyahu's prayer during the drought.[3] A
prophet's prayers seem to possess a special power in that they are never
completely rejected.

This rule – that a prophet's prayer never meets with total rejection
– has only one exception: Moshe Rabbenu. He had the priesthood and
lost it. He prayed for kingship and it was not given to him.[4] Finally, God
rejected his plea to be allowed to enter Eretz Yisrael. It would appear,
then, that the idea that a prophet's prayers are always answered does not
apply to Moshe. This is a tragedy not only for Moshe but also for the
entire Jewish people. Had God accepted Moshe's plea and allowed him
to enter the Promised Land, Jewish history would have taken a totally
different course. At the same time, perhaps the fact that Moshe was not
permitted to enter Eretz Yisrael allowed him to assume the role of *rebbi*
of the Jewish people.

---

1 Genesis 20:7.
2 Isaiah 38:1–5, II Kings 20:1–11.
3 I Kings 18:36–39.
4 BT *Zevahim* 102a.

✌ Receiving the *Torah She'beal Peh*

In the same way that Parashat Yitro describes the giving of the Written Law to Moshe, Parashat Ki Tisa describes the giving of the *Torah she'beal peh* – the Oral Law.

> ויאמר ה' אל משה כתב לך את הדברים האלה כי על פי הדברים האלה כרתי אתך
> ברית ואת ישראל.

God said to Moshe, "Write these words for yourself, for according to these words I have sealed a covenant with you and Israel."[5]

The breaking of the tablets demonstrated that the Written Law is not permanent. Only through the Oral Law could God make a lasting covenant with the Israelites. The Talmud in Tractate *Gittin* states, לא כרת הקב"ה ברית עם ישראל אלא בשביל דברים שבעל פה – "God made a covenant with the Jewish people exclusively around the Oral Law."[6] The Oral Torah is to be transmitted in two ways only: through *kabbalah* (received tradition) and *masorah* (transmission from generation to generation).

While we celebrate the revelation of the Written Law on Shavuot, Yom Kippur is the revelation of the Oral Torah. The Oral Law, which was given to Moshe in the context of the second *luhot* (tablets), enabled him to become the *rebbi* of the Jewish people. It is very difficult, if not impossible, to achieve scholarship in *lomdut* – in the intricacies of the Oral Law – without a *rebbi*. It is almost impossible to find a person wholly self-taught who became a Torah giant and was able to impart his learning to others.

---

5 Exodus 34:27.
6 BT *Gittin* 60b.

﹖ A Radiance Unique to the Oral Law

In Parashat Ki Tisa, the Torah relates, ויהי ברדת משה מהר סיני ושני לחת העדת ביד משה ברדתו מן ההר ומשה לא ידע כי קרן עור פניו בדברו אתו – "When Moshe descended from Mount Sinai with the two tablets of testimony, in the hands of Moshe as he descended from the mountain, Moshe did not know that the skin of his face had become radiant when He had spoken to him."[7] Moshe's face began to radiate light because he spoke frequently with God.

Why did Moshe develop this quality on Yom Kippur rather than on Shavuot, when God spoke with him? The answer lies in the difference between the Oral Law and the Written Law. In receiving the Written Law, Moshe was a worthy messenger uniquely qualified for this purpose. However, his personality was not yet intertwined with the Torah. The quality of radiance implies that Moshe absorbed the Torah into the essence of his personality – that he now personified the Torah and, in effect, had been transformed into a living *sefer Torah*. This happened only on Yom Kippur when he received the Oral Torah.

The *Beit ha-Levi* (Rabbi Yosef Dov Baer Halevi Soloveitchik) contends that true identification with the Torah, which leads to *kedushat ha-guf* (inner sanctity), cannot be reached through the Written Law, but only through the Oral Law. The radiance that emanated from Moshe was a function of *kedushat ha-guf*. Through his acquisition and transmission of the Oral Torah, Moshe became a *keli sharet* (ministering vessel) that is not subject to redemption. This is because the *keli sharet* has *kedushat ha-guf*, and this sanctity is an inherent part of the vessel.[8]

From the moment Moshe achieves this *kedushat ha-guf* and becomes the *rebbi* of *Klal Yisrael*, God becomes concerned with Moshe's prestige. From now on, any infringement upon it is an infringement upon the

---

7 Exodus 34:29.
8 *Beit ha-Levi al ha-Torah,* Parashat Yitro, Derashot of the Beit Halevi; 17–18.

Torah itself. Therefore, when Miriam and Aaron criticized Moshe, God told them that Moshe's stature was unique.

לא כן עבדי משה בכל־ביתי נאמן הוא: פה אל־פה אדבר־בו ומראה ולא בחידות ותמונת יהוה יביט ומדוע לא יראתם לדבר בעבדי במשה.

Not so is my servant Moshe. Of all my house, he is the trusted one. Mouth to mouth I speak to him, in a clear vision and not in riddles. He gazes at the image of God. Why, then, did you not fear to speak against my servant Moshe?[9]

The background for that description of Moshe is this very *parashah,* Ki Tisa.

✺ Mesirut Nefesh

Why did Moshe become the *rebbi* of *Klal Yisrael*? Had he not become their *rebbi*, *Klal Yisrael* would not have survived. Only Moshe, as the transmitter and embodiment of the Oral Law, could bring them through the crisis that occurs in the *parashah.*

How does *rebbi* ensure Jewish survival? Parashat Ki Tisa deals with this question as well. After the Israelites' sin, Moshe told God, ועתה אם תשא חטאתם ואם אין מחני נא מספרך אשר כתבת – And now, if You will forgive their sin – but if not, erase me now from the book that You have written."[10] The ultimate criterion for a *rebbi* is his willingness to engage in *mesirut nefesh* (self-sacrifice) for his students. When Moshe shows his willingness to sacrifice himself for the Jewish people, he becomes a model of *mesirut nefesh* for every future *rebbi.*

---

9 Numbers 12:7–8.
10 Exodus 32:32.

Ki Tisa II: The Sin of the Golden Calf and Its Aftermath

⊰ Illegitimate Religious Expression

IN CONSIDERING THE Sin of the Golden Calf, the *Rishonim* (early commentators) point out that the Israelites had not desired to engage in idol-worship. Rather, they were panic-stricken over Moshe's disappearance and sought a mediator between themselves and God (see Ramban[1] and Ibn Ezra[2]). They wanted a place in which God could dwell.

In his work, *The Kuzari,* Rav Yehuda Halevi asked how a nation that had witnessed the miracles of the redemption from Egypt and the divine revelation at Mount Sinai could sink so low as to construct an idol. He explained that the Israelites had simply wanted something concrete to replace Moshe. They believed that a spirit would come and reside in the Golden Calf, which would assume the role of a Tabernacle for them.[3] However, there is a big difference between the Tabernacle and the Golden Calf. God commanded every detail of the Tabernacle's construc-

---

1 Exodus 32:1.
2 Exodus 31:18.
3 *Kuzari,* 1:97.

tion, as the verses in *Vayakhel–Pekudei* emphasize: "As God commanded Moshe." On the other hand, God never commanded the construction of the Golden Calf. The Golden Calf was created by the people alone.

The Golden Calf epitomizes individuals throughout the ages who have sought to create new forms of religious experience and expression. Although many such efforts may be well-intentioned, they are not legitimate because they lack a divine mandate. This was the essence of the sin of the Golden Calf. Tampering with prayer, the priestly blessings, the synagogue or any other form of religious service is another form of that sin. At the time, the Israelites offered sacrifices to God. However, because God had not commanded such service, it was illegitimate and unacceptable. Therefore, we can see how critical it is that we maintain tradition, particularly regarding prayer. It is important to our survival as a people.

℘ Moshe's Plea for the Jewish People: Pardon or Reprieve

There is a fascinating controversy among the Torah commentators about the timing of Moshe's initial petition to God following the sin of the Golden Calf:

וידבר ה' אל משה לך רד כי שחת עמך אשר העלית מארץ מצרים: סרו מהר מן
הדרך אשר צויתם עשו להם עגל מסכה וישתחוו לו ויזבחו לו ויאמרו אלה אלהיך
ישראל אשר העלוך מארץ מצרים . . . ויחל משה את פני ה' אלהיו ויאמר למה ה'
יחרה אפך בעמך אשר הוצאת מארץ מצרים בכח גדול וביד חזקה . . . וינחם ה' על
הרעה אשר דבר לעשות לעמו.

God said to Moshe, "Go, descend, for your people that you brought up from the land of Egypt has become corrupt. They have strayed quickly from the way that I have commanded them. They have made themselves a molten calf, prostrated themselves to it and sacrificed to it, saying, 'This is your god, O Israel, that brought you up from the land of Egypt . . .'"
Moshe pleaded before the Lord his God and said, "Why, O

God, should your anger flare up against your people whom you brought out of Egypt with great power and a strong hand?" ... God reconsidered the evil that He had declared He would do to His people.[4]

According to the Ibn Ezra, the scene in which Moshe entreats God (*"va-yahel Moshe"*) does not belong here. Its rightful place is after verse 30, which states: ויהי ממחרת ויאמר משה אל העם אתם חטאתם חטאה גדלה ועתה אעלה אל ה' אולי אכפרה בעד חטאתכם – On the next day, Moshe said to the people, "You have committed a grievous sin! Now I shall ascend to God – perhaps I can obtain atonement for your sin."[5] This occurs after the seventeenth of Tammuz, on which Moshe ascended and prayed to God for forty days. However, the Torah there refers to these prayers in a single verse.

Alternatively, the Ramban contends that *"va-yahel Moshe"* was Moshe's immediate response to God's command that he descend because his nation had become corrupt.[6] Moshe began to pray even though he had not yet seen or rejoined the Israelites after their sin. However, when God told him what had happened, Moshe feared that God's anger would be catastrophic, so he responded immediately. Therefore, according to the Ramban's approach, God retracted His decision to destroy the Israelites before Moshe descended from the mountain. Afterward, Moshe descended from the mountain and broke the tablets upon seeing the Golden Calf. Then he returned to God to ask for atonement for this sin.

The Ibn Ezra argues that Moshe could not have prayed immediately because one cannot ask God to forgive a transgression that is still being committed. This can be compared to immersing in a *mikveh* while holding a *sheretz* (a kind of insect that conveys ritual impurity). Moshe had to

---

4   Exodus 32:7–8, 11, 14.
5   Exodus 32:30.
6   See Ramban on Exodus 32:11.

destroy the idol and punish the idolators first. According to the Ramban, what was the logic of Moshe praying while the idol still existed?

It seems logical to suggest that the controversy between the Ibn Ezra and Ramban concerns whether Moshe's entreaties were a prayer for pardon or a reprieve. According to the Ramban, Moshe was saying, "I am not asking for forgiveness, but for *erech apayim*" (forbearance and patience). Afterward, the Ramban says that Moshe went down and destroyed the Golden Calf, and only then did he pray for forgiveness. However, the Ibn Ezra contends that Moshe's prayer was for forgiveness, so while it belongs elsewhere in the Torah, it was placed here based on the rabbinic dictum אין מוקדם ומאוחר בתורה (there is no precise chronology in the Torah).

❧ The Need for God's Personal Involvement after the Sin

Parashat Ki Tisa contains a dialogue between Moshe and God (Exodus 33:12–16) in which Moshe insists that God accompany the Jewish people personally and not send an angel instead.

ויאמר אליו אם אין פניך הולכים הלכים אל תעלנו מזה.

He [Moshe] said to Him, "If your Presence does not go, do not take us forth from here."[7]

However, in Parashat Mishpatim, when God says that He will send an angel to accompany the Jewish people on their way, Moshe does not object:

הנה אנכי שלח מלאך לפניך לשמרך בדרך ולהביאך אל המקום אשר הכינותי.

Behold, I send an angel before you to protect you on the way and to bring you to the place that I have prepared.[8]

---

7 Exodus 33:15.
8 Exodus 23:20.

Why does Moshe react differently in each instance? Also, in Mishpatim, God sends an angel. In Ki Tisa, He grants Moshe's request, saying, ויאמר ה' אל משה גם את הדבר הזה אשר דברת אעשה כי מצאת חן בעיני ואדעך בשם – God said to Moshe, "Even of this thing of which you spoke I shall do, for you have found favor in my eyes, and I have known you by name."[9]

There is a basic difference between the two instances. In Parashat Mishpatim, the Israelites had not sinned. Therefore, Moshe felt that an angel could guide them to their destination. But in Ki Tisa, when the Israelites committed a terrible sin, Moshe felt that they needed God to guide them. The reason for this is that angels, who epitomize the attribute of strict judgment (*middat ha-din*), cannot relate to the idea of *teshuvah*, which is rooted in the attribute of mercy (*middat ha-rahamim*).

In Parashat Mishpatim, the Torah warns of this attribute of angels in the text: השמר מפניו ושמע בקולו אל תמר בו כי לא ישא לפשעכם כי שמי בקרבו – Beware of him, obey him and do not rebel against him, for he will not forgive your willful sin because My name [the attribute of strict judgment] is within him."[10] In Ki Tisa, God taught Moshe the covenant of the thirteen attributes of mercy, which emphasizes God's compassion toward sinners. That is why Moshe insisted that God, and not an angel, guide the Israelites after the sin of the Golden Calf.

---

9 Exodus 33:17.
10 Exodus 23:21.

Vayakhel I: Shabbat and the Tabernacle, Sanctuaries in Time and Space: Two Intertwined Concepts

ויקהל משה את כל עדת בני ישראל ויאמר אלהם אלה הדברים אשר צוה ה'
לעשת אתם.

Moshe gathered the entire assembly of the children of Israel and said to them: These are the things that God has commanded to do them.[1]

THE VERSE USES the plural to introduce the subsequent topics: "*Eleh ha-devarim*" (These are the things). Immediately afterwards, the Torah describes the Sabbath:

ששת ימים תעשה מלאכה וביום השביעי יהיה לכם קדש שבת שבתון לה' כל
העשה בו מלאכה יומת.

For six days, do your work, but the seventh day shall be sacred to you, a sabbath of sabbaths for God. Whoever does work on it shall be put to death.[2]

---

1 Exodus 35:1.
2 Exodus 35:2.

Subsequently, the Torah describes the collection of *terumah* – donations for the *Mishkan*. Therefore, one must conclude that the plural expression *eleh ha-devarim* introduced both the Shabbat and the Tabernacle. In fact, the Torah introduces the discussion of the *Mishkan* using the same language as in the first sentence of the *parashah,* זה הדבר – "This is the thing."[3] This terminology assumes a connection between Shabbat and the building of the *Mishkan*. Let us look at three other places in the Torah where Shabbat and the Tabernacle are connected.

In Parashat Ki Tisa, after describing Betzalel and Oholiav, the Torah returns to the subject of Shabbat, stating, אך את שבתתי תשמרו – "However, you must observe my Sabbaths."[4] We see the same linkage between the Tabernacle and the Sabbath, with the only difference being the order of its presentation. In Parashat Ki Tisa, the Tabernacle precedes the exposition of the Sabbath, while in Parashat Vayakhel, the order is reversed. The sages are concerned with the exegesis of the expression *ach*.[5] They concluded that despite the people's excitement over the construction of the Tabernacle, the Tabernacle does not override the Sabbath. In Parashat Kedoshim, the Torah reiterates this link. את שבתתי תשמרו ומקדשי תיראו אני ה' – "You shall observe my Sabbath and revere my sanctuary: I am the Lord."[6] Again, the sages interpret this verse as enjoining us from constructing the sanctuary on the Sabbath.[7] Finally, Parashat Behar ends with the verse את שבתתי תשמרו ומקדשי תיראו אני ה' – "You shall observe my Sabbaths and revere my sanctuary: I am the Lord."[8] Thus, there are four places where the Torah links the Sabbath with the Tabernacle.

What is the nature of these intertwined concepts? The answer is fundamental: both Shabbat and the Tabernacle constitute sanctuaries. One is a sanctuary in time while the other is a sanctuary in space. God

---

3 Exodus 35:4.
4 Exodus 31:13.
5 See Rashi on Exodus 31:13.
6 Leviticus 19:30.
7 Rashi on Leviticus 19:30; *Torat Kohanim* 78:6–7.
8 Leviticus 26:2.

wants Jews to establish a residence for him both in space and in time. The Jew who has prepared properly for the Sabbath and is about to light his candles finds himself in the same position as the Jew of two thousand years ago preparing to enter the Sanctuary. Through *tzimtzum* (self-contraction), God squeezed infinity into finitude and chose to dwell among human beings, first in the *Mishkan* and later in the *Beit ha-Mikdash*. On the one hand, infinity separates the human being from God. On the other hand, God is immanent and close to his people.

Shabbat embodies a similar idea. On Friday night, as we sing "Lecha Dodi," God pays us a visit. The festivals and Shabbat are different in that on Shabbat, God visits the Jewish people, while on the festivals, we visit God. "Lecha Dodi" represents the *Shechinah* knocking on our door. The Talmud[9] records two versions of a story about Rav Yannai. In one version, he would wrap himself in his garment, turn and say, "Come, O Bride!" In the other, he would walk to the edge of the field to greet the Sabbath Queen. The idea of a sanctuary in space and sanctuary in time makes it clear why the Torah, in four different places, linked the sanctity of the Sabbath and that of the Tabernacle.

THE ALMIGHTY IN NATURE VS. THE SUPERNATURAL

There is difference between the sanctity of Shabbat and that of the Tabernacle and the Temple. The sanctity of the *Mikdash* can never disappear, for although the physical Temple was destroyed, the *Shechinah* is always there.[10] The *Shechinah* of the *Mikdash* was of a transcendental nature. At the end of Parashat Pekudei, as soon as the *Mishkan* was completed, a cloud of glory hovered over it by day and a pillar of fire by night. The *Shechinah* was both a physical light and a spiritual experience. It was outside of nature and defied the laws of causality, for the *Mishkan* was nothing less than an ongoing miracle that transcended the natural order.

---

9 BT *Shabbat* 119a, *Bava Kamma* 32a.
10 BT *Megilah* 28a.

In contrast, Shabbat demonstrates God's presence on a natural level. Just as God reveals himself through his transcending the causal order through supernatural miracles, God also reveals himself in the order of nature. One can experience God through the blue sky and the flowering bush. All this is enhanced by the awareness of Shabbat, which epitomizes the natural order at rest. God has no desire to interfere with the natural order. Each individual must pause, as did Rav Yannai, to take God's presence within the natural order into account.

ᴖ The Supremacy of Shabbat

Shabbat and the *Mikdash* are two antithetical poles. Shabbat embodies the natural while the *Mikdash* embodies the supernatural. When we read the story of how God gave Moshe the blueprint for the Tabernacle, we encounter the word *ach,* from which our sages derive that the construction of the Tabernacle does not override Shabbat. We have survived two thousand years without the *Beit ha-Mikdash,* but we could never have survived without Shabbat. In light of this distinction, God's words to Moshe at the beginning of Parashat Vayakhel are apt. אלה הדברים אשר צוה ה' לעשת אתם – "These are the things that God has commanded to do them."[11] There are two principal commandments – Shabbat and construction of the *Mishkan.* However, Jewish survival is not bound up with the *Mishkan.* While the *Mishkan* is a lofty and important place, we must remember: *ach* – Shabbat, which is essential to Jewish survival, is stronger. Of course, we pray, that soon, in our day, we will experience both.

---

11 Exodus 35:1.

ויקהל

Vayakhel II: Witnesses on God's Behalf

ויקהל משה את כל עדת בני ישראל ויאמר אלהם אלה הדברים אשר צוה ה'
לעשת אתם.

Moshe gathered the entire assembly of the children of
Israel and said to them: These are the things that God has
commanded to do them.[1]

ASHI COMMENTS THAT the day after Yom Kippur, Moshe
assembled the nation to tell them about the construction of the
Tabernacle. Why was this public assembly necessary, and why
did Moshe hold it the day after Yom Kippur?

There are two kinds of transgressions: public and private. Rav
Yohanan ben Zakkai ruled that a *ganav* – one who steals in secret, such
as a thief or burglar – must be punished more severely than a *gazlan* – a
bandit who engages in open robbery.[2] Why is this so?

A *gazlan* is not hypocritical about his ethics. He fears neither God
nor human beings. However, while a *ganav* fears human beings, he does
not fear God. The behavior of the *ganav* is therefore more offensive to
God than that of the *gazlan*.

---

1 Exodus 35:1
2 Rashi on Exodus 21:37.

However, the Shabbat is treated in the reverse way. One who violates Shabbat within the four walls of his home does not fall into the same category as an apostate. Since desecrating Shabbat in public borders on arrogance, it is considered more severe than doing so in private. For example, Elisha ben Avuyah, in an act of defiance, rode a horse in public on a Yom Kippur that fell on Shabbat.[3] Why is there a difference in attitude between acts of public and private desecration?

The answer lies in the essence of Shabbat, which testifies that God created the world in six days and rested on the seventh. By observing the Sabbath, every observant Jew testifies to God's creation of and sovereignty over the world. The court that hears the testimony is the universe itself. Therefore, a Jew who desecrates the Sabbath testifies, in effect, that the world created itself. Therefore, the act of desecration is tantamount to apostasy.

Now we can understand why Moshe gathered the entire assembly of Israel. He had to teach this profound aspect of Shabbat – that the Jew is commanded to act as a witness. This mission is contained in the phrase "Vayakhel Moshe et kol adat benei Yisrael." The word *edah*, of which *adat* is the construct form, comes from the word *ed*, which means witness. Thus, the entire Jewish people acted as witnesses when Moshe gathered them. Rashi's deduction that this happened the day after Yom Kippur is therefore appropriate. Once the Jewish people had repented and received forgiveness, they were worthy of being witnesses to God's sovereignty over the universe as it is reflected in the holy Sabbath day.

---

3   BT *Hagigah* 15a.

✑ פקודי ✑

Pekudei: The *Luhot* Provide the Ark with Its Very Identity

✑ The Placement and Removal of the Staves

IN PARASHAT PEKUDEI, the Torah states:

ויקח ויתן את העדת אל הארן וישם את הבדים על הארן ויתן את הכפרת על הארן מלמעלה.

He took and placed the testimony into the Ark *and placed the staves on the* Ark, and he placed the lid on the Ark from above.[1]

Thus, it would seem that the staves used for carrying the Ark were originally placed in the rings in Parashat Pekudei. However, the Torah states in Parashat Vayakhel that the staves were already inserted into the rings:

ויעש בצלאל את הארן עצי שטים . . . ויצק לו ארבע טבעת זהב על ארבע פעמתיו ושתי טבעת על צלעו האחת ושתי טבעות על צלעו השנית. ויעש בדי עצי שטים ויצף אתם זהב. ויבא את הבדים בטבעת על צלעת הארן לשאת את הארן.

Betzalel made the *Ark* of acacia wood ... He poured for it four golden rings on its four corners: two rings on one side

---

1   Exodus 40:20.

and two rings on the other side. He made staves of acacia wood and covered them with gold. He inserted the staves in the rings on the side of the aron to carry the aron.[2]

It would appear that the staves, which had already been placed in the rings, as discussed in Parashat Vayakhel, were removed at some point. Now, in Parashat Pekudei, they were placed into the rings once again. How is it possible that the staves were removed from the Ark? When God commands Moshe to insert the staves into the rings on the side of the *Aron,* he says: בטבעת הארן יהיו הבדים לא יסרו ממנו – "The staves shall remain in the rings of the Ark; they shall not be removed from it."[3] Rashi,[4] citing the Talmud in Tractate *Yoma,*[5] notes that there is a prohibition against ever removing the staves from the Ark. Therefore, once they had been inserted into the Ark, how could they have been removed and then inserted yet again?

☙ The Approach of Tosafot

The Tosafot ask a related question in Tractate *Yoma*[6] about of the manner in which the covering of the Ark was set in Parashat Bamidbar. The Torah states:

ובא אהרן ובניו בנסע המחנה והורדו את פרכת המסך וכסו בה את ארן העדת. ונתנו עליו כסוי עור תחש ופרשו בגד כליל תכלת מלמעלה ושמו בדיו.

Aharon and his sons shall come when the camp journeys. They shall take down the partition of the screen and cover the Ark of the Testimony with it. They shall place a covering

---

2 Exodus 37:1, 3–5.
3 Exodus 25:15.
4 Rashi on Exodus 25:15.
5 BT *Yoma* 72a.
6 Tosafot, BT *Yoma* 72a, ד"ה כתיב בטבעות בארון.

made of *tahash* hide upon it and spread a cloth entirely of turquoise wool over it and set its staves.[7]

How could the staves be positioned or set when they could not be removed even when the *Mishkan* was standing? The Tosafot presents a bold interpretation. He suggests that there were actually two sets of four rings each, making a total of eight. Thus, two staves, which were permanently affixed, could not be removed. However, two additional staves were inserted whenever the Israelites traveled and were removed when the Ark was at rest.

❧ The Distinction between the Ark and the Other Vessels

The Rav suggested another approach to resolve the difficulty. In Parashat Pikudei, when the Torah describes the construction of the *Mishkan* and the placement of the various utensils, there is a pronounced difference between all the other utensils and the Ark. The *shulhan* was installed in its proper place, and only afterwards was the *lehem ha-panim* placed upon it. The lights were kindled only after the *menorah* had been placed in its position. However, when it came to the Ark, the order was reversed. At first, the Torah states, ושמת שם את ארון העדות – "There you shall place the Ark of Testimony,"[8] but it is put into position only afterwards. There, the Torah says:

ויקח ויתן את העדת אל הארן וישם את הבדים על הארן ויתן את הכפרת על הארן מלמעלה. ויבא את הארן אל המשכן.

He took and placed the testimony into the Ark, inserted the staves on the Ark and placed the cover on the Ark from above. He brought the Ark into the *Mishkan*.[9]

---

7 Numbers 4:5–6.
8 Exodus 40:3.
9 Exodus 40:20–21.

In other words, first he placed the *luhot* into the Ark. Only afterwards were the staves inserted, and then the Ark was positioned inside the *Mishkan*.

✿ Fulfillment of *Mitzvot* vs. Name-Identity

Rav Soloveitchik explained in the name of his father, Rav Moshe Soloveitchik, *zt"l*, that there is a fundamental distinction between the other utensils, such as the *shulhan,* the *menorah* and the Ark. The table and the candelabrum are considered utensils respectively even without the presence of the *lehem ha-panim* and the kindling of the lights. These actions are the *mitzvah fulfillment* of these respective utensils. However, the *luhot ha-edut* provide the Ark with its purpose and identity. Without them, the Ark is not considered an Ark at all.

The full description of the Ark is *aron ha-edut* with the *luhot* inside. We can find proof of this distinction in the fact that there was no Ark in the Second Temple. The reason that there was no Ark was because there were no *luhot*. But could the people not have constructed an Ark without *luhot*? We must therefore conclude that without the *luhot,* there is no *shem aron* – it is no longer appropriate to describe the item as an *aron*. Therefore, one would gain nothing by placing an empty Ark in the Second Temple.

This theory also explains why, according to the Rambam, the Ark was not included in the commandment to construct the *Beit ha-Mikdash,* while the making of the other utensils was included.[10] Why is this? The answer is that the Ark differs from the other utensils of the Temple. The other utensils are used for specific purposes, while the Ark is merely a repository for the *luhot*. Therefore, the command to construct the Ark in the *Mishkan* was a distinct, autonomous *mitzvah* – that of building the Ark to contain the *luhot,* and is not included in the commandment to construct the *Beit ha-Mikdash.*

---

10 Rambam, *Sefer ha-Mitzvot,* Mitzvat Aseh 20.

We can also understand a Rashi in Parashat Terumah in light of the above. The Torah says:

וְנָתַתָּ אֶת הַכַּפֹּרֶת עַל הָאָרֹן מִלְמָעְלָה וְאֶל הָאָרֹן תִּתֵּן אֶת הָעֵדֻת אֲשֶׁר אֶתֵּן אֵלֶיךָ.

You shall place the lid on the Ark from above, and you shall place the testimony that I give you into the Ark.[11]

Rashi comments:

לֹא יָדַעְתִּי לָמָּה נִכְפַּל, שֶׁהֲרֵי כְּבָר נֶאֱמַר וְנָתַתָּ אֶל הָאָרוֹן אֶת הָעֵדוּת.

I don't know why this has been repeated, for it has already been stated: "You shall put the Testimony into the *Ark*."[12]

One might say that the repetition of the placement of the Testimony is to teach that when the *Aron* is uncovered, Moshe should lay the testimony in it and then place the lid on top. Indeed, we find that when Moshe built the *Mishkan*, the text states, "He put the testimony into the Ark," and only afterwards does it say "and he put the lid of the Ark on top." This is Rashi's intent: that without the *luhot*, the Ark is not considered an Ark. Only after the *luhot* have been placed inside it does it acquire a *shem aron*, and then the next phrase, "and he put the lid on the *aron*," makes sense.

Rav Soloveitchik used the basis of this principle – that the *aron* draws its identity from the *luhot* – to answer the initial difficulty in Parashat Pekudei. The prohibition against removing the staves only applied after Moshe placed the *luhot* into the Ark. Prior to that, the item was not considered an Ark, and was not subject to any prohibition. The removal of the staves between Parashat Vayakhel and Parashat Pekudei was not a sin because it occurred before the *luhot* were placed in the Ark.

---

11 Exodus 25:21.
12 Rashi on Exodus 25:21.

℘ Sefer Vayikra

ויקרא

Vayikra: The Korban as Expression of the Jew's Essence

I N THE BEGINNING of *Sefer Vayikra*, the *Torah* states:

ויקרא אל משה וידבר ה' אליו מאהל מועד לאמר: דבר אל בני ישראל ואמרת אלהם אדם כי יקריב מכם קרבן לה' מן הבהמה מן הבקר ומן הצאן תקריבו את קרבנכם.

He called to Moshe and Hashem spoke to him from the Tent of Meeting, saying: "Speak to the Children of Israel and say to them: When a man among you brings an offering to Hashem: from animals, from the cattle or from the flock shall you bring your offering."[1]

The *Midrash Rabbah* says:

רבי יהושע דסכנין בשם רבי לוי אמר אף הכתובים חלקו לישראל כמה דתימא אדם כי יקריב מכם אבל כשהוא בא לדבר בדבר של גנאי ראה מה כתוב אדם מכם כי יהיה בעור בשרו אין כתיב כאן אלא כי יהיה בעור בשרו.

Rav Yehoshua de-Sikhnin said in the name of Rav Levi: Even Scripture shows honor to the Jewish people, as it is written:

---

1   Leviticus 1:1–2.

"When a man among you brings an offering . . ." But when the text speaks pejoratively, look what it says. It does not say: "If a person among you has on his flesh . . ." Rather, the text says: "If a person has on his flesh . . ."[2]

Rav Soloveitchik suggested that the *Midrash* conveys a deeper meaning. When the Torah refers to the *mitzvah* of bringing an offering, it uses the term מכם – *mikem* – "from you," from your essence. However, in the context of a skin affliction such as *tzaraat,* the Torah does not use the term *mikem.* This is because the religious devotion of a Jew emanates from an inner heartfelt drive that reflects his fundamental nature, while any transgression he performs is a function of external whims only. This idea is encapsulated in a famous passage in Rambam's *Mishneh Torah,* which contains a statement of great psychological import in the mindset of a Jew.

◦ Compelling Someone Until He Performs an Act Voluntarily (כופין אותו עד שיאמר רוצה אני)

The Rambam states:

מי שהדין נותן שכופין אותו לגרש את אשתו ולא רצה לגרש, בית דין של ישראל בכל מקום ובכל זמן מכין אותו עד שיאמר רוצה אני ויכתוב הגט והוא גט כשר ... שאין אומרים אנוס אלא למי שנלחץ ונדחק לעשות דבר שאינו מחוייב מן התורה לעשותו אבל מי שתקפו יצרו הרע לבטל מצוה או לעשות עבירה והוכה עד שעשה דבר שחייב לעשותו או עד שנתרחק מדבר שאסור לעשותו אין זה אנוס ממנו אלא הוא אנס עצמו בדעתו הרעה. לפיכך זה שאינו רוצה לגרש מאחר שהוא רוצה להיות מישראל רוצה הוא לעשות כל המצות ולהתרחק מן העבירות ויצרו הוא שתקפו וכיון שהוכה עד שתשש יצרו ואמר רוצה אני כבר גרש לרצונו.

If Jewish law mandates that a Jew is forced to divorce his wife and he refuses to do so, a Jewish court of law in any place

---

and at any time may subject him to lashes until he agrees to write a *get*. That *get* is valid . . . (Why is the *get* not invalidated because it is written out of coercion?) . . . Because an act performed under coercion is only invalid if one is forced to do something that the Torah does not obligate him to do. However, one whose evil inclination has compelled him to repudiate a *mitzvah* or to perform a transgression and who is given lashes until he does as he is obligated to do or until he stops performing the forbidden act – this is not deemed to be acting under coercion, but rather he himself has engaged in self-coercion with his spurious outlook. Therefore, one who does not wish to give a *get* – since he wishes to be a Jew and wants to fulfill all the *mitzvot* and avoid transgressing – his evil inclination has overcome him. Once he receives lashes until his evil inclination is weakened and he says "I am willing," he is considered to have given the *get* voluntarily.[3]

The soul of a Jew always wishes to fulfill God's commandments. It is only the evil inclination that can overcome him and compel him to sin or fail to fulfill a *mitzvah*. In this situation, he is considered to have acted under duress, not of his own free will. When he is freed, even by force, from the pull of the evil inclination, he may act as a free being once again.

This is the explication of the *Midrash*. When a Jew offers a sacrifice, fulfills *mitzvot* and lives a life of sanctity according to Torah principles, this is considered to be מכם – *mikem,* from within you, from your essence, from the depths of your personality. The Torah shows honor to the Jewish people by pointing out that the good deeds that we do emanate from our inner persona, as it is written: אדם כי יקריב מכם קרבן לה' – "When a man among you brings an offering to God."[4] When a Jew

---

3 Rambam, *Mishneh Torah,* Hilchot Gerushin 2:20.
4 Leviticus 1:2.

offers a sacrifice to God, an inner drive motivates him. When he sins, Scripture says, אדם כי יהיה בעור בשרו – "If a person should have upon his flesh"[5] (a disease such as *tzaraat*), implying that the transgression is only on the surface of his flesh.

ﻙ **Resilience of the Pure Spirit**

The Rav developed this idea further in an analysis of a *midrash* on a verse in Aharei Mot:

... ונשא השעיר עליו את כל עונתם אל ארץ גזרה

The male goat shall carry all their iniquities to an uninhabited land ...[6]

There is an exegesis of the *Midrash*:

... אלא ונשא השעיר עליו זה עשו שנאמר 'הן עשו אחי איש שעיר', את כל עונתם את כל עונות תם, שנאמר ויעקב איש תם.

The *sa'ir* will carry upon itself – that is Esau, as it is written, "But my brother Esau is a hairy man." All their iniquities – the iniquities of the *tam*, as it is written: "*Yaakov ish tam*" (a wholesome man).[7]

How are we to understand "the iniquities of the *tam?*" If this refers to sins (עונתם), where is the *temimut* (wholesomeness)? How can these two opposing terms be paired in this description?

Furthermore, on Yom ha-Kippurim it says כי ביום הזה יכפר עליכם לטהר אתכם – "For on this day he shall provide atonement for you to cleanse you ..."[8] Rashi, on the verse in Vayishlah, כי אמר אכפרה פניו – "For he

---

5 Leviticus 13:2.
6 Leviticus 16:22.
7 *Midrash Rabbah*, Bereshit 65:15.
8 Leviticus 16:30.

said: I will appease him"[9] – says: ונראה בעיני שכל כפרה שאצל עוון וחטא ואצל פנים כולן לשון קנוח והעברה הן – "It seems to me that all atonement that has to do with sin or transgression or to the face refers to wiping away or removal."[10]

We can answer these questions in light of the aforementioned principle that the Jew, at his essence, always seeks to fulfill *mitzvot*. Despite his transgression and even at the very moment that he is committing it, a Jew remains in some way *tam* – wholesome and pure. Sin does not come from his inner personality, but is external to him. Often, it is a product of environmental influences and the cultural ambience of the non-Jewish world around him. Since the sin is not internal or inherent, it is compared to a particle of dirt that lodges in one's garment or skin. This requires only a wiping away – *kapparah* – to remove it. Therefore, on Yom ha-Kippurim, we ask for *kapparah*.

This is the source of our perpetual ability to do *teshuvah,* as well as the foundation of the *korbanot* introduced in Parashat Vayikra. Deep down, a Jew only wants to fulfill God's will. Therefore, sin is not rooted in his soul. It is merely a response to external stimuli. Since the Jew's desire to do God's will is stronger than any other impulse within him, it generates a permanent ability to overcome the evil inclination and return wholeheartedly to God.

---

9   Genesis 32:21.
10 Rashi on Genesis 32:21.

צו

The Juxtaposition of Parashat Tzav and the Festival of Passover

I T IS NOT coincidental that the festival of Passover always follows Parashat Tzav. The practice of reading a particular section of the Torah in connection with a specific holiday dates back to Moshe Rabbenu. Tzav is read before Pesah, Bamidbar before Shavuot, Vaethanan after Tisha be-Av and Nitzavim before Rosh ha-Shannah. The Rav suggested two reasons for the reading of Parashat Tzav before Pesah.

✺ The Cleansing of Utensils

The first and most important explanation relates to the concepts of *biur hametz* – cleansing one's home and utensils. The Torah mentions this act twice: in Parashat Tzav and later in Parashat Matot. Parashat Tzav, which sets forth the laws of kosherizing metal utensils that have absorbed the taste of a sacrifice, contains the basic *halachot*.[1] In the *Beit ha-Mikdash,* the meat of a sin-offering must be eaten within a single day and night. The cooked meat of a *korban shelamim* must be eaten within two days and one night. After this time, the meat becomes *notar,* which

---

1 Leviticus 6:21.

is forbidden. Therefore, the taste absorbed in the pot must be removed by means of *hagalah* – immersion in boiling water.[2]

In the *Mishneh Torah,* the Rambam distinguishes between an ordinary utensil that became *treif* (by absorbing the taste of a forbidden food) and a utensil intended for use on Passover. An ordinary *treif* vessel requires only *hagalah*. However, when one cleanses a Passover utensil, immersion alone is not enough. The vessel must also be rinsed in cold water.[3] This process, which is called *shetifah,* is derived from a verse in Tzav: ומרק ושטף במים – "purged and rinsed in water."[4]

Tosafot, on the other hand, maintains that *shetifah* is not necessary to make utensils kosher for Passover. Tosafot contends that *merikah* (scalding) and *shetifah* are required only in the *Beit ha-Mikdash*.[5] Since vessels with an absorption of קדשים (sanctified items) must not be removed from the Temple court, a distinctive procedure of *shetifah was* introduced, as it is written: ומרק ושטף במים.[6]

Tosafot's opinion seems to make sense. If Temple vessels require a formal additional procedure, then this could be any type of procedure, regardless of whether it contributes to the removal of the absorbed matter. However, the Rambam, who says that this is also required for Passover, is difficult to understand. *Merikah* is the equivalent of *hagalah* which is in boiling water, but *shetifah* is in cold water and isn't capable of removing that which was absorbed. The process of *merikah* (scalding) is understandable, since it constitutes additional cleansing. However, *shetifah* does not affect cleansing. Why, then, should it be required for kashering utensils for Passover? What does the Rambam say about it? Apparently, utensils that are used for Passover require additional cleansing beyond *hagalah*. A utensil that is used for *hametz* throughout the year

---

2   Numbers 31:23 and BT *Avodah Zarah* 75b.
3   See Mishneh Torah, Hilchot Hametz u-Matzah 5:23 and Hilchot Maachalot Assurot 17:4.
4   Leviticus 6:21.
5   Tosafot on BT *Zevahim* 96b; ד"ה לא צריכא.
6   See Ramban Leviticus 6:20.

requires a dispensation in order to be used for Passover. This is derived from *merikah* and *shetifah* of sacred vessels. Performing *shetifah* provides the dispensation that allows us to use the utensil during Passover.

Merikah and *shetifah* are the model for the special התיר כלים (dispensation) of Pesah. *Merikah* and *shetifah* don't only purge the כלי (vessel), but serve as a מתיר (dispensation) for its use again. Similarly on Pesah, there is a special rabbinic prohibition to use *chametz* vessels even if they would not transfer טעם (the taste).

ࠒ The Paschal Sacrifice as the Quintessential Offering

The Rav gave a second reason for reading Parashat Tzav before Passover. Like Parashat Vayikra, Parashat Tzav contains many descriptions of sacrifices. Most of the time, the Torah describes sacrifices offered by individuals. The paschal lamb, as the first communal offering, represents a shift. It thus serves as both a herald of and a key to the redemption of the Jewish people because it emphasizes the sense of community among *Klal Yisrael.*

ࠒ Excision as Penalty for Not Fulfilling
a Positive Commandment

Only two positive commandments in the Torah must be fulfilled on pain of *karet* (excision)[7]: the *korban Pesah* and *brit milah*. We can understand the penalty for not observing *brit milah* because circumcision is the mark of identification of male Jews, which sets them apart from all other nations. However, one might ask why the failure to offer the paschal sacrifice carries such a severe penalty. Regarding all other *mitzvot,* if we fail to fulfill them, we receive no reward, but we are not punished either.

---

7 According to Rashi (Leviticus 17:9), the sinner's children die and he himself dies prematurely.

Why would the Torah impose such a severe punishment for failure to offer the paschal sacrifice?

✥ Pesah Mitzrayim as the *Brit Milah* of the Jewish Collective

The answer, said the Rav, is that *Pesah Mitzrayim* serves the identical function of *brit milah* throughout our history. It is more than a single positive commandment; it is the mark of our collective identity. We were slaves in Egypt, and many Israelites did not want to leave Egypt. God commanded Moshe to tell each household to offer the paschal lamb – the only sacrifice that needs no *mizbeah* (altar). We were commanded to place the lamb's blood upon the door posts and lintels, an act akin to sprinkling the sacrificial blood on the corners of the altar. This act, which demonstrates complete obedience to God, is a sign of faith that is similar to *matzah*.

According to Rashi, only one-fifth of the Jewish people left Egypt.[8] Like the *korban Pesah,* the journey required a leap of faith. Those who refused to offer the paschal lamb showed contempt for God's commandments and a lack of faith in God. These severe transgressions required a severe punishment: *karet.* The *korbanot* are introduced in Parashat Vayikra and completed in Tzav, coinciding with the Passover festival, in order to emphasize this element of faith.

✥ The Message of the *Haftarot* of *Vayikra* and *Tzav*

It is rare for the *parshiyot* and *haftarot* to be out of sync. However, this phenomenon occurs in Vayikra and Tzav. While these two *parshiyot* concern the sacrifices, in both *haftarot*, the prophets protest against a mistaken understanding of sacrifices. Their messages appear to undermine rather than reinforce the importance of the *korbanot*.

---

8   Rashi on Exodus 13:18.

In the *haftarah* of Vayikra, Isaiah says:

לא הביאת לי שה עלתיך וזבחיך לא כבדתני לא העבדתיך במנחה ולא הוגעתיך
בלבונה: לא קנית לי בכסף קנה וחלב זבחיך לא הרויתני אך העבדתני בחטאותיך
הוגעתני בעונתיך.

You did not bring me sheep for your burnt offerings, nor did
you honor me with your peace offerings; I did not burden you
with a meal offering, nor did I weary you with frankincense.
You brought me no cinnamon with silver, nor did you satisfy
me with the fat of your offerings, but you burdened me with
your sins. You wearied me with your iniquities.[9]

In effect, God says: I do not need your *korbanot* and never demanded
them. Similarly, in the *haftarah* of Tzav, Jeremiah says:

כה אמר ה' צבא־ות א־להי ישראל עלותיכם ספו על זבחיכם ואכלו בשר: כי לא
דברתי את אבותיכם ולא צויתים ביום הוציאי אותם מארץ מצרים על דברי עולה
וזבח: כי אם את הדבר הזה צויתי אותם לאמר שמעו בקולי והייתי לכם לא־להים
ואתם תהיו לי לעם והלכתם בכל הדרך אשר אצוה אתכם למען ייטב לכם.

So said the Lord, Master of Legions, God of Israel: Pile your
burnt offerings upon your peace offerings and eat flesh. For I
did not speak with your forefathers nor did I command them
on the day I took them out of the land of Egypt concerning
burnt offerings or peace offerings. Rather, I commanded them
regarding only this matter, saying: Hear my voice so that I
may be a God unto you and you will be a people unto me, and
you shall follow along the entire path in which I command
you, so that it may go well for you.[10]

Although Isaiah and Jeremiah never told the people to stop bringing
sacrifices, they were more concerned with ethical principles. They said,

---

9 Isaiah 43:23–24.
10 Jeremiah 7:21–23.

in effect: If you think that *korbanot* automatically wipe away sin, you are mistaken. This is the message of the two *haftarot*. When we fulfill the obligation of the *korbanot*, we must be careful to do so within the context of *kedushah*. The *korbanot* must be not an isolated procedure followed by rote, but rather part of a larger effort to obey God's will. We all pray for the restoration of the *Beit ha-Mikdash*, but until it is rebuilt, our sages in their wisdom replaced the focus on *korbanot* with a focus on the values of the Oral Law.

When we read the account of the *Avodah* on Yom Kippur, we see that it centers upon the *korbanot*. In the Mishnah at the end of *Masechet Yoma*,[11] Rabbi Akiva tried to cheer the sad and weary Jewish nation by telling them that it is God who cleanses them. He changed the focus of Yom Kippur from the *korbanot* to prayer, allowing the people to experience the day with as much passion and exaltation as they had felt when the Temple was still standing.

This was not the theme of the messages of Isaiah and Jeremiah. According to them, we must first attain a state of *kedushah*, and only then can we offer sacrifices. We must understand that offering a *korban* is not a perfunctory, meaningless ritual but that it requires us to be in a state of holiness. We have survived without the *Beit ha-Mikdash* for over nineteen hundred years, and yet we could not have lasted for one hundred years without Shabbat, *tzniut* (modesty) and *kashrut*. These are the major principles that define our existence, and in this sense they are more fundamental than *korbanot*.

However, the *korban Pesah* symbolizes a collective experience, a communal endeavor. In this sense it is the *korban* that most openly captures the broader values of Judaism, of *mesirat nefesh* (self-sacrifice) and *arevut* (interdependency). Why was it necessary for the Jewish people to offer this sacrifice at the moment of the exodus? The reason is that a slave usually is focused only upon himself and loses interest in his fellow slaves. It

---

11 BT *Yoma* 85b.

is said that one of the great tragedies of the concentration camps during the Holocaust was that some of the inmates stopped caring about even their own children and could only focus on themselves.

The purpose of a collective offering, such as the paschal lamb, is to instruct us to have compassion upon each other. It symbolizes our surrender as Jews to the will God. God remembers how we followed him into the desert, shed our status as slaves and became a community. This is why *korban Pesah* is so important, and why failure to offer it results in *karet* – being ripped away from the Jewish destiny. This is also why the *parshiyot* of the *korbanot*, Vayikra and Tzav, are linked to the Passover festival.

‏ שמיני ‏

Shemini: The Transgression of Nadav and Avihu

I N PARASHAT SHEMINI, the Torah recounts the deaths of Nadav and Avihu, the two older sons of Aharon the High Priest. Two questions come to mind: why were they punished so swiftly, and what was their sin?

God Is Slow to Anger

One of God's attributes is that he is slow to anger – מאריך אף – especially with ordinary human beings. This example of the divine attribute of *rahamim* – mercy – allows people the opportunity to do *teshuvah*. However, when God employs the attribute of *din* or *emet* (justice or truth), then he metes out punishment swiftly.

In the aftermath of the sin of the Golden Calf, the Torah states:

ויאמר ה' אל משה ראיתי את העם הזה והנה עם קשה ערף הוא: ועתה הניחה לי ויחר אפי בהם ואכלם ואעשה אותך לגוי גדול.

God spoke to Moshe as follows: I have seen this nation, and see, it is stiff-necked. Now leave me alone, and my anger will wax hot against them. I shall destroy them and make of you a great nation.[1]

---

1 Exodus 32: 9–10.

The language of "leave me alone" implies that God would punish the people after Moshe's departure. Thus the door was left open for Moshe to intercede on their behalf. Moshe seized that opening, providing the Israelites with the opportunity to do *teshuvah*.

On the other hand, the Torah tells us that Moshe failed to circumcise his second son Gershom. Here, God told him:

לך שב מצרים כי מתו כל האנשים המבקשים את נפשך ... בלכתך לשוב מצרימה ראה כל המפתים אשר שמתי בידך ... ויהי בדרך במלון ויפגשהו ה' ויבקש המיתו.

Go, return to Egypt, for those who sought your life are dead ... When you go to return to Egypt, see all the wonders that I have put into your hand ... It was on the way, in the inn, that God encountered him and sought to kill him.[2]

Before God commanded Moshe to appear before Pharaoh to demand the Jewish people's release, Moshe was, as it were, an ordinary person. While that was still true, God was slow to anger. The moment that Moshe took up the rod, however, he became a charismatic leader. Now, failure to comply with divine commands is an offense subject to immediate punishment.

We recall that years later, when Uzzah, the son of Aminadav, took hold of the Holy Ark containing the Tablets, he died instantly.[3] A similar event occurred when Aharon's two sons perished on the day of their consecration.[4] Had they been ordinary individuals, they would have been given the chance to do *teshuvah*. But because they were prominent figures in the community, they were held to a higher standard. In short, there is a large difference between how God relates to the misbehavior of a person chosen for a divine mission and that of an ordinary person.

---

2 Exodus 4:19, 21, 24.
3 II Samuel 6:7.
4 Leviticus 10:1.

The actions of the former are subject to close scrutiny, while the latter is given the chance to mend his ways.

℘ The Nature of the Sin of Nadav and Avihu

The second question relates to the nature of the sin of Nadav and Avihu. The sages and the Rishonim differ as to the essence of the sin and the reason why they died. Some said that it was because of their insolent question (referring to Moshe and Aharon): "When will these old men die so that we may assume leadership?"[5] Others assert that they showed insolence by issuing a halachic opinion in Moshe's presence.[6] Still another opinion asserts that they drank wine and became intoxicated before performing the service in the *Mishkan.*[7] All these opinions are stated in the *Midrash* and by some of the Rishonim.

However, the Torah states, ויקרבו לפני ה' אש זרה אשר לא צוה אתם – "They offered strange fire that they had not been commanded."[8] On the day of their installation, wearing their priestly vestments, they were overcome by ecstasy and by the need to express their emotions. The incense that they burned was identical to that which their father, Aharon, had offered. But there is one significant difference. Aharon was obeying God's will, while Nadav and Avihu performed an action that God had not commanded.

℘ Ceremony vs. Religious Experience

According to the simple meaning of the text, the sin of Nadav and Avihu illustrates a dichotomy in one's approach to religious observance: religious divine service, with its accompanying discipline, versus ceremonial experience. A *mitzvah* is not only a perfunctory action or divine

---

5 *Yalkut Shimoni,* Shemini, 524.
6 BT *Eruvin* 63a and *Yalkut Shimoni,* Shemini, 524.
7 *Yalkut Shimoni,* Parashat Shemini, 524.
8 Leviticus 10:1.

performance. It must also translate into experiential terms. The Torah demands that we experience joy and satisfaction when we perform a *mitzvah*. In Parashat Ki Tavo, the Torah provides the reason for our suffering and exile as תחת אשר לא עבדת את ה' א-לוהיך בשמחה ובטוב לבב מרב כל – "Because you did not serve the Lord your God amid gladness and goodness of heart when everything was abundant."[9] A Jew fasts on Yom Kippur because God commanded it. However, the result of such obedience to God must be an ecstatic, illuminating experience that transforms his personality.

ᴦ The Torah Approach

There are two ways to achieve that exalted state: the Jewish way and the pagan way. The Jewish way requires us to fashion our lives according to God's discipline, as illustrated by the word *ve-tzivanu*. The reason that we perform the *mitzvah* is our absolute surrender to God's will. However, we must progress from that surrender to a profound spiritual experience that encompasses our entire being. Prayer begins as an obligatory, even compelled act, with rigid requirements of time, location, and behavior. We are particularly aware of this during the winter or in inclement weather when we must venture out into the cold for *minyan* early in the morning and at night. However, as we progress in our relationship to prayer, we feel the rewards of intimate communion with God.

The eating of *matzah* on seder night is initially a response to God's command, בערב תאכלו מצות – "On this night you shall eat *matza*."[10] As the evening evolves, however, eating the *matza* becomes an act of love for God. Likewise, Yom Kippur begins with total surrender to the will of God, but as it progresses, we move toward a joyful catharsis. In brief, the road consists of two steps: obedience to God's command and discovering the spiritual treasures inherent in it.

---

9 Deuteronomy 28:47 and Rambam, *Hilchot Lulav* 8:15.
10 Exodus 12:18.

The *Mishnah* in *Sukkah*[11] requires us to remove the furniture from the *sukkah* on Shemini Atzeret in order to demonstrate that the *mitzvah* no longer applies. The Vilna Gaon made Havdalah over beer at the end of Passover in order to demonstrate that his sole motivation for not benefiting from *hametz* on the holiday was God's prohibition.[12] These practices also show the importance of the personal experience in fulfillment of the *mitzvah*.

✒ The Pagan Approach

The pagan approach, which is the antithesis of the Torah approach, begins with excitement and culminates in sin and disillusionment. It very much parallels the approach of the modern world, where one uses drugs or alcohol in order to create an artificial feeling of euphoria, masking one's actual life situation of disappointment and futility.

✒ Korah's Error

Korah erred in this matter, confusing the ceremonial with God's command. According to the sages, Korah attempted to discredit Moshe by posing two questions: 1) If a person wears a garment that is made entirely of *techelet* (the biblically-mandated blue of the *tzitzit* fringe), is it valid for the fulfillment of the *mitzvah* of *titztzit*? 2) If a house is filled with sacred books, must a *mezuzah* still be affixed to its door post?[13] When Moshe said yes to both questions, Korah mocked him. Korah's error was his undue focus on the ceremonial aspect of the *mitzvah* while ignoring the aspect of God's command, which is the most important.

---

11 BT *Sukkah* 48a.

12 *Maaseh Rav, Hilchot Pessah* 185. See also *Torah Temimah,* Exodus 12:168 and *Shulhan Aruch Orah Hayyim* 296:2 in the Rama, and the glosses of the *Biur ha-Gra*. See further Rav Shlomo Zalman Auerbach's comment in *Halichot Shlomo,* Pesah, 10:24.

13 *Yalkut Shimoni,* Korah 750 (beginning of Parashat Korah).

✣ The Golden Calf vs. the Mishkan

The primary distinction between the Golden Calf and the *Mishkan* was the fact that construction of the *Mishkan* was commanded by God, while that of the Golden Calf was not. The recurring expression in Parashat Pekudei, כאשר צוה ה' את משה – "As God commanded Moshe"[14] – illustrates this premise. Each act of the *Mishkan*'s construction was accompanied by a phrase that conferred sanctity upon it. The construction of the Golden Calf was an act of idolatry because God had not ordered its construction.

King David wanted to express his gratitude to God by building him a Temple. However, he was not permitted to do so because God wanted his son, King Solomon, to construct it. Therefore, the transgression of Nadav and Avihu, whom the Torah describes as sanctified, was that "they offered a strange fire concerning which they had not been commanded." The divine command and our discipline in obeying that command are the only healthy routes to religious inspiration. Any deviation, especially by *tzaddikim,* is unacceptable and ultimately doomed to failure.

---

14 Exodus 40.

Tazria: The Three Expressions of Negaim

THE SAGES SEE the *negaim* – the afflictions of *tzaraat* – as
punishment for a series of transgressions, including *lashon ha-ra*
(derogatory speech), *ayin ha-ra* (envy) and *shefichut damim*
(bloodshed).[1] The Rav examined the deeper meaning of *negaim* through
the three different terms used to describe them: *seit, sapahat* and *baheret*.

The *Midrash Rabbah* in Tazria explicates the three terms of *se'et,
sapahat* and *baheret*.

שאת זו על בבל על שום ונשאת המשל הזה על מלך בבל ואמרת איך שבת נוגש
שבתה מדהבה רבי אבא בר כהנא אמר שבתה מדהבה מלכות שהיא אומרת מדוד
והבא, ספחת זו מדי שהעמידה המן הרשע ששף כנחש על שום על גחונך תלך,
בהרת זו יון שהיתה מבהרת בגזרותיה על ישראל ואומרת להן כתבו על קרן השור
שאין לכם חלק בא-להי ישראל, נגע צרעת זו אדום.

Se'et [A rising] is Babylonia, as it is written: "You will recite
this parable about the king of Babylonia, and you will say:
How has the oppressor come to an end, the arrogance
has been ended. Rabbi Aba the son of Kahana said, "The
arrogance has been ended – a kingdom that says 'Count!'

---

1 BT *Arachin* 16a.

[referring to money and golden dinarim] and 'Bring!'" [to the royal treasury]. *Sapahat* [a scab] is [the kingdom of the] Medes, which raised Haman the wicked, who crawled like a snake, as it is written, "On your belly you shall go." *Baheret* [a bright spot] is Greece, which made herself conspicuous in its decrees against the Jewish people and told them, "Write on the horn of an ox that you have no share in the God of Israel." A *tzaraat* affliction is Edom.[2]

❧ *Se'et* – the Sin of Arrogance

The Talmud in Tractate *Shavuot*[3] connects *se'et* with "heights." Nebuchadnezzar, the king of Babylonia, set up a golden idol of himself and commanded everyone to prostrate themselves to it. The affliction of *tzaraat* is related to *gaavah* (arrogance). Our sages contended that arrogance lies at the root of all sin and compared an arrogant person to an idol-worshipper.[4] The Talmud in Tractate *Sanhedrin*[5] describes Yeravam ben Nevat as being one of the foremost Torah scholars of his generation. If that was true, then why did he erect two idols of gold in Dan and Beit El? He feared that if the Jewish people fulfilled the *mitzvah* of the thrice-annual pilgrimage to Jerusalem, they would return to the ranks of Rehavam.

In other words, the entire thought process was a function of *gaavah* and ego. The Talmud concludes with an astounding statement:

ויאמר ירבעם בלבו עתה תשוב הממלכה לבית דוד. אם יעלה העם הזה לעשות
זבחים בבית ה' בירושלם ושב לב העם הזה אל אדניהם אל רחבעם מלך יהודה
והרגני ושבו אל רחבעם מלך יהודה.

Yeravam then thought: Now the kingship may revert to the

---

2 *Midrash Rabbah,* Tazria 15:9.
3 BT *Shavuot* 6b.
4 BT *Sotah* 4b.
5 BT *Sanhedrin* 102a.

house of David. If this nation should ascend to bring offerings in the Temple of God in Jerusalem, the heart of this people will revert to their ruler, to Rehavam, king of Judah. They will kill me and return to Rehavam, king of Judah.[6]

⟿ Yeravam Chooses Earthly Honor and Pragmatism over Divine Favor

אמר רבי אבא: אחר שתפשו הקדוש ברוך הוא לירבעם בבגדו, ואמר לו: חזור בך, ואני ואתה ובן ישי נטייל בגן עדן, אמר לו, מי בראש. בן ישי בראש. אי הכי לא בעינא.

Rav Aba said: God seized Yeravam by his garment and told him to retract, saying: [If you do so], I and you and the son of Yishai will take a stroll in Gan Eden. He [Yeravam] said: Who will be first? He [God] answered: The son of Yishai will be first. [Yeravam replied:] If so, I am not interested.[7]

Yeravam was caught in a web of *gaavah* from which he could not detach himself. As a result, to this day he remains the symbol of a wicked king who ended as a pariah. He was unwilling to share any honor with Rehavam. His pride was so strong that he even passed up an opportunity to walk with God in the Garden of Eden because he would not be in the lead. Because of his arrogance, Yeravam missed an opportunity to establish himself in Jewish history.

This is also the intent of the above-mentioned *midrash* in which Babylonia was represented by the king in the counting house. While a king's job is to protect his people, this king is interested only in himself and seeks only to amass material wealth. Our sages deplore such behavior. "Blessing is not to be found in something that is weighed or

---

6 I Kings 12:26–27. See BT *Sanhedrin* 101b.
7 BT *Sanhedrin* 102a.

counted or measured, but rather in that which is remote from sight."[8] A person must nurture an appreciation for things that cannot be counted in terms of material wealth, such as Jewish values. Yeravam gave up a chance to take a stroll with God in Paradise for a *narisher kavod* – a silly and worthless honor.

This phenomenon is strongly reflected in the lives of some Jews who see Judaism only from a utilitarian, pragmatic perspective. The reason that Torah education in America often failed is that parents opted for a Judaism that could be measured and quantified but lacked the experiential dimension – the walk with God in Paradise. This outlook does not see the value of Shabbat, prayer and connection to God. Such parents send their children to the most prestigious secular schools because they are the quintessence of *tachlit* (*telos*). What is the *tachlit* of a human being, according to the Rambam? Is there any greater purpose than a connection with God? Unfortunately, the *tachlit* of many Jews has become the motto of Yeravam – Will I be in charge? Who takes the lead? This is the model of Esau in the verse ויאמר עשו אל יעקב הלעיטני נא מן האדם האדם הזה כי עיף אנכי על כן קרא שמו אדום – "Pour into me some of that red, red stuff, for I am exhausted,"[9] the model of immediate gratification. The fact that he gave up the birthright and paradise is irrelevant to him.

A father and mother who have no appreciation for or sense of the future will not give their child a religious education. This is the subset of *tzaraat* entitled *se'et*. Everything is measured by a *grubber tachlis* (a practical telos). One result of such an upbringing is that children neglect the obligation to honor their parents when they become elderly and infirm. They have absorbed only too well the idea that only people who have pragmatic value matter, so when their parents can no longer meet their needs, their respect for their parents dissipates. Children who have been brought up this way also discard synagogue attendance and Shabbat observance once they feel that these are not practical. True,

---

8 BT *Taanit* 8b and *Bava Metzia* 42a.
9 Genesis 25:30 and Ramban on Genesis 25:34.

Jews are a practical people and must make a living, but this is not our main purpose. Our day-to-day activities are the means toward the higher goal of bonding with God.

✺ Sapahat – the Sin of Loss of Dignity

The second type of *tzaraat* is *sapahat,* which is identified with מדי (the Medes). Their scion is the wicked Haman, who slithered like a snake but was puffed up with arrogance. A fawning personality, he lacked dignity. His sycophantic behavior resulted in his becoming prime minister to King Ahashverosh. Yet Haman was no leader. A weak and spineless man, he used flattery in order to get ahead. Thinking that it would save his life, he behaved in a servile manner toward Esther even after she exposed him. Like other haughty people, he did not realize how base he was, that he was actually a form of *sapahat.*

✺ Gaavah – Arrogance vs. Ge'ut – Grandeur

There are two characteristics related to the root גאה, which means pride or honor. One, *gaavah* – arrogant pride – is a negative character trait, a form of spiritual *tzaraat.* However, there is a positive form: *ge'ut,* which is a characteristic of God, as we see in the verse from Psalms: ה' מלך גאות לבש – "The Lord will have reigned; He will have donned grandeur."[10] The principle of *imitatio dei* demands that we emulate God's attributes. Therefore, we must avoid *gaavah* and be careful not to behave like Haman, who thought that only he was worthy of honor. ויאמר המן בלבו למי יחפץ המלך לעשות יקר יותר ממני – "Haman said in his heart: 'Whom would the king wish to honor more than myself?'"[11] Haman dreamed of grandeur even though he did not deserve it.

---

10 Psalms 93:1. See also *Yemei Zikaron* of Rav Yosef Dov Soloveitchik by Moshe Krona, 9–11, 20–21, 208–209.

11 Esther 6:6.

ויאמר המן אל המלך איש אשר המלך חפץ ביקרו: יביאו לבוש מלכות אשר לבש

בו המלך וסוס אשר רכב עליו המלך ואשר נתן כתר מלכות בראשו: ונתון הלבוש

והסוס על יד איש משרי המלך הפרתמים והלבישו את האיש אשר המלך חפץ

ביקרו והרכיבהו על הסוס ברחוב העיר וקראו לפניו ככה יעשה לאיש אשר המלך

חפץ ביקרו.

Haman said to the king, "The man whom the king desires to honor: let them bring him royal attire that the king has worn and a horse upon which the king has ridden, one with a royal crown placed on his head. Then let the attire and the horse be given into the hand of one of the king's most noble officials. Let them dress the man whom the king desires to honor and have him ride on the horse through the city square as they proclaim before him: 'This is what shall be done to the man whom the king desires to honor!'"[12]

Unlike Haman, Mordechai was not excited by the prospect of honor. He had to allow it even though he had not sought it, and after his ride through the city, he resumed wearing his sackcloth and returned to the palace gate.[13] Since Mordechai had *ge'ut* and a clear philosophy of life, the royal horse and finery had no meaning for him.

Rav Menachem Mendel of Kotzk, the Kotzker Rebbe, remarked that a human being has, in a manner of speaking, two pockets. In one is a slip of paper on which is written ואנכי עפר ואפר - "I am but dust and ashes."[14] The second pocket contains a slip of paper bearing the words ותחסרהו מעט מא־להים וכבוד והדר תעטרהו - "Yet you have made him but slightly less than the angels and crowned him with soul and splendor."[15] Both hands are in both pockets. There is a dialectical tension between the self-respect and self-esteem that healthy people possess – in other words,

---

12 Esther 6:7–9.
13 See Rashi on Esther 6:12.
14 Genesis 18:27.
15 Psalms 8:6.

ge'ut and in sharp contradistinction the sort of *gaavah* – arrogance – that leads to behavior like Haman's. In its most extreme form it leads to the sort of megalomania that characterized two of the worst tyrants and mass-murderers of recent history, Stalin and Hitler.

↝ *Baheret* – The Sin of Superficiality

The third type of *tzaraat* is *baheret*. In the Midrash cited above, *baheret* is represented by ancient Greece, which said, "Write on the horn of an ox that you have no share in the God of Israel.[16] The Mishnah in Tractate *Bikkurim*[17] describes the procession of people bringing their first fruits to the Temple, while an ox adorned with gold, with a garland of olives on its horns, walked before them.

Why did the Greeks write on the horn of an ox? The ox is a symbol of agriculture. The Greeks and Hellenist sympathizers did not want to uproot Judaism completely. Instead, metaphorically speaking, they wanted Judaism to be inscribed on the horns of an ox. In other words, they preferred a style of Judaism that was external and superficial, defined by its aesthetics rather than by its inner essence. This is *baheret*.

The Greeks contended that form is more important than content. One's feelings are not important, but rather what one shows outwardly. The Talmud in Tractate *Arachin*[18] describes Temple vessels and musical instruments that dated back to Moshe's time. Because they had been used for so many years, they were becoming worn out. Although the sages brought craftsman from Alexandria to repair the utensils and artisans to adorn them with gold, they did not succeed in restoring the vessels and musical instruments to their former state. However, once the adornments were removed, the vessels and musical instruments worked properly once again.

---

16 *Midrash Rabbah,* Tazria 15:9.
17 Mishnah *Bikkurim* 3:3.
18 BT *Arachin* 10b.

While the outside world focuses on the beauty of an item, Judaism is concerned with the inner essence. We would rather have a vessel that is somewhat worn but still genuine than one that is beautiful but fake.

The Rav pointed out that some of the greatest rabbis were not the greatest of orators. His grandfather, Rav Chaim Soloveitchik, was a great pedagogue but did not often engage in public speaking. He spoke twice a year, on Shabbat ha-Gadol and Shabbat Shuvah. He used to explain why he usually avoided public speaking by asking: How can I tell other Jews to repent when I must repent first? From 1892 to 1918, all we have is one *derashah* of *teshuvah* by Rav Chaim Soloveitchik. Nevertheless, he had tremendous influence on the city of Brisk, even without public oratory.

Rav Yitzchak Elchonon Spektor gave the same *derashah* every Shabbat Shuvah. He would begin by quoting the confessional prayer, "We are foolish and have committed transgressions." Then he would begin to weep, and the congregation would weep together with him. The Hatam Sofer was famous for his outstanding *derashot*. Even though the Lithuanian rabbis generally were not orators, they had a great deal of influence on their communities because their strength lay not in speaking but in their moral character.

Bilaam was an excellent speaker. Had the Jews of his time been *baheret* Jews, they would have flocked to him. But Jews avoid such manifestations of *se'et, sapahat* and *baheret*. Although Moshe Rabbenu was no orator – in fact, he suffered from a speech impediment[19] – he loved the Jewish people to the depths of his soul. In his humility, he realized an important lesson that we, too, would do well to learn: that often, speaking words of sanctity in public may actually constitute a desecration. Sometimes it is proper to leave them unsaid.

The Rav said that while his father kissed him only on the hand, his profound love for his son was beyond doubt. American Zionists speak

---

19 Exodus 4:10.

glowingly of Israel, yet they stay where they are – abroad. Jews of centuries past did not talk much about Eretz Yisrael except on the seder night or at the end of Yom Kippur, when they recited "Next year in Jerusalem" with all their hearts. Judaism is much more profound than the *baheret* Judaism, the artificial, surface Judaism inscribed on the horns of the ox.

The disease of spiritual *tzaraat,* then, takes three forms: *se'et,* a *puster narisher gaavah* (vapid, foolish arrogance); *sapahat* – an inferiority complex and lack of dignity, and *baheret* – artificial speech and behavior that lack depth. In the near future, we hope and pray that God will cleanse the Jewish people of all of these afflictions.

Metzora: The Kohen as a Public Servant

The Kohen's Responsibility regarding *Negaim*

AS WE EXPLORE Parashat *Metzora,* we encounter a peculiar phenomenon: the Kohen is charged to perform tasks that appear out of his ordinary jurisdiction. He is given the role of diagnostician, nurse, and adjudicator of ritual purity or impurity. He is given sole discretion in the matter of *negaim.* Usually, a Kohen must distance himself from all forms of ritual impurity. Yet when it comes to this particular form of *tumah,* the Torah states, ועל פיהם יהיה כל ריב וכל נגע – "Every grievance and every plague shall be decided according to their word."[1] The Navi also states, ואת עמי יורו בין קדש לחל ובין טמא לטהור יודעם – "They shall instruct my people concerning [the differences] between holy and profane. Let them inform them of [the difference] between impure and pure."[2] Why is this role conferred upon the Kohen?

The answer lies in the Judaic concept of service. The role of the Kohen as defined by the prophet Ezekiel in the *haftarah* of Parashat Emor encompasses several different tasks: he serves as a member of the Sanhedrin, judging cases brought before them. He is responsible for

---

1 Deuteronomy 21:5.
2 Ezekiel 44:23.

declaring the holidays by establishing the months. He must teach the people, and he serves in the Temple.

ঙ The Underlying Spirit of the Kohen

However, a single spirit underlies these three roles: a strong sense of love, friendship and concern for every person. One of the most important conditions of a valid priestly blessing is that it be done with love, and this condition forms part of the blessing that is recited prior to performing this act. The *Zohar* remarks that a Kohen who feels enmity toward any member of the congregation may not participate in the blessing, and there is a danger if he does so.[3]

Judaism recognizes only one authority figure: the *rebbe* or teacher. We have never entrusted our people to politicians or statesmen. According to Isaiah, the ideal king in Messianic times will be a great teacher.[4] A *talmid* looks to his *rebbe* with profound reverence and love. Thus, although the kohanim are teachers and leaders, they are primarily friends who share in the community's sorrows and joys. The Kohen is the key to providing for the needs of one who suffers from *tzaraat*.

ঙ The *Metzora*: Isolated but Not Abandoned

Let us analyze the leper's social status. Leprosy instilled the type of anxiety and social ostracism that a malignancy or severe illness does today in many societies. The moment one developed the outward symptoms of leprosy, he was quarantined. He had no contact with other human beings and was stripped of his dignity. As a carrier of *tzaraat,* which was viewed as a contagious disease, he became a *persona non grata* and was banished to a place outside the camp. His food was given to him from a distance. We have examples in the Orient where people who suffered

---

3 Zohar, Parashat Naso, 147. *Mishnah Berurah Orah Hayyim* 128:37.
4 Isaiah 2:3.

from the disease were required to shout "Leper, leper" to warn people away. Often, people behaved cruelly and mercilessly toward lepers. The Torah tells us:

איש צרוע הוא טמא הוא טמא יטמאנו הכהן בראשו נגעו: והצרוע אשר בו הנגע בגדיו יהיו פרמים וראשו יהיה פרוע ועל שפם יעטה וטמא טמא יקרא: כל ימי אשר הנגע בו יטמא טמא הוא בדד ישב מחוץ למחנה מושבו.

> He is a man afflicted with *tzaraat*; he is contaminated. The Kohen shall declare him contaminated, and his affliction shall be on his head. As for the person who suffers from *tzaraat,* his garments shall be rent, the hair of his head shall be unshorn and he shall cloak himself up to his lips. He is to call out, "Contaminated, contaminated." All the days that the affliction is upon him he shall remain contaminated; he is contaminated. He shall dwell in isolation; his dwelling shall be outside the camp.[5]

The Torah's approach to lepers is much more humane and merciful. It was designed to maintain and restore the leper's sense of dignity even though he must be isolated from the rest of the population. The Torah effectively prescribes a form of mourning for the leper; he must be separated from society at large. However, he is not excluded completely. The immediate, initial reaction was to summon a Kohen to diagnose the malady,[6] and the Kohen must be in constant contact with him. In fact, the leper could ask to be seen by the Kohen Gadol himself, whose sanctity was so strong that he could not attend the funerals of his closest relatives.

Yet if a leper asked to see him, he had to go. The Torah acted to prevent the loss of dignity. On the one hand, the leper must be isolated for seven days, while on the other, the Kohen, a leader and an authority figure,

---

5   Leviticus 13:44–46.
6   Leviticus 14:2–3.

does everything possible to connect with the leper and heal him. Both Tazria and Metzora emphasize the message that God wants someone of exalted stature, the Kohen, to associate with the leper.

Priest and Prophet

The Rav compared the role of the Kohen with that of the prophet. The prophet was also charged with the task of becoming a friend and confidant. Besides his role as deliverer of God's word, he also had the mission of helping people as a father would. Ramban derives this from the dialogue between Moshe Rabbenu and his father-in-law, Yitro: כי יהיה להם דבר בא אלי ושפטתי בין איש ובין רעהו והודעתי את חקי הא־להים ואת תורתיו[7] – "When they have a matter, one comes to me and I judge between a man and his fellow. I announce God's decrees and teachings."[8] Ramban interprets the verse as if Moshe is saying: Whenever they need me, I am there. I am constantly ready to pray to God for a sick child, day or night.

Elisha as the Embodiment of Human Compassion

A clear reflection of this definition is seen in the handiwork of the prophet Elisha, who was a farmer. When the prophet Eliyahu first met him, he was plowing. When Eliyahu cast his mantle upon him[9], Elisha said, ויאמר אשקה נא לאבי ולאמי ואלכה אחריך ויאמר לו לך שוב כי מה עשיתי לך – "'Please let me kiss my father and mother, and then I shall go after you.' But he said to him, 'Go, return, for what have I done to you?'"[10] What was the nature of that statement? It meant that he was now resolved to total dedication to his people. Elisha was a consultant to the king, had a voice in all state matters and was revered by the entire nation. He knew

---

7 Ramban on Exodus 18:15.
8 Exodus 18:16.
9 I Kings 19:19.
10 I Kings 19:20.

prophetically what God was planning, and his job was to keep the king updated. Yet despite his high status, he never abandoned the common people.

When an impoverished widow was threatened with the sale of her children into slavery, Elisha worked a miracle that gave her enough oil to sell in order to cover her debts.[11] He prayed for a barren woman who subsequently gave birth to a son, and resuscitated him from death several years later.[12] These qualities of the prophet are a manifestation of *imitatio dei,* just as a fundamental dialectic of God is his simultaneous transcendental and immanent nature.

אמר רבי יוחנן: כל מקום שאתה מוצא גבורתו של הקדוש ברוך הוא אתה מוצא
ענוותנותו . . . שנוי בנביאים דכתיב – כה אמר רם ונשא שכן עד וקדוש שמו מרום
וקדוש אשכון ואת דכא ושפל רוח להחיות רוח שפלים ולהחיות לב נדכאים.

Rabbi Yohanan said, "Wherever you find God's greatness, there you find his humility . . . It is repeated in the Prophets, as it is written: 'So says the exalted and uplifted One, Who abides forever and Whose name is holy: I abide in exaltedness and holiness but am with the contrite and lowly of spirit, to revive the spirit of the lowly and to revive the heart of the contrite.'"[13]

ﻰ Elisha and Naaman

The *haftarah* of Tazria tells the story of Naaman, the field marshal of Aram (present-day Syria), who was stricken with leprosy. A young Jewish girl who had been taken captive and now served Naaman's wife told her mistress that there was a prophet in Israel, Elisha, who might be able to cure him. The king of Aram sent a message to the Jewish king together

---

11 II Kings 4:1–7.
12 II Kings 4:14–37
13 BT *Megillah* 31a.

with gifts of gold, silver and fine clothing, with a request to help Naaman. The king of Israel was terrified, but Elisha told Naaman to bathe seven times in the waters of the Jordan River. Initially, Naaman was indignant, but ultimately he obeyed Elisha and was cured. His gratitude was such that he offered the prophet great riches. Elisha refused because the cure had not come from him, but from God. Naaman then declared that the God of Israel was the sole God and renounced the idols of Aram.

Gehazi Undermines the Kiddush ha-Shem

Elisha's servant, Gehazi, was a base man. He could not bear to see the gifts withdrawn and pursued Naaman in order to receive them himself. This act of dishonesty, which negated the sanctification of God's name that Elisha had performed, earned Gehazi his master's curse: the very disease that had afflicted Naaman.

Elisha had said, יבא נא אלי וידע כי יש נביא בישראל – "Let him come to me now and he will realize that there is a prophet in Israel."[14] Naaman's response to his cure was to say, ויאמר הנה נא ידעתי כי אין א‑להים בכל הארץ כי אם בישראל ועתה קח נא ברכה מאת עבדך – "Behold, now I know that there is no God in the whole world but in Israel. Now, please accept a tribute from your servant."[15]

Why did Elisha say "a prophet in Israel"? He wanted Naaman to know that God was all-powerful and had great prophets who, despite their honored place in Jewish society, never abandoned a suffering person. True, Naaman was no ordinary person. However, since Aram engaged in guerrilla warfare with Israel, Elisha's act of kindness was particularly self-sacrificing and even dangerous. Despite the ongoing state of war, Elisha sanctified the divine name by curing Naaman.

When Elisha later encountered Hazael, who was destined to become the king of Aram, he wept. When Hazael asked him why, he answered,

---

14 II Kings 5:8.
15 II Kings 5:15.

כי ידעתי את אשר תעשה לבני ישראל רעה – "Because I know what evil you will do to the children of Israel."[16] Aram was Israel's sworn enemy, and yet earlier, Elisha had cured its field marshal, Naaman, of leprosy. This was tantamount to aiding and abetting the enemy. Naaman must have been astonished by Elisha's selfless act.

Naaman wanted to give Elisha rich gifts, but Elisha invoked an oath in refusal. Had he accepted the gifts, he would have negated the effect of his act. Unfortunately, that is precisely what happened when Gehazi pursued Naaman in order to receive the gifts himself. Had Gehazi not done so, the miracle might have influenced Naaman to become Jewish himself. The entire country of Aram might have converted with him, ending the war and spreading the teachings of Judaism far and wide. Gehazi's act may well have caused Naaman to doubt Elisha's honesty and the integrity of the entire Jewish faith.

The powerful thread that links priest and prophet is that both commit themselves, with absolute devotion, to assist all people, including potential enemies, regardless of their station.

16 II Kings 8:12.

Aharei Mot: The Interdependence
of *Hok* and *Mishpat*

T HE *PARSHIYOT* OF Aharei Mot and Kedoshim are usually combined and read on a single Shabbat. During a leap year, they are
read separately. The joint reading of these two *parshiyot* is not
only a function of practical necessity but also of thematic commonality.
The beginning of Aharei Mot is devoted to the Yom Kippur service in
the Temple. The next chapter is devoted to the sacrifices. Subsequently,
Parashat Aharei Mot lists a series of forbidden sexual relationships that
is expanded further in Parashat Kedoshim. In Parashat Aharei Mot, the
Torah states the prohibitions. In Parashat Kedoshim, it lists the punish-
ments for violating them.

Most of these laws of forbidden relationships fall under the category
of *hok*. One may offer explanations, but the many restrictions and their
rigid enforcement defy human logic. However, the *parashah* of Kedoshim
also includes some of the best examples of *mishpatim* – *mitzvot* that may
be readily understood by human reason.

The Sequence of *Hok* vs. *Mishpat*

In *Aharei Mot*, the Torah introduces the laws of sexual morality with
the following verse: את משפטי תעשו ואת חקתי תשמרו ללכת בהם אני ה' א-להיכם

– "Obey my laws and make sure that you follow my decrees. I am the Lord your God."[1] In this verse, *mishpat* (law) precedes *hok* (decree). However, in the next verse, the order is reversed: ושמרתם את חקתי ואת משפטי אשר יעשה אתם האדם וחי בהם אני ה' – "You shall observe my decrees and my laws, which man shall carry out and by which he shall live – I am the Lord."[2] Here, *hok* precedes *mishpat*. Why is there a reversal in the order? The first verse implies that *mishpat* is primary and logically precedes *hok*. The second verse would seem to imply the opposite.

✺ Trust as the Basis of All Relationships

At first, God created the first human being in a state of aloneness. Then he created Hava, for a lonely existence without existential companionship is pragmatically undesirable. The *Etz Hayyim*, Rav Hayyim Vital, provides a deeper understanding. God, who is all good, wanted to bestow his lovingkindness upon humanity and therefore created the first human being. However, the existence of man as a solitary being negated the need for two great virtues, love and trust. To be alone is to undermine the purpose of existence, for the ability to invite others to share in one's existence enables and fosters love and trust. Love is a noble quality and trust expresses the very essence of humanity.

Halachah illustrates trust using the principle of *hazakah*. I trust my fellow human being unless he is found guilty. Only then does he lose my trust. God created man to trust the decency of his neighbor. Character assassination, which undermines this basic trust, threatens the foundation of human relations and is therefore unconscionable. But beyond the principle of *hazakah* lies a more fundamental principle: that God created humanity in his image, which automatically presupposes intelligence and trust. Otherwise, the fabric of society would unravel and all social cohesion would disintegrate. No one would want to step outside

---

1 Leviticus 18:4.
2 Leviticus 18:5.

his home for fear of being harmed by his neighbor. Suspicion lies at the root of economic depression and upheaval. An economy's viability depends on mutual trust.

✌ Trust through Deduction and Induction

The ability to trust one's neighbor is founded upon two logical principles. First, since human beings were created in God's image, they are worthy of trust because of their essential goodness. This is the principle of deduction. If God is just and good and human beings are created in God's image, then they are also good. The second is based on empirical observation. When we observe a particular person acting in a trustworthy manner again and again, we trust this person. This is inductive reasoning.

If human beings were commanded to have faith and trust in their fellows, the same would certainly be expected between human beings and their Creator, God. In addition, the Jewish people must have trust in the Torah itself. Human beings must have faith that the Torah is honest and reasonable and that it would not obligate us to do something harmful. What, then, is the basis of my trust in the Torah? The two principles cited above apply. First, based on deduction, if God is all-wise and all-just, then his Torah must be also. Second, by observing the many specific rules of the Torah, we conclude, using induction, that it, too, is just and reasonable.

✌ Equating *Hok* with *Mishpat*

In Parashat Kedoshim, the Torah presents a list of commandments, both prescriptive and prohibitive, and sums them up with the following concluding verse: 'ושמרתם את כל חקתי ואת כל משפטי ועשיתם אתם אני ה – "You shall observe all my decrees and all my ordinances, and you shall perform them: I am the Lord."[3] What are some of these laws? Reverence for par-

---

3   Leviticus 19:37.

ents, the laws of *peah* (leaving the corners of the field for the poor) and *leket* (leaving the gleanings of the sheaves for the poor). All of these laws seem beautiful, noble and understandable. What else do we encounter among the laws in Kedoshim? Do not steal from your neighbor, do not embezzle, do not oppress a worker, pay wages on time, do not place a stumbling block before the blind; do not hate your brother in your heart, love your fellow human being as yourself. The Torah expects us to lead a dignified and honorable life because it is a book of reasonable laws. So why does it mingle *hok* and *mishpat*?

This mingling carries with it an additional message. The *hukim*, which are seemingly unreasonable and presented in enigmatic language, also have a meaning that we cannot grasp. We ultimately trust that *hukim* are as reasonable as the *mishpatim*. In fact, they may even be more reasonable. The highest of the *mishpatim* is to love your fellow human being as yourself. The Torah says, as it were: I have another group of *mitzvot* called *hukim* that are not as comprehensible, such as *shaatnez* (the mixing of wool and linen in a garment). God says: Trust me in everything. If I can trust my neighbor, why should I not trust God and his Torah?

Since one might have been inclined to dismiss the *hukim* categorically, the verse ends with the phrase "I am the Lord your God." In other words, God tells us: I am the God who gave you both *hukim* and *mishpatim*. Why would I give you laws that are unreasonable? God gave the nations of the world the seven Noahide laws, which are readily understood, but he did not give them *hukim*, which are not. Our special relationship with God obligates us to go beyond our logic and trust God completely. Later, in retrospect, we may understand. Why, for example, does the State of Israel suffer so much? This question, too, is on the level of *hok*, which requires complete trust in God.

✣ The Frailty of Human Reason

If human beings are unable to accept commandments that they do not understand, then it will be hard for them to accept even the most reasonable *mishpatim*. Human thinking and subjective judgment are constantly in flux and vulnerable to self-deception. That which is reasonable today can easily become absurd tomorrow. Human beings are basically selfish. While they are capable of great kindness, they are also capable of hypocrisy. When they believe that something which is considered the norm restricts them, they will find a way to reject even that which is most reasonable.

This tension between fixed morality and human judgment is captured vividly in Dostoyevsky's classic work, *Crime and Punishment*. It depicts a young, intelligent man who is aware that murder is wrong. Yet he is desperately in need of funds. He meets a pawnbroker whom he sees as mean and vile, of no use to anyone – and who has the money that he needs. His reasoning changes abruptly. From his perspective, the pawnbroker's life is worthless, while he can put the money to good use. Now he reasons that the law forbidding murder is unreasonable, though he felt that it was reasonable the day before. Only after he has committed the murder does he realize the enormity of his crime.

The same problem exists today regarding euthanasia and abortion. The argument goes: why stand by and allow a person to suffer needlessly? Also, in a world with finite resources, it seems reasonable that some must die so that others may live. Regarding abortion, why let the fetus live when any reasonable person knows that it is not yet a human being? This is relatively easy to rationalize. Indeed, the Rav lamented the fact that in Eretz Yisrael today, abortion has taken the lives of many future citizens. Such acts represent the categorical rejection of *hukim*. Once we dismiss *hukim*, the entire system collapses, for one who ignores *hukim* will ultimately ignore *mishpatim* as well. We must teach society to move away from that which is wrong even if it seems to be pleasurable and even sensible. Modern society suffers from an inability to distance itself from evil in this way.

⌁ The Observance of *Mishpatim* Depends upon *Hukim*

Towards the conclusion of Aharei Mot, the Torah provides us with an example of three prohibitions in sequence: (a) ואל אשה בנדת טמאתה לא תקרב לגלות ערותה – "Do not approach a woman during her menses to uncover her nakedness";[4] (b) ואל אשת עמיתך לא תתן שכבתך לזרע לטמאה בה – "Do not lie with your neighbor's wife to contaminate yourself with her";[5] and (c) ומזרעך לא תתן להעביר למלך ולא תחלל את שם א-להיך אני ה' – "You shall not present any of your children to pass through for Molech, and do not profane the name of your God – I am the Lord."[6] The first two prohibitions relate to sexual morality and therefore fall into the classification of *hukim*. The third, which pertains to the ritual murder of children, is clearly in the category of *mishpatim*. What is the nature of the transition between these two groups? When the Rav described an actual case in which parents were willing to put their own child up for adoption rather than compromise their lifestyle, he declared that this was a modern-day example of giving one's child to Molech.

The conceptual connection is very clear. If people observe the *hukim* of sexual morality, they will also love their children. If they do not preserve sexual morality in their lives, it will inevitably lead to Molech – disdain for and hatred of children. Sexual morality from a Torah perspective is definitely a *hok*: difficult to understand and accept. It calls for strong discipline and sacrifice. Often, when couples wish to live as observant Jews, they have no objection to Shabbat, kashrut or the festivals. The greatest obstacle is accepting the laws of family purity as prescribed by the Torah and by our sages. Those who observe *hukim* out of surrender to the will of God will always observe the *mishpatim*. However, those who reject the *hukim* will one day abandon the *mishpatim* as well.

---

4   Leviticus 18:19.
5   Leviticus 18:20.
6   Leviticus 18:21.

~ קדושים ~

Kedoshim: The Duality of Shabbat Observance and Honoring Parents

IN PARASHAT KEDOSHIM, the Torah states: איש אמו ואביו תיראו ואת שבתתי תשמרו אני ה' א־להיכם – "Every man shall revere his mother and father and keep my Sabbaths: I am the Lord your God."[1] The Torah has linked the two commandments of revering one's parents and observing Shabbat. What is the nature of that equation? The Talmud explains[2] that these are combined in order to convey the following legal principle. It is proper to obey one's parents when their request accords with Torah law. However, if their request violates Torah law, we may not obey. Rashi notes that if a parent commands a child to violate one of the Torah's commandments, the child is obligated to obey God first and may not obey the parent. One might ask: why did the Torah choose Shabbat specifically to make this point? The same principle could have been derived from any other *mitzvah*.

~ *Mitzvot* That Occur on Two Levels

Rav Soloveitchik suggested that this particular combination contains a deeper meaning, which we may see in the Zohar's interpretation. In

---

1 Leviticus 19:3.
2 BT Bava Metzia 32a.

249

general, the Torah mentions Shabbat in the singular: שמור את יום השבת
לקדשו, זכור את יום השבת לקדשו – "Safeguard the Sabbath day to sanctify
it,"[3] or "Remember the Sabbath day to sanctify it."[4] Parashat Kedoshim
contains the possessive plural *shabbetotai*, "my Sabbaths," which we find
in two other places in the Torah. At the end of Parashat Be-har, the Torah
states, את שבתתי תשמרו ומקדשי תיראו אני ה' – "You shall observe my Sabbaths
and revere my sanctuary: I am the Lord."[5] In Parashat Ki Tisa, the Torah
says: אך את שבתתי תשמרו– "However, you must observe my Sabbaths."[6]

The Zohar recounts a conversation that took place between Rav
Shimon and Rav Abba as they traveled with a Bedouin man. They
were discussing the word *shabbetotai*. One Sabbath, said the Bedouin, is
related to the *Shabbat le-ela* (the supernal Sabbath), while one is related
to the *Shabbat le-tata* (the earthly Sabbath). The *Ke-gavna* prayer, which
hasidim recite on Friday night, contains the same idea.

The Blessing vs. the Holiness of Shabbat

The nature of this twofold Sabbath is explicit in the Torah's text. The
earthly Shabbat is a day that God blessed, while the supernal Shabbat is a
day that God hallowed and consecrated. We find in Genesis: ויברך א־להים
את יום השביעי ויקדש אתו – "God blessed the seventh day and sanctified it."[7]
In other words, Shabbat was both blessed and sanctified.

Lifting the Curse

When Adam ate the forbidden fruit, God cursed him. When a day is
blessed, any curse becomes nullified. Therefore, on Shabbat, no curse

---

3 Deuteronomy 5:12.
4 Exodus 20:8.
5 Leviticus 26:2.
6 Exodus 31:13.
7 Genesis 2:3.

applies. Human beings have the power to extend this blessing by prolonging Shabbat. The purpose of Shabbat is to lift the curse under which we labor.

Adam's curse contains four components. The first is hard labor: בזעת אפיך תאכל לחם – "By the sweat of your brow shall you eat bread."[8] The second is endless, uninterrupted work that has no telos. The Bible uses two terms to describe work: *amal* and *avodah*. *Amal* is pointless labor, as in the verse: ופניתי אני בכל מעשי שעשו ידי ובעמל שעמלתי לעשות והנה הכל הבל ורעות רוח ואין יתרון תחת השמש – "Then I regarded all my deeds that my hands had wrought and upon the toil at which I had labored, and behold everything was vanity and frustration, and there is no profit under the sun."[9] The third component of the curse is *itzavon*:[10] the restlessness, fear and suffering that characterize competitive society, or the conflict between human beings. A person in need of a livelihood is always frightened that someone will take his possessions away from him. The Marxist concept of the class struggle for existence reflects this anxiety. The fourth component is our mortality – כי עפר אתה ואל עפר תשוב – "For you are dust and to dust shall you return."[11] Therefore, the curse of Adam is a composite of four segments: continuous, exhausting and pointless labor that is by nature unproductive, conflict between human beings and, ultimately, death.

The blessing of Shabbat releases us from this curse. During the week, human beings find themselves on the same level as animals, working in order to survive. In the course of his daily regimen, they may lose their sense of dignity and act in an animalistic fashion. Work is dignified and ennobling as long as we know when to stop. The Torah tells us about God's work so that we may learn to imitate him, as it is written: כי בו שבת

---

8 Genesis 3:19.
9 See Ecclesiastes 2:11 and Metzudat Dovid there.
10 Genesis 3:17.
11 Genesis 3:19.

מכל מלאכתו – "Because on [that day] he abstained from all his work."[12] The Torah tells us that God rested on the seventh day in order to convey the importance of work on the one hand and the necessity for rest on the other.

֎ Kedushah

Shabbat is more than a day filled with specific duties and prohibitions. It means not only that we rest, but also that we must stop whatever it is that we do during the week. Whatever we do on Shabbat should be different from what we do on other days. Maimonides writes that on Shabbat, one should wear special clothing that is different from one's weekday attire.[13] If he wears short clothing during the week, he should wear longer clothing on Shabbat. Whenever Rosh ha-Shannah or Yom Kippur falls on Shabbat, we recite different liturgical poems during the service. By setting Shabbat apart in all the ways that the Torah and the sages teach, we fulfill the *mitzvah* of remembering it as the day of blessing. Shabbat releases us from Adam's curse by alleviating the weariness and boredom of the workday world that can lead to despair and, in extreme cases, to suicide. It is for good reason, then, that Shabbat is the goal and the high point of our week.

֎ Shabbat Le-tata: Torah, Community and Family

Jews are commanded to study and to develop their minds and intellects. How much time should a person devote to study in view of his need to make a living? On Shabbat, we not only refrain from working, but we also study Torah. This is a reflection of *Shabbat le-tata*.

Another dimension of Shabbat is community. God told Moshe to assemble the people on Shabbat and preach to them, and said that this

---

12 Genesis 2:3.
13 Maimonides, *Mishneh Torah,* Hilchot Shabbat 30:3.

would be a model for future generations. Being together with others renews the individual's personality. On Shabbat, we are released from the monotony, jealousy and rancor that are often a part of mundane pursuits. Even though God cursed Adam on that mysterious Friday when he ate the fruit from the forbidden tree, he gave him respite from the curse on the following day – Shabbat.

Endless work estranges people from their families. The Torah commands that the family rest together. Ties between parents and children are renewed on Shabbat. All members of the family are released from the curse of competition and alienation from their neighbors. The Talmud tells us of the Sambatyon River, which is so turbulent and dangerous during the week that no one can cross it, but becomes calm every Shabbat.[14]

༯ Shabbat Le-ela: Release from the Curse of Mortality

For all its many blessings, Shabbat does not release us from death. The animal soul of a human being dies, but his higher soul, his *neshama,* does not. This is *Shabbat le-ela,* which, according to the Zohar, is not only blessed but also sanctified. All evil forces depart, and a shelter of rest and peace descends from heaven and rests on earth.

In the Friday night prayers, we ask God to spread his *sukkat shalom,* his shelter of peace, over us. Adam's sin drove a wedge between God and humanity, but on the Sabbath, God appears to us and we are reconciled with him, and all evil departs. When this occurs, then the world will be free of suffering. In such a world, there will be no place for death. This is the eschatological Shabbat of which the prophet says, ביום ההוא יהיה ה' אחד ושמו אחד – On that day Hashem will be One and His Name will be One.[15] This is the meaning of the phrase *shabbetotai tishmoru,* which the Bedouin in the Zohar interpreted.

---

14 BT *Sanhedrin* 65b.
15 Zechariah 14:9.

✑ The Duality of Honoring Parents

The same duality applies to the *mitzvah of kibbud av va-em* (honoring one's father and mother). Again, there is a double connotation. There is the *kibbud av va-em le-ela* and *kibbud av va-em le-tata*. The commandment to honor one's parents falls into the category of both *mishpatim* and *hukim*. As we remember, *mishpatim* are those commandments which the human mind itself would have understood even if God had not commanded them.

Why does *kibbud av va-em* fit into this category? It is founded upon the ideas of reciprocity and gratitude, since parents make many sacrifices for their children. Parents' love for their children is indescribably profound, all-encompassing and expects nothing in return. If their grown children have any sense of responsibility, they will treat their elderly parents with love. This is a matter of simple *menschlichkeit,* as well as *middah ke-neged middah* – measure for measure. We must show our parents the same boundless devotion that they showed us when we were children. This is *kibbud av va-em le-tata.*

What, then, is *kibbud av va-em le-ela*? Here, the commandment is worded not in the language of *kibbud* – honor – but of *yira* – reverence.[16] The Hebrew word for fear is *pahad.* The word *yira* is the same word that is used regarding God. As we treat God, so shall we treat our parents. The Talmud tells us of one of our sages, Rabbi Yosef, that whenever his mother approached and he heard her footsteps, he would rise from his seat with reverence.[17] The Torah teaches that the penalty for blaspheming God[18] or cursing one's parents[19] is death. Why are there so many

---

16 Leviticus 19:3.
17 BT *Kiddushin* 31b.
18 Leviticus 24:16.
19 Exodus 21:17.

parallels between how we must relate to God and how we must treat our parents?

The reason is that according to our tradition, we see God's reflection in our fathers and that of the *Shechinah* – the Divine Presence – in our mothers. Our fathers never enter a room alone. God always accompanies them. Likewise, the *Shechinah* accompanies our mothers wherever they go. We rise for them as we would rise for God. Raising a hand against one's father or mother is tantamount to raising a hand against God. The key to this analogy lies in the transmission of tradition. Just as Moshe Rabbenu received the Torah at Mount Sinai and transmitted it to subsequent generations, our parents pass the tradition from one generation to another. Parents are the link between the past and the future. Thus, they are representatives of God and deserve our reverence. This is how we may understand the connection between *kibbud av va-em* and Shabbat on two levels, *le-ela and le-tata,* above and below.

⚜ אמר ⚜

Emor: The Essence of Yom Kippur

וידבר ה' אל משה לאמר: אך בעשור לחדש השביעי הזה יום הכפרים הוא מקרא
קדש יהיה לכם ועניתם את נפשתיכם והקרבתם אשה ל ה': וכל מלאכה לא תעשו
בעצם היום הזה כי יום כפרים הוא לכפר עליכם לפני ה' א־להיכם.

God spoke to Moshe saying: But the tenth day of this month
is the Day of Atonement. You shall hold a holy convocation
and you shall afflict yourselves. You shall offer a fire-offering
to the Lord. You shall do no work on this day, for it is the
Day of Atonement to grant you atonement before the Lord
your God.[1]

WHY IS THE Day of Atonement termed *Yom ha-Kippurim*
instead of, for example, *Yom ha-Kapparah* or *Yom ha-Kapparot*? Had it been termed Yom ha-Kapparah, it would
have had a double connotation, since the word *kapparah* has two main
meanings. It can denote an actual sacrifice such as an *asham* or a *hatat*
offered by the individual sinner or by a community, and it also refers
to atonement or pardon. The verb *kaper* connotes erasing or blotting
out the sin. In this context, it relates to a divine act of forgiveness, as we
recite during the Yom Kippur service: ועל כולם א־לוה סליחות סלח לנו מחל לנו

---

1 Leviticus 23:26–28.

כפר לנו – "For all these, O God of forgiveness, forgive us, pardon us, atone for us."[2] Had the day been called Yom Kapparah, then its sacred nature would have expressed itself either in the offering of many sacrifices or in a divine act of pardon and erasure of our sins. However, the emphasis on sacrifices is certainly incorrect. The Torah never associates the holiday of Sukkot, which contains more sacrifices than Yom ha-Kippurim does, with atonement. The power of Yom Kippur transcends the sacrifices that were offered on it. We see that its greatness and sanctity remain intact even though no sacrifices have been offered for the last nineteen hundred years.

✥ The Message of Rabbi Akiva

On Yom Kippur we describe the Temple service that took place on that day, and remember it with more longing than we do even on Tisha be-Av. However, we also recall the message of Rabbi Akiva, who said, אמר רבי עקיבא אשריכם ישראל לפני מי אתם מטהרין מי מטהר אתכם אביכם שבשמים – "Rabbi Akiva said: Fortunate are you, O Israel! Before whom do you cleanse yourselves? Who makes you pure? Your Father in Heaven!"[3] Rabbi Akiva was speaking to the survivors of the destruction of the Temple, who could not imagine the process of *teshuvah* without the *Beit ha-Mikdash*. Rabbi Akiva told them: Although we have lost the sacred stones of our Temple, we have not lost our Father in Heaven. Even if we are now slaves who witnessed the deaths of thousands of our people, including our loved ones and our scholars, God remains with us. It is not the High Priest, but God, who removes sin, pardons and grants atonement.

---

2 From the Yom Kippur liturgy.
3 BT *Yoma* 85b.

The Centrality of Teshuvah

The second conclusion that we might draw from the name Yom Kapparah, which emphasizes God's wiping away our sins, does no justice to the essence of this day either. The Rambam writes[4] that while the Temple stood, the sacred service that took place there on Yom Kippur expiated our sins. Now that there is no longer an altar of atonement, it is Yom Kippur itself, together with *teshuvah,* that effects atonement. The most important requirement for atonement is to stand before God in sincerity. Therefore, the term Yom Kapparah would be misleading because it does not include the element of *teshuvah.*

Teshuvah as the *Mitzvah* of the Day

Jewish tradition does not define the festivals as much by when they fall on the calendar as it does by the *mitzvot* that they involve. Passover is termed *hag ha-matzot* rather than *hag yetziat Mitzrayim* (The Holiday celebrating the Exodus from Egypt). *Shavuot* is *zeman matan Toratenu,* the time when the Torah was given to us. Rosh ha-Shannah is *Yom Teruah,* the day that the shofar is sounded. The fact that it is also a *yom ha-din,* a day of judgment, refers to God's role rather than ours. Similarly, on Yom Kippur, kapparah is the divine result, but the *mitzvat ha-yom* is *teshuvah.*

Our sages taught that when the Temple altar still stood, it atoned for sins. Our dining tables now fill that role.[5] While *kapparah* is pure atonement, it involves and even demands a great deal of effort and perseverance. When Jacob sent gifts to Esau, the Torah tells us: כי אמר אכפרה פניו – "He said, 'I will appease him.'"[6] Could Esau grant atonement? Of

---

4 *Mishneh Torah,* Hilchot Teshuvah 1:3.
5 BT *Hagigah* 27a.
6 Genesis 32:21.

course he could not. It was the effort that Jacob expended that was so important. *Kapparah* is what God does. *Kippur* refers to our own effort, our introspection and contrition. While it is true that atonement is ultimately a divine act of *hesed,* it still requires *teshuvah.* Without *teshuvah,* there can be no divine response. Rav Menahem Mendel of Kotzk said that if Yom Kippur is preceded by *teshuvah,* it becomes the sweetest day of the year, full of splendor and beauty. The phrase *"mizbeah mechaper"* means that the altar was the way to receive *kapparah* when the Temple stood. Today, our dining tables make atonement for us. The word *kippur,* however, is the *pe'eil,* or causative, form and requires supreme effort on our part.

The more profound our experience of Yom Kippur, the stronger the forgiveness that we receive. ותתן לנו ה' א-להינו באהבה את יום הכפרים הזה קץ ומחילה וסליחה על כל עוונותינו – "You have given us, O Lord our God, with love, this Day of Atonement as a deadline, pardon and forgiveness for all our iniquities."[7] Our liturgy refers to the day as Yom ha-Kippurim rather than as Yom ha-Kapparah in order to distinguish between the two terms. If we make proper use of the ten days between Rosh ha-Shannah and Yom Kippur by doing *teshuvah,* then we will be privileged to receive *mehilah, selihah* and *kapparah.*

✺ The Multiple Paths of Teshuvah

Why does the Torah refers to the day in the plural, as Yom ha-Kippurim? The answer is that one may do *teshuvah* in many ways, and God accepts all of them. *Teshuvah* may be sincere, turbulent, or exultant. Whether it is *teshuvah me-ahavah* – repentance motivated by love – or *teshuvah mi-yirah* – repentance motivated by fear – God in His mercy accepts it.[8]

The plural phrase Yom ha-Kippurim reflects the diverse world of *teshuvah* whether it arises from reflection, joy or sadness. The Rav said

---

7   From the Yom Kippur Neilah service.
8   BT *Yoma* 86b.

that in Germany, the *viddui* was sung as a triumphant, joyous march, while in Lithuania, congregations wept as they recited it.

Yom Kippur itself is a dialectical experience. On the one hand, it is a festival. The *geonim* said that it was a *mitzvah* to be joyful on Yom Kippur.[9] On the other hand, it is a solemn day of supplication, a genuine communal fast day that includes the recitation of *Avinu Malkeinu.* On Yom Kippur, we chant festive prayers such as *Ha-aderet ve-ha-emunah,* just as we do on the purely joyous festival days of Shemini Atzeret and Simhat Torah.

Our sages struggled over this issue, asking whether we should give preference to Yom Kippur's characteristics as a festival day or as a solemn communal fast day. When the Rambam speaks of *vidui,* he always uses the expression "*lifnei ha-Shem,*" which emphasizes its element of joy. According to Chabad philosophy, Rosh ha-Shannah is a day of awe and dread, while Yom Kippur is a day of joy. On Yom Kippur, we celebrate the fact that every single one of us has access to God if we desire it.

৵ Seeking *Mehilah* from God

ותתן לנו ה' א־להינו באהבה את יום הכפורים הזה למחילה ולסליחה ולכפרה ולמחל בו את כל עונותינו.

You have given us, O Lord our God, with love, this Day of Atonement for pardon, forgiveness, and atonement and to pardon all our iniquities.[10]

Of the three terms, *mehilah* – a human term that describes human action – is the most easily translated into everyday language. *Selihah* and *kapparah* are theological notions. Only God can absolve us of sin through *selihah* and wipe away our sin through *kapparah.* Human beings

---

9   See Radak on Hoshea 2:13 in the name of Rav Saadya Gaon. See also the *Sheiltot de-Rav Ahai Gaon,* no. 15.

10 From the Yom Kippur Mussaf service.

do not have this power. On the other hand, *mehilah* is a human concept with a twofold connotation. It is a legal act of renouncing the right to collect a debt, and on an emotional level, it is related to a perception of pain. To ask for and receive *mehilah* says, in effect, that we no longer feel humiliated and that we have forgotten the transgression, whatever it may have been. According to the laws that govern interactions between human beings, to cause someone pain or offend his or her dignity is worse than theft. Therefore, it makes sense for us to seek *mehilah* from those whom we may have offended. But how can we seek *mehilah* from God?

⌇ Our Friendship with God

Human beings are in contact with God on two levels. On Rosh ha-Shannah, we approach God as an Omnipotent Creator. Our relationship to Him is one of *im ka-avadim* – as servants. On Yom ha-Kippurim, our relationship to God takes on additional dimension, one of intimate friendship. God is both the father and mother of *Knesset Yisrael.* Our transgressions not only undermine God's authority, but they also harm our friendship with him.

Judaism sees the impact of sin on two levels. First, it is personal and social. Sin defiles the human personality and expresses itself in *tumah.* Moreover, it causes pain to God and damages the connection between human beings and God.

The purpose of *mehilah* is to repair the friendship. *Selihah* and *kapparah* have to do with repairing the metaphysical impact of sin. Yom Kippur is a day of reconciliation between human beings, and between human beings and God.

The liturgy that we recite after the recounting of the Yom Kippur service in the Temple captures this dual function:

אבל עונות אבותינו החריבו נוה, וחטאותינו האריכו קצו. אבל זכרון דברים תהא
סליחתנו, ועֵנוי נפשינו תהא כפרתנו. על כן ברחמיך הרבים נתת לנו את יום צום

261

הכפרים הזה, ואת יום מחילת העוון הזה, לסליחת עוון ולכפרת פשע. יום אסור
באכילה, יום אסור בשתיה, יום אסור ברחיצה, יום אסור בסיכה, יום אסור
בתשמיש המטה, יום אסור בנעילת הסנדל. יום שימת אהבה ורעות, יום עזיבת
קנאה ותחרות, יום שתמחל לכל עוונותינו.

But our ancestors' iniquities destroyed the Temple and our
own sins have delayed the final redemption. However, the
remembrance of these things shall constitute our pardon and
our self-affliction shall be our atonement. Therefore, in your
abundant mercy, you have given us this fast day of atonement
and this day of pardon of transgression, for forgiveness of
iniquity and atonement of willful sin – a day when eating
is forbidden, a day when drinking is forbidden, a day when
washing is forbidden, a day when applying oil is forbidden, a
day when marital relations are forbidden, a day when wearing
leather footgear is forbidden, a day of implanting love and
friendship, a day of forsaking jealousy and competition, a day
when you will pardon all our iniquities.[11]

The *Shulhan Aruch* accepts the viewpoint that on *Yom Kippur eve,*
one must apologize even for a minor insult because Yom Kippur is a day
for promoting love, friendship and peace, and eliminating envy.[12] We
behave the same way toward God, working to repair our relationship
with our treasured friend.[13]

---

11 From the Yom Kippur Mussaf service.
12 Shulhan Aruch, Orah Hayyim, 606:1.
13 See Parashat Nitzavim: Two Levels of Mehilah.

Behar: Ish El Ahuzato: Eretz Yisrael as a Living Heritage

THE RAV ANALYZED the order of presentation of themes related to *Eretz Yisrael* in Parashat Behar:

֍ Restoring the Land to Its Original Owner

At the beginning of Parashat Behar, the Torah introduces the laws of *shemittah* and *yovel*.

וידבר ה' אל משה בהר סיני לאמר: דבר אל בני ישראל ואמרת אלהם כי תבאו אל הארץ אשר אני נתן לכם ושבתה הארץ שבת לה'... וספרת לך שבע שבתת שנים שבע שנים שבע פעמים והיו לך ימי שבע שבתת השנים תשע וארבעים שנה... וקדשתם את שנת החמשים שנה וקראתם דרור בארץ לכל ישביה יובל הוא תהיה לכם ושבתם איש אל אחזתו ואיש אל משפחתו תשבו... בשנת היובל הזאת תשבו איש אל אחזתו.

The Lord spoke to Moshe on Mount Sinai, saying: Speak to the children of Israel and say to them: When you come into the land that I give you, the land shall observe a Sabbath rest for the Lord ... You shall count for yourself seven cycles of sabbatical years seven years seven times; the years of the seven cycles of sabbatical years shall be for you forty-nine years

... You shall sanctify the fiftieth year and proclaim freedom throughout the land for all its inhabitants. It shall be the Jubilee year for you. You shall return each man to his ancestral village and you shall return each man to his family ... In this Jubilee year, you shall return each man to his ancestral heritage.[1]

Rashi interprets the phrase תשבו איש אל אחזתו as referring to the fields that were sold, but must now revert to their original owners.[2] The text then becomes somewhat puzzling, for the Torah might have formulated it: ישובו אחזתו אל האיש – that the ancestral heritage should be returned to each man.[3] Why is the language reversed?

✂ A. The Law of *Onaah*

Afterward, the Torah sets forth two categories of *onaah: onaat mammon* (monetary deception) and *onaat devarim* (verbal harassment). The Ramban understands the verse וכי תמכרו ממכר לעמיתך או קנה מיד עמיתך אל תונו איש את אחיו – "When you sell an item to your fellow or purchase something from your fellow, do not aggrieve one another,"[4] as referring to *onaat mammon*. The Ramban understands the subsequent verse, במספר שנים אחר היובל תקנה מאת עמיתך במספר שני תבואת ימכר לך – "According to the number of years after the Jubilee year shall you buy from your fellow; according to the number of crop-years shall he sell to you,"[5] as referring to financial victimization in the context of real estate. The Ramban cites the sages' ruling that there is no law of *onaah* regarding real estate or property.

---

1 Leviticus 25:1–13.
2 Rashi, Leviticus 25:13.
3 See Siftei Hachamim, Leviticus 25:10.
4 Leviticus 25:14.
5 Leviticus 25:15.

B. Concern and Reassurance Regarding *Shemittah*

Subsequently, the Torah states:

> ונתנה הארץ פריה ואכלתם לשבע וישבתם לבטח עליה: וכי תאמרו מה נאכל
> בשנה השביעת הן לא נזרע ולא נאסף את תבואתנו: וצויתי את ברכתי לכם בשנה
> הששית ועשת את התבואה לשלש השנים.

> The land will give its fruit and you will eat your fill; you will
> dwell securely upon it. If you will say: "What will we eat in
> the seventh year? Behold! We will not sow and not gather in
> our crops?" I will ordain my blessing for you in the sixth year
> and it will yield a crop sufficient for the three years.[6]

C. The Land Shall Not Be Sold in Perpetuity

The Torah then continues: והארץ לא תמכר לצמיתת כי לי הארץ כי גרים ותושבים
אתם עמדי – "The land shall not be sold in perpetuity, for the land is mine.
You are sojourners and residents with me."[7] The location of this last
verse is puzzling because it actually belongs near verse 13, בשנת היובל הזאת
תשבו איש אל אחזתו "In this Jubilee Year you shall return each man to his
ancestral heritage," which is supported by the prohibition of not selling
the land in perpetuity. Why was this verse placed at the end?

Parallels to Parashat Aharei Mot

We may understand these passages in light of verses found at the end
of Parashat Aharei Mot. There, the Torah introduces the frightening
spectre of exile. The Torah warns us to be particularly careful regarding
our behavior in the Land of Israel. The Ramban emphasizes the fact that

---

6 Leviticus 25:19–21.
7 Leviticus 25:23.

Eretz Yisrael cannot abide transgressors, particularly in the three cardinal areas of sexual immorality, idolatry and murder.[8] The Torah says:

ותטמא הארץ ואפקד עונה עליה ותקא הארץ את ישביה... ולא תקיא הארץ
אתכם בטמאכם אתה כאשר קאה את הגוי אשר לפניכם.

The land became impure and I recalled its iniquity upon it, and the land spewed forth its inhabitants . . . Let not the land spew you forth for having made it impure, as it spewed out the nation that preceded you.[9]

✺ The Sensitivity of Eretz Yisrael

Rashi compares Eretz Yisrael to a prince with a delicate constitution who needs a specific dietary regimen.[10] Furthermore, the Torah in Parashat Behukotai reiterates the punishment of exile for not observing the laws of *shemittah*. כל ימי השמה תשבת את אשר לא שבתה בשבתתיכם בשבתכם עליה – "All the days of its being desolate it will rest for the period that it did not rest during your sabbatical years when you dwelled upon it."[11] In the preceding verse, the Torah says: אז תרצה הארץ את שבתתיה כל ימי השמה ואתם בארץ איביכם אז תשבת הארץ והרצת את שבתתיה – "Then the land will be appeased for its sabbaticals during all the years of its desolation while you are in the land of your foes. Then the land will rest and it will appease for its sabbaticals."[12]

✺ Eretz Yisrael as a Living, Almost Human Entity

Is it only the Land of Israel that cannot abide transgressions, while other countries are capable of bearing them? How shall we understand the Land

---

8 Ramban, Leviticus 18:25.
9 Leviticus 18:25–28.
10 Rashi on Leviticus 18:28.
11 Leviticus 26:35.
12 Leviticus 26:34.

of Israel's special sensitivity to sin? The Torah speaks of a land "defiled" and of a land "resting" and "observing its sabbatical years." The Land of Israel possesses a distinct personality. It is likened to a human being who can be defiled, can be sanctified, can rest and can be appeased. Just as a Jew observes the Sabbath once a week, the Land of Israel observes the Sabbath once every seven years. In this way, the Land of Israel takes on human dimensions. Kabbalistically, the Land of Israel embodies the *sefirot,* or attributes, of *malchut* and *shechinah.*

Therefore, when Jews abstain from cultivating the land every seventh year and the Torah mentions our question as to how we will survive economically, the Land of Israel itself provides the answer. It will increase its yield by providing three years' worth of harvest in one. In other words, the land itself will respond to the need of the Jewish people and extend itself to help us. This emphasizes the almost human quality of the land.

✣ The Nature of Reward and Punishment

The Rambam in chapter nine of *Hilchot Teshuvah* queries as to the nature of reward and punishment in the Torah. If we obey the Torah's commandments, we will be rewarded, and if we do not, then we will be punished. The Torah seems to define reward and punishment in physical terms: economic prosperity or famine, peace or war, kingship or subjugation, dwelling at home in the Land of Israel or, God forbid, in exile. On the surface, the emphasis on physical conditions seems to overlook the deeper spiritual attainments symbolized by *olam ha-ba,* the World to Come.

The Rambam explains that if we obey the Torah's commandments, God will bless us with the ability to acquire the World to Come in ease and comfort. However, if we are sinful, he will send us obstacles such as sickness, war or famine that will impede our ability to acquire the World to Come. The Land of Israel is an integral part of this system of reward and punishment. If we follow God's ways, then Eretz Yisrael will be fruitful and prosperous. If we do not, then the land will become an obstacle, economically and otherwise. The Torah supports this by describing Eretz Yisrael in living terms as a land that will "rest" or be "very productive."

❧ The Sequence in our Parashah

The sequence of the Torah can be understood in light of the above. In Parashat Aharei Mot, the Torah describes a land filled with sanctity that cannot abide transgression and that assists those who are sensitive to its sanctity.[13] Parashat Behar expands on this theme in the discussion of the *mitzvot* of *shemitta* and *yovel.* Eretz Israel is under God's direct providence. ארץ אשר ה' א־להיך דרש אתה תמיד דרש עיני ה' א־להיך בה מרשית השנה ועד אחרית שנה – "A land that the Lord your God seeks out. The eyes of the Lord your God are always upon it from the beginning of the year to the year's end."[14] Since Eretz Yisrael is under God's direct ownership, it cannot be sold in perpetuity.

Thus, when we express concern about the ability to observe *shemittah,* the Torah reminds us that Eretz Yisrael is not an ordinary land. It will respond to the needs of the Jewish people just as a caring individual responds to the needs of a loved one. Eretz Yisrael has a vibrant, vital personality that distinguishes it from all other lands.

❧ A Prohibition both Personal (*Gavra*) and Material (*Heftza*)

The Torah introduces the principle of not selling land in perpetuity in two different contexts. The first is at the beginning of the parashah, with the phrase תשבו איש אל אחזתו – Each man shall return to his ancestral heritage (which, according to Rashi, refers to the restoration of land that had been sold by its original owner). The second is והארץ לא תמכר לצמיתות – the prohibition of selling land in perpetuity. Why? This is because

---

13 Leviticus 18:28, 26.
14 Deuteronomy 11:12.

the prohibition of not selling the land in perpetuity contains a double aspect. First, it devolves upon the seller or the buyer, or both, never to sell the land in perpetuity. This constitutes a *hovat gavra,* a duty that a person must fulfill. Second, the prohibition also applies to the Land of Israel itself. It constitutes a prohibition on the *heftza* of Eretz Yisrael being sold. This is also why the Torah used the language in the initial passage, "Each man shall return to his ancestral heritage," rather than vice versa. This is meant to emphasize that the restoration is far more than a financial-legal process. Jews may not act in a manner that implies the slightest contempt for the Land of Israel. He may not discard it in any way, and must return to his ancestral heritage. By religious obligation, he must return to and bond with his land.

After this, the Torah describes the human, personal characteristics of the Land of Israel. It then sets forth the prohibition that the land may never be sold in perpetuity because of its human sensibilities. One may never show disrespect to the Land of Israel by selling it in perpetuity.

בחוקתי

Behukotai: The Distinctions
between the Two Tochahot

THERE ARE SEVERAL distinctions between the *tochaha* in Parashat Behukotai and the *tochaha* of Parashat Ki Tavo in Devarim. We can readily understand the rationale for these distinctions, and we will see that many of them are interdependent.

1. Shavuot vs. Rosh ha-Shannah

Ezra decreed that the blessings and curses of Behukotai must be read before Shavuot, and those of the Mishnah Torah (Sefer Devarim) before Rosh ha-Shannah.[1] There are two different sets of *tochahot*, one at the conclusion of Sefer Vayikra and one towards the end of Sefer Devarim in Parashat Ki Tavo. An examination of the Rambam's exposition regarding this matter reveals that there are two other readings that fit into this general set of laws. One is in Parashat Tzav, which is read before Pesah, and the other occurs in Parashat Vaethanan, which is read after Tisha be-Av. In *Hilchot Tefillah,* the Rambam writes as follows:

---

1 BT *Megillah* 31b.

עזרא תקן להם לישראל שיהו קורין קללות שבספר ויקרא קודם עצרת ושבמשנה
תורה קודם ראש השנה והמנהג הפשוט שיהו קוראין במדבר סיני קודם עצרת
ואתחנן אחר תשעה באב. אתם נצבים קודם ראש השנה צו את אהרן קודם פסח
בשנה פשוטה.

Ezra decreed that the Jewish people must read the imprecations of Sefer Vayikra before Atzeret [Shavuot] and the imprecations of Mishnah Torah [Sefer Devarim] before Rosh ha-Shannah. The basic custom is to read *Be-midbar Sinai* before Atzeret and Vaethanan after Tisha be-Av, *Atem nitzavim* before Rosh ha-Shannah, and *Tzav et Aharon* before Pesah in a regular year.[2]

The Rambam combined Ezra's two decrees concerning the *tochahot* before Shavuot and Rosh ha-Shannah with the readings of Va-ethanan and Tzav after Tisha be-Av and before Pesah.

The sequence is that the *parshiyot* preceding a Yom Tov should reflect the theme of that Yom Tov. The link between Parashat Tzav and Pesah is the topic of *hagalat kelim,* a major theme of Pesah. (A discussion of the laws of *merikah* and *shetifah* may be found in Parashat Tzav.) Before Pesah, Shavuot and Rosh ha-Shannah, we announce the approaching festival. These thematically-related *parshiyot* usually precede the special day. However, we read Tisha be-Av's special *parashah,* Vaethanan, after the day itself. This is due to the Talmudic rule that states: אקדומי פורענות לא מקדמי – "We try to defer imminent catastrophe."[3] Even though Parashat Vaethanan contains words of consolation intended to strengthen and comfort the Jewish people after Tisha be-Av, it would go against this ruling to introduce the theme of Tisha be-Av before the day itself.

---

2 *Mishneh Torah,* Hilchot Tefillah, 13:2.
3 BT *Megillah* 5a.

৵ 2. The Written Law and the Oral Law

The blessings and curses of Parashat Behukotai are an expression of our acceptance of the yoke of the commandments before *Matan Torah,* since both the blessing and the curse are coterminous with an oath. Shavuot represents the divine meeting when we received the Torah and made a covenant with God. Some contend that one should even learn Masechet Shavuot between Pesah and Shavuot in order to prepare for *Matan Torah.*[4]

In contrast to Behukotai are the blessings and curses of Sefer Devarim, which are read before Rosh ha-Shannah. This symbolizes our prayer that the curses of the old year end and the blessings of the new year begin.[5] The blessings and curses at the end of Devarim that we recite before Rosh ha-Shannah precede Yom Kippur which, according to the Beit ha-Levi, was an acceptance of the Oral Torah. In Tractate *Gittin,* Rav Yohanan tells us that God sealed a covenant with the Jewish people over the Oral Law.[6] This covenant was formulated in Ki Tavo–Nitzavim. In contrast, the blessings and curses in Behukotai, which relate to the acceptance of the Written Torah, are read before Shavuot.

৵ 3. Moshe's Role in the Written Law vs. the Oral Law

Rav Soloveitchik noted a distinction between Moshe's role as the receiver of the Torah, in which he served as a scribe taking dictation from God, and as a *shaliah le-holacha,* where he gave the Torah to the Jewish people. The Rav said that this was similar to the verse in Jeremiah:

ויאמר להם ברוך מפיו יקרא אלי את כל הדברים האלה ואני כתב על הספר בדיו.

---

4   Minhagei Hatam Sofer.
5   BT *Megillah* 31b.
6   BT *Gittin* 60b.

Baruch replied to them from his own mouth that he would dictate all these words to me and I would write on the book with the ink.[7]

However, Moshe's role was different regarding the Oral Law, which was was engraved on Moshe's heart, so to speak, and sanctified him. The rays of light that illumined his face reflected this sanctity, which he acquired only after he received the second set of tablets in Ki Tisa. Therefore, Ezra decreed that before Rosh ha-Shannah and Yom Kippur, we must read the blessings and curses of Ki Tavo, which are relevant to the Oral Law.

ᴈ 4. Interrupting the Curses

The Gemara in Tractate *Megillah*[8] in which the *Mishnah* rules that one may not interrupt the reading of the curses and that they must be read in their entirety by one person is qualified by Abaye[9] as applying only to the curses of Vayikra (Behukotai) and that one may interrupt the curses in Sefer Devarim.

אמר אביי לא שנו אלא בקללות שבתורת כהנים אבל קללות שבמשנה תורה פוסק מאי טעמא הללו בלשון רבים אמורות ומשה מפי הגבורה אמרן והללו בלשון יחיד אמורות ומשה מפי עצמו אמרן.

Abaye said: This rule was taught only regarding the curses found in the Book of Leviticus but regarding the curses found in the Book of Deuteronomy, one may interrupt.

What is the reason for this difference?

The Gemara explains that the curses of Vayikra were uttered in the plural and Moshe recited them in God's name, while those in Devarim

---

7 Jeremiah 36:18.
8 BT *Megillah* 31a.
9 BT *Megillah* 31b.

were uttered in the singular and *Moshe* recited them on his own. Why should this make any difference with regard to interruption?

Rashi explains that in Vayikra, *Moshe* acted as God's emissary, saying: God said this to me, and the formulation is: "I will give . . . I will send the one who has the ability to act." But in Sefer Devarim, Moshe uttered it by himself . . . Tosafot immediately comments that it means that Moshe uttered them with *ruah ha-kodesh*.

From the Gemara and Rashi, it is clear that the grammatical form in Sefer Devarim is the third person, while in Behukotai it is the first person, where God addresses himself directly to the Jewish people. What was Moshe's role in Behukotai? He was a part of the Jewish people, who were under oath. In Parashat Ki Tavo, Moshe is the one who, together with God, administers the oath.

Behukotai relates to the Written Law, and Moshe, together with the rest of the Jewish people, are under its strictures. Here, he was simply a messenger. In Sefer Devarim, he operated as *rabban shel Yisrael,* for without Moshe there is no Oral Law. In summary, in Torat Kohanim (Sefer Vayikra), in which God reads the *tochaha,* there may be no interruption. In Sefer Devarim, where Moshe, so to speak, is the *baal kore,* interruptions are allowed. The proof to this can be adduced from the terminology of the text in Parashat Ki Tavo. The Torah says:

אלה דברי הברית אשר צוה ה' את משה לכרת את בני ישראל בארץ מואב מלבד הברית אשר כרת אתם בחרב.

These are the words of the covenant that God commanded Moshe to seal with the Children of Israel in the land of Moab in addition to the covenant that he sealed with them at Horeb.[10]

In Horeb, or Mount Sinai, God was the *baal kore,* so to speak, and in Sefer Devarim, it was Moshe who sealed the covenant.

---

10 Deuteronomy 28:69.

৵ 5. The Inclusion of Consolation

The Rav noted still another difference between Behukotai and Ki Tavo.
The sages ruled that harsh words of rebuke must be accompanied by
words of consolation. We find such words at the end of Behukotai.

וזכרתי את בריתי יעקוב ואף את בריתי יצחק ואף את בריתי אברהם אזכר והארץ
אזכר.

I will remember my covenant with Jacob and also my
covenant with Isaac and also my covenant with Abraham will
I remember and I will remember the land.[11]

Yet in Ki Tavo, at the end of the *tochaha,* we encounter no words of
consolation. Instead, we read:

והשיבך ה' מצרים באניות בדרך אשר אמרתי לך לא תסיף עוד לראתה והתמכרתם
שם לאיביך לעבדים ולשפחות ואין קנה.

God will return you to Egypt in ships on the way that I said
that you would never see again. There you will offer yourselves
for sale to your enemies as male and female slaves, but no one
will want to buy you.[12]

Where are the words of consolation?

The answer may be found in Parashat Netzavim, which contains
words of consolation:

והיה כי יבאו עליך כל הדברים האלה הברכה והקללה אשר נתתי לפניך והשבת
אל לבבך בכל הגוים אשר הדיחך ה' א-להיך שמה: ושבת עד ה' א-להיך ושמעת
בקלו ככל אשר אנכי מצוך היום אתה ובניך בכל לבבך ובכל נפשך.

It will be that when all these things come upon you, the

---

11 Leviticus 26:42.
12 Deuteronomy 28:68.

blessing and the curse that I have presented before you, then you will take it to your heart among all the nations where the Lord your God has dispersed you. And you will return to the Lord your God and listen to his voice according to everything that I command you today, you and your children, with all your heart and all your soul.[13]

ꝏ 6. The First and Second Temples

The difference can be explained based on the Ramban, who wrote that the first *tochaha* of *Behukotai* relates to the First Temple and the second *tochaha* of Ki Tavo relates to the Second Temple.[14] In the First Temple, God said that after seventy years, we would be redeemed and return to Eretz Yisrael. He would remember the covenant that he made with the patriarchs, and our return would not depend upon *teshuvah*. Therefore, Behukotai concludes with *nehama (consolation)*. However, after the destruction of the Second Temple, no time frame was given for redemption. The Rambam wrote that the Jewish people would only be redeemed by means of *teshuvah*.

כל הנביאים כולן צוו על התשובה ואין ישראל נגאלין אלא בתשובה, וכבר הבטיחה תורה שסוף ישראל לעשות תשובה בסוף גלותן ומיד הן נגאלין שנאמר והיה כי יבאו עליך כל הדברים וגו' ושבת עד ה' א־להיך ושב ה' א־להיך וגו'.

All the prophets commanded concerning *teshuvah,* and the Jewish people will only be redeemed by means of *teshuvah.* The Torah has already promised that ultimately, the Jewish people will do *teshuvah* at the end of their exile and be redeemed immediately, as it is written: "When these things

---

13 Deuteronomy 30:1–2.
14 Ramban on Leviticus 26:16.

come upon you ... and you return to your God, God will return ..."[15]

For this reason, there could be no consolation in Ki Tavo, since in Parashat Nitzavim, we have the *parashah* of *teshuvah,* and this redemption is dependent exclusively upon our doing *teshuvah.*

---

15 *Mishneh Torah,* Hilchot Teshuvah 7:5.

❧ Sefer Bamidbar

❧ במדבר ❧

Bamdibar I

PARASHAT BAMIDBAR OPENS with God's command to Moshe to take a census of all the tribes of the Jewish people.

וידבר ה' אל משה במדבר סיני באהל מועד באחד לחדש השני בשנה השנית לצאתם מארץ מצרים לאמר: שאו את ראש כל עדת בני ישראל למשפחתם לבית אבתם במספר שמות כל זכר לגלגלתם: מבן עשרים שנה ומעלה כל יצא צבא בישראל תפקדו אתם לצבאתם אתה ואהרן.

The Lord spoke to Moshe in the wilderness of Sinai, in the Tent of Meeting, on the first of the second month, in the second year after their exodus from the land of Egypt, saying: "Take a census of the entire assembly of the Israelites according to their families, according to their father's household, by number of the names, every male according to their head count. From twenty years of age and up, everyone who goes out to the army in Israel, you shall count them according to their legions, you and Aharon."[1]

Rashi notes:

---

1   Numbers 1:1–3.

מתוך חיבתן לפניו מונה אותם כל שעה. כשיצאו ממצרים מנאן, וכשנפלו בעגל מנאן לידע מנין הנותרים. כשבא להשרות שכינתו עליהן מנאם. באחד בניסן הוקם המשכן ובאחד באייר מנאם.

Because of [Israel's] dearness before Him, He counts them at all times. When they left Egypt, He counted them, and when they fell at the sin of the Golden Calf, He counted them in order to know how many remained. When He wanted to rest his *Shechinah* upon them, He counted them. On the first day of the month of Nisan, the Tabernacle was erected and on the first day of Iyyar, He counted them.[2]

The Ramban asks:

לא הבינותי טעם המצוה הזאת למה צוה בה הקב"ה, כי היה צורך שיתיחסו לשבטיהם בעבור הדגלים, אבל ידיעת המספר לא ידעתי למה צוה שידעו אותו.

I do not understand the reason for this mitzvah. Why did God demand this count? There was a need that they should be counted by tribes for the purpose of [encamping according to] the divisions; but I do not know why God commanded that the total number be known.[3]

The Ramban answers this question:

אולי להודיעם חסדו עליהם כי בשבעים נפש ירדו אבותיהם מצרימה ועתה הם כחול הים, כך וכך בני עשרים. ואחרי כל דבר ומגפה ימנם, להודיע כי הוא משגיא לגויים ימחץ וידיו תרפינה. וזהו שאמרו רבותינו מרוב חבתם מונה אותם כל שעה. ועוד כי הבא לפני אב הנביאים ואחיו קדוש ה' והוא נודע אליהם בשמו יהיה לו בדבר הזה זכות וחיים, כי בא בסוד העם ובכתב בני ישראל וזכות הרבים במספרם, וכן לכולם זכות במספר שימנו לפני משה ואהרן כי ישימו עליהם עינם לטובה, יבקשו עליהם רחמים.

Perhaps [He did so] in order to let them know them of His

2   Rashi on Numbers 1:1.
3   Ramban on Numbers 1:45.

kindness to them, for they descended to Egypt seventy souls, and now they were numerous as the sand of the sea with such and such numbers of those who were twenty years old. After every plague He counts them in order to inform us that He makes nations numerous [and that] He crushes but [then] His hands heal, and our sages say that out of affection, He counts them constantly. Furthermore, one who comes before the father of all prophets [Moshe] and his brother, God's holy one [Aharon], and is known to them by name shall have merit and life, because he entered into the counsel of the people and in the written record of the Jewish nation and [so he will share] in the merit of the census of the multitudes. Everyone has merit in the numbers that were counted before Moshe and Aharon, for they [Moshe and Aharon] will look upon them favorably and seek God's mercy for them . . .[4]

The words of the Ramban require an explanation.

Every census has two goals. *One goal is to ascertain the total numbers of the Jewish people.* This is similar to taking an inventory of our possessions in order to know the total number of assets that we possess. In the context of the *mitzvah* of *sefirat ha-omer,* I count fifty days according to the Torah, and at the same time, I wish to count up to a certain number of weeks. *The second goal is to count in order to get to know each individual.* How was Moshe able to accomplish this second goal? Moshe was familiar with the public in general, but did not know them on an individual basis.

After the sin of the Golden Calf, Moshe prays to God on the nation's behalf. However, after the construction of the *Mishkan*, this method was no longer acceptable. Had the first *luhot* not been broken, then Moshe would have functioned as the agent of the Jewish people and simply required the consent of the sender, the Jewish people as a whole. After

---

4 Ramban on Numbers 1:45.

the breaking of the *luḥot* and the division of the Written and the Oral Law, Moshe became the rebbe of the entire Jewish people, and a rebbe must know all his students. In Parashat Ki Tisa, the Torah says: ויאמר ה' אל משה כתב לך את הדברים האלה כי על פי הדברים האלה כרתי אתך ברית ואת ישראל – "God said to Moshe: Write these words for yourself, for by these words I have sealed a covenant with you and Israel."[5] This covenant entailed a commitment to the Oral Law.[6]

Therefore, God commanded Moshe at the beginning of Sefer Bamidbar: שאו את ראש כל עדת בני ישראל למשפחתם לבית אבתם במספר שמות כל זכר לגלגלתם – "Take a census of the entire assembly of Israel according to their families, according to their father's household *by number of the names every male according to their head count*."[7] God's intent was a dual one. It was not enough for Moshe to know the total number of the Jewish people. He had to perform a head count in order to get to know each person as an individual with their own background and life experience. Moshe's additional obligation emanates from the fact that he was *rabban shel Yisrael,* the *rebbe* of the entire Jewish nation, and therefore had to know every Jew by name. It was as though God were telling him: Moshe, when you pray, you will pray not only for the general public, but also for every Jew in his or her moments of joy and pain. This duality, specifically the focus on the individual, was the Ramban's true intent.

---

5 Exodus 34:27.
6 BT *Gittin* 60b.
7 Numbers 1:2.

במדבר ⊰

Bamidbar II: Kedushat ha-Mahanot
of Sefer Bamidbar

OSAFOT ON TRACTATE *Megillah*[1] cite Ezra's decree that the blessings and curses of Sefer Vayikra must be read before Shavuot and the blessings and curses of Sefer Devarim must be read before Rosh ha-Shannah. *Tosafot* is troubled by the question as to why we divide the *parshiyot* of Nitzavim and Vayelech when there are two Shabbatot between Rosh ha-Shannah and Sukkot. In conclusion, Tosafot suggest that we divide them because we want the Shabbat before Rosh ha-Shannah to contain a reading without curses so as not to associate the approaching new year with them. For this reason, we also read Parashat Bamidbar before Shavuot so as not to juxtapose the curses of *Behukotai* with the festival of Shavuot. Parashat Nitzavim contains the assurance that we will ultimately do *teshuvah,* while Parashat Behukotai tells us that God will remember the covenant that he made with the Patriarchs. Yet we are still left wondering about the significance of Parashat Bamidbar in this context. Which *halachah* does Parashat Bamidbar contain?

In examining the structure of the banners, one sees a tripartite

---

1 BT *Megillah* 31b; ד"ה קללות שבתורת כהנים.

structure of *mahaneh Shechinah, mahaneh Leviya* and *mahaneh Yisrael.*
The Rambam states in *Hilchot Beit ha-Behira*:

שלש מחנות היו במדבר, מחנה ישראל והוא ארבע מחנות ומחנה לויה שנאמר
בה וסביב למשכן יחנו, ומחנה שכינה והוא מפתח חצר אהל מועד ולפנים, וכנגדן
לדורות, מפתח ירושלים עד הר הבית כמחנה ישראל, ומפתח הר הבית עד פתח
העזרה שהוא שער ניקנור כמחנה לויה, ומפתח העזרה ולפנים מחנה שכינה.

There were three camps in the wilderness: *mahaneh Yisrael,*
which consisted of four camps, and *mahaneh Leviya,* of which
it is written: "They will encamp around the *Mishkan,*" and
mahaneh Shechinah, which extends from the entrance of the
courtyard of the Tent of Meeting to its inner portion. This
corresponds to all generations. The land from the entrance
of Jerusalem to the Temple Mount is analogous to *mahaneh
Yisrael.* The land from the entrance of the Temple Mount to
the entrance of the courtyard, which is the Nicanor Gate,
is analogous to *mahaneh Leviya.* From the entrance of the
courtyard inward is *mahaneh Shechinah . . .*[2]

The Rambam's intent is that for posterity, the sanctity shall be that of
kedushat mahanot. In other words, the sanctity of the Temple increases
by degrees. According to this concept, Jerusalem which is an extension
of the Temple, carries the sanctity of *mahaneh Leviya.*

These degrees constitute the halachic substratum of Sefer Bamidbar.
Therefore, Mount Sinai also possessed the sanctity of the Temple with
its varying degrees of sanctity. There was a sector for Moshe that was
endowed with the sanctity of *mahaneh Shechinah,* a sector for Aharon
that possessed the sanctity of *mahaneh Leviya* and a sector for the entire
Jewish people that possessed the sanctity of *mahaneh Yisrael.* The Torah
in Parashat Yitro constantly reminds us of the lines of demarcation.

2 *Mishneh Torah,* Hilchot Beit ha-Behirah, 7:11.

Without *kedushat mahanot,* the whole enterprise of *kabbalat ha-Torah* is negated. Therefore, we read Sefer Bamidbar before Shavuot.

The Talmud asks: When the *Mishkan* was in transit from place to place, why wasn't the *lehem ha-panim* invalidated with the *pesul* of *yotzei* (the disqualification that occurs when something leaves its appropriate environs)? The Talmud answers that even when the *Mishkan* was in transit, it retained its sanctity. "The Tent of Meeting, the camp of the Levites, shall journey in the midst of the camps . . ." Even when the Tent of Meeting travels, it remains the Tent of Meeting, with all that it implies.[3]

This is the secret power of the Jewish people throughout the millennia. During the periods in our history that we were engulfed by the nations of the world, the fact that we never left the Temple protected us. The Temple is not merely an area that is circumscribed by *kedushat mehitzot,* but we were constantly traveling with *kedushat mahanot.* Therefore, before we are introduced to *kedushat ha-Torah,* it is critical that we read of the ongoing sanctity that accompanied us in all of our wanderings.

---

3   BT *Menahot* 95a.

≈ נשא ≈

Naso: The Priestly Blessing as
Hashraʾat ha-Shechinah

THE SECTION OF *birkat kohanim* reads:

וידבר ה' אל משה לאמר: דבר אל אהרן ואל בניו לאמר כה תברכו את בני
ישראל אמור להם: יברכך ה' וישמרך: יאר ה' פניו אליך ויחנך: ישא ה' פניו
אליך וישם לך שלום: ושמו את שמי על בני ישראל ואני אברכם.

The Lord spoke to Moshe saying: Speak to Aharon and his
sons, and tell them: This is how you shall bless the Children
of Israel. You shall say to them: May the Lord bless you and
safeguard you. May the Lord illuminate his countenance
for you and be gracious to you. May the Lord lift up his
countenance to you and grant you peace. They shall place my
name upon the Israelites, and I shall bless them.[1]

The Talmud in Tractate *Sotah* describes a dispute about how the
congregation should conduct themselves when they receive the blessing
of *the kohanim*:

---

1 Numbers 6:22–27.

בזמן שהכהנים מברכים את העם, מה הן אומרים? אמר ר' זירא אמר רב חסדא:
ברכו ה' מלאכיו גבורי כח וגו', ברכו ה' כל צבאיו משרתיו עושי רצונו, ברכו ה' כל
מעשיו בכל מקומות ממשלתו ברכי נפשי את ה'.

במוספי דשבתא מה הן אומרים? אמר רבי אסי: שיר המעלות הנה ברכו את ה' כל
עבדי ה' וגו', שאו ידיכם קדש וברכו את ה', ברוך ה' מציון שוכן ירושלים הללויה . . .

במנחתא דתעניתא מאי אמרי? . . .

בנעילה דיומא דכיפורי מאי אמר? . . .

א"ר חייא בר אבא: כל האומרן בגבולין אינו אלא טועה. אמר רבי חנינא בר פפא:
תדע דבמקדש נמי לא מיבעי למימרינהו, כלום יש לך עבד שמברכין אותו ואינו
מאזין?

When the kohanim bless the people, what do [the people]
say? Rav Zeira said in the name of Rav Hisda: [They say:]
"Bless the Lord, all his angels . . . Bless the Lord, all his legions,
his servants who do his will. Bless the Lord, all his works, in
all the places of his dominion. Bless the Lord, O my soul."

[When the kohanim bless the people] In the mussaf
service on Shabbat, what do they say? Rav Assi said: A song
of ascents. Behold, bless the Lord, all you servants of the Lord
. . . Lift your head in sanctity and bless the Lord. Blessed is the
Lord from Zion, who dwells in Jerusalem . . .

[When the kohanim bless the people during] *minhah* of a
fast day, what do they say? . . . During Neilah of Yom Kippur,
what do they say? . . . Rav Hiyya bar Abba said: Whoever
recites these verses outside the Temple is making a mistake.
Rav Hanina bar Papa said: Know that it should not be said in
the Temple either. Does a servant receive a blessing and not
listen? Rav Abba bar Hanina said: Does a servant receive a
blessing and not show gratitude?[2]

---

2   BT *Sotah* 39b–40a.

The aforementioned Gemara is worthy of explication. What is the source for reciting these verses? Rashi explains that those who receive blessings must demonstrate their gratitude for them. Doing so, as Rashi explains later, shows that we appreciate God's blessings and that they are beloved to us, and that we will somehow repay our master for them. This simple intent is clear, but what is Rashi's underlying meaning?

Further, why is there a differentiation (according to Rav Hiyya bar Abba) between the Temple proper and the area outside it? Why are these verses recited only in the Temple? Rashi explains that communal blessings were recited in response to the uttering of the Tetragrammaton, which was said only in the Temple. Here, again, we are challenged to understand the deeper significance of this distinction.

⌘ The Dual Nature of the Priestly Blessing

To answer these questions, we must elucidate the true nature of *birkat kohanim*. One can propose that this *mitzvah* has two distinct elements: the transmission of a direct blessing from God and *hashra'at ha-Shechinah*. *Birkat kohanim* is more than a transmission of blessing. It is a direct meeting with the Shechinah. It presents us with an intimate encounter in which we come face to face with God. The Rav, in classic fashion, explained these aspects through careful analysis of specific *halachot* attached to the *mitzvah* of *birkat kohanim*, as well as other related ones.

⌘ The Requirement of a *Minyan* for *Birkat Kohanim*

The *Mishnah* in Tractate *Megillah*[3] includes *birkat kohanim* in the list of items that require a *minyan*. The Gemara there cites as the source for this requirement the verse ונקדשתי בתוך בני ישראל – "I shall be sanctified in the midst of the Israelites."[4] The Gemara derives the principle that

---

3 Mishnah *Megillah* 23b.
4 Leviticus 22:32.

any *davar she-bi-kedushah* – a dialogue that takes place between the initiator, usually a *sheliah tzibbur,* and the community that responds to him – must be recited only in the context of a *minyan.* Since it is a fulfillment of the *mitzvah* of *kiddush ha-Shem,* it requires a *minyan.* Prima facie, the implication is that this is the relevant source for *birkat kohanim.* The Ran, in his commentary on the Rif,[5] notes that the need for a quorum of ten men for *birkat kohanim* is derived from the language of *bnei Yisrael,* which is mentioned at the beginning of the *parashah of birkat kohanim.* However, when the Rambam codifies this law, he writes clearly that the reason that a quorum of ten men is required for *birkat kohanim* is that it is a *davar she-bi-kedushah.*[6] Why is it so clear that *birkat kohanim* is a *davar she-bi-kedushah*? This is because of the aspect of *hashra'at ha-Shechinah.*

II. A *kohen hedyot* (simple priest) is qualified to bless the people

The Rambam discusses the *halachah* that nearly all *kohanim* (with specific exceptions), may perform *birkat kohanim* even if they are not scholars or righteous people:

ואל תתמה ותאמר ומה תועיל ברכת הדיוט זה, שאין קבול הברכה תלוי בכהנים אלא בהקדוש ברוך הוא . . . הכהנים עושים מצותן שנצטוו בה והקב"ה ברחמיו מברך את ישראל כחפצו.

Do not be amazed and say: How could the blessing of an ordinary person have any value? After all, the acceptance of the blessing does not depend upon the *kohanim* but on the Holy One, blessed be He . . . The *kohanim* perform the mitzvah that God commanded them, and God in his mercy blesses the Jewish people.[7]

---

5 Rif, Folio 13b.
6 *Mishneh Torah,* Hilchot Tefillah, 8:5–6.
7 *Mishneh Torah,* Hilchot Tefillah 15:7.

Here the Rambam states clearly that the blessing in *birkat kohanim* comes not from the *kohen* but directly from God. This is why the *kohen* who recites the blessing does not require any special level of sanctity. This point is actually very clear from the verse, ואני אברכם – "I shall bless them."[8] Contrary to appearances, *birkat kohanim* is not only a relaying of the heavenly blessing, but also a direct enactment of *hashra'at ha-Shechinah*. *Nesiat kapayim* (the "raising of the hands," as in the priestly blessing) – a face-to-face encounter between God and the Jewish people – leads to *hashra'at ha-Shechinah*. It reflects God's act of extending kindness. If we do not demonstrate our immediate appreciation for this *beracha*, then we show ingratitude to God.

III. Blessing with Fingers Outstretched

The Rambam, in *Hilchot Tefillah*, states as follows:

כיצד היא נשיאת כפים בגבולין בעת שיגיע שליח צבור לעבודה כשיאמר רצה כל הכהנים העומדים בבית הכנסת נעקרין ממקומן והולכין ועולין לדוכן ועומדים שם פניהם להיכל ואחוריהם כלפי העם ואצבעותיהם כפופות לתוך כפיהם עד שישלים שליח ציבור ההודאה ומחזירין פניהם כלפי העם ופושטין אצבעותיהן ומגביהין ידיהם כנגד כתפיהם ומתחילין יברכך . . . כשישלימו הכהנים ג' פסוקים מתחיל ש"ץ ברכה אחרונה של תפלה שהיא שים שלום והכהנים מחזירין פניהם כלפי הקדש וקופצין אצבעותיהן ועומדין שם.

How is the priestly blessing recited outside the Temple? When the leader of the congregation reaches the blessing, "May you be pleased," all the *kohanim* standing in the synagogue leave their places and ascend the dais. They stand there facing the Holy Ark with their backs to the congregation, their fingers clenched against their palms until the leader of the congregation completes the blessing, "We thank you." They

---

8 Numbers 6:27.

then turn their faces toward the people, spread out their fingers, lift their hands shoulder-high and begin to recite, "May God bless you ..." When the *kohanim* conclude the three verses, the leader of the congregation begins the final blessing of the *Shemoneh Esreh*, "Grant peace." The *kohanim* face the Ark and close their fingers and remain standing on the dais...[9]

We learn from the Rambam that the *kohanim* maintain closed fists up until the moment they begin to recite *birkat kohanim*. Then they spread their open fingers while reciting *birkat kohanim* and clench them again once they are finished. Rashi explains that the basis for the prohibition of not looking at the *kohanim* as they bless the people is that the *Shechinah* rests upon their fingers.[10] This is also Rashi's explanation why the *kohanim* in the Temple lifted their hands above their heads: because they blessed us with the Divine Name and the *Shechinah* rested over their fingers.[11] The conclusion is that the spreading of the fingers was an integral part of the *mitzvah* because it facilitated *hashra'at ha-Shechinah*. This is the reason that the *kohanim* spread their fingers only after they complete the *birkat ha-mitzvah* – אשר קדשנו בקדושתו של אהרן, which they recite immediately before יברכך.

א IV. The Requirement of *Kavanah*

The concept of *hashra'at ha-Shechinah* has a specific connection to the Temple, where the *kohanim* must spread their hands above their heads. There, the presence of the *Shechinah* serves as the basis for the prohibition against looking at the *kohanim* as they recite the blessing. However,

---

9   Hilchot Tefillah 14:3–4.
10 Rashi on BT *Hagigah* 16a: ד"ה ומברכים.
11 Rashi on BT *Sotah* 38a, ד"ה ובמקדש.

it appears that this notion of *hashra'at ha-Shechinah* also applies outside the Temple, as the Rambam explains:

כשיהיו הכהנים מברכין את העם לא יביטו בעם ולא יסיחו דעתן אלא יהיו עיניהם
כנגד הארץ כעומד בתפלה, ואין אדם רשאי להסתכל בפני הכהנים בשעה שהן
מברכין את העם כדי שלא יסיחו דעתם, אלא כל העם מתכוונין לשמוע הברכה
ומכוונים פניהם כנגד פני הכהנים ואינם מביטים בפניהם.

When the *kohanim* bless the people, the *kohanim* should not look at them nor should the *kohanim* become unfocused, but their eyes should be directed downwards as if they were standing in prayer. One may not look at the faces of the *kohanim* when they are blessing the people so that the *kohanim* will not be distracted, but the people should have in mind to hear the blessing and direct their attention to the *kohanim* and not look at their faces.[12]

The Rambam's rationale is היסח הדעת – concern that looking at the faces of the *kohanim* will distract the *kohanim* and interfere with their concentration. However, we may ask why *kavanah*, which is a requirement for prayer, should be required for receiving *birkat kohanim*. The answer is that *birkat kohanim* is also a kind of prayer. The people are standing in the presence of the *Shechinah,* and this demands *kavanah* even outside the Temple.

ᴘ Why the Need for a Verbal Response? The Obligation of *Shirah*

Whenever a person stands in God's presence, whenever he senses the lustre of the *Shechinah,* he must engage in *shirah* (joyful song). There are many *parshiyot* throughout the Tanach that support this principle. וירא ישראל את היד הגדלה אשר עשה ה' במצרים – "Israel saw the great hand

---

12 *Mishneh Torah,* Hilchot Tefillah 14:7.

294

that God inflicted upon Egypt,"[13] is followed by אז ישיר משה ובני ישראל את השירה הזאת לה' – "Then Moshe and the Children of Israel chose to sing this song to God." [14]זה א‑לי ואנוהו, א‑להי אבי וארוממנהו – "This is my God and I will build him a sanctuary, the God of my father and I will exalt him."[15]

In Parashat Shemini, we read: ותצא אש מלפני ה' ותאכל על המזבח את העלה ואת החלבים וירא כל העם וירנו ויפלו על פניהם – "A fire went forth from before the Lord and consumed the burnt offering and the fats upon the altar. The people saw and sang glad song and fell upon their faces."[16] Targum Onkelos translates וירנו – "and sang glad song" as ושבחו – "they praised God with glad song." In explanation of the *mitzvah* of Hallel on Yom Tov, the Ramban in his glosses on Rambam's *Sefer ha-Mitzvot* explains that the element precipitating Hallel is the joy of Yom Tov.[17] That simcha is a function of the perceived presence of God, which grants a person peace of mind so that he does not suffer from anxiety at night. Why do the Levites recite *shirah* daily over the sacrifices? They do so because the *Shechinah* is present in the Temple. The recital of the additional prayers of *Malchuyot, Zichronot* and *Shofarot* on Rosh ha-Shannah is a recitation of *shirah* to God, while the blowing of the shofar heralds the revelation of the *Shechinah,* the divine presence.

Therefore, *birkat kohanim* mandates *shirah* because it is a medium through which we merit a face-to-face encounter with God. The Jewish people cannot be silent when the priests who are God's own emissaries pronounce the blessing. We must demonstrate our gratitude by reciting verses of praise and thanksgiving to our master. This is the intent of the above-mentioned Gemara: "Is there a servant who receives a blessing and does not show gratitude?"

---

13 Exodus 14:31.
14 Exodus 15:1.
15 Exodus 15:2.
16 Leviticus 9:24.
17 Ramban's commentary on *Sefer ha-Mitzvot, Shoresh Rishon,* gloss 9.

✌ Inside vs. Outside the Temple

We now see how the centrality of *hashra'at ha-Shechinah* in *birkat kohanim* accounts for the need to respond with song and praise. However, what is the basis for distinguishing between inside and outside the Temple? *Birkat kohanim* in the Temple takes on a heightened aspect of *hashra'at ha-Shechinah* because of the use of the Tetragrammaton. We may ask: what level of divine presence creates the obligation to respond with song and praise? According to Rav Hiyya bar Abba in the Gemara, only the highest level of *giluy Shechinah*, which is found only in the Temple itself, merits this response. Outside the Temple, the congregation listens silently as they receive the blessing.

✳ בהעלותך ✳

Be'haalotcha I: Kivrot ha-Taavah
and the Peril of Hedonism

✷ Moshe's Despair with Klal Yisrael

ARASHAT BE'HAALOTCHA DESCRIBES the rebellion of the rabble at Kivrot ha-Taavah:

> והאספסף אשר בקרבו התאוו תאוה וישבו ויבכו גם בני ישראל ויאמרו מי
> יאכלנו בשר.

The rabble among them cultivated a craving, and the Children of Israel wept again, saying, "Who will feed us meat?"[1]

They go on to complain about the manna and God responds with great anger. Moshe's response is uncharacteristic:

> ויאמר משה אל ה' למה הרעת לעבדך ולמה לא מצתי חן בעיניך לשום את משא
> כל העם הזה עלי: האנכי הריתי את כל העם הזה אם אנכי ילדתיהו כי תאמר אלי
> שאהו בחיקך כאשר ישא האמן את הינק על האדמה אשר נשבעת לאבתיו: מאין
> לי בשר לתת לכל העם הזה כי יבכו עלי לאמר תנה לנו בשר ונאכלה: לא אוכל אנכי

---

1   Numbers 11:4.

לבדי לשאת את כל העם הזה כי כבד ממני: ואם ככה את עשה לי הרגני נא הרג אם
מצאתי חן בעיניך ואל אראה ברעתי.

Moshe said to God: "Why have you done evil to your servant?
Why have I not found favor in your eyes, that you place the
burden of this entire people upon me? Did I conceive this
entire people or give birth to it that you say to me: Carry
them in your bosom, as a nurse carries a suckling, to the land
that you swore to his forefathers? Where shall I get meat to
give to this entire people when they weep to me, saying, 'Give
us meat that we may eat'? I cannot carry this nation alone, for
it is too heavy for me. And if this is how you deal with me,
then kill me now, if I have found favor in your eyes, and let me
not see the evil that shall come to me."[2]

Moshe lived through many crises and stressful moments. The worst
was the sin of the Golden Calf, which shook the relationship between
God and Israel and almost ended it entirely. Yet Moshe never faltered or
panicked. He never complained about Israel's shortcomings, but instead
asked God's forgiveness. ויחל משה – "Moshe pleaded."[3] Later, the term
ואתחנן – "I implored"[4] – captured the element of boldness in Moshe's
petitioning of God on Israel's behalf. The sages used the following metaphor vis a vis the sin of the Golden Calf:

מלמד, שתפסו משה להקדוש ברוך הוא כאדם שהוא תופס את חברו בבגדו,
ואמר לפניו: רבונו של עולם, אין אני מניחך עד שתמחול ותסלח להם.

It shows us that Moshe seized God by his garments as one
seizes his friend by his garments and said to him: Master

---

2 Numbers 11:11–15.
3 Exodus 32:11.
4 Deuteronomy 3:23.

of the Universe, I will not let you go until you grant them pardon.[5]

In Parashat Be'haalotcha, we see a change in Moshe's usual way of doing things. Here, the people complain, and instead of defending them, Moshe points an accusing finger.

Moshe had made similar statements in his mission to Pharaoh, which ended in failure. Then he returned to God, saying:

וישב משה אל ה' ויאמר א־דני למה הרעתה לעם הזה למה זה שלחתני: ומאז באתי אל פרעה לדבר בשמך הרע לעם הזה והצל לא הצלת את עמך.

My Lord, why have You done evil to this people? Why have You sent me? From the time I came to Pharaoh to speak in Your Name, he has done evil to this people, but You did not rescue Your people.[6]

There, Moshe's frustration was not with Israel but with God. Moshe was then a young man with limited experience. He did not express this level of doubt until now. It is unlike Moshe to condemn Klal Yisrael out of fear and resignation, but here, he does.

✺ The Moral Failure of Hedonism

The reason for this shift in Moshe's demeanor may be found in the sin of the rabble's rebellion and in the sin of Kivrot ha-Ta'avah.

והאספסף אשר בקרבו התאוו תאוה וישבו ויבכו גם בני ישראל ויאמרו מי יאכלנו בשר: זכרנו את הדגה אשר נאכל במצרים חנם את הקשאים ואת האבטחים ואת החציר ואת הבצלים ואת השומים: ועתה נפשנו יבשה אין כל בלתי אל המן עינינו.

The rabble among them cultivated a craving, and the Children of Israel wept again, saying, "Who will feed us meat? We

---

5 BT *Berachot* 32a.
6 Exodus 5:22–23.

remember the fish that we would eat in Egypt free of charge and the cucumbers, and the melons, the leeks, the onions and the garlic. But now our life is parched. There is nothing. We have nothing before our eyes but the manna."[7]

The Jewish people were seized by a greedy craving that aroused God's anger. Why did Moshe not pray to God, as he had done after the sin of the Golden Calf? The answer is that the two events were different. The sin of the Golden Calf was the result of fear, since the people thought that Moshe had died. Feeling terrified and abandoned, they committed the sin of idolatry. However, there were mitigating circumstances, since they intended the Golden Calf to serve as a substitute for Moshe Rabbenu.[8]

This is different from the incident at Kivrot ha-Taavah, which stemmed from a desire for a pagan way of life, with its insatiable desires, unlimited lusts, and complete absence of boundaries. This pagan lifestyle is the antithesis of Judaism, which demands self-discipline. The Torah therefore detests paganism because, unlike idolatry – the worship of a short-lived object of wood or clay or metal – paganism is often infectious. Somewhat later in this *parashah,* the Torah describes the behavior that followed:

ויקם העם כל היום ההוא וכל הלילה וכל יום המחרת ויאספו את השלו הממעיט אסף עשרה חמרים וישטחו להם שטוח סביבות המחנה.

The people rose up all that day and all the night and all the next day and gathered up the quail – the one who took least gathered in ten chomers – and they spread them out all around the camp.[9]

The people, mad with desire, abandoned all restraint and gave in to

---

7   Numbers 11:4–6.
8   Ramban on Exodus 32:1.
9   Numbers 11:32.

their desires. Indeed, the pagan lifestyle that they adopted was a veritable "grave of the voluptuary." This is in stark contrast with the Jewish disciplined way of life as evidenced in the story of the manna. ויצא העם ולקטו דבר יום ביומו – "Let the people go out and pick each day's portion on its day . . ."[10] ועשו כן בני ישראל וילקטו המרבה והממעיט: וימדו בעמר ולא העדיף המרבה והממעיט לא החסיר איש לפי אכלו לקטו – "The children of Israel did so. Some gathered more and some less. When they measured it against an omer, whoever had gathered more had nothing extra, and whoever had taken less had no lack. Everyone had enough to eat."[11] This self-discipline is the root of the Jewish approach.[12]

∾ The Remedy: Moshe's Transformation from Rebbe to Nursing Mother

This moral breakdown of the Israelites made it clear to Moshe that his role as teacher of the Jewish people would no longer be sufficient. This role had begun in Egypt and culminated at the revelation at Mount Sinai, when a slave society was transformed into a kingdom of priests and a holy nation. However, the incident at Kivrot ha-Taavah required a transformation from Moshe. He was now called upon to assume not only the rule of a teacher but also that of a nursing mother. כאשר ישא האמן את הינק – "As a nurse carries a suckling."[13] A nursing mother bonds with and teaches her baby, but mainly carries him in her bosom. While a father may teach his child and provide discipline, the child does not necessarily become a part of him. Yet a baby becomes a part of its mother, who nurses him and protects him from the unfriendly outside world. A baby's mother has no life of her own. She belongs to her infant.

Moshe Rabbenu now discovered that it was not enough for him to

---

10 Exodus 16:4.
11 Exodus 16:17–18.
12 Ramban on Leviticus 19:2.
13 Numbers 11:12.

be a teacher. As a Jewish leader, he had to become a nursing mother, guessing his baby's needs, feeling pain when his baby cried and happy when he was cheerful. האנכי הריתי את כל העם הזה אם אנכי ילדתיהו כי תאמר אלי שאהו בחיקך כאשר ישא האמן את הינק... – "Did I conceive this entire people or did I give birth to it that You say to me, carry them in your bosom as a nurse carries a suckling? ..."[14] According to the Rav, Moshe realized that from now on he no longer had a life of his own or any rights at all. He was not entitled to enjoy the life of an ordinary individual because he was now the mother of the Jewish people.

✍ The Sin of Miriam

Moshe's new role of nursing mother might explain the connection with the last segment of the *parashah,* which describes Miriam's sin and her punishment. Her offense requires a deeper understanding. How did Moshe's devoted and loyal sister become his accuser? As a young girl, Miriam had stood on the shore of the Nile River and followed the course of the floating ark. She had faith in her brother's survival and was ready to endanger herself to save him.[15] While everyone else – her mother and father and everyone around them – had resigned themselves to losing him, she persevered. ותתצב אחתו מרחק לדעה מה יעשה לו – "His sister stationed herself at a distance to learn what would happen to him."[16] How did her devotion turn to criticism?

The sages explain that Miriam criticized Moshe's withdrawal from family life.[17] She did not understand that Moshe now had to expand his role as leader to the extent that he could no longer carry on a normal family life. Just as a nursing mother is devoted to her child to the exclusion of any life of her own, Moshe felt that he could have no life of his

---

14 Numbers 11:12.
15 Rambam, *Mishneh Torah,* Hilchot Tumat Tzaraat 16:10.
16 Exodus 2:4.
17 Rashi on Numbers 12:1.

own. His foremost concern was to be father and mother to the Jewish people. Miriam knew that in most cases, this behavior was contrary to the Jewish approach, which holds family life to be an essential aspect of religious expression.

What of Moshe's Own Children?

This interpretation also sheds light on another question that puzzled the sages and biblical commentators: the conspicuous absence of Moshe's children from the limelight. In the beginning of Bamidbar, the Torah states:

> ואלה תולדת אהרן ומשה ביום דבר ה' את משה בהר סיני: ואלה שמות בני אהרן
> הבכור נדב ואביהוא אלעזר ואיתמר.

> These are the offspring of Aharon and Moshe on the day that the Lord spoke with Moshe at Mount Sinai. These are the names of the sons of Aharon, the firstborn was Nadav and Avihu, Elazar and Itamar.[18]

The passage only mentions the children of Aharon, not those of Moshe. In the Bible, Moshe's children are described by the term *"bnei Menashe."*

> ויקימו להם בני דן את הפסל ויהונתן בן גרשם בן מנשה הוא ובניו היו כהנים לשבט
> הדני...

> The children of Dan set up for themselves the carved image and Jonathan son of Gershom son of Menashe – he and his children – were priests for the tribe of Dan...[19]

This is not only because of their involvement in the incident of

---

18 Numbers 3:1–2.
19 Judges 18:30.

Micha's idol, but perhaps because Moshe became the father of all the children of the Jewish people.

The separation of Moshe from his family really occurred at the moment of divine revelation on Mount Sinai, when God told him, לך ... אמר להם שובו לכם לאהליכם: ואתה פה עמד עמדי ואדברה אליך – "Go, say to them: Return to your tents. But as for you, stand here with me and I shall speak to you . . ."[20] The realization of this surfaced once again during the incident at Kivrot ha-Taavah, and this is what disturbed Miriam and Aharon. Does prophecy require a man's alienation from his family? Why did Moshe have to dedicate himself solely to his people? ויאמרו הרק אך במשה דבר ה' הלא גם בנו דבר וישמע ה' – "They said: Is it only to Moshe that God speaks? Does he not speak to us as well? And Hashem heard."[21] In other words, they said, we are also prophets and yet we live with our husbands, children and relatives, and our family life does not interfere with our devotion to our people. God's answer to them is: There is a great difference between you and Moshe. You, as ordinary people, do not have to give up ordinary family life, but Moshe is in a different category altogether.

A Lesson for Our Generation

Today as well, the Jewish people suffers from the problem of hedonism, of unrestrained desire. The only way to combat this phenomenon is to become nursing parents. The covenantal community is a teaching community. It not only teaches and instructs but also gives love and devotion to the child. Rabbinic leadership must adopt the message of כאשר ישא האמן את הינק – "As a nurse carries a suckling."[22] Moshe, when he realized

---

20 Deuteronomy 5:26–27. See *Mishneh Torah,* Hilchot Yesodei ha-Torah 7:6.
21 Numbers 12:2.
22 Numbers 11:12.

and recognized the magnitude of his task, felt that he was incapable of accomplishing it.

The battle for traditional Judaism in America has not been won yet despite our great progress in the realm of day schools, youth conclaves and the growth of Hasidut and yeshivot. Our ongoing challenge is to grapple with a society plagued by *mitonenim* and *mitavim* –hedonism. The model we must invoke is the one that Moshe used.

Be'haalotcha II: The Halting of the Triumphant March

I T I S O U R duty to learn the Bible's principles. However, the Rav believed that the most vexing issue in Be'haalotcha was the seeming lack of continuity in the *parashah*. There is no systematic development in the continuum of the narrative. There are many stories with no apparent thread of continuity.

We may understand all the seemingly disjointed events of Parashat Be'haalotcha in the context of the moral failure of Kivrot ha-Taavah. This was not merely a transgression. This was a pivotal event in the derailing of Jewish history – the halting of a triumphant march to the building of the Temple in Eretz Yisrael and the beginning of a long and painful detour. Let us note the sequence of events.

(A) *Kiddush ha-leviim* (the sanctification of the Levites) and *parashat ha-menorah* (the section of the Torah that deals with the candelabrum) that is juxtaposed to the previous *parashah* of the *Nesiim* (the leaders of the tribes). Therefore, Be'haalotcha begins as follows: והעמדת את הלוים לפני אהרן ולפני בניו והנפת אתם תנופה לה' – "You shall stand the Levites before Aharon and before his sons and wave them as a wave-offering before the Lord."[1]

---

1   Numbers 8:13.

(B) *Pesah sheni* (the second paschal offering). The Torah records that some individuals had been rendered ritually impure and therefore unable to bring the first paschal offering. God therefore instituted *Pesah sheni* for their benefit.[2] What is the connection between *Kiddush ha-leviim* and *Pesah sheni*? At first glance, it is inexplicable.

(C) The description of the pillar of cloud that guided the people in their journeys: ולפי העלות הענן מעל האהל ואחרי כן יסעו בני ישראל ובמקום אשר ישכן שם הענן שם יחנו בני ישראל – "Whenever the cloud lifted from above the tent, afterwards the Children of Israel would journey. Wherever the cloud rested, there the Children of Israel encamped."[3]

(D) The commandment of the two silver trumpets and their use in assembling the people and in their journeying. The Torah describes various kinds of trumpet blasts.[4] Afterwards, the Torah resumes describing the journeys and the order of the tribes as they marched.

(E) A puzzling conversation between Moshe and his father-in-law. Moshe humbly extends an invitation to his father-in-law to join the Jewish people in their trek to the promised land – ויאמר משה לחבב בן רעואל המדיני חתן משה נסעים אנחנו אל המקום אשר אמר ה' אתו אתן לכם לכה אתנו והטבנו לך כי ה' דבר טוב על ישראל – "Moshe said to Hobab son of Reuel, the Midianite, the father-in-law of Moshe, 'We are journeying to the place of which the Lord has said: I shall give it to you. Go with us and we shall treat you well, for the Lord has spoken of good for Israel.'"[5]

(F) The *parashah* beginning with the phrase ויהי בנסע הארן "Va-yehi binsoa ha-aron"[6] (when the Ark would journey), which consists of two verses. An inverted *nun* appears at the beginning and the end of the two verses in order to show that it appears out of context. One may ask: if that is the case, why was the phrase inserted here? These two

---

2   Numbers 9:6–14.
3   Numbers 9:17.
4   Numbers 10:1–10.
5   Numbers 10:29.
6   Numbers 10:35.

verses would have served as an appropriate sequel to the end of Parashat Pekudei, following the verse כי ענן ה' על המשכן יומם ואש תהיה לילה בו לעיני כל בית ישראל בכל מסעיהם – "The cloud of God was over the Tabernacle by day and fire was over it at night, before the eyes of all the house of Israel throughout their journeys."[7]

(G) The episode at *Kivrot ha-Taavah*, where they were overcome by a craving and wept. Although Moshe himself was not threatened by them, their complaint could have had a devastating effect. They remembered the "good old days" in Egypt. Such complaints were reflective of modern man. They are the grave of desire that pleasure-seekers dig for themselves.

(H) The final episode relates to Miriam and Aharon.

We are not sure whether the events of this *parashah* constitute one story with an underlying unity or are an amalgam of several stories. The Rav, who used to say that this particular *parashah* could be compared to a bee flying from flower to flower on a clear summer morning, gathering nectar, felt strongly the need to restore its unity. He sensed that an inverted historical process was occurring that was tragic and, unfortunately achieved its goal. The inverted *nunim* represent history that was thwarted.

Moshe's task was to liberate the Israelites. That act would reach its peak with the Divine revelation of the Torah. וזה לך האות כי אנכי שלחתיך – בהוציאך את העם ממצרים תעבדון את הא-להים על ההר הזה – "This is your sign that I have sent you. When you take the people out of Egypt, you will serve God on this mountain."[8] What did God mean by that? The *Sefer ha-Hinuch*[9] contends that God was referring to the giving of the Torah at Mount Sinai. A consequence of *matan Torah* was the construction of the Tabernacle, which took place after Moshe's descent from Mount Sinai. Had the Jews not succumbed to the rabble, they would have accomplished those two goals earlier. Moshe would have descended on

---

7   Exodus 40:38.
8   Exodus 3:12.
9   *Sefer ha-Hinuch*, Parashat Emor, Mitzvah 306 (*sefirat ha-omer*).

the seventeenth of Tammuz, and the construction of the Tabernacle would have begun. Instead, Moshe spent eighty days in prayer and descended from Mount Sinai on Yom ha-Kippurim. The construction of the Tabernacle, which was delayed, lasted until Rosh Hodesh Nisan, followed by the eight days of consecration. Once these two goals had been accomplished, the people had no further reason to remain in the Sinai Desert, and their sojourn could end.

In Parashat Naso, we read of the offerings made by the *nesiim,* the tribal leaders, at the dedication of the Tabernacle. In the beginning of Parashat Be'haalotcha, we read of the sanctification of the Levites. Once the sanctification of the Levites and dedication of the *Mishkan* had been completed, the Jewish people were ready to leave the desert. The tribal leaders began to make their offerings on Rosh Hodesh Nisan, and after twelve days we had reached the thirteenth of the month. We were ready for the march to the Promised Land, but the cloud did not ascend because the next day was *erev Pesah,* when the paschal lamb must be offered, and so the march was postponed until after the festival. God instructed Moshe regarding the offering of the paschal lamb:

וידבר ה' אל משה במדבר סיני בשנה השנית לצאתם מארץ מצרים בחדש הראשון לאמר: ויעשו בני ישראל את הפסח במועדו.

God spoke to Moshe in the wilderness of Sinai in the second year from their exodus from the land of Egypt, in the first month, saying: The Children of Israel shall make the Passover offering in its appointed time.[10]

At that point, those who were defiled asked what they must do regarding the paschal offering. In response, God introduced *Pesah sheni.* There is perfect continuity.

The march to Eretz Yisrael was now supposed to begin. How long was it supposed to last? Rashi in Devarim cites the calculation:

---

10 Numbers 9:1–2.

"אחד עשר יום מחרב." אמר להם משה ראו מה גרמתם, אין לכם דרך קצרה
מחורב לקדש ברנע כדרך הר שעיר ואף הוא מהלך אחד עשר יום, ואתם הלכתם
אותו בשלשה ימים, שהרי בעשרים באייר נסעו מחורב שנאמר (במדבר י:יא) ויהי
בשנה השנית בחדש השני בעשרים בחדש וגו' ובכ"ט בסיון שלחו את המרגלים
מקדש ברנע, צא מהם שלושים יום שעשו בקברות התאוה, שאכלו הבשר חדש
ימים, ושבעה ימים שעשו בחצרות להסגר שם מרים, נמצא בשלשה ימים הלכו
כל אותו הדרך, וכל כך היתה שכינה מתלבטת בשבילכם למהר ביאתכם לארץ,
ובשביל שקלקלתם הסב אתכם סביבות הר שעיר ארבעים שנה.

"Eleven days from Horeb." Moshe said to them: See what you
have caused! There exists no shorter route from Horeb to
Kadesh Barnea than the route of Mount Seir, and even that
is a journey of eleven days. Yet you traversed it in three days.
On the twentieth of Iyyar, they traveled from Horeb, as it is
written: It was in the second year in the second month on the
twentieth of the month, and so on, and on the twenty-ninth
of Sivan they sent the spies from Kadesh Barnea. Deduct
from them thirty days, which they spent at *Kivrot ha-Taavah*,
for they ate the meat there for a month, and deduct another
seven days which they spent at Hazerot when Miriam was
quarantined there. What emerges is that they went that entire
route in three days. The Shechinah struggled so much for your
sake in order to expedite your arrival in the land, but because
you acted improperly, he took you roundabout Mount Seir
for forty years.[11]

The Torah therefore reveals to us the details of the march. The guide
was the the pillar of cloud, as the Torah already indicated in Parashat
Beshalah: וה' הלך לפניהם יומם בעמוד ענן לנחתם הדרך – "The Lord went before
them by day in a pillar of cloud to lead them on the way . . ."[12] Now the
Torah describes the encampment for the march, which tribes were in

---

11 Rashi on Deuteronomy 12:.
12 Exodus 13:21.

the vanguard and which tribes were in the rear guard. (Dan, the *measef le-chol ha-mahanot,* served as the rear guard of all the camps). The Torah uses the phrases *al tzeva* and *le-tzivotam* (their legions). The accompaniment of the two trumpets also presages the communication signals for the journey. When we read the verses carefully, we feel an increasing tempo, a mood of tension and expectancy, and a sense of mobilization and order. All conditions have been met, and the promise to Avraham Avinu that was made so long ago will now be fulfilled.

ויהי בשנה השנית בחדש השני בעשרים בחדש נעלה הענן מעל משכן העדת: ויסעו בני ישראל למסעיהם ממדבר סיני וישכן הענן במדבר פארן.

It was in the second year, in the second month, on the twentieth of the month, the cloud was lifted from over the Tabernacle of Testimony. The children of Israel went on their journeys from the wilderness of Sinai, and the cloud rested in the wilderness of Paran.[13]

The Torah continues:

ויסעו מהר ה' דרך שלשת ימים וארון ברית ה' נסע לפניהם דרך שלשת ימים לתור להם מנוחה.

They journeyed three days' distance from the Lord's mountain, and the Ark of God's Covenant journeyed a three-day distance before them to seek out a resting place for them.[14]

At that juncture, a conversation ensues between Moshe and his father-in-law, Yitro, which gives us a glimpse into the mood of Moshe.

It was supposed to be the final journey, the journey that would take them to the promised land. Moshe was excited and expected great things. There was a sense of determination in the atmosphere. Moshe said to his father-in-law, נסעים אנחנו אל המקום אשר אמר ה' אתו אתן לכם לכה אתנו והטבנו

---

13 Numbers 10:11–12.
14 Numbers 10:33.

לך כי ה' דבר טוב על ישראל – "We are journeying to the place of which the Lord said: I shall give it to you. Go with us and we shall treat you well, for the Lord has spoken of good for Israel."[15] The emotional level had reached its peak, and the Israelites were assured of reaching their final destination. The Torah's language reflects the excitement by using the present tense, "We are journeying,"[16] rather than "We will journey."

Moshe's invitation to Yitro was not merely a personal one, but that it included all proselytes for all generations. The Midrash in Kohelet interprets the verse, כל הנחלים הלכים אל הים והים איננו מלא – "All the rivers flow into the sea, yet the sea is not full"[17] – as a reference to all potential proselytes who come to Eretz Yisrael in order to convert. All of them could have joined the march to the Promised Land and Moshe would have become the Messiah. The *parashah* is so moving that one could weep. Moshe speaks in the first person plural: "We are journeying." "Go with us and we shall treat you well." "It shall be that if you come with us." Moshe was certain that he and all those who had left Egypt would enter the Promised Land. It was not necessary to send out spies, for intelligence data is necessary only if there are doubts or uncertainties, and here there were none. ויסעו מהר ה' דרך שלשת ימים וארון ברית ה' לפניהם דרך שלשת ימים לתור להם מנוחה – "They journeyed a distance of three days from the mountain of the Lord, and the Ark of God's Covenant journeyed a three-day distance before them in order to seek out a resting place for them."[18] Rashi cites the *Sifrei* that they traveled a distance of three days in a single day because God wanted to bring them to Eretz Yisrael immediately. It is no wonder that the verses that tell of the journeying of the Ark now appear. Had things been otherwise, there would have been no need for two inverted *nunim*.

Suddenly, something totally unexpected happened: the episode of the

---

15 Numbers 10:29.
16 Numbers 10:29.
17 Ecclesiastes 1:7, Kohelet Rabbah 1:6
18 Numbers 10:33.

Mitonenim leading to *Kivrot ha-Taavah*. Moshe was unable to come to the defense of the Jewish people. He saw the messianic vision of Jewish redemption unraveling before his eyes as the triumphant march ended almost before it began.

Those who reject self-discipline are not worthy to enter the land. For this reason, the verses that speak of the Ark's journeying – "*va-yehi binsoa ha-aron*" – are dislocated. The distance to the land suddenly grew greater, and Moshe realized that the great march had come to an end.[19]

When the *mitonenim* began to complain, Moshe despaired of seeing Eretz Yisrael. He said to God, ואם ככה את עשה לי הרגני נא הרג אם מצאתי חן בעיניך ואל אראה ברעתי – "If this is how you are going to treat me, then kill me now if I have found favor in your eyes, and let me not see the evil that has come upon me."[20]

In their commentary on the verse, אלדד ומדד מתנבאים במחנה – "Eldad and Medad are prophesying in the camp,"[21] the sages noted that their prophecy consisted of the following statement: אמרו: משה מת, יהושע מכניס את ישראל לארץ – "They said: Moshe will die and Joshua will bring Israel into the land."[22] According to their prophecy, Moshe would never enter the Land of Israel. The *nunim* were inverted, the march was halted and the Jewish people were distanced further from Eretz Yisrael.

We can now understand the continuity of the *parashah* in light of the above interpretation. All of its segments led to the fulfillment of God's promise to bring us to the Promised Land. The incident at *Kivrot ha-Ta'avah* then pulled Jewish history off course.

Thus, all of Parashat Be'haalotcha is one continuous unit. It is the

---

19 Here, Rav Soloveitchik added a personal note. He said that during his wife's illness, which lasted for four years, he had faith that she would recover. However, on the Yom Kippur before she passed away, the Rav was holding a Torah scroll during the Kol Nidrei service, and gave it to a student of his to replace in the Ark. The Torah scroll slipped and fell into the Ark, and at that moment, the Rav felt a premonition that his wife would not recover. He said, "Don't ask me how, but I just felt it." Unfortunately, this turned out to be the case.

20 Numbers 11:15.

21 Numbers 11:27.

22 BT *Sanhedrin* 17a.

story of the march to Eretz Yisrael that was about to take place and that would have culminated in the fulfillment of the verse וְהָיָה ה׳ לְמֶלֶךְ עַל כָּל הָאָרֶץ בַּיּוֹם הַהוּא יִהְיֶה ה׳ אֶחָד וּשְׁמוֹ אֶחָד – "The Lord will be king over all the world; on that day, the Lord shall be one and his name shall be one."[23] Yet because of the people's lack of self-discipline and surrender to hedonism, they and so many future generations were denied this great blessing.

---

23 Zechariah 14:9.

שלח ≈

Shelah

PARASHAT SHELAH OPENS with the words: וידבר ה' אל משה לאמר: – שלח לך אנשים ויתרו את ארץ כנען אשר אני נתן לבני ישראל "The Lord spoke to Moshe, saying: Send forth men and let them spy out the land of Canaan that I give to the Children of Israel..."[1] Rashi comments למה נסמכה פרשת מרגלים לפרשת מרים, לפי שלקתה על עסקי דבה שדברה באחיה, ורשעים הללו ראו ולא לקחו מוסר – "Why was the episode of the spies juxtaposed to that of Miriam? When she was punished for having spoken against her brother, these wicked people saw [what happened to her] and did not learn their lesson." In order to understand the episode of the spies, we must understand the nature of Miriam's transgression, since there is a connection between them.

Why was Miriam punished? In Parashat Ki Tetze, we are commanded: זכור את אשר עשה ה' א-להיך למרים בדרך בצאתכם ממצרים – "Remember what the Lord your God did to Miriam on the way when you left Egypt."[2] Every Jew is obligated to remember six things: the exodus from Egypt, the revelation at Sinai, Amalek, our wanderings in the desert, Shabbat and the episode of Miriam. In Ki Tetze,[3] Rashi connects the episode of

---

1 Numbers 13:1–2.
2 Deuteronomy 24:9.
3 Rashi on Deuteronomy 24:9.

Miriam with the sin of *lashon ha-ra*. Why did the Torah emphasize the prohibition against *lashon ha-ra* more than all the other commandments that have to do with our treatment of our fellow human beings? Why is Miriam's sin so important in Jewish history?

The Rav referred to a classification of the Rambam in his preamble to *Seder Zeraim*. The Rambam mentions פירושים מקובלים מפי משה "explanations that were accepted from Moshe Rabbenu." He means there are different ways of explaining the Torah, such as *peshat* and *Midrash* and so on. However, regarding some things in the Torah, there is no freedom of interpretation. The classic example, according to the Rambam, is the commandment of עין תחת עין – "an eye for an eye,"[4] which the sages commanded that we never interpret literally, but only in terms of monetary compensation.[5] Any other understanding of the verse constitutes heresy.

Another example is the verse about the four species that we take on Sukkot. According to the Rambam in his preamble to *Seder Zeraim*, the phrase פרי עץ הדר[6] – "the fruit of a beautiful tree"[6] – refers only to an etrog and nothing else. The Rambam states strongly that this interpretation is the only valid one, and no other interpretation is permitted. A third example is the verse וקצתה את כפה – "You shall cut off her hand,"[7] which, according to the sages, also referred solely to compensation.[8] The Rambam writes that anyone who interpreted the verse differently is considered an *apikorus*. The prevalent rule is that only the explanations that were accepted from Moshe Rabbenu are authentic.[9]

The Rav said that his father, *zt"l*, had received an oral tradition from his grandfather, Rav Chaim Halevi, *zt"l*, that the episode of Miriam's sin and punishment was also included in that category. Anyone who

---

4 Exodus 21:24.
5 BT *Bava Kamma* 84a, *Mishneh Torah*, Hilchot Hovel u-Mazik 1:5–6.
6 Leviticus 23:40.
7 Deuteronomy 25:12.
8 Rashi on Deuteronomy 25:12.
9 See "U-vikashtem mi-sham,"n. 1, in which the Rav elaborates on the allegorical nature of Shir ha-Shirim and then relates to this category of the Rambam.

interpreted the verse כי אשה כשית לקח – "for he had married a Cushite woman"[10] – contrary to the sages' interpretation that it referred to Tzipporah's beauty, which was unparalleled in her generation, was an *apikorus*. Rashi quotes a tradition from the sages that Moshe divorced her.[11] The reference is to the verse in Parashat Vaethanan that states, לך אמר להם שובו לכם לאהליכם. ואתה פה עמד עמדי ואדברה אליך – "Go, say to them: Return to your tents. But as for you, stand with me and I shall speak to you."[12] After the giving of the Torah, God ordered Moshe to separate from his wife and to devote himself solely to him. The rest of the Jewish people could return to normal family life.[13]

When Miriam spoke about "the Cushite woman" that Moshe had married, she was critiquing this decision, for she felt that Moshe should also resume normal family life. She spoke about this with Aharon, her brother. ויאמרו הרק אך במשה דבר ה' הלא גם בנו דבר – "They said: Was it only to Moshe that the Lord spoke? Did he not speak to us as well?"[14] What is so unique and distinctive about Moshe that he had to separate from his wife? Why weren't we instructed to act similarly when we are also prophets?

God answered Miriam and Aharon as follows:

ויאמר שמעו נא דברי אם יהיה נביאכם ה' במראה אליו אתודע בחלום אדבר בו: לא כן עבדי משה בכל ביתי נאמן הוא: פה אל פה אדבר בו ומראה ולא בחידת ותמנת ה' יביט.

He said: "Hear now my words. If there be prophets among you, I, the Lord, shall make myself known to them in a vision; I shall speak with him in a dream. Not so is my servant Moshe, the most trusted of all my household. Mouth to mouth do I speak to him, in a clear vision and not in riddles. He gazes upon God's image . . ."[15]

---

10 Numbers 12:1.
11 Rashi on Numbers 12:1.
12 Deuteronomy 5:27–28.
13 See *Mishneh Torah*, Hilchot Yesodei ha-Torah, 7:6.
14 Numbers 12:2.
15 Numbers 12:6–8.

What is the connection between the complaint of Miriam and Aharon and God's response? Here, God was saying not only that Moshe was greater and more sanctified than other prophets, but that as a prophet, he was unique. No other prophet could compare to him. This is what Miriam and Aharon failed to understand.

The Rambam explains the difference between the stature of Moshe Rabbenu and that of other prophets in *Hilchot Yesodei ha-Torah* as follows:

כל הדברים שאמרנו הם דרך נבואה לכל הנביאים הראשונים והאחרונים חוץ ממשה רבינו רבן של כל הנביאים, ומה הפרש יש בין נבואת משה לשאר כל הנביאים שכל הנביאים בחלום או במראה ומשה רבינו מתנבא והוא ער ועומד שנאמר ובבא משה אל אהל מועד לדבר אתו וישמע הקול מדבר אליו, כל הנביאים על ידי מלאך, לפיכך רואים מה שהם רואים במשל וחידה, משה רבינו לא על ידי מלאך שנאמר פה אל פה אדבר בו, ונאמר ודבר ה' אל משה פנים אל פנים, ונאמר ותמונת ה' יביט כלומר שאין שם משל אלא רואה הדבר על בוריו בלא חידה ובלא משל, הוא שהתורה מעידה עליו במראה ולא בחידות שאינו מתנבא בחידה אלא במראה שרואה הדבר על בוריו. כל הנביאים יראים ונבהלים ומתמוגגין ומשה רבינו אינו כן הוא שהכתוב אומר כאשר ידבר איש אל רעהו כלומר כמו שאין אדם נבהל לשמוע דברי חבירו כך היה כח בדעתו של משה רבינו להבין דברי הנבואה והוא עומד על עומדו שלם, כל הנביאים אין מתנבאים בכל עת שירצו משה רבינו אינו כן אלא כל זמן שיחפוץ רוח הקודש לובשתו ונבואה שורה עליו ואינו צריך לכוין דעתו ולהזדמן לה שהרי הוא מכוון ומזומן ועומד כמלאכי השרת, לפיכך מתנבא בכל עת.

All that we have said above refers to the nature of prophecy for all earlier and later prophets except Moshe Rabbenu, the master of all prophets. What is the difference between the prophecy of Moshe and other prophets? All the prophets saw in a dream or a vision and Moshe prophesied when he was alert and standing, as it says, "When Moshe came to the Tent of Meeting to speak with him and he heard the voice speaking to him."[16] All prophets [see their prophecy] through an

---

16 Numbers 7:89.

angel; therefore they see what they see in parables and riddles. Moshe Rabbenu didn't see prophecy through the medium of an angel as it says "Mouth to mouth do I speak to him," and it says "The Lord spoke to Moshe face to face," and it says "He gazes upon God's image," meaning that there is no parable but that he [Moshe] sees everything with total clarity without having recourse to parables or riddles. That is what the Torah testifies about him when it states, "In a clear vision and not in riddles" – that he doesn't prophesy in riddles but he sees everything with total clarity. All prophets are seized by a fear that overtakes and confounds them, while Moshe [saw and understood the prophetic words of God without fear]. That is what the verse refers to when it states, "As a man speaks with his friend," meaning that a person isn't frightened to hear the words of his friend. So, too, Moshe Rabbenu had the strength of mind to understand the words of prophecy and remain totally lucid (with all of his faculties aware). All other prophets cannot prophesy when they desire, but Moshe could do so any time he wished. He was "clothed" with *ruah ha-kodesh* and it hovered over him. He did not require a precise reorienting of himself in order to prophesy, for he was in a perpetual state ready to receive prophecy, akin to the angels. Therefore, he was able to prophesy at any time he wished."[17]

In short, the Rambam draws a firm distinction between Moshe and the rest of the prophets, as reflected in the words לא כן עבדי משה – "Not so is my servant Moshe."[18]

The quality of Moshe's prophecy is more than mere description. It is the seventh of the thirteen articles of faith as laid down by the Rambam. In the sixth article, the Rambam states the doctrine of true prophecy,

---

17 *Mishneh Torah,* Hilchot Yesodei ha-Torah 7:6.
18 Numbers 12:7.

and in the seventh, he mentions Moshe's unique prophetic role. Moshe was the father of all prophets before and after him. This is one of the fundamental principles of prophecy.

Another fundamental principle in Judaism is that of *behirah* (chosenness). We believe that God chose the Jewish people from among all nations. One who denies this denies all of Judaism. The Torah uses two expressions to describe this state of chosenness: *behirah* and *segulah*.

ועתה אם שמוע תשמעו בקלי ושמרתם את בריתי והייתם לי סגלה מכל העמים
כי לי כל הארץ.

And now, if you listen well to me and keep my covenant, you shall be to me the most beloved treasure of all people, for the entire world is mine.[19]

A *segulah* is a unique, desirable item. A person may own many precious items that are all dear to him, but one of them may hold a special place in his heart. An example would be Jacob's love for Rachel. Even though the verse states וירא ה' כי שנואה לאה – "God saw that Leah was hated,"[20] it does not refer to actual hatred. It means only that compared to the overwhelming love that Jacob had for Rachel, his love for Leah was of a lesser nature.[21] So, too, Jacob loved all of his children. However, his love for Joseph was far stronger. This is *segulah*.

Aharon and Miriam did not understand that Moshe possessed the *segulah* level of prophecy. When the Torah states זכור את אשר עשה ה' א־להיך למרים בדרך בצאתכם ממצרים – "Remember what the Lord your God did to Miriam on the way when you left Egypt,"[22] it does not mention that the incident occurred in Hazerot but rather states "בצאתכם ממצרים" – "when you left Egypt."[23] Only Moshe, the consummate leader with his unique

---

19 Exodus 19:5.
20 Genesis 29:31.
21 See Ramban on Genesis 29:31.
22 Deuteronomy 24:9.
23 Deuteronomy 24:9.

relationship with God, could have accomplished the exodus from Egypt. Therefore, the sin for which Miriam was punished was that she did not realize that Moshe was on the level of *segulah*.[24]

A halachic ramification of this principle is: שאין נביא רשאי לחדש דבר מעתה – "A prophet cannot introduce a new innovation."[25] A prophet who innovates a new *halachah* and states that he is doing so as a prophet is defined as a false prophet. Only Moshe Rabbenu was authorized to establish *halachah* in God's name. In the book of Zechariah, someone asked how to observe the fast days after the building of the second Temple.[26] The prophet's response was:

> כה אמר ה' צבאות צום הרביעי וצום החמישי וצום השביעי וצום העשירי יהיה לבית יהודה לששון ולשמחה ולמעדים טובים והאמת והשלום אהבו.

> Thus says the Lord, Master of Legions: The fast of the fourth, the fast of the fifth, the fast of the seventh and the fast of the tenth shall be, for the House of Judah, times of joy and gladness and for happy festivals, love truth and peace.[27]

Here, God instructs the prophet regarding fast days that are rabbinic in nature rather than of Torah origin. No prophet except Moshe Rabbenu has the authority to innovate *halachah*.

---

24 *Mishneh Torah*, Hilchot Tumat Tzaraat 16:10.
25 BT *Megillah* 2b.
26 See BT Rosh ha-Shannah 18b.
27 Zechariah 8:19.

שלח

Shelah II: The Episode of the Meraglim

ETURNING TO THE story of the spies, we must ask the purpose of their mission. The Torah in Parashat Shelah does not use the term מרגלים (*meraglim*) but rather uses the verb form, לתור (*latur*).[1] The word *rigul* implies a military reconnaissance mission designed to find strategic locations and strong and weak points in the enemy's territory. Joseph uses similar words when he accuses his brothers of being spies: ויאמר אלהם מרגלים אתם לראות את ערות הארץ באתם – "You are spies! To see the land's nakedness have you come."[2] Yet here, the spies' mission was not of a military nature but rather *latur* – to gather information about the nature of the inhabitants of Eretz Canaan, the climate, topographical conditions and the economy.

Why was it necessary to send out spies when God had already promised that the land would be conquered? Rav Soloveitchik provided a halachic perspective on the matter. In Tractate *Kiddushin*, the Talmud states: אסור לאדם שיקדש את האשה עד שיראנה – "One may not marry a woman until he has seen her."[3] We find that when Eliezer returned from his mission of finding a wife for Isaac, the Torah says: ויבאה יצחק האהלה

---

1   Numbers 13:2.
2   Genesis 42:9.
3   BT *Kiddushin* 41a.

שרה אמו – "Yitzhak brought her into the tent of his mother Sarah."[4]
He wanted to see whether Rebecca would be a worthy successor to his
mother Sarah. Rashi comments based on the *Midrash:*

ויבאה האהלה והרי היא שרה אמו, כלומר ונעשית דוגמת שרה אמו, שכל זמן
שׁשׂרה קיימת היה נר דלוק מערב שבת לערב שבת, וברכה מצויה בעיסה, וענן
קשׁור על האהל, ומשׁמתה פסקו, וכשׁבאת רבקה חזרו.

> He brought her into the tent and behold, she was Sarah, his
> mother; that is to say, then she became the image of Sarah,
> his mother. For all the time that Sarah was alive a lamp would
> be lit continuously from erev Shabbat to erev Shabbat and
> a blessing would be found in the dough and a cloud would
> be stationed over the tent. When she died, they stopped, and
> when Rebecca arrived, they resumed.[5]

Although Isaac trusted Eliezer, his father's faithful servant, he wanted
to observe the commandment of marrying a woman only after he had
seen her. Marriage is more than a mutual commitment of two partners.
It is a sharing of pleasures and anxieties, of moments of happiness and
stress. All this is included in the category of "seeing." Of course, it is
reciprocal, since the woman must see her potential bridegroom as well.

In Parashat Be'haalotcha,[6] Moshe Rabbenu invites his father-in-law
to accompany them into the land and the destiny that God promised
the Israelites. This promise, in essence, is a kind of merger – a betrothal
and marriage – between a nation and its land. Therefore, the law of not
marrying until one sees one's potential spouse applies to the Land of
Israel as well. Moshe wanted the Israelites to recognize it intimately, in
an all-encompassing and detailed way. That was why he decided to send
them on a mission to "see the land."

---

4 Genesis 24:67.
5 Rashi on Genesis 24:67.
6 Numbers 10:29.

Jacob sends Joseph to Shechem and instructs him: לך נא ראה את שלום
אחיך ואת שלום הצאן והשבני דבר וישלחהו מעמק חברון ויבא שכמה – "'Go now,
ascertain the welfare of your brothers and the welfare of the flock, and
bring me word.' So he sent him from the valley of Hebron and he arrived
at Shechem."[7] Rashi comments, הלא חברון בהר, שנאמר ויעלו בנגב ויבא עד
חברון, אלא מעצה עמוקה של אותו צדיק הקבור בחברון, לקיים מה שנאמר לאברהם בין
הבתרים כי גר יהיה זרעך – "But is not Hebron on a mountain? It is written:
'They ascended in the south.' He arrived in Hebron, but here it means
from the deep counsel of that righteous one, Abraham, who is buried in
Hebron, in fulfillment of that which had been told to Abraham at the
Covenant between the Pieces: 'Your offspring shall be sojourners.'"[8]

Taking his cue from the Midrash, Rashi found symbolism in the
expression "the valley of Hebron." One who is in a deep valley sur-
rounded by mountains cannot see very far because the mountains block
his view. But a person who is standing on the peak of a mountain can see
very far indeed.

Therefore, Jacob escorted Joseph down the mountains of Hebron and
together they came to "the valley of Hebron." Here, Jacob left Joseph
and sent him alone towards Shechem. Why did Jacob escort Joseph?
Apparently, divine providence intervened. At that moment, Jacob didn't
know how Joseph's mission would end, for he spoke metaphorically
about "the valley," where his vision of the future was blocked. Jacob knew
that Joseph's brothers disliked him, yet he sent Joseph to them anyway.
Two things were hidden from Jacob: that he would not see Joseph for
the next twenty years, and that while he thought that he was sending
Joseph only to Shechem, he was actually sending Joseph as the harbinger
of the Egyptian exile.

When Moshe sent the spies to Canaan, he told them ועליתם את ההר
– "Climb the mountain."[9] This was the same mountain that Jacob and

---

7 Genesis 37:14.
8 Rashi on Genesis 37:14.
9 Numbers 13:17.

Joseph had descended when Joseph left his father's home and the Land of Israel. Now Moshe told the spies to climb it in order to connect the nation to the land once again. Moshe wanted the spies to understand the land's majesty and spiritual grandeur. He wanted them to realize that the land of Israel and the nation of Israel were bound, even betrothed, to each other. Moshe was convinced that the land itself was waiting for its people to return.

Moshe believed that the spies would be affected by the land where God had made his original covenant with Abraham, the Covenant between the Pieces, and would realize that the divine presence rested there. In other words, Moshe sent out the spies on the basis of the *halachah* that a man may not marry a woman until he has seen her. What did the spies do? ויעלו בנגב ויבא עד חברון – "They ascended in the south and he arrived in Hebron . . ."[10] Because they had not climbed the mountain as Moshe had commanded, they did not see what they were supposed to see. Since they were short-sighted, they did not see the land's quality as a *segulah*. This was what Rashi meant at the beginning of Parashat Shelah, when he noted that the reason that the episode of the spies is so close to that of Miriam is because the spies did not learn their lesson from her punishment. Just as Miriam did not see the *segulah* quality of her brother, the spies did not see the *segulah* quality of Eretz Yisrael.

While many Jewish values are precious in themselves, other values are priceless. One has to know how to distinguish between them. Even *halachah* contains elements that are on the level of *segulah*. Shabbat, the most precious of all days, transcends even the sanctity of Yom Tov. In a manner of speaking, even God has this quality. The Rambam often writes that God is not only one, but that he is unique in his unity and oneness.[11]

One of the paradoxes of our faith is that on the one hand, God is the source of the present. He is existence par excellence, and any existence

---

10 Numbers 13:22.
11 *Mishneh Torah,* Hilchot Yesodei ha-Torah 1:7.

in this world emanates from him. There is absolute unity between the creator and his creation. On the other hand, the creator is one and alone. He not only created and sustains the universe, but he also negates the world as a singular entity. The only authentic existence is His, and none can compare to Him. For us, He is immanent and transcendent simultaneously. We cannot exist without him.

Since human beings were created "in the image of God," there is a dialectic character to their existence. They are an integral part of the world order, and at the same time they are also in their own category. Moreover, regarding human relationships, the Torah demands that we practice *hesed* (kindness), be open-hearted and reach out to all humankind. At the same time, we are obligated to preserve our privacy and individuality.

Moshe Rabbenu was a great leader. He worked among the people and loved them to the point of his willingness to be erased from the Torah entirely (after the sin of the Golden Calf).[12] At other times, his *segulah* quality demanded that he remain apart. ומשה יקח את האהל ונטה לו מחוץ למחנה הרחק מן המחנה וקרא לו אהל מועד – "Moshe would take the tent and pitch it outside the camp, far from the camp, and call it the Tent of Meeting."[13] In Moshe, the elements of *reshut ha-yahid* (private property) and *reshut ha-rabim* (public property) were combined. This duality of Moshe emanates from the Divine dictum of *imitatio dei*. This duality is also reflected in the relationship between the Jewish people in Israel and in the Diaspora with the land and its segulah character. Our bond with the land of Israel is not based only on logic. It is also emotional and spiritual. Jews who live in the Diaspora are also sensitive to the land of Israel's *segulah* character and do not relate to it only with logic. We do not fully understand the riddle of our being the "chosen nation," nor do we fully understand the mystery of the "chosen land." Why did we have to live in exile for so very long?

---

12 Exodus 32:32.
13 Exodus 33:7.

The section of the Torah that talks about *tzitzit* alludes to the fact that Jews are dialectical beings. The white and the blue are inextricably intertwined. The white threads symbolize clarity. The blue thread, the *techelet,* symbolizes the hidden and obscure. *Techelet* is compared to the heavens and to the sea.[14] The combination of white and blue symbolizes the Jew's dialectic *segulah* personality and, simultaneously, our recognition that we lack clarity in many areas but are ultimately dependent upon God. Indeed, the Jewish people constitutes an *am segulah* par excellence.

---

14 BT *Menahot* 43b.

❧ קרח ❧

Korah I

KORAH'S REBELLION: THE FIRST CONSPIRACY

KORAH'S REBELLION WAS not just an incident that took place during the Israelites' desert wanderings. Rather, it was a watershed event that is relevant to our own time and from which we can learn many lessons. Before Korah's rebellion, the Israelites complain constantly, but always out of need or other distress. Examples are the story of Amalek, the serpents and the sojourn in the wilderness.

❧ The Character of Previous Protests

In order to emphasize the uniqueness of Korah's rebellion, the Rav provided additional examples of reactive rebellions and explained that there are many such phenomena in the Torah. Four examples follow:

I. ופרעה הקריב וישאו בני ישראל את עיניהם והנה מצרים נסע אחריהם וייראו מאד
ויצעקו בני ישראל אל ה'.

Pharaoh approached. The Israelites raised their eyes, and behold – Egypt was journeying after them. They were very frightened, and the Israelites cried out to the Lord.[1]

---

1   Exodus 14:10.

Fear prompted their reaction.

II.   וילונו כל עדת בני ישראל על משה ועל אהרן במדבר: ויאמרו אלהם בני ישראל
מי יתן מותנו ביד ה' בארץ מצרים בשבתנו על סיר הבשר באכלנו לחם לשבע כי
הוצאתם אתנו אל המדבר הזה להמית את כל הקהל הזה ברעב.
The entire assembly of the Israelites complained against
Moshe and Aharon in the wilderness. The Israelites said to
them: "If only we had died by the hand of the Lord in the
land of Egypt as we sat by the pot of meat when we ate bread
to satiety! You have taken us out to this wilderness in order to
kill this entire congregation by famine."[2]

III.   ויסעו כל עדת בני ישראל ממדבר סין למסעיהם על פי ה' ויחנו ברפידים ואין מים
לשתת העם: וירב העם עם משה ויאמרו תנו לנו מים ונשתה.
The entire assembly of the Children of Israel journeyed from
the wilderness of Sin to their journeys according to the word
of the Lord. They encamped in Rephidim, and there was no
water for the people to drink. The people contended with
Moshe, saying, "Give us water that we may drink . . ."[3]

None of the situations mentioned above were political disputes or
ideological controversies. They stemmed from the people's concerns
over their immediate and basic physical needs: water and food.

Not even the incident of the Golden Calf stemmed from a desire
for idolatry or a weakening of the Israelites' moral fiber. It was a reaction to their terror and perceived abandonment. Thinking that Moshe
Rabbenu, their leader, was gone forever, they feared for their survival.[4]

---

2 Exodus 16:2–3.
3 Exodus 17:1–2.
4 See Ibn Ezra on Exodus 31:18 and Ramban's commentary on Exodus 32:1.

IV. וירא העם כי בשש משה לרדת מן ההר ויקהל העם על אהרן ויאמרו אליו קום
עשה לנו א־להים אשר ילכו לפנינו כי זה משה האיש אשר העלנו מארץ מצרים
לא ידענו מה היה לו.

The people saw that Moshe had delayed in descending the
mountain and the people gathered around Aharon and said
to him rise up, make for us gods that will go before us, for this
man Moshe who brought us up from the land of Egypt we do
not know what became of him.[5]

The First Conspiracy

As we have seen, until Korah's rebellion, all the quarrels among the
Israelites were unorganized, spontaneous reactions to frightening situations. They were marked by a mob mentality, which is easily excited and
can also be calmed within a short time. Korah's rebellion was different in
several ways. First, its purpose was not to gratify basic drives such as hunger or to assuage panic. Second, the majority of the Jewish people were
not involved. Only several hundred followers of Korah, mostly of the
intellectual aristocracy, participated. The Torah calls them נשיאי עדה קראי
מועד אנשי שם – "leaders of the assembly, those summoned for meeting,
men of renown."[6] This rebellion was neither emotional nor spontaneous, but deliberate and well planned. It was a premeditated conspiracy.

Korah Capitalizes on the Tragedy of the Meraglim

The Ramban, in his commentary on the Torah, traced the origin of
Korah's rebellion. Korah's hostility began when Aharon was appointed
high priest and the Levites were chosen to function as servants in the
sanctuary. Although this had taken place a year earlier and undoubtedly made Korah angry then, he bided his time, not daring to come out

---

5 Exodus 32:1.
6 Numbers 16:2.

publicly against Moshe at that time. At that point, the people were loyal to Moshe and would have met any attempt to undermine him with anger and resistance. והנה היו אוהבים אותו כנפשם ושומעים אליו. ואילו היה אדם מורד על משה בזמן ההוא היה העם סוקלים אותו – "Behold, they loved him [Moshe] as themselves and they listened to him. Had anyone rebelled against Moshe at that time, the people would have stoned him [the rebel]."[7] Korah waited patiently for an opportunity to undermine Moshe's status. This moment arrived earlier than he had anticipated.

The incident of the *meraglim* and God's subsequent decree that the generation that had left Egypt would die in the desert were devastating to the Israelites. Moshe's prestige in the eyes of the people suffered as well. When the Israelites were still slaves in Egypt, he had promised them that they would reach the Promised Land. Indeed in Parashat Be'haalotcha, in the second year after leaving Egypt, Moshe told his father-in-law, נסעים אנחנו אל המקום אשר אמר ה' אתו אתן לכם לכה אתנו והטבנו לך כי ה' דבר טוב על ישראל – "We are journeying to the place regarding which God said: 'I shall give it to you. Go with us and we shall treat you well, for the Lord has spoken of good for Israel.'"[8] The people were filled with hope and excitement. Then, as a result of the incident of the *meraglim*, God extended their sojourn in the desert by another thirty-nine years. Their hopes were shattered, and Moshe's popularity plummeted.

Korah seized this opportunity to recruit disaffected Israelites and organize his opposition. The Ramban felt that the fact that the Torah tells the stories of both incidents so close together shows that the incident of the spies was the cause of the rebellion. This differs from the approach of the Ibn Ezra, who claims that the rebellion occurred after the *bechorim* were replaced by the Levites.[9] The Ramban's position is both intuitively and textually correct. When Datan and Aviram refused Moshe's summons, they said:

---

7 Ramban, Numbers 16:1.
8 Numbers 10:29.
9 Ibn Ezra, Numbers 16:1.

המעט כי העליתנו מארץ זבת חלב ודבש להמיתנו במדבר . . . אף לא אל ארץ זבת
חלב ודבש הביאתנו ותתן לנו נחלת שדה וכרם.

Is it not enough that you have brought us up from a land
flowing with milk and honey to die in the wilderness? . . .
*Moreover, you did not bring us to a land flowing with milk and
honey,* nor did you give us a heritage of field and vineyard . . .[10]

In other words, they told Moshe: You have made promises that you
could not keep. Your promises are false and empty.

The most significant phrase here is *va-yikah Korah*. Rashi explicates it
as follows: לקח את עצמו לצד אחד להיות נחלק מתוך העדה לעורר על הכהונה – "He
took himself from the community by raising objections regarding the
priesthood."[11] Why was the tribe of Reuven involved? Rashi answers that
it was because he lived near Korah, as it is written: אוי לרשע, אוי לשכנו
– "Woe to the wicked; woe to his neighbor." The Ramban notes that
Korah harbored a grudge against Moshe for having deprived them of the
priesthood, the levitical role and the kingship.[12] They also bore a grudge
against Moshe for having taken away their privileges as the first-born.
Here, too, Korah took advantage of the weaknesses and ill feelings of
others in order to foment rebellion.

---

10 Numbers 16:13–14.
11 Rashi on Numbers 16:1.
12 Ramban on Numbers 16:1.

קרח

Korah II: Korah's Fault

Korah's First Argument: The Social Equality of Sanctity

ALL MOVEMENTS NEED a basic ideology in order to succeed. Korah provided several in order to support his rebellion. The most powerful of his arguments was the first one that the Torah mentions: רב לכם כי כל העדה כלם קדשים ובתוכם ה' ומדוע תתנשאו על קהל ה' – "You have taken too much upon yourself. The entire community – everyone – is holy, and the Lord is among them. Why, then, do you exalt yourselves above the Lord's congregation?"[1]

Since Korah felt that Moshe had usurped power, he challenged Moshe's authority. First, he used logic. The whole community is holy. Every Jew has sanctity. As far as covenantal holiness and choseness are concerned, there is no difference between Moshe Rabbenu and a woodcutter. In this sense, Korah stated a basic Jewish belief.

---

1 Numbers 16:3.

❧ The Dual Nature of Human Holiness

Korah's mistake was that he did not understand the dual character of *kedushat Yisrael*. The community of Israel is more than an assembly of people or a covenantal community with a genetic code of *kedushah*. That is indeed one aspect of its sanctity. A baby born to a Jewish mother is Jewish, and inherits his sanctity from his forebears. However, there is another source of *kedushah* at the individual level. If that source of *kedushah* did not exist, individuals would be deprived of their initiative, creativity, originality and uniqueness. Individual *kedushah* is part of one's personality.

Our sages speak of each individual's uniqueness.[2] The verse in Deuteronomy emphasizes the dual nature of *kedushah*.

כי עם קדוש אתה לה' א־להיך בך בחר ה' א־להיך להיות לו לעם סגלה מכל העמים אשר על פני האדמה – "You are a holy nation to the Lord your God, and the Lord has chosen you for himself to be a treasured people from among all the nations on the face of the earth."[3] The verse speaks of a twofold sanctity: one that relates to the covenantal community and one that relates to the individual endowment, which is an expression of individual greatness.[4] As far as communal *kedushah* is concerned, we are all of equal stature. Regarding individual chosenness and *kedushah*, the idea of equality cannot apply and in fact is absurd. Korah frequently uses the term *edah*, referring to communal *kedushah*, while Moshe emphasizes its individual component.

בקר וידע ה' את אשר לו ואת הקדוש אליו והקריב אליו ואת אשר יבחר בו יקריב אליו.

In the morning, the Lord will make known the one who is his

---

2 *Midrash Tanhuma* Pinhas; see also BT *Berachot* 58a and BT *Sanhedrin* 38a.
3 Deuteronomy 7:6.
4 See Rashi on Deuteronomy 14:2; קדושת עצמך מאבותיך ועוד ובך בחר ה'.

own, and the one who is sanctified. He will draw him close to himself; whomever he chooses he will draw close to himself.[5]

Moshe uses the term *"boker"* (in the morning). The medieval grammarians draw a parallel between the words *boker* and *levaker,* which means to discriminate, to accentuate individual distinctiveness.

✺ Korah Overlooked the Quality of Rebbi

Furthermore, Korah was wrong about something else as well. Korah thought that the covenantal community was identical to a political community, in which the central figure is the king and the others are his subjects. This is not so. The covenantal community is a singular teaching community. At its center is not the king, warrior or high priest, but rather the teacher, or *rebbi.* A political community often uses compulsion to enforce obedience. The covenantal community is founded upon a commitment by its disciples to their master and teacher.

Judaism historically disapproved of all forms of human government. A human king is, at best, a *melech evyon,* a pitiful figure, destined for death and the grave. Even though *Moshe* had the halachic authority of a king,[6] throughout our history we have referred to him as Moshe Rabbenu, the *rebbi* par excellence of the Jewish people and the father of all prophets.

Aharon, for his part, is not merely the high priest. He is also a great teacher and expositor of learning. כי שפתי כהן ישמרו דעת ותורה יבקשו מפיהו כי מלאך ה' צבאו־ת הוא – "The lips of the *kohen* should safeguard knowledge. People should seek teaching from him because he is an agent of the Lord, Master of Legions."[7] Korah did not realize that the importance of Moshe and Aharon went far beyond political power. Their roles as

---

5 Numbers 16:5.
6 See *Mishneh Torah,* Hilchot Beit ha-Behirah 6:11; Ramban on Deuteronomy 33:5; Rashi on Shir ha-Shirim 7:4.
7 Malachi 2:7.

teachers and spiritual role models were what made Korah's challenge so preposterous.

✺ Korah's Second Argument: The Fallacy of Common Sense

The Torah does not mention Korah's second argument – that Halachah must be interpreted based on a common-sense approach – explicitly. Rather, it is derived from our sages. Rashi refers to one such example that Korah cites in order to demonstrate the irrationality of the halachic process.

In the example that Rashi cites, Korah gave his followers cloaks dyed in *techelet*. Then he asked Moshe whether the cloaks required *tzitzit*. When Moshe said that they did, Korah and his followers ridiculed him. They argued that if a cloak made from a different type of cloth could be exempt by one thread of *techelet*, a cloak made entirely of *techelet* should certainly be exempt.[8]

Korah also asked Moshe whether a house filled with Torah books required a *mezuzah*. When Moshe answered that it did, Korah laughed at him.[9]

Korah and his followers appealed to common sense and logic. However, the Oral Law is not based on common sense. It has its own methodology, categories and schemata. It has its own method of conceptualization, which was developed by *gedolei Yisrael* such as Rabbi Akiva Eiger, the Hatam Sofer, the authors of the Ketzot and Netivot, and Rav Chaim Brisker. The *halachah* works like a mathematician in an a priori world. Its constructs are ideal. It prepares abstract schemata and applies them to the world of sense. *Halachah* is entitled to formulate its own logical, epistemological approach. *Korah* pleaded the case for common sense, arguing that every Jew should have the ability to determine *Halachah* in common sense categories.

---

8   Rashi on Numbers 16.1.
9   Bamidbar Rabbah 18:3.

The Rav cited members of the women's liberation movement who argue that *Halachah* discriminates against women. One of their arguments is that women are ineligible to serve as witnesses in a court of law. If we examine the matter in terms of common sense, we must conclude that the Halachik status of women is inferior to men. However, this argument is false because a Jewish king, even if he were the Messiah himself, may not serve as a witness – and one could never say that the king, or the Messiah, was inferior to any other Jew.

Both male and female were created in God's image, and equality is a basic premise. The exclusion of both women and the Messiah from serving as witnesses has its own halachic underpinnings that have nothing to do with the common-sense approach of human logic. The paradox is that we derive the *halachot* of prayer from Hannah,[10] and yet women may not be counted in a *minyan*. This also presupposes an autonomous halachic methodology that is not subject to human common sense.

Ritual committees often employ common sense to reach halachic decisions. All Reform movements, from the Sadducees to contemporary religious liberals, pleaded the cause of common sense. Korah also operated with a common-sense methodology. Moshe replied that Korah's criteria were irrelevant because *Halachah* has its own, independent methodology and logos. Only a scholar who has mastered its conceptual structure can understand this logic.

↭ Korah's Third Argument: The Primacy of Emotional Experience

Finally, Korah argued that emotional experience was paramount in the performance of *mitzvot*. This approach contends that the *mitzvah* itself is secondary to the inner feeling that its performance generates. A *mitzvah* is primarily designed to evoke a certain mood. Korah said if the goal

---

10 BT *Berachot* 31a.

of *techelet* was to remind us of God, why limit it to a single thread? He placed emphasis on the inner emotional experience. The Torah warned us against confusing the religious experience of performing a *mitzvah* with an aesthetic or hedonistic experience. A classic example is the use of an organ – which is not an instrument of a religious experience but an aesthetic one – in the synagogue.

Our primary interest is in the *mitzvah* itself, which must be fulfilled carefully. We also would like to experience the emotions that stem from performing the *mitzvah*, but this is a secondary outcome. The pure, objective performance of a *mitzvah* puts us on solid footing, while emotions are constantly in flux and subject to change. *Halachah* cannot give emotions the kind of credibility that it gives to the fulfillment of a *mitzvah*. Since human emotions are constantly changing, the halachic requirement for a religious experience demands a concrete form of discipline that is not subject to such changes. If we were to give in to emotions and to experiential criteria, we would not be able to distinguish properly between the religious experience of *devekut* and both pagan and secular hedonism.

The Orthodox Jew moves from action to feeling and not the reverse.[11] Korah did not understand this. He could not grasp the profundity of the halachic system or the methodology of Moshe Rabbenu. The lessons of Parashat Korah are extremely valuable because they provide the foundations for the covenantal community and enable it to continue into the future.

---

11 See Parashat Shemini for an analysis of these two phenomena.

Hukat I: The Incomprehensibility of Hok

T HE WORD *HUKAH* refers to the category of laws that we do not understand. It is not that such laws are difficult to comprehend, but that they are intrinsically incomprehensible and not subject to human logic. The human being is incapable of assimilating these laws. They are therefore subject to ridicule from our foes.

Our sages ruled that one must accept a *hok* as a whole with all of its seeming contradictions.[1] For example, they acknowledged the distinctive character of the *parah adumah*, and called for the suspension of judgment regarding it. When we suspend our judgment on such matters, we act in accordance with the inscrutable will of God even though our logical minds may be confused. Nevertheless, we must suspend our judgment.

∼ Interpretation vs. Explanation

Rashi cites Rav Moshe ha-Darshan, who provided an interpretation of the *parah adumah*.[2] But don't such interpretations go against the spirit of a *hok*? The answer is no because there is a difference between an

---

1   Rashi on Numbers 19:2.
2   Rashi on Numbers 19:22.

explanation and an interpretation. Even though we are forbidden to ask for an explanation for a *hok*, we may inquire about its interpretation. An explanation answers the question *why*, which is not a scientific question but rather a metaphysical one that science does not address. Science explains the *how* or *what* of the event, not the *why*. In other disciplines, the important question is *what*, and the answer is interpretive or descriptive. Botany and zoology, classifications of the plant and animal worlds, relate almost exclusively to the *what* question.

With regard to *hukim*, to ask *why* is foolish, but we can and must ask *what*. The question *why* refers to the motivation and the ultimate explanation. It is beyond our ken, especially since God is involved. The answer to *why* is "Because God wills it." When one asks *why* God created the world, the answer is because he willed it.[3] The realization of God's will is the greatest goal. However, even in the context of *hok*, we can and must ask the question of *what*. "What is the *parah adumah*?" is a valid question, as is "What does this *hok* tell me?" Neither of these questions asks why God ordained that law. Here we are only asking, "What is the spiritual message of the *parah adumah* that I can assimilate into my world view?"

ᴈ The Importance of Interpretation and Understanding in Avodah she-ba-lev

The Rav discussed the element of *Avodah she-ba-lev* (worship of the heart) as a spiritual modality that tells us how to live and worship God. *Avodah she-ba-lev* must be present in the ritual and moral spheres of every religious act. Each human being is commanded to be an *oved Elohim*, which connotes commitment, emotional warmth, joy and love for God. The Hasidic movement added the emphasis on the emotional

---

3 See the Kaddish: "*Yitgadel ve-yitkadesh sheme rabba ba-olma di-vera ki-re'uteh*" (In the world that he created according to his will).

element of serving God. The Ba'al ha-Tanya cites a Gemara in Tractate *Hagigah*:

א"ל בר הי הי להלל מאי דכתיב ושבתם וראיתם בין צדיק לרשע בין עובד א-להים
לאשר לא עבדו היינו צדיק היינו עובד א-להים היינו רשע היינו אשר לא עבדו א"ל
עבדו ולא עבדו תרוייהו צדיקי גמורי נינהו ואינו דומה שונה פרקו מאה פעמים
לשונה פרקו מאה ואחד. א"ל ומשום חד זימנא קרי ליה לא עבדו א"ל אין

Bar Hei Hei said to Hillel: What is the meaning of that which
is written: You will return and see the difference between a
righteous person and a wicked person, between one who
serves God and one who does not serve Him? A righteous
person is the same as one who serves God, and a wicked person
is the same as one who does not serve him! Hillel answered
Bar Hei Hei: One who serves God and one who does not
serve him are both completely righteous. Nevertheless, there
is no comparison between one who reviews his learning one
hundred times and one who reviews his learning one hundred
and one times. Bar Hei Hei said to Hillel: And because [he
failed to review his studies that] one [extra] time, he is called
one who does not serve God? Hillel answered him: Yes![4]

Rav Shneur Zalman of Liadi understands it in these terms – one must
not merely discharge one's duty but also rejoice and love the *mitzvah*.

וכן אף מי שאינו מתמיד בלמודו בטבעו רק שהרגיל עצמו ללמוד בהתמדה גדולה
ונעשה ההרגל לו טבע שני די לו באהבה מסותרת זו אלא אם כן רוצה ללמוד
יותר מרגילותו ובזה יובן מה שנאמר בגמרא דעובד א-להים היינו מי ששונה פרקו
מאה פעמים ואחד ולא עבדו היינו מי ששונה פרקו מאה פעמים לבד והיינו משום
שבימיהם היה הרגילות לשנות כל פרק מאה פעמים כדאיתא התם בגמרא משל
משוק של חמרים שנשכרים לעשר פרסי בזוזא ולאחד עשר פרסי בתרי זוזי מפני
שהוא יותר מרגילותם. ולכן זאת הפעם המאה ואחת היתרה על הרגילות שהורגל

---

4   BT *Hagigah* 9b.

מנעוריו שקולה כנגד כולן ועולה על גביהן ביתר שאת ויתר עז להיות נקרא עובד
א־להים מפני שכדי לשנות טבע הרגילות צריך לעורר את האהבה לה' על ידי
שמתבונן בגדולת ה' במוחו לשלוט על הטבע שבחלל השמאלי המלא דם הנפש
הבהמית שמהקליפה שממנה הוא הטבע וזו היא עבודה תמה לבינוני. או לעורר את
האהבה המסותרת שבלבו למשול על ידה על הטבע שבחלל השמאלי שזו נקרא
גם כן עבודה להלחם עם הטבע והיצר על ידי שמעורר האהבה המסותרת בלבו
מה שאין כן כשאין לו מלחמה כלל אין אהבה זו מצד עצמה נקראת עבודתו כלל.

So, too, is one who, although by nature not an assiduous
student, has yet accustomed himself to study with great
diligence, so that the habit has become second nature with
him; for him, too, suffices the innate love, unless he wishes to
study more than his wont. This will explain the statement in
the Gemara that "one who is serving God" refers to him who
revises his lesson 101 times, while "one who serves him not"
refers to him who revises his lesson no more than 100 times.
This is because in those days it was customary to revise each
lesson one hundred times, as, indeed, illustrated in the Gemara,
ibid., by the example taken from the market where donkey-
drivers used to hire themselves out at a rate of ten parasangs
for a zuz, but for eleven parasangs charged two zuzim, because
that exceeded their customary practice. For the same reason,
the 101st revision, which is beyond the normal practice to
which the student had been accustomed since childhood, is
considered equivalent to all the first one hundred times put
together, and even surpassing them in endurance and effort,
hence entitling him to be called "one who is serving God." For
in order to change his habitual nature, he must arouse the love
of God by means of meditation in his mind on the greatness
of God, in order to gain mastery over the nature that is in the
left part [of the heart] which is full of the animal soul's blood
originating in the *kelipah*, whence comes his nature. This is a
perfect service for a *benoni*. Or, he must awaken the hidden

love in his heart to control, through it, the nature that is in the left part, for this, too, is called service – the waging of war against his nature and inclination, by means of exciting the love that is hidden in his heart. However, if he has no war at all to wage, the said love in itself can in no way be credited to his service.[5]

Avodat Elokim is not attainable unless the *hok* conveys a message to us. In order to offer God my heart and soul and to serve him, I must understand and be involved in the logos of the *maaseh ha-mitzvah*. Since we are rational beings, we cannot experience the bliss of the divine commandment if the logos is excluded from that involvement – not the *why* but the *what*. We therefore have a duty to interpret *hukim* even though we cannot explain them.

✄ The Interpretation of Shiluah ha-ken

The Ramban in Parashat Ki Tetze[6] makes a similar point regarding the *mitzvah* of *shiluah ha-ken* (which is not a *hok*). The Talmud[7] tells us that this *mitzvah*, which emanates from a divine decree, is not a function of His mercy, suggesting that we may not speculate about reasons. The Ramban asks: Does this mean that I cannot say that because the Torah forbids taking the offspring from the mother, it is therefore concerned with human mercy and kindness? The Ramban's point is that it depends on how one asks the question: as *why* or as *what*. Although we do not find this vocabulary in the Ramban's lexicon, this is what he means. We do not know, and it is pointless to ask, why God created the *mitzvah*. However, we are duty-bound to ask what it means and formulate an intelligent response.

---

5 *Likutei Amarim Tanya*, Ch. 15, translated by Nissan Mandel, "Kehot" Publication Society.
6 Nahmanides on Deuteronomy 22:6.
7 BT *Berachot* 33b.

✥ Parah Adumah as Hok Par Excellence

Let us proceed to raise the *what* question regarding *parah adumah* – the question that Rav Moshe ha-Darshan (quoted by Rashi) described. To Rav Moshe ha-Darshan, the *parah adumah* meant atonement for the sin of the Golden Calf, which had such a devastating effect upon Jewish history. How do we experience the verse זאת חקת התורה – "And this is the statute of the Torah"?[8] When I say *Shema Yisrael,* my experience is one of closeness to God. What about *parah adumah*? What is its central motif?

What is unique about that *parashah* of the *parah*? The sages speak of the *hukat ha-parah*. Why only *parah*? True, the *Midrash* and Rashi mention *shatnez*, and the Ramban mentions the sacrifices – for example, the goat that was sent into the wilderness on Yom Kippur, which is an excellent example of a non-rational *mitzvah*. But the sages saw the *parah adumah* as the central *hok*: גזירה היא מלפני ואין לך רשות להרהר אחריה – "It is a statute issued by Me, and you may not question it."[9] This is indicative of all *hukim,* and the question of what is so incomprehensible in this *hok* begs to be asked. The popular answer has to do with the ceremony of the *parah adumah*. The mere fact that it is a sacrifice offered outside the three camps already sets it apart because in all other cases, Jewish law forbids slaughtering an animal outside the sacred precincts. The burning of the *parah* to ashes, which are then mixed with spring water – all these aspects of the ritual are surely mystifying. However, it is not these ceremonial aspects which explain the singularity of the *parah adumah,* but rather that the *mitzvah* of *parah adumah* captures the tragedy of the human condition. (See the following essay: "*Parah Adumah:* The Tragedy of the Human Condition.")

---

8 Numbers 19:2.
9 Rashi on Numbers 19:2.

ﺣﻮﻗﺖ

Hukat II: Parah Adumah: The Tragedy of the Human Condition

The Placement of Parah Adumah

ACCORDING TO OUR tradition, the *parashah* of the *parah adumah* was revealed to Moshe together with the section regarding the Tabernacle.[1] The first red heifer was offered on the eighth day of the *miluim* (the consecration of the Tabernacle). Therefore, the section regarding the red heifer should have been inserted either in the context of the *parshiyot* about the *Mishkan* (Tzav, Shemini, or Terumah) or those that contain the rules regarding ritual purity and impurity (Tazria and Metzora). The red heifer, which is related to *tumat met* (ritual impurity that comes from contact with a corpse), belongs in that context. The insertion of the section dealing with the red heifer between Parashat Korah and Miriam's death in Parashat Hukat is incomprehensible.

The following two questions are to be raised:

What is the continuity between the *parah adumah* and the account of Miriam's death?

---

1 BT *Gittin* 60b and JT *Megillah* 3:5.

345

How are we to understand the sequence of the three *parshiyot:* Shelah, Korah and Hukat?

↝ The Unique Quality of Tumat Met

To answer these questions we need to first understand the unique quality of *tumat met.* In other portions of the Torah, such as Emor, we have an inkling of *tumat met:* לנפש לא יטמא בעמיו – "One shall not defile oneself for a soul"[2] – and Naso: על נפש מת לא יבא – "He shall not come near a dead person,"[3] but we could not derive the principle of *tumat met* from them. These *parshiyot* contain the prohibition against entering the tent of the dead, perhaps without consequences. The first time we encounter the fact that a corpse is a source of ritual impurity is the section that deals with the red heifer – and this is its uniqueness.

What is unique about *tumat met?* The answer is the wondrous expression of *hukah.* The Torah never said "This is the law concerning a person who becomes contaminated by a creeping insect, by a person suffering from a discharge or one afflicted with *tzaraat.*" However, regarding *tumat met,* the Torah, with the same solemnity of the statement "This is a law of the Torah," says: זאת התורה אדם כי ימות באהל – "This is the law concerning one who dies in a tent."[4] Why? The reason is that *tumat met* is different from other sources of ritual impurity. It is obvious that a kohen may have contact with a creeping insect, a person suffering from a discharge and a person afflicted with *tzaraat,* but he may not come into contact with a corpse.

↝ The Requirement of Immersion vs. Sprinkling

Another area in which *tumat met* differs from other kinds of ritual impurity is the method of purification. In all cases of ritual impurity, the

---

2 Leviticus 21:1.
3 Numbers 6:6.
4 Numbers 19:14.

method of purification is immersion in a *mikveh* (ritual bath). The only exception to this is *tumat met,* in which immersion in a *mikveh* comprises only part of the cleansing. The person who has contracted *tumat met* must also be sprinkled with the water of purification on the third and seventh days after contracting the *tumah.* Otherwise, he remains ritually impure and may not enter the Temple.

Why is *tumat met* so different from other instances of ritual impurity?

הוא יתחטא בו ביום השלישי וביום השביעי יטהר ואם לא יתחטא ביום השלישי וביום השביעי לא יטהר.

He shall purify himself with it on the third day, and on the seventh day he shall become pure. Yet if he does not purify himself on the third day, then he will not become pure on the seventh day.[5]

✌ The Tragedy of the Human Condition

The text contains a message regarding the metaphysical uniqueness of humanity. The human state comprises both greatness and tragedy. The difference between the two cleansing methods, immersion in a *mikveh* and being sprinkled with the water of purification, symbolize two different experiences. Immersion is done by the person who requires cleansing, while sprinkling is done by someone else. The person who has contracted *tumat met* cannot purify himself by his own efforts. A human being defiles himself, and therefore must cleanse himself. Immersion, which symbolizes human freedom, creativity, capability and initiative, is an important example of free will.

Sprinkling is the antithesis of immersion. The individual who has contracted *tumat met* cannot sprinkle the cleaning water upon himself. והזה הטהר על הטמא – "The one who is ritually pure must perform the

---

5 Numbers 19:12.

sprinkling upon the one who is ritually impure . . .".[6] The one who defiled himself cannot purify himself. Someone who is already ritually pure must do it for him. Why can people cleanse themselves from all other forms of ritual impurity simply by immersing in a *mikveh*? Today one of the reasons that it is religiously problematic for Jews to ascend the Temple Mount is that we have neither a red heifer nor a ritually pure person who can perform the sprinkling for us, for we are all ritually impure. *Tumat met* is therefore unique.

∼ Two Approaches to Teshuvah

Our sages equated the process of *teshuvah* with *taharah* – purification. In the Mishnah, in Tractate *Yoma*, Rabbi Akiva used the *mikveh* as a metaphor for God. Just as a *mikveh* cleanses those who have become ritually impure, God cleanses the Jewish people.[7] The prophet Yehezkel used sprinkling of water as a metaphor as well: וזרקתי עליכם מים טהורים וטהרתם מכל טמאותיכם ומכל גלוליכם אטהר אתכם – "I will sprinkle pure water upon you, and you shall be purified. I will cleanse you of all your defilements and abominations."[8] Teshuvah presupposes both methods. The initiative lies with the transgressor. If he is too arrogant to admit that he sinned, if he cannot bow his head and bend his knee in order to immerse in the *mikveh*, then he cannot repent. If the transgressor takes the initiative, then God will complete the final act of *teshuvah*, of purification.

∼ Tumah: An Encounter with Ugliness
vs. an Encounter with Tragedy

Other kinds of ritual impurity include that which can be contracted from a *sheretz* (creeping animals), *nevalah* (the carcass of an animal), or

---

6 Numbers 19:19.
7 BT *Yoma* 85b.
8 Ezekiel 36:25.

a *zav* or *zavah* (a man or woman who suffers from a discharge). These kinds of *tumah* cause revulsion. They are simply aesthetically ugly.

Tumat met occupies an independent category. Certainly a human corpse is as subject to decay as an animal carcass is, but we feel differently when we must deal with a human. In the animal kingdom, death simply destroys the functionality of the organism. However, the death of a human being is not only physical; there is a spiritual dimension as well. It ends the existence of an individual who was driven by vision and hope, who experienced joy and sorrow. When a human being dies, an individual who was capable of creating and destroying worlds is gone forever.

✂ The End of a Spiritual World

Human death therefore constitutes the destruction of a world. The most tragic experience of a human being is to know that after his death, he cannot continue serving God. Rebbi – who was also known as Rabbi Yehuda ha-Nasi, the redactor of the *Mishnah* – wept before his death. When his students asked him why he was weeping, he replied that he was grieved over the Torah and *mitzvot*.[9] Even the blissful life of the hereafter does not compare to the joy of learning Torah and performing *mitzvot* in this world. This is unlike the animal world, in which the individual animal exists only as a representative of a species. As long as the species survives, the individual death is not so great a tragedy. For human beings, who merit the highest levels of Divine Providence and each of whom is a microcosm, death is an existential tragedy. Maimonides developed this idea further in his work *The Guide for the Perplexed*.[10]

---

9 BT *Ketubbot* 103b.
10 Maimonides, *Guide for the Perplexed*, vol. 3, Chapter 17.

֍   The Jewish Value of Human Life

The Rav related an astounding story in this regard that was heard from a European behind the Iron Curtain. Nicolae Ceauşescu, the prime minister of Romania, visited Egyptian Prime Minister Anwar Sadat in the fall of 1973 and discussed the imminent war that everyone but the State of Israel knew about. Ceauşescu warned Sadat not to start the war because the Israeli army was far superior to the Egyptian one. Sadat acknowledged this, but stated that there was another reason to start the war. Taking an Israeli newspaper from a drawer, he showed it to the Romanian prime minister, who remarked that he could not read it. Sadat then showed him a picture of a young man in an army uniform who had been killed, and the article that showed that the entire country of Israel mourned for him. Sadat said: A nation like this cannot survive a war of attrition for long. If every individual is so dear to them, and if they continue to mourn for each of their fallen as deeply as the article and picture indicate, they will lose the war no matter how superior their weaponry may be.

In Israel, the urge to save a young life takes precedence over every other consideration. When one Jew dies, the world collapses. Therefore, *tumat met* is not a result of the death of the body but of the departure of the soul. It is a response to human helplessness, which is a traumatic existential experience. The verse in Ecclesiastes states: כי מקרה בני האדם ומקרה הבהמה ומקרה אחד להם – "The fate of human beings and the fate of beasts are one and the same ..."[11] Hence, *tumat met* represents the tragedy of the human condition, from which no one can escape. A person may cleanse himself of ordinary *tumah* on his own, but purification from *tumat met* demands two distinct forms of cleansing: immersion and sprinkling. God then completes the purification process. When will

---

11 Ecclesiastes 3:19.

this occur? It will take place during the end of days, when בלע המות לנצח וכו' ומחה ה' א־להים דמעה מעל כל פנים – "He will eliminate death forever, and the Lord God will wipe tears from all faces,"[12] and so on. Then the whole world will be cleansed of death, since death will be no more. Until that time comes, we must struggle with death and try to defeat it.

Judaism, which holds human life as sacred, honors the human effort to provide healing and preserve life. Physicians, who have a divine mandate to heal, may decide matters of religious significance that fall within their purview, such as whether a patient may fast on Yom Kippur.[13] Judaism believes that human beings, with God's help, will defeat death eventually. Therefore, immersion by a human being in order to cleanse himself of ritual impurity is appropriate. However, Judaism is not naïve enough to teach that human beings are already immortal. Only God will save us from death. If this is so, how can we redeem ourselves from the ritual impurity that death causes? Through ritual immersion, we can limit the power of death. Through sprinkling, we can place our trust in God and hope that the day will arrive soon when death will be defeated. The *Midrash ha-gadol* comments on the verse:

ואסף איש טהור את אפר הפרה והניח מחוץ למחנה במקום טהור והיתה לעדת בני ישראל למשמרת למי נדה חטאת היא.

A man who is ritually pure shall gather the ashes of the cow and place them outside the camp in a pure location. For the assembly of Israel it shall be kept safely as water of sprinkling; it is for purification.

The *Midrash* says:

ואסף איש טהור זה הקב"ה דכתיב טהור עינים מראות רע (חבקוק א:יג) את אפר הפרה אלו גליותיהן של ישראל והניח מחוץ למחנה במקום טהור זו ירושלים שהיא טהורה. והיתה לעדת בני ישראל למשמרת לפי שבעולם הזה ישראל

---

12 Isaiah 25:8.
13 Shulhan Aruch, Orah Hayyim 618:1.

מיטמאין ומיטהרין על פי כהן גדול אבל לעתיד לבוא הקב״ה עתיד לטהרן שנאמר
וזרקתי עליכם מים טהורים וטהרתם (יחזקאל לו:כה) כן יאמר רחום.

A pure man shall gather [the ashes of the cow]. This refers
to God, as it is written: "Your eyes are too pure to see evil"
(Habakuk 1:13). "The ashes of the cow": These are the exiles
of Israel. "Place it outside the camp in a pure location": That
is Yerushalayim, which is pure. "For the assembly of Israel it
shall remain kept safely," because in this world Israel becomes
defiled and purified through the agency of the High Priest,
but in the future, God will purify them, as it is written: "Then
I will sprinkle pure water upon you that you may become
cleansed" (Ezekiel 36:25). So will the Merciful One say.[14]

Humanity cannot defeat death by itself. God must complete the task.
So what is the great *hukah*? The great mystery is death, which human
beings cannot grasp. אדם כי ימות באהל – The corpse of "one who dies
in a tent" renders others ritually impure not because they experienced
something ugly but rather because they suffered a trauma. כל הבא אל האהל
וכל אשר באהל יטמא שבעת ימים – "Whoever enters the tent and whatever is
in the tent shall be rendered ritually impure for seven days."[15] How can
one cleanse oneself of such powerful impurity? ולקחו לטמא מעפר שרפת
החטאת ונתן עליו מים חיים אל כלי – "They shall take for the one who is ritually
impure from the ashes of the burnt sacrifice and pour spring water upon
it in a vessel."[16]

❧ A Bridge during Thirty-Eight Years of Hester Panim

How then does the section regarding the *parah adumah* serve as the
introduction to the verse ויבאו בני ישראל כל העדה מדבר צן – "The children of

---

14 *Midrash ha-Gadol,* Parashat Hukat, Parah Adumah 19:21.
15 Numbers 19:14.
16 Numbers 19:17.

Israel, the whole assembly arrived at the wilderness of Zin"?[17] Between the episode of Korah and the death of Miriam there is a gap of thirty-eight years. The *Rishonim* dispute as to whether Korah's rebellion occurred before or after the story of the spies.[18] However, we know that it happened in the second year after the exodus from Egypt. Miriam died in the fortieth year, after the generation of the desert had passed on.[19] The Torah does not record anything of what happened during those thirty-eight intervening years, so that period of time remains mysterious and even frightening. Where can we find a clue as to what happened during that time? If so much had happened in only two years, then one can only imagine how much transpired over the next thirty-eight, but the Torah provides no details. The bridge to these thirty-eight years apparently lies in the *hok* of the *parah adumah*.

The *Torah* in *Sefer Devarim* summarizes these thirty-eight years.

ותשבו ותבכו לפני ה' ולא שמע ה' בקלכם ולא האזין אליכם: ותשבו בקדש ימים רבים כימים אשר ישבתם :ונפן ונסע המדברה דרך ים סוף כאשר דבר ה' אלי ונסב את הר שעיר ימים רבים.

Then you retreated and wept before God, but God did not listen to your voice, nor did he hearken to you. You dwelt in Kadesh for many days, as many days as you dwelt. We turned and journeyed to the wilderness towards the Sea of Reeds, as the Lord had commanded me, and we circled Mount Seir for many days."[20]

The journey described reflects an aimless kind of wandering without any directedness.

---

17 Numbers 20:1.
18 See Ramban and Ibn Ezra on Numbers 16:1.
19 See Rashi on Numbers 20:1–2 and Ramban on Numbers 20:1.
20 Deuteronomy 1:45–46, 2:1.

והימים אשר הלכנו מקדש ברנע עד אשר עברנו את נחל זרד שלשים ושמנה שנה
עד תם כל הדור אנשי המלחמה מקרב המחנה כאשר נשבע ה' להם: וגם יד ה'
היתה בם להמם מקרב המחנה עד תמם: ויהי כאשר תמו כל אנשי המלחמה למות
מקרב העם: וידבר ה' אלי לאמר.

The days that we traveled from Kadesh Barnea until we
crossed the Zered Brook were thirty-eight years until the end
of the entire generation, the men of war, from the midst of the
camp, as Hashem swore to them. Even the hand of Hashem
was on them to confound them from the midst of the camp
until their end. So it was that the men of war finished dying
from amidst the people . . . Hashem spoke to me, saying . . .[21]

ﻉ The Jewish People as Circling Stars

These thirty-eight years were a time of *hester panim*. It was an era of
spiritual decay and lack of accomplishment. The circling of Mount Seir
led to the Rambam's description of the stars and other heavenly bodies
that also move in a circle.[22] According to the Rambam, these heavenly
bodies are endowed with intelligence. They are attracted by the love of
God and want to approach Him, but they fail and are compelled to start
anew. The Jewish nation's travels, too, had no destination. The nation
was completely alienated from God, and there was no communication.
Our sages describe that period in fearful terms:

כל ט' באב היו עושין קבריהן ושוכבין בתוכן ולמחר הכרוז יוצא הבדלו החיים
ואותה השנה שכלתה הגזרה קמו כולם והיו סבורים שמא טעו בחודש עד שראו
הלבנה מלאה ואז ידעו שכלתה הגזרה ועשו יו"ט.

Every year on the ninth day of the month of Av, they
would dig their graves and lie in them. In the morning, the

---

21 Deuteronomy 2:14–17.
22 See *Mishneh Torah*, Hilchot Yesodei ha-Torah, Chapter 3.

announcement was made: "Let the living separate" [from those who had died during the night]. The year that the decree was rescinded, they all rose and thought that they erred in the calculation of the month till they saw the full moon. Then, knowing that the decree had been rescinded, they held a celebration.[23]

The Midrash paints a horrific picture for us of thousands of people who dug their own graves every year and died. Theirs was a life with no hope or future. No one prayed for fulfillment, for everyone knew what his ultimate fate would be. People did not understand the *hester panim,* just as our generation does not understand the Holocaust. Existence seemed irrational and absurd to them, since they were living in order to die. This thirty-eight-year period was one of the most paradoxical in Jewish history. Not even Moshe Rabbenu could communicate with God then. The community waited for God's intervention and his redeeming grace.

The Eventual Purification of the Jewish People

At the conclusion of the story of the *meraglim,* the Torah sets forth the laws of *hallah* and wine libations. These laws, which are applicable only in the Land of Israel, convey a message of hope: no matter how long the delay, we will eventually arrive there and enjoy its bounty. Yet the people had to endure the darkness first.

The Period of Zot Hukat ha-Torah

This dark period came to an end in the fortieth year. In a manner of speaking, God performed the act of sprinkling, purifying all those who were *tamei met* (defiled by contact with the dead). This is how the

---

23 Tosafot, *Taanit* 30b, ד"ה יום שבו כלו מתי מדבר.

parashah of the *parah adumah* serves as the bridge that spans the river flowing into oblivion. The dark thirty-eight-year period would become known as *zot hukat ha-Torah*, when human beings suspended their judgment and surrendered their rationality to God, just as one must surrender one's rationality in order to accept the *hok* of *parah adumah*.

Only at the end of that period, when the people stopped digging their graves, did their conversation with God resume. The symbol of that period is the *hukat ha-parah*. Is there a more dramatic story of the thirty eight years than אדם כי ימות באהל – "One who dies in a tent"?[24] What did the Jewish people do during those thirty-eight years besides dig their graves and die? The fact that Moshe Rabbenu died without having been allowed to enter the Land of Israel, as he so desired, is also part of *zot hukat ha-Torah*, one of the mysteries before which a Jew can only bow his head in submission and surrender to God's will.

---

24 Numbers 19:14.

יָּ בלק ָּיָ

Balak: Two Kinds of Prophets, Two Forms of Prophecy

HE RAV ANALYZED the character of two prophets, Moshe Rabbenu and Bilaam. In order to illustrate the differences between them, he cited imagery from his classic *derashah* on Parashat Bereshit, עלי תאנה וכותנות אור – "Fig Leaves and Clothes of Light."[1]

The verse says, ולא קם נביא עוד בישראל כמשה אשר ידעו ה' פנים אל פנים – "Never again did there arise in Israel a prophet like Moshe, whom the Lord knew face to face."[2]

The sages comment:

בישראל לא קם אבל באומות העולם קם ואיזה זה בלעם בן בעור.

One never arose among the Jewish people, but among the non-Jews, such a prophet did arise – Bilaam son of Beor.[3]

This indicates that from a certain perspective, Moshe and Bilaam

---

1 For this *derashah* in its entirety, the reader is referred to *Yemei Zikaron,* 199–214.
2 Deuteronomy 34:10.
3 *Yalkut Shimoni* 966 on Deuteronomy 34:10.

were comparable. However, the sages[4] made a strong distinction between them:

משה לא היה יודע מי מדבר עמו ובלעם היה יודע מי מדבר עמו שנא' נאם שומע
אמרי אל . . . משה לא היה מדבר עמו אלא כשהוא עומד שנאמר ואתה פה עמוד
עמדי ובלעם היה מדבר עמו כשהוא נופל שנא' אשר מחזה שקי יחזה נופל וגלוי
עינים.

Moshe did not know who was speaking with him. Bilaam knew who was speaking with him, as it is written: "The words of one who hears the sayings of God . . ." Moshe only spoke with God when he was standing, as it says, "But as for you, stand here with me . . ." Bilaam spoke with him when he was falling, as it is written: "Who sees the vision of Shaddai while fallen and with uncovered eyes."[5]

ꙮ The Language of Prophecy

The prophecy of Bilaam differs from that of Moshe Rabbenu in terms of the mellifluous language, use of metaphor and panoramic vision of the end of days. Who can compare to Bilaam in his polished and elegant speech? His words were even integrated into the *mussaf* prayer of Rosh ha-Shannah. לא הביט און ביעקב ולא ראה עמל בישראל ה' א־להיו עמו ותרועת מלך בו – "He perceived no iniquity in Jacob and saw no perversity in Israel. The Lord his God is with him, and the friendship of the king is in him."[6] When a Jew enters the synagogue each morning, he recites a verse of Bilaam's prophecy: מה טבו אהליך יעקב משכנתיך ישראל – "How goodly are your tents, O Jacob, your dwelling places , O Israel."[7] Only Moshe Rabbenu used such beautiful words when he prophesied.

---

4 Ad loc.
5 Sifrei Zuta 7:89.
6 Numbers 23:21.
7 Numbers 24:5.

✺ Fig Leaves vs. Garments of Leather

This aspect of the garb of prophecy is illustrated with an example from Parashat Bereshit. Before Adam and Hava ate the forbidden fruit, the Torah states that they were naked.‑ויהיו שניהם ערומים האדם ואשתו ולא יתב "ששו " – "They were both naked, the man and his wife, and they were not ashamed."[8] After they sinned, the Torah states, ותפקחנה עיני שניהם וידעו כי עירמם הם ויתפרו עלה תאנה ויעשו להם חגרת – "Then the eyes of both of them were opened. They realized that they were naked and they sewed fig leaves together, making aprons for themselves."[9] Suddenly, they found nakedness objectionable and wanted to cover themselves. Toward the end of the chapter, the Torah indicates God's displeasure with the fig leaves, as it says ויעש ה' א‑להים לאדם ולאשתו כתנות עור וילבשם – "The Lord made for Adam and his wife garments of skin and he clothed them in it."[10] In brief, the Torah describes two kinds of clothing that Adam and Hava wore: that which they prepared themselves – the fig leaves and what God used to clothe them – the garments of skin.

Clothing and nakedness relate not only to the human body but also to one's *neshama*, one's soul, as the Zohar explains.

> ת"ח, כד קריבו אינון יומין קמי מלכא קדישא, אי הוא זכאה, האי, בר נש דנפיק מעלמא, סליק ועאל באינון יומין, ואינון לבושי יקר, דמתלבשא בי נשמתיה ואינון יומין הוו, דזכה בהו, ולא חב בהו.

Come and see: When these days approach before the holy King, if the individual who passed away was a righteous person, he ascends and enters in these days. His *neshamah*

---

8 Genesis 2:25.
9 Genesis 3:7.
10 Genesis 3:21.

[soul] is clothed with garments of splendor and these days transpire because he was righteous and did not transgress.[11]

The clothing that Adam and Hava used were not solely for the purpose of covering their bodies. Their main purpose was to cover their souls. Isaiah speaks of *bigdei yesha* (clothing of salvation) – שוש אשיש בה׳ תגל נפשי בא־להי כי הלבישני בגדי ישע מעיל צדקה יעטני – "I will rejoice exceedingly with the Lord. My soul will exult with my God, for he has clothed me in the raiment of salvation; in a cloak of righteousness he has robed me …"[12] The clothing of salvation is worn by someone whose soul is filled with joy over being in God's presence. A soul that is naked, ungirded with faith, is exposed to the hardships of chance and to nature's whims. People in that situation suffer from loneliness, especially when they become older and lose close relatives. Only God can provide the clothing of solace and warmth for a naked and vulnerable soul. A Jew who is clothed in *bigdei yesha* is girded with faith and the warmth of the creator.

✌ Robes of Light

The *Midrash Rabbah*[13] distinguishes between two types of garb: כתנות עור with an *ayin*, which means "leather garments" and כותנות אור with an *aleph* – an additional homiletic connotation – meaning "robes of light." These two kinds of clothing reflect both ordinary human clothing and spiritual clothing expressed through the cloak of the divine light. This is illustrated this through two figures from the Talmud, Elisha ben Abuya and Rabbi Akiva. Elisha ben Abuya had the protection of the Roman government. He could sleep at night without worrying that thieves would steal his belongings. He was clothed in the comfort of *kotnot or* with an *ayin*. However, he abandoned Jewish tradition and was left

---

11 Zohar, Vayehi 299.
12 Isaiah 61:10.
13 Genesis Rabbah 20:21.

friendless. Thus he lacked *kotnot or* with an *aleph* – he had no cloak of salvation.

In comparison, Rabbi Akiva had no *kotnot or* with an *ayin*. Subject to imprisonment by the Roman authorities, he had to keep constant vigilance. In his later years, he was a homeless fugitive. In the end, he died a cruel death, his flesh scraped from his body by iron combs. Yet despite his difficult life and terrible death, he was enrobed in *kotnot or* with an *aleph*. When he recited the *shema* for the last time before he died, he was accompanied by God and by *Knesset Yisrael*. His cloak was not only one of salvation but also of righteousness, steeped in Torah knowledge and wisdom.

The Garb of Speech

This dualism also manifests itself in a person's speech – the logos of a human being and his most distinctive element, which reflects the *tzelem Elokim*. Unlike the other beings of the animal kingdom, a human being is a *medaber*, one who articulates thoughts and ideas. The speech of a person who expresses deep thoughts and transcendental feelings of holiness is compared to a "cloak of light." Yet all too often, human speech is only a fig leaf that barely conceals a lack of thought and emotion. Such a person's inner character has little of substance. Even if he is articulate and possesses oratorical skills, he has nothing of value to say.

Moshe vs. Bilaam

The difference between Moshe's prophecy and Bilaam's is compared to the difference between the cloaks of light and the fig leaves. "Moshe did not know who was speaking to him . . . Moshe only spoke with God when he was standing." In other words, when Moshe delivered the word of God, he was expressing the emotions and thoughts of his own soul. Experientially, his prophecy emanated from the depths of his spirit. His standing up represents his asserting his own personality rather than being a passive channel. His personality merged with his prophecy into a single identity.

When Moshe said, בצר לך ומצאוך כל הדברים האלה – "When you are in distress and all these things have befallen you,"[14] he felt anguish over the Jewish people's suffering. When he consoled his people and said

ושב ה' א-להיך את שבותך ורחמך ושב וקבצך מכל העמים אשר הפיצך ה' א-להיך שמה – "Then the Lord your God will bring back your captivity and have mercy upon you. He will gather you in from all the peoples among which the Lord your God has scattered you,"[15] his soul overflowed with joy for those who would return to Zion after a thousand years. Moshe's prophecy was thus a clear reflection of his lofty soul, capacity for displaying his self-sacrifice and unparalleled devotion that was his hallmark as the *rebbi* of all of Israel.

Genuine prophecy is a "cloak of light," for it expresses the grandeur of the prophet's personality and his inner sanctity. However, there were false prophets whose words were nothing but fig leaves. Their opening phrase, כה אמר ה' צבאו-ת א-להי ישראל לאמר – "Thus spoke the Lord, Master of Legions, God of Israel, saying . . ."[16] was only the routine, regimented language of a personality devoid of content.

But Bilaam's words had no connection with his cold personality. His entire prophecy was a "fig leaf" that hid his ugly spirit. Our sages say of him: בלעם היה יודע מה הקב"ה עתיד לדבר עמו שנ' ויודע דעת עליון – "Bilaam knew what the Lord was going to tell him, as it is written: 'The words of one who hears the sayings of God . . .'"[17] In other words, Bilaam knew perfectly well that the prophetic words that he spoke were not his. He did not feel inside himself what his mouth uttered, nor did he appreciate the beauty of the words that flowed mechanically from his mouth.

---

14 Deuteronomy 4:30.
15 Deuteronomy 30:3.
16 Jeremiah 28:2.
17 Sifrei Zuta 7:89.

Unlike Moshe, Bilaam did not stand up to meet with and participate in the divine prophecy.

On the words ויקר ה' אל בלעם וישם דבר בפיו – "The Lord happened upon Bilaam and put an utterance in his mouth,"[18] Rashi comments, ונתן לו הקב"ה רסן וחכה בפיו כאדם הפוקס בהמה בחכה להוליכה אל אשר ירצה – "God placed a bridle and hook in his mouth, as a person bridles an animal with a fishhook in order to lead it where he wishes."[19] In short, Bilaam was compelled to speak the words of God even as he remained himself, unchanged: Bilaam the sorcerer, a fallen misfit.

18 Numbers 23:16.
19 Rashi on Numbers 23:16.

Pinhas: Joshua – The Next Link in the Chain of the Mesorah

❧ He Who Guards the Fig Tree

IN PARASHAT PINHAS, the Torah describes the qualifications of a Jewish leader and the process of succession to Moshe Rabbenu.

וידבר משה אל ה' לאמר: יפקד ה' א-להי הרוחת לכל בשר איש על העדה: אשר
יצא לפניהם ואשר יבא לפניהם ואשר יוציאם ואשר יביאם ולא תהיה עדת ה'
כצאן אשר אין להם רעה: ויאמר ה' אל משה קח לך את יהושע בן נון איש אשר
רוח בו וסמכת את ידך עליו: והעמדת אתו לפני אלעזר הכהן ולפני כל העדה
וצויתה אתו לעיניהם: ונתתה מהודך עליו למען ישמעו כל עדת בני ישראל: ולפני
אלעזר הכהן יעמד ושאל לו במשפט האורים לפני ה' על פיו יצאו ועל פיו יבאו
הוא וכל בני ישראל אתו וכל העדה: ויעש משה כאשר צוה ה' אתו ויקח את יהושע
ויעמדהו לפני אלעזר הכהן ולפני כל העדה: ויסמך את ידיו עליו ויצוהו כאשר דבר
ה' ביד משה.

Moshe spoke to the Lord, saying: Let the Lord, God of the spirits of all flesh, appoint a man over the assembly who shall go out before them and come in before them, who shall take them out and bring them in, and let God's assembly not be like sheep without a shepherd. The Lord said to Moshe: Take to yourself Joshua the son of Nun, a man in whom there is spirit, and lean your hand upon him. You shall stand him before Elazar the Kohen and before the entire assembly and command him before their eyes. You shall place some of your majesty upon him so that the entire assembly of the Children of Israel will pay heed. He shall stand before Elazar the Kohen, who shall ask the judgment of the Urim before the Lord. At his word shall they go out and at his word shall they come in, he and all the children of Israel with him and the entire assembly. Moshe did as the Lord had commanded him. He took Joshua and stood him before Elazar the Kohen and before the entire assembly. He leaned his hands upon him and commanded him as the Lord had spoken through Moshe.[1]

The Mishnah in *Pirkei Avot* states, משה קבל תורה מסיני ומסרה ליהושע – "Moshe received the Torah from Sinai and transmitted it to Joshua . . ."[2] The sages ask why the Torah was given to Joshua when others, such as Pinhas and Elazar, had greater intellectual gifts. In answer, the Midrash[3] quotes a verse in Proverbs: "The one who guards the fig tree will merit eating from its fruits."[4] Joshua was chosen as Moshe's successor because he had served Moshe by arranging the chairs and spreading the mats before his *shiur*. Because of his devoted service, he was the appropriate candidate to replace Moshe Rabbenu.

Often, a leader's successor was chosen not only because of his intellectual prowess but also because of his devoted service to his teacher. Two examples of this are when the Baal Shem Tov passed away, the mantle of leadership was not given to Rav Yaakov Yosef, a Torah giant and the author of the *Toldot*. Rather, it was passed to the Magid of Mezeritch, who had served the Baal Shem Tov with great devotion and loyalty.

---

1   Numbers 27:15–23.
2   Mishnah *Avot* 1:1.
3   *Midrash Tanhuma,* Parashat Pinhas #11. See also Rashi's citation of the Midrash in his commentary on Numbers 27:16.
4   Proverbs 27:18.

Similarly, Rav Chaim Volozhin became the successor to his teacher, the Vilna Gaon, partly because he was his confidant to a greater degree than his other disciples.

This principle of the transmission of leadership can be derived from an excerpt of the Rambam's prologue to the *Mishneh Torah* in which he writes:

כל המצות שניתנו לו למשה בסיני בפירושן ניתנו . . . והמצוה שהיא פירוש התורה

לא כתבה אלא צוה בה לזקנים וליהושע ולשאר כל ישראל . . . ואלעזר ופנחס

ויהושע שלשתן קבלו ממשה וליהושע שהוא תלמידו של משה רבנו מסר תורה

שבעל פה וצוהו עליה.

All the *mitzvot* that were given to Moshe at Mount Sinai were given with their explanation . . . and the mitzvah which is the explanation of the Torah was not written but he commanded it to the elders, to Joshua and to the rest of Israel . . . Elazar, Pinhas and Joshua all received the Torah from Moshe, and to *Joshua, who was the disciple of Moshe Rabbenu,* he gave the Oral Law and commanded him regarding it.[5]

There seems to be a tautology in the Rambam's language. First, he states that Elazar, Pinhas and Joshua all learned under the tutelage of Moshe Rabbenu. Then, he states that Joshua, who was his disciple, received the Oral Law. What is the reason for the Rambam's apparent repetition? The Rambam's intent was apparently to explain that even though Moshe had many disciples, only Joshua merited receiving the tradition from Moshe Rabbenu. He became one of the *baalei ha-mesorah* because he was the foremost *talmid.*

---

5   The Rambam's introduction to the *Mishneh Torah.*

ﮊ The Acquisition of the Torah and the Harvest of Figs

It was no accident that this *midrash* mentions a fig tree. Other trees, such as olives, grapes, and dates, have a single, defined term of harvest, while the fig tree's fruits ripen over a much longer period of time. So, too, a person acquires the Torah not overnight, but over a protracted period of time. One who guards the fig tree will merit eating its fruits – the fruits of Torah and of kingship. This is precisely what happened to Joshua.

Joshua served Moshe day and night, as the verse indicates לא ימיש מתוך האהל – "He did not leave the tent."[6] Therefore, God honored him. Because Joshua served Moshe, he merited to receive the gifts of *ruah ha-kodesh* and prophecy. This is because the *mitzvah* of serving Torah scholars is greater than that of learning Torah.[7] Therefore, Joshua was granted the *mesorah* of Moshe's *regesh* and *hashkafa*, and the tradition of the Torah was transmitted to him exclusively. His level as a *baal mesorah* was beyond that of Elazar and Pinhas because he was Moshe's foremost disciple. Even though Pinhas learned directly from Moshe, the Rambam notes that Pinhas received the Torah from Joshua. In order for Pinhas to transmit the *mesorah* to Eli ha-Kohen, he had to receive it from Joshua.

The above-mentioned verse, וצויתה אתו לעיניהם – "And command him before their eyes," serves as the source for this Rambam. The *Sifrei Zuta* contends that this commanding refers to words of Torah.[8] Moreover, the *Pesikta Zutrata* on the verse in Deuteronomy, וצו את יהושע וחזקהו ואמ־ צהו – "But you shall command Joshua and strengthen him and give him resolve,"[9] states specifically that this command refers to *divrei Talmud* – the transmission of the Oral Law.[10]

---

6 Exodus 33:11.
7 BT *Berachot* 7b.
8 *Sifrei Zuta,* Numbers 27:19.
9 Deuteronomy 3:28.
10 *Yalkut Shimoni,* Vaethanan 3.

The Rambam also codifies the duality of receiving the Oral Torah and being part of the chain of tradition, one of the *baalei ha-mesorah*. He speaks of one type person who denies the Torah, together with a second type who denies its expounders.[11] One is a heretic in the explanation of the Oral Law, while the other is a heretic against the bearers of our tradition. The novel idea of Parashat Pinhas is that Joshua is not merely a successor to Moshe Rabbenu but rather one who stepped into his shoes as a full *baal mesorah*. The most important prerequisite of Joshua's succession as leader was his devotion to Moshe Rabbenu. It was thanks to his total commitment to Moshe that he became the Israelites' next leader.

---

11 *Mishneh Torah,* Hilchot Teshuvah 3:8.

מטות ⁓

Matot: The Distinction between a Neder and a Shevuah

⁓ "By the Life of the King" vs. "By the King"

IN TWO PLACES in Humash, the Ramban[1] differentiates between a *neder* (a vow) and a shevuah (an oath). The Ramban says that *nedarim* are taken בחיי המלך, "by the life of a king," while a *shevuah* is an oath taken כנשבע במלך עצמו, "by the king himself." The source is a *Sifrei*.[2] What is the intent of this distinction?

⁓ Hatfasa: The Extension of a Prohibition vs. the Creation of a New Prohibition

Rav Soloveitchik explained that the *Sifrei* is focused on the *halachah* of *hatfasah* (the transfer or extension of an existing prohibition) in *nedarim* and the mention of the name of God in a *shevuah*. A *neder* does not require mention of the name of God. However, a *neder* must be connected to a sacrifice or object consecrated to God. Therefore,

---

1 Ramban on Genesis 2:7 and Numbers 30:3.
2 *Sifrei*, Matot 153.

369

the verse reads, '"איש כי ידר נדר לה'" – "If a man makes a vow to God."[3] A person can cause something to be forbidden by *hatfasa*, connecting it to an item that was sanctified to God. In this sense, he is making a vow *to* God. *Nedarim* constitute a prohibition of *konamot*, which is a form of *hekdesh*. Otherwise, it would not be possible to confer a prohibition on an article. One must include the particular article among other articles of *hekdesh* via the medium of *hatfasa*.

A *shevuah* does not require the medium of *hatfasah* because it is an *issur gavra*, a prohibition that devolves upon the person. A person may enact a prohibition upon himself. A *neder*, by contrast, is an *issur heftza*, a prohibition that devolves on an object in question. Without *hatfasa*, which connects the item to a sacrifice to God, there is no way to confer a prohibition on the item. In comparison to a *shevuah*, in which the prohibition relates to a particular person, one cannot use a *neder* to transform that object into something forbidden. The object is not legally in one's possession because the earth and all that it contains belongs to God. Only when a person invokes *hatfasa*, connecting the object to a sacrifice to God, may he confer a prohibition upon it.

With this distinction, we can now understand the *Sifrei*. A *neder* is taken in the life of a king. *Nedarim* take effect upon the object to which they refer exclusively outside of the individual's identity and agency. In this sense, a *neder* is taken in the life of the king, in the entire creation where the creator of the world is revealed. On the other hand, a *shevuah* is taken in the king himself. The human being who is created in the image of God places himself under a prohibition. A person created in the image of God has the authority to impose the strictures of a *shevuah* upon himself if he invokes the names of God. In this way, he invokes the prohibition upon himself with the force of the creator who conferred upon him the title of human being and endowed him with the *tzelem Elokim*.

---

3   Numbers 30:3.

✂ When a Gavra Acts as a Heftza

When we say that a *neder* is an *issur heftza*, this refers not only to an inanimate object. A *neder* may also refer to an individual. By means of a *neder,* a person may prohibit himself from eating bread or meat or from drinking water. In this sense, the person addresses his body as a *heftza* and imposes on himself a prohibition against eating specific foods. He may do this through the statement, קונם עלי כל אוכל שבעולם "Konam upon me all food in the world" or קונם פי מאכילה "Konam my mouth from eating." Or, for example, if a person wants to prohibit himself from reading a book, he may do so in one of two ways: by accepting a *konam* of books on himself or by accepting a *konam* upon himself from reading.

On the other hand, when a person uses a *shevuah*, he does not require a precise formula. He simply forbids himself from performing a certain action, as in: I will not read, I will not eat. In short, when we say that a *neder* is an *issur heftza*, the term *heftza* can encompass the individual himself, who may be transformed into a *heftza*. However, he may also use a *shevuah*, which refers to the *gavra* – the person himself.

✂ A Major Difference

An entire world view is embedded in the differences between a *neder* and a *shevuah*, a *heftza* and a *gavra*. This difference is a fundamental principle in all the systems of logic and syntax. In every sentence and every logical utterance, there is a subject that is active (*gavra*) and an object (*heftza*), which is the recipient of the action. When I say that I am writing a letter, I am the *gavra*, the subject of the action, while the letter is the *heftza*, the object of the action. The *gavra* is the *mashpia*, the one who influences, while the *heftza* is the *mushpa*, the one being influenced. A physician who says, "I cured Reuven" is the subject of the sentence, the *gavra*. Reuven, the patient, is the *heftza*.

✒ The Dual Nature of Human Existence

However, all of these distinctions are significant not only in *halacha*, logic and grammar alone but also in the realm of realistic human existence. All of human existence can be divided according to the criteria of *gavra* and *heftza*. Sometimes a person acts as a *gavra* and sometimes as a *heftza*. For example, when a person climbs a mountain, he attempts to attach himself to the rocks as closely as possible. The slightest shift in the rocks on which he leans could mean his death. Should this occur, he would become a *heftza*. In other words, a *gavra* is active and vibrant, and sometimes acts against the laws of gravity. A *gavra* is energized and courageous, operating in accordance with his free personality. By contrast, a *heftza* is not active, but rather acted upon.

✒ The Ascent and Descent of Moshe at Har Sinai

ויאמר ה' אל משה עלה אלי ההרה והיה שם ואתנה לך את לחת האבן והתורה והמצוה אשר כתבתי להורתם – "God said to Moshe: Ascend to me upon the mountain and remain there, and I shall give you the stone tablets and the teaching and the commandment that I have written, that you may teach them."[4] God commands Moshe to ascend as a *gavra*, with his own strength, in order to receive the Torah. After the sin of the Golden Calf, God says, לך רד כי שחת עמך אשר העלית מארץ מצרים – "Go, descend, for your people whom you brought up from the land of Egypt …"[5] Suddenly Moshe, in his descent, takes on, temporarily, the characteristics of a *heftza*.

---

4 Exodus 24:12.
5 Exodus 32:7.

✌ The Throwing Down of the Tablets

In the Torah, we read: ויהי כאשר קרב אל המחנה וירא את העגל ומחלת ויחר אף משה
וישלך מידיו את הלחת וישבר אתם תחת ההר – "It happened, as he drew near the camp and saw the calf and the dancing, that Moshe's anger flared up. He threw down the tablets from his hands and shattered them at the foot of the mountain."[6]

The sages disagree about the breaking of the tablets. Many hold that Moshe broke them deliberately because he did not want to give them to idol-worshippers. The Talmud tells us in Tractate *Shabbat* that Moshe received divine approval for his actions.[7] Other opinions hold that Moshe did not throw the tablets down deliberately, but dropped them unintentionally. The *Yalkut Shimoni*[8] comments on the verse, "It happened as he drew near the camp," that Moshe looked at the tablets and saw that the writing was flying away. The tablets then became very heavy in Moshe's hands, and they fell from his hands and broke.[9] This opinion gives rise to a question. Later, we find at the second giving of the Torah, that Moshe remained on the mountain. He was told:

> פסל לך שני לחת אבנים כראשנים וכתבתי על הלחת את הדברים אשר היו על
> הלחת הראשנים אשר שברת: והיה נכון לבקר ועלית בבקר אל הר סיני ונצבת לי
> שם על ראש ההר . . . ויפסל שני לחת אבנים כראשנים וישכם משה בבקר ויעל
> אל הר סיני כאשר צוה ה' אתו ויקח בידו שני לחת אבנים.

> Carve for yourself, on two stone tablets, the words that were on the first tablets which you shattered. Be prepared in the morning; ascend Mount Sinai and stand by me there on the mountaintop . . . So he carved out two stone tablets like the

---

6 Exodus 32:19.
7 BT *Shabbat* 87a.
8 *Yalkut Shimoni*, Ki Tisa 393.
9 Exodus 32:19.

first ones. Moshe arose early in the morning and ascended to Mount Sinai as God had commanded him, and he took two stone tablets in his hand.[10]

Which is more difficult: to carry a burden up or down a mountain? If Moshe was able to carry the tablets on his ascent of the mountain, it follows that he could carry them on his descent. However, during the ascent to Mount Sinai, Moshe was overcome with love and anticipation of the news of God's forgiveness. He was acting as a *gavra* who could overcome any obstacle, up to and including the law of gravity. On that cold, gray morning, he was ready to climb the mountain to God, to the source of all. Therefore, potentially, he could carry not only the two tablets, but also the entire world. No obstacle could block his ascent.

However, when Moshe was jarred and pushed off the mountain as a consequence of לך רד כי שחת עמך – "Go, descend, for your people have become corrupt"[11] – his trek down the mountain took place with lack of self-control, rendering him incapable of carrying the tablets any longer. In that moment, the *gavra* became a *heftza*, an object, who could not support the tablets, which in turn became too heavy for him to carry and shattered at the foot of the mountain.

If a human being is to act as an emissary of God, then he must be a *gavra*, constantly moving upward. Only an active *gavra* with free will and a strong personality can carve out tablets and ascend a mountain. A *gavra*'s ability to influence and carry tablets of stone given to him for safekeeping is a realization of his *tzelem Elokim*. Therefore, according to our tradition, a *shevuah* is administered to each person at birth[12] that obligates him to be a *gavra*.

---

10 Exodus 34:1–2, 4.
11 Exodus 32:7.
12 BT *Niddah* 30b.

✍ The Oath Taken by Every Newborn

The Rav often focused on the difference between the ideal that God envisions for each person and the reality that falls short of this ideal. The Talmud, in a statement in Tractate *Niddah,* illustrates the gap between God's ideal and the actual reality with respect to a fetus. An oath is administered to the fetus who is about to emerge from the womb of its mother:

תהי צדיק ואל תהי רשע, ואפילו כל העולם כולו אומרים לך צדיק אתה, היה בעיניך כרשע –

"Be a righteous person and do not be a wicked one, and even if the entire world tells you that you are righteous, see yourself as a wicked person."[13]

This dialectic can also be found in the Ramban's commentary on the mystery of *tzelem Elokim,* a merger of the heavenly and earthly domains.[14] The Ramban can be interpreted as saying that *tzelem Elokim* refers to a person's desire to realize his goals even though he often fails to do so. Each individual has a mission which, while it may be clear and precise on the one hand, is sure to end in frustration on the other. *Tzelem Elokim* is manifest in a person's desire to achieve his dreams and aspirations.

Based on the above explanation of human nature, which vacillates between *heftza* and *gavra*, we understand the secret of this *shevuah,* תהי צדיק ואל תהי רשע – "Be a righteous person and do not be a wicked one."[15] Even if ineluctable circumstances compel a person to the brink of sin, he must withstand temptation and stand firm to the oath he took. Is it possible for a person to abide by that oath? The answer is yes, for the *shevuah* epitomizes the dynamic activism of the *gavra*. A *shevuah* that is taken in "the king himself" expresses the divine personality of the human being, of the Eternal King who constricts his infinity into the human *neshama*. This is the guarantee of the *shevuah* that serves as the guarantor for a *tzelem Elokim*.

---

13 BT *Niddah* 30b.
14 Ramban's commentary on Genesis 1:26.
15 BT *Niddah* 30b.

ּ מסעי ּ

Masei: Two Paradigms of
Rabbinic Leadership

ּ The Death of Aharon

T HE TORAH RECORDS the death of Aharon, the High Priest,
in two different places. In Parashat Hukat, the Torah states:

ויסעו מקדש ויבאו בני ישראל כל העדה הר ההר: ויאמר ה' אל משה ואל אהרן
בהר ההר על גבול ארץ אדום לאמר: יאסף אהרן אל עמיו כי לא יבא אל הארץ
אשר נתתי לבני ישראל על אשר מריתם את פי למי מריבה... ויראו כל העדה כי
גוע אהרן ויבכו את אהרן שלשים יום כל בית ישראל.

They journeyed from Kadesh and the Children of Israel
arrived – the entire assembly – at Mount Hor. God spoke to
Moshe and Aharon at Mount Hor by the border of the land
of Edom, saying, "Aharon shall be gathered to his people, for
he shall not enter the land that I have given to the Children of
Israel because you defied my word at Mei Merivah." ... When
the entire assembly saw that Aharon had died, the whole
house of Israel wept for Aharon for thirty days.[1]

---

1 Numbers 20:22–24, 29.

376

In Parashat Masei we read the following:

ויסעו מקדש ויחנו בהר ההר בקצה ארץ אדום: ויעל אהרן הכהן אל הר ההר על
פי ה' וימת שם בשנת הארבעים לצאת בני ישראל מארץ מצרים בחדש החמישי
באחד לחדש: ואהרן בן שלש ועשרים ומאת שנה במתו בהר ההר.

They journeyed from Kadesh and encamped in Mount Hor,
at the edge of the land of Edom. Then Aharon the Kohen
went up to Mount Hor at God's word and died there, in the
fortieth year after the Children of Israel went forth from the
land of Egypt in the fifth month on the first of the month.
Aharon was one hundred and twenty-three years old at his
death upon Mount Hor.[2]

✌ A Pair of Pearls

In Tractate *Keritut,* the Talmud states:

ת"ר: כשמן הטוב היורד על הראש וגו' – כמין שתי טיפין מרגליות היו תלויות
לאהרן בזקנו. אמר רב כהנא, תנא: כשהוא מספר עולות ויושבות בעיקרי זקנו,
ועל דבר זה היה משה רבינו דואג, שמא חס ושלום מעלתי בשמן המשחה! יצתה
בת קול ואמרה: כטל חרמון שיורד על הררי ציון, מה טל אין בו מעילה, אף שמן
שיורד על זקן אהרן אין בו מעילה, ועדיין אהרן היה דואג, שמא משה לא מעל ואני
מעלתי! יצתה בת קול ואמרה לו: הנה מה טוב ומה נעים שבת אחים גם יחד, מה
משה לא מעל, אף אתה לא מעלת.

The Rabbis taught in a *baraita*: Scripture states: Like the
precious oil upon the head [running down, etc.], upon the
beard, the beard of Aharon, that runs down over his garments
[as part of Aharon's investiture as High Priest], Moshe
poured the anointing oil on his head; this verse teaches that
two drops of it hung at the end of Aharon's beard like two

---

2 Numbers 33:37–39.

pearl drops. Rav Kahana said (and regarding these drops of oil): A *baraita* taught that when Aharon spoke [with other people], the drops [miraculously] ascended and lodged in the roots of his beard, and regarding this matter [the two drops of anointing oil in Aharon's beard], Moshe was worried. He said: Perhaps, God forbid, I committed *me'ilah* with the anointing oil. A heavenly voice emerged and proclaimed: [Like the precious oil upon the head running down upon the beard, the beard of Aharon] like the dew of Hermon that runs down the mountains of Zion [the drops of anointing oil on Aharon's beard are comparable to drops of dew]. Just as dew is not subject to *me'ilah*, so too the anointing oil that runs down Aharon's beard is not subject to *me'ilah*. Nevertheless, Aharon was worried, thinking: Perhaps Moshe did not commit *me'ilah*, but I did commit *me'ilah*. A heavenly voice emerged and proclaimed to him: Behold how good and how pleasant is the dwelling of brothers together. Just as Moshe did not commit *me'ilah*, you did not commit *me'ilah* either.[3]

⤳ The Difference in Mourning for Moshe and Aharon

From this passage, we see that the destiny of Moshe and Aharon was intertwined and that they functioned together in harmony. We also see that their stature in terms of righteousness is similar in some ways. However, the Torah also shows distinctions between them. Perhaps the most prominent is the difference in its depiction of the deaths of Moshe and Aharon. Moshe was mourned by a select group of men, while Aharon was mourned by "the entire house of Israel," all men and women.[4] Why?

The difference lies in the fact that Moshe chastised the people and meted out true judgment, while Aharon never rebuked any man or

---

3 BT *Keritut* 5b.
4 Rashi on Deuteronomy 34:8.

woman directly. He pursued peace and instilled love between quarreling parties, particularly between husband and wife.[5]

✥ Two Models of Leadership

Moshe and Aharon serve as paradigms of leadership for future generations. The nation, in its simplicity, did not appreciate Moshe as a leader and caretaker. Those who perceived things on a superficial level did not grasp Moshe's greatness or understand the depth of his love for them. This was because Moshe often scolded them and even accused them of being rebels. Therefore, the Israelites could not appreciate his commitment to them.

The masses also failed to appreciate Moshe's anguish over the troubling events that befell them. They seemed to forget the exodus from Egypt, the splitting of the sea, and the divine revelation when they received the Torah. They forgot their own quarrelsome behavior. They forgot how Moshe had prayed to God on their behalf for forty days and nights. They forgot how he had asked God to strike his name from the Torah rather than harm them. They did not understand the soul of Moshe and therefore did not weep at his death. They did not understand the nature of what they had lost.

However, they not only understood Aharon, but also venerated him. They saw him as the leader of the people as well as the high priest who constantly carried the judgment of the Children of Israel before God in his heart. They felt his love and devotion to them. This was not true of Moshe. He sat alone, his tent pitched outside the Israelite camp. Why was there such a difference in their attitudes toward Moshe and Aharon? It was because Moshe reprimanded the people, while Aharon never did.

---

5 *Avot de-Rebbe Natan* 12:3. See also Rashi on Deuteronomy 34:8.

✢ Different Pearls: The Obvious vs. the Obscure

Two drops of oil hung upon Aharon's beard like two pearls. All the people respected Aharon as the Kohen Gadol. They all saw the oil of consecration, the symbol of leadership, priesthood and kingship, in his beard – that is, in his personality and his features. Everyone could see the physiognomy of the high priesthood in Aharon, but only the very discerning could see two similar pearls in Moshe's beard – the features of the master of all prophets.

The Talmud, in Tractate *Keritut*, is telling us homiletically that Aharon's popularity allowed him no rest. Aharon asked himself how it could be that the people did not appreciate Moshe. After all, even though Moshe was God's devoted servant and the master of all prophets, he still encountered much opposition. How is it, he asked himself, that I receive such great love and respect from the Israelites while my brother does not?

Aharon was worried. He thought to himself: Maybe I sinned with the oil of consecration. Maybe I do not carry the crown of the priesthood properly. Perhaps I pursued peace too much. Maybe I made too many concessions. Maybe I treated the people too leniently so that they would like me. Perhaps, Aharon thought to himself, the only reason for my success is that I committed *me'ilah* with the oil of consecration. Perhaps my popularity has come at the cost of diluting and offending the holiness of the *Kehuna*, which is, in a sense, an act of *me'ilah*. Perhaps I blemished the priesthood. Is Moshe himself not proof of this? After all, the entire House of Israel is displeased with him. Does this not prove that an uncompromisingly honest message would have also led to my being unpopular?

A divine voice replied, "How good and how pleasant is it for brothers to dwell together." Do not be frightened, Aharon, the divine voice said. You did not compromise on anything. Your Kohen's lips observed judgment, and you never engaged in any type of inappropriate behavior. You did not shower superfluous compliments upon the people. You pursued peace *le-shem Shamayim* (for the sake of Heaven). Your success in winning the people's hearts was decreed by Heaven no less than Moshe's lack of it. You did not deviate from the right path in any way. You are the Kohen Gadol, "an angel of God." Just as Moshe did not sin, neither did you.

ᔏ The Need for Introspection among Rabbanim

The Rav drew a parallel between Aharon's fear that he had sinned to the role of rabbinic leaders. We must be concerned a fortiori. If Aharon, a prophet, was worried that he had sinned with the oil of consecration, then we ordinary mortals who do not have the gift of prophecy should certainly be worried. When a rabbi is successful with his congregation, when his congregation loves and reveres him, he should ask himself the question that Aharon asked. He should think to himself as Aharon did: Perhaps I have transgressed in some way and need to engage in introspection. Have I fulfilled my communal duties faithfully? Success in the rabbinate, receiving accolades and cheers, often conceals signs of possible transgression.

The Talmud speaks of a Torah scholar who is unanimously beloved, saying that his congregation's love for him might be due to the fact that he does not give his congregation reproof when necessary. אמר אביי האי צורבא מרבנן דמרחמין ליה בני מתא לאו משום דמעלי טפי אלא משום דלא מוכח להו במילי דשמיא – "This rabbinic scholar who is liked by the people of his town: it is not because they think that he is of such fine character. Rather, it is because he does not rebuke them in matters of Heaven."[6] The Rav said that he was suspicious that the heavenly voice only went forth in the time of Aharon, a prophet of truth. In our day, it is a tacit presumption that a rabbi who is popular with his congregation is guilty

---

6   BT *Ketubbot* 105b.

of trespassing with the "oil of consecration." The two "drops of pearls" that are suspended upon the rabbi's beard testify that the anointing oil never fell upon his head and entered his soul or character, but remained outside, upon his beard.

On the other hand, a rabbi may have difficulty with his congregation and sense that he is unpopular. His enemies may make life difficult for him, and he may feel as though he is not successful. A rabbi in this situation should not despair or become disillusioned. His lack of success may be testimony to the fact that the Divine Presence hovers over him, that he committed no transgression and the "drops of oil that fell on his head" have been absorbed by his mind and his spirit. The Rav said, "Don't curtail your prophecy." Don't hide from the people. Teach them about the six hundred and thirteen commandments, the questions of Abaye and Rava, the code of Jewish law and its interpreters, the restrictions of Shabbat and forbidden foods.

The Rav continued to emphasize this idea. He remarked that the rabbinate requires people who have a spark of the true prophet in them, strong-minded individuals, valorous soldiers who are not looking for accolades, flattery or adulation – which are often not genuine anyway. Authentic Judaism seeks religious leadership that will reprove the people, that will lead and not be led, that will be bold enough to articulate the word of God and *halachah*, that will carry a *Sefer Torah* in the streets and spread its light. The rabbinate is not a refuge for the faint of heart. Let those who are frightened go home.[7]

---

7   See Devarim 20:8.

❧ Sefer Devarim

‮דברים‬ ❧

Devarim I: A Tragic Demise

❧ ‮בגללכם‬ – **Because of You**[1]

IF DEATH IS an unsettling and perplexing experience, then the death of an individual as an atonement of others is incomprehensible. In such a case, an individual is found guilty not because he sinned but because he is the representative of a guilty group. How can we understand such an idea? In Parashat Devarim, Moshe points out this tragic quality of his own demise. ‮גם בי התאנף ה' בגללכם לאמר גם אתה לא תבא שמה‬ – "With me, as well, Hashem became angry *because of you*, saying: 'You too shall not come there [to the Land of Israel].'"[2] Why did Moshe die without being granted the opportunity to enter the Land of Israel? Was he not the redeemer who had sacrificed his private life for the people? Was he not the one who had received the Torah? Why, then, was he condemned to remain outside the land in life and in death?

Later, in Parashat Vaethanan, the Torah states how much Moshe yearned to enter Eretz Yisrael:

---

1 Deuteronomy 1:37.
2 Ibid.

ואתחנן אל ה' בעת ההוא לאמר: א־דני ה' אתה החלות להראות את עבדך את
גדלך ואת ידך החזקה אשר מי א־ל בשמים ובארץ אשר יעשה כמעשיך וכגבורתך:
אעברה נא ואראה את הארץ הטובה אשר בעבר הירדן ההר הטוב הזה והלבנן.

I implored the Lord at that time saying, Lord God, you
have begun to show your servant your greatness and your
strong hand. What power is there in heaven and earth that
can perform according to your deeds and according to your
mighty acts? Please, let me cross over and see the good land
that is on the other side of the Jordan, this good mountain
and Lebanon.[3]

Although Moshe's prayer was filled with love and longing, God
forbade him to repeat it. Not only did God deny Moshe's petition,
but Moshe was forbidden to pray. No such prohibition had ever been
imposed upon anyone else. ויתעבר ה' בי למענכם ולא שמע אלי ויאמר ה' אלי
רב לך אל תוסף דבר אלי עוד בדבר הזה – "But the Lord became angry with
me because of you and he did not listen to me. The Lord said to me:
'Enough! Speak to me no more about this matter.'"[4]

The death of Moshe falls into the category of *hok*. It is impossible
for us to grasp the secret of his death. The text emphasizes the fact that
Moshe died not for his sake but rather on account of the Jewish people:
גם בי התאנף ה' בגללכם לאמר גם אתה לא תבא שם – "With me, as well, Hashem
became angry *because of you*, saying: You, too, shall not come there."[5]
ויקציפו על מי מריבה וירע למשה בעבורם – "They provoked at the Waters of
Merivah, and Moshe suffered *because of them*."[6]

What is the meaning of the phrases "because of you" and "because
of them"? Why wasn't Moshe himself responsible for the transgression?

---

3 Deuteronomy 3:23–25.
4 Deuteronomy 3:26.
5 Deuteronomy 1:37.
6 Psalms 106:32.

According to Rashi,[7] his transgression consisted of hitting the rock instead of speaking to it. If this is the case, on what grounds could the Israelites be blamed? Was it because they had pressured Moshe Rabbenu? Nevertheless, Moshe is responsible for his own actions. We could ask the same type of question regarding all the other theories about Moshe's guilt. In what way, then, are the children of Israel responsible for Moshe's death outside the Land?

✧ A Generation Unworthy of its Leader

Moshe's life was a tragedy – not only because he was not permitted to enter the Land of Israel, but because, as a teacher, he became too great for his disciples, too exalted for his generation. Moshe's life was the tragedy of the teacher with boundless knowledge – breadth, depth, and great emotional warmth – whose contemporaries misunderstood him. Perhaps this was what Moshe meant when he said that the people had caused his failure.

Of course, there were exceptions: Joshua, Elazar and Pinhas, who appreciated Moshe's greatness, received his Torah and carried on his tradition. They reflected Moshe's glory and majesty. פני משה כפני חמה, פני יהושע כפני לבנה – "The face of Moshe is likened to the face of the sun and the face of Yehoshua is likened to the face of the moon."[8] *Darshanim* have explained that Moshe's face radiated his own light while Joshua's reflected Moshe's, as the moon reflects the light of the sun. However, Moshe was the teacher of the generation of the desert, the generation that merited growing up under his personal tutelage. How could it be that he had only three primary disciples rather than an entire nation of them?

---

7   Rashi on Numbers 20:12.
8   BT *Bava Batra* 75a.

✂ The First vs. the Second Generation

Why did the first generation that left Egypt fall short on so many levels? Why did they not conduct themselves with dignity and perseverance during lean times? Why did they allow themselves to be drawn after the desires of the mixed multitude and those who constructed the Golden Calf?

Moshe argued before God: למה ה' יחרה אפך בעמך אשר הוצאת מארץ מצרים בכח גדול וביד חזקה – "Why, Lord, should Your anger flare up against Your people, whom you took out of the land of Egypt with great power and a strong hand?"[9] What do you expect from a nation whose background is pagan and that has never been taught proper morality? It takes time to rehabilitate them and teach them new values.

Moshe's defense of the people when they made an idol was sound, for they were understandably frightened. Since those who had left Egypt could not be considered Moshe's disciples, he had no reason to be discouraged.

At Mei Merivah and in Shittim, however, it was the next generation that rebelled out of fear. Moshe had raised them himself. How could they now use the same language that their parents had used forty years earlier?

ולמה העליתנו ממצרים להביא אתנו אל המקום הרע הזה לא מקום זרע ותאנה וגפן ורמון ומים אין לשתות.

And why did you bring us up from Egypt to bring us to this evil place – a place of no seed, fig, grape or pomegranate, and no water to drink?[10]

Why did the people whom Moshe had led forty years later speak the same language of newly-liberated slaves? In effect, Moshe said: I failed because I did not succeed in implanting in them proper faith, morals and

---

9 Exodus 32:11.
10 Numbers 20:4; see also Exodus 16:3.

restraint. Therefore, in Shittim, Moshe weeps.[11] He does not do this during the crises of the Golden Calf or of the spies. What is the difference? The answer is that during those times, Moshe was able to offer a defense for the Israelites' behavior. They were not yet his disciples. It was too soon. However, he could not offer this defense for the next generation.

So what can be said about the second generation? It was not Moshe who had failed. It was that he was too great for his generation. His vision was too penetrating, his depth almost superhuman. They failed to understand him. Therefore, Moshe said, "Because of you," "because of them." In other words, he was saying: Had you, the Jewish people, understood the teachings I offered you over of the past forty years, nothing like this could have happened, and I would have been allowed to enter the Promised Land; There would have been no need for the incident at Mei Merivah. A kingdom of Kohanim and a holy nation would not have behaved the way you did at Mei Merivah. The people were guilty not only of succumbing to temptation, but of not absorbing Moshe's teachings and becoming his true disciples.

✺ Why Must the Teacher Suffer the Consequences?

It is still difficult to understand why Moshe had to suffer the consequences of his people's failure. The answer may be found in a somewhat obscure *halachah* in Tractate *Makkot*. There we learn that if a pupil commits manslaughter and flees to a city of refuge, his teacher goes into exile with him.[12] The bond between teacher and disciple defies all circumstances and must be preserved at all costs. It is based on this principle that Moshe had to remain with his disciples, who were in exile either physically or spiritually. The Israelites sinned by closing their minds and hearts to Moshe's personality and message. Of course, Moshe's death remains a mystery to us. He should have attained immortality. Instead, his life ends in disappointment.

---

11 Numbers 25:6.
12 BT Makkot 10a; Mishneh Torah, Hilchot Rotzeah 7:1.

❧ דברים ❧

Devarim II: The Delay of the Messianic Era

❧ A King Who Did Not Achieve Leadership

OSHE'S FAILURE TO cross into the Land of Israel was more than a personal tragedy or a tragedy for his generation. Had Moshe entered the land, Jewish history would have been completely transformed. Had the Israelites absorbed his Torah properly, he would have entered the Land of Israel and become the Messiah, and Jewish history would have found its fulfillment immediately.

It is clear from many sources that Moshe Rabbenu was worthy to be the Messiah.

Moshe's level of prophecy was even higher than that of the Messiah. The seventh of Maimonides' Thirteen Principles of Faith states that Moshe was the greatest of all prophets: ושהוא היה אב לנביאים לקודמים לפניו ולבאים אחריו – "He was the father of the prophets both of those who preceded him and those who followed him."[1] Among those who are to follow him is the Messiah himself. The Rambam writes in *Hilchot Teshuvah*: מפני שאותו המלך שיעמוד מזרע דוד בעל חכמה יהיה יתר משלמה, ונביא גדול הוא קרוב למשה רבינו – "Because that king who will arise from the scion of

---

1 The seventh of the Rambam's Thirteen Principles of Faith.

390

David will be of greater wisdom than king Solomon and a great prophet approaching the stature of Moshe Rabbenu."[2] Since no prophet in the past or in the future can surpass the prophetic level of Moshe, he should have been crowned as the Messiah, since the Messiah is chosen from among everyone. ואני נסכתי מלכי על ציון הר קדשי: אספרה אל חק ה' אמר אלי בני אתה אני היום ילדתיך – "I myself have anointed my king over Zion, my holy mountain. I am obliged to proclaim that the Lord said to me: You are my son. I have begotten you this day."[3]

If Moshe was qualified to be the Messianic king, why did Divine Providence decide against it? Had Moshe entered Eretz Yisrael, the land would have been endowed with sanctity and could never have been captured or destroyed. The sanctity of Joshua was only of a temporary nature, but Moshe's sanctity would have been permanent. Why did the Israelites lose this opportunity?

The answer is that the rule of the Messianic king depends upon the people's readiness. Had the people become Moshe's true disciples and treated him with the love and reverence of a student for his Torah master, then Moshe would have become the Messianic king. Unfortunately, the nation could not forget the fleshpots of Egypt even after forty years. Therefore, the Messianic Era was postponed for many centuries. Moshe died, and his teachings were entrusted to Joshua. When the entire Jewish nation accepts Moshe and his teachings and demonstrates its readiness, the redemption will take place.

✧ The Death of Moshe and the Confrontation with Edom

After the episode at Mei Merivah, in Parashat Hukat, God told Moshe and Aharon that they would not bring the assembly of Israel into the Promised Land.[4] At that juncture, the Torah should have told us about

---

2 *Mishneh Torah,* Hilchot Teshuvah 9:2.
3 Psalms 2:6–7.
4 Numbers 20:12.

the death of Aharon. Instead, it tells the story of the refusal of the King of Edom to allow the Israelites to cross his borders on their way to the Promised Land.[5] This sequence of events is astounding, for logically, this story should have been connected to similar episodes regarding the kings, Sihon and Og, who also did not allow the Israelites to pass through their territory. When these stories are recalled here in Parashat Devarim, they are connected. Why is there a pause before Aharon's death in Parashat Hukat?

When Sihon and Og refused to allow the Israelites to pass through their kingdoms, Moshe declared war upon them and defeated them.[6] Yet when the king of Edom refused to allow the Israelites to pass through his kingdom, the Israelites had to go around his kingdom, which, the Torah tells us, was a frustrating and wearying experience. ויסעו מהר ההר דרך ים סוף לסבב את ארץ אדום ותקצר נפש העם בדרך – "They journeyed from Mount Hor by way of the Sea of Reeds to go around the land of Edom and the people grew impatient on the way."[7] Edom was not touched by the Israelites. Following that incident, the Torah tells us the story of the venomous snakes. Why was there any difference between the way we behaved toward Sihon and Og, whom the Torah depicts as kings of mighty kingdoms in Parashat Devarim, and Edom, whose kingdom seems to have been smaller? Why were we firm with Sihon and Og, yet forgiving with Edom? The text in Devarim tells us:

ואת העם צו לאמר אתם עברים בגבול אחיכם בני עשו הישבים בשעיר וייראו מכם ונשמרתם מאד: אל תתגרו בם כי לא אתן לכם מארצם עד מדרך כף רגל כי ירשה לעשו נתתי את הר שעיר.

You shall command the people, saying: You are passing through the boundary of your brothers, the children of Esau who dwell in Seir. They will fear you, but you should be very

5 Numbers 20:14–21.
6 Numbers 21:21–24.
7 Numbers 21:4.

careful. You shall not provoke them, for I will not give you even the right to set foot in their land, for I gave Mount Seir as an inheritance to the children of Esau.[8]

In other words, no Jew has the right to enter Edom's territory. Is this a permanent decree? It does not appear so, for regarding the end of days, we are told: ועלו מושעים בהר ציון לשפט את הר עשו והיתה לה' המלוכה – "Saviors will ascend Mount Zion to judge the mountains of Esau, and the kingdom will be the Lord's."[9] Thus we are barred from Edom's territory until Messianic times, when we will be allowed to acquire this territory. How shall we understand this prohibition, and why will it expire with the beginning of the Messianic era?

﹃ Jacob's Promise to Esau

Our sages comment that when Esau showed Jacob his willingness to travel together with him, he said to Jacob, ויאמר נסעה ונלכה ואלכה לנגדך – "He said, 'Travel on and let us go. I will proceed alongside you.'"[10] Jacob answered:

ויאמר אליו אדני ידע כי הילדים רכים והצאן והבקר עלות עלי ודפקום יום אחד
ומתו כל הצאן: יעבר נא אדני לפני עבדו ואני אתנהלה לאטי לרגל המלאכה אשר
לפני ולרגל הילדים עד אשר אבא אל אדני שעירה.

But he said to him: "My lord knows that the children are tender and the nursing flocks and cattle are upon me. If they are driven hard for a single day, then all the flocks will die. Let my lord go ahead of his servant. I will make my way at a slow pace, according to the pace of the cattle before me and the pace of the children, until I come to my Lord at Seir."[11]

---

8 Deuteronomy 2:4–5.
9 Obadiah 1:21.
10 Genesis 33:12. See Rashi on Genesis 33:14 and on Numbers 24:19.
11 Genesis 33:13–14.

The Midrash[12] notes that a close inspection of the entire Tanach mentions no instance in which Jacob went to visit Esau. Is it possible that Jacob broke his promise to his brother? This would go against everything we understand about his character. The Midrash explains that Jacob's intent was not that he would arrive in Seir in his own lifetime, but that he would come in the end of days. This will happen only in the Messianic era.

Esau is the symbol of hostility towards the Jew. Edom has been our chief opponent throughout the long and dreary night of *galut*. During this time, we may not enter Edom. Yet at the time of the redemption, this prohibition will be lifted, and Edom will play its part in the messianic vision.

With this insight, the following explanation for the interruption in the flow of the narrative described above can be proposed. Until the time that he heard from God that he would not enter the Land of Israel, Moshe retained the hope that the Messianic visions would be fulfilled immediately, which would mean that the Israelites were destined to enter Edom and conquer it. Once he was told that he would die in the desert, Moshe understood that he was no longer destined to be the Messianic king. Thus the hope for a swift fulfillment for the Messianic vision was lost. As a result, the territory of Edom became inviolable. Had Moshe become the Messianic king, he would have conquered Edom and the redemption would have been completed. Therefore, when Moshe is told that he shall not enter the Promised Land and that the redemption will be delayed, the Torah immediately mentions the story of Edom. Now the Israelites will have to bypass this kingdom. They will have to wait for the fulfillment of the Messianic prophecy.

---

12 Genesis Rabbah 78:14.

ואתחנן

Vaethanan: The Experience
of Ma'amad Har Sinai

PARASHAT VAETHANAN DESCRIBES the giving of the Torah and the meeting between God and the people of Israel.

את הדברים האלה דבר ה' אל כל קהלכם בהר מתוך האש הענן והערפל קול
גדול ולא יסף ויכתבם על שני לחת אבנים ויתנם אלי: ויהי כשמעכם את הקול
מתוך החשך וההר בער באש ותקרבון אלי כל ראשי שבטיכם וזקניכם: ותאמרו הן
הראנו ה' א-להינו את כבדו ואת גדלו ואת קלו שמענו מתוך האש היום הזה ראינו
כי ידבר א-להים את האדם וחי: ועתה למה נמות כי תאכלנו האש הגדלה הזאת
אם יספים אנחנו לשמע את קול ה' א-להינו עוד ומתנו: כי מי כל בשר אשר שמע
קול א-להים חיים מדבר מתוך האש כמנו ויחי: קרב אתה ושמע את כל אשר יאמר
ה' א-להינו ואת תדבר אלינו את כל אשר ידבר ה' א-להינו אליך ושמענו ועשינו.

The Lord spoke these words to your entire congregation on the mountain, from the midst of the fire, the cloud and the thick cloud, a great voice, never to be repeated, and he inscribed them on two stone tablets and gave them to me. It happened that when you heard the voice from the midst of the darkness and the mountain was burning in fire, that you, all the heads of your tribes and your elders, approached me. They said: "Behold, the Lord has shown us his glory and his greatness, and we have heard his voice from the midst of the fire. In this way, we saw that the Lord could speak to a person and that the person could live. But now, why should we die when this great fire consumes us? If we continue to hear the voice of the Lord our God any longer, we shall die. For is there any human who has heard the voice of the living God speaking from the midst of the fire, as we have heard, and lived? You should approach and hear whatever the Lord our God says, and you should tell us whatever the Lord our God says to you. Then we shall listen and we shall obey."[1]

From the description of how the Israelites saw God's glory and heard his voice, it is clear that they merited the revelation of the Divine Presence and actually became prophets. That is the ultimate goal of a Jew's life: to merit divine revelation. The revelation at Mount Sinai was therefore a watershed event, for during that face-to-face encounter with God, He told us that we must adopt a distinctive lifestyle.

In Parashat Yitro, during the preamble to the giving of the Torah, the Israelites are raised to the status of a kingdom of priests and a holy nation.[2] The people answer, ויענו כל העם יחדו ויאמרו כל אשר דבר ה' נעשה – "Everything that the Lord has spoken, we will do."[3] Then the Lord tells Moshe, ויאמר ה' אל משה הנה אנכי בא אליך בעב הענן בעבור ישמע העם בדברי עמך וגם בך יאמינו לעולם – "Behold, I come to you in the thickness of the cloud so that the people will hear as I speak to you *and they will also believe in you forever*."[4] The Ramban, in his commentary,[5] cites the Ibn Ezra that some Jews doubted Moshe's prophecy. Even though earlier, the Torah tells us, ויאמינו בה' ובמשה עבדו – "they believed in the Lord and in Moshe his servant,"[6] their acceptance was not universal. This, the Ibn Ezra

---

1 Deuteronomy 5:19–24.
2 Exodus 19:6.
3 Exodus 19:8.
4 Exodus 19:9.
5 Ramban on Exodus 19:9.
6 Exodus 14:31.

says, is borne out by the statement in Parashat Vaethanan, היום הזה ראינו כי ־ידבר א־להים את האדם וחי – "This day, we saw that the Lord will speak to a person and he may live,"[7] implying that heretofore not all of them had believed in God to that point, and now they would experience the nature of prophecy concretely.

The Ramban disagrees with the Ibn Ezra, contending: God forbid that the seed of Abraham should be ambivalent regarding the truth of prophecy.

> והנכון בעיני שאמר אני בא אליך בעב הענן, שתגש אתה אל הערפל בעבור ישמע העם דברי, ויהיו הם עצמם נביאים בדברי, לא שיאמינו מפי אחרים, כמו שנאמר באמור ה' אלי הקהל לי את העם ואשמיעם את דברי למען ילמדון ליראה אותי כל הימים.

What appears to me to be correct is that the Almighty said I will come to you in the thickness of the cloud. The Lord instructed Moshe to enter into the thickness of the cloud, so that the people will hear when I speak to Moshe, and they themselves will become prophets rather than believe the statements of others, as it is written: "When the Lord said to me: Gather the people to me, and I shall let them hear my words so that they shall learn to revere me all the days that they live on the earth …"[8]

According to the Ramban, all the Jewish people received the gift of prophecy and heard the *Aseret ha-Dibrot* directly from God – with one qualification. When God uttered the first two commandments, the Israelites heard God's word directly from him, exactly as Moshe heard God's word. Afterwards, the people heard God's word without understanding it, and they needed Moshe to interpret each commandment. In short, the Ramban argues that as far as the first two commandments

---

7   Deuteronomy 5:21.
8   Ramban on Exodus 19:9.

were concerned, the entire Jewish nation became prophets. In a sense, this widespread gift of prophecy is relevant to the entire Torah because these two commandments constitute the foundation for all Torah and *mitzvot*.

Even according to the Ibn Ezra's interpretation, it must be true that the Israelites attained some level of prophecy. Only if they became prophets themselves would they be able to confirm their belief in Moshe's prophecy. If they did not, then how could they be so confident that what Moshe was hearing was indeed prophecy from God?

✑ Unworthy of Prophecy?

The Israelites, in both Yitro[9] and Vaethanan,[10] asked that Moshe speak to them as an intermediary. They felt they were not on a high enough level for direct contact with the Divine. God answered they had spoken well,[11] suggesting that he found their reasoning acceptable. The Midrash comments that the Israelites' "speaking well" was akin to the cleaning of the lamp in the Temple and to the ascent of the incense in smoke.[12] The Midrash understands that the Israelites felt that they were unworthy of the gift of prophecy. How could they compare themselves to Moshe, who had prepared himself to become a prophet? Prophecy is meant for *yehidei segulah* – distinctive individuals whose character traits are flawless. Their language – כי מי כל בשר אשר שמע קול א־להים חיים מדבר מתוך האש כמנו ויחי – "For is there any human being who has heard the voice of the living God speaking from the midst of the fire, as we have, and lived?"[13] – contains elements both of *hakarat het* (recognition of sin) and *viddui* (confession).

---

9 Exodus 20:16.
10 Deuteronomy 5:24.
11 Deuteronomy 5:25.
12 *Midrash Rabbah*, Parashat Emor, 32:2.
13 Deuteronomy 5:23.

God indicated that this feeling of unworthiness is a proper one, for the Midrash cited above teaches that lighting the menorah presupposes *hatava*, its cleaning. Just as the burning of the incense requires preparation, so does prophecy.

During the incident of Eldad and Medad, who prophesied in the camp,"[14] Joshua immediately reacted with a statement ויאמר אדני משה כלאם – "He said: 'My lord Moshe, incarcerate them.'"[15] Moshe replies, ומי יתן כל עם ה' נביאים כי יתן ה' את רוחו עליהם – "Would that the entire people of God might be prophets! If only the Lord would but place his spirit upon them!"[16]

What was the source of Moshe's statement? The answer is from the verse in Yitro and the Ramban's interpretation of it. בעבור ישמע העם בדברי עמך וגם בך יאמינו לעולם – "So that the people will hear as I speak to you, and they will also believe in you forever."[17] At that juncture, they realized that they were unworthy of the gift of prophecy, but the text indicates that in the future, they will be; this indication occurs in Parashat Vaethanan. It will also happen in the end of days, as the prophet Yoel states:

והיה אחרי כן אשפוך את רוחי על כל בשר ונבאו בניכם ובנותיכם זקניכם חלמות יחלמון בחוריכם חזינות יראו.

And so it shall happen after this that I will pour out my spirit upon all flesh, and your sons and daughters will prophesy, your elders will dream [prophetic] dreams and your young men will see visions.[18]

---

14 Numbers 11:26.
15 Numbers 11:28.
16 Numbers 11:29.
17 Exodus 19:9.
18 Yoel 3:1.

עקב

Ekev: The Commandment of Birkat ha-Mazon (the Blessing after the Meal)

THE VERSE IN Parashat Ekev states: ואכלת ושבעת וברכת את ה' א-להיך על הארץ הטבה אשר נתן לך – "You will eat and be satisfied, and you will bless the Lord your God for the good land that he gave you."[1] The Rambam in *Hilchot Berachot* notes in the heading that there is one positive Torah commandment: מצות עשה אחת והיא לברך את השם הגדול והקדוש אחר אכילה – There is one positive Torah commandment to bless his "great and sanctified name" after eating.[2] Why did the Rambam add these two descriptions, great and sanctified? Why not simply bless his name?

The *paytan* in the mussaf Avodah of Yom Kippur writes: והכהנים והעם העומדים בעזרה כשהיו שומעים את השם הנכבד מפרש יוצא מפי כהן גדול בקדשה ובטהרה – "The priests and the people, when they heard the honored and awesome Ineffable Name . . . uttered by the High Priest in holiness and purity . . ."[3] Why did they use the "honored and awesome" [name of the Lord]? When the ineffable name of the Lord is pronounced, there is an obligation to kneel and prostrate oneself, and the utterance of God's

---

1 Deuteronomy 8:10.
2 *Mishneh Torah*, Hilchot Berachot, heading caption of Chapter 1.
3 Mussaf Avodah of Yom Kippur, based on Mishnah *Yoma* 6:2.

ineffable name gives rise to this obligation. Prostrating oneself is the manifestation of total surrender to God. However, in the context of *birkat ha-mazon*, why does the Rambam use these two descriptions of "great" and "sanctified"?

In the first *halachah* in his codex in *Hilchot Berachot*, the Rambam writes:

> מצות עשה מן התורה לברך אחר אכילת מזון שנאמר ואכלת ושבעת וברכת את
> ה' א-להיך על הארץ הטבה אשר נתן לך.

> There is a positive Torah commandment to bless [God] after eating, as it is written: You will eat and be satisfied, and bless the Lord your God for the good land that he gave you.[4]

Unlike the *mitzvah* of prayer, concerning which there is a controversy among the Rishonim as to whether it is of Torah or of rabbinic origin, it is universally accepted that *birkat ha-mazon* is a Torah obligation. The sages debated as to whether women's obligation to recite the grace after meals is from the Torah or is rabbinic in nature.[5] The well-known aggadic passage in Tractate *Berachot* also indicates that *birkat ha-mazon* is of biblical origin.

> דרש רב עוירא: אמרו מלאכי השרת לפני הקדוש ברוך הוא: רבונו של עולם,
> כתוב בתורתך אשר לא ישא פנים ולא יקח שחד ... אמר להם: וכי לא אשא
> פנים לישראל? שכתבתי להם בתורה: ואכלת ושבעת וברכת את ה' א-להיך, והם
> מדקדקים [על] עצמם עד כזית ועד כביצה.

> Rav Avira expounded: The angels said before God: It is written in your Torah, "Who does not show favor to the Jewish people, as it is written: 'May the Lord lift his countenance to you ... The Lord said to them [the angels] shall I not lift my countenance to the Jewish people, for I wrote in the Torah,

---

4 *Mishneh Torah*, Hilchot Berachot 1:1.
5 BT *Berachot* 20b.

You will eat and you will be satisfied and bless the Lord
your God: "And they are meticulous with themselves to the
amount of a *ke-zayit* and a *ke-betzah*."[6]

It is universally assumed that *birkat ha-mazon* is of Torah origin. The
Talmud in Tractate *Berachot* cites an argument if the *beracha* of *ha-tov
va-hametiv* is of Torah origin or not.[7] Which components of *birkat ha-
mazon* are of Torah origin? This is an argument among the Rishonim.
The first position, expressed by both the Rambam and the Ramban, is
that the blessings themselves are rabbinic and only the overall obligation
is of Torah origin.

The Rambam writes in *Hilchot Berachot*:

סדר ברכת המזון כך היא: ראשונה ברכת הזן, שנייה ברכת הארץ, שלישית בונה
ירושלים, רביעית הטוב והמטיב. ברכה ראשונה משה רבינו תקנה, שנייה תיקן
יהושע, שלישית תיקן דוד ושלמה בנו, רביעית חכמי משנה תקנוה.

The order of *birkat ha-mazon* is as follows. The first blessing
is *birkat ha-zan,* the second is *birkat ha-aretz,* the third is
boneh Yerushalayim, and the fourth is *ha-tov ve-ha-metiv.*
The first blessing was enacted by Moshe Rabbenu, the second
by Joshua, the third by David and his son Solomon, and the
fourth by the sages of the Mishnah.[8]

It would seem that according to the Rambam, all the *berachot* are
rabbinic in nature. The question then arises: What exactly is of Torah
origin? In his critical glosses to the Rambam's *Sefer ha-Mitzvot* (*Shoresh
One*), the Ramban writes:

וכן אמרו משה תיקן ברכת הזן יהושע תקן ברכת הארץ שלמה תקן בונה ירושלם.
וכולן אין מטבען תורה אבל נצטוינו מן התורה שנברך אחר אכילתנו כל אחד כפי

---

6 BT *Berachot* 20b.
7 BT *Berachot* 46a.
8 *Mishneh Torah,* Hilchot Berachot 2:1.

דעתו, כענין ברכת בנימין רעיא שאמר בריך רחמנא מאריה דהאי פיתא ובאו
הנביאים ותקנו לנו נוסח מתוקן הלשון וצח המליצה ושנינו בו אנחנו עוד בגלות
ומלכות בית דוד משיחך מהרה תחזירנה למקומה ותבנה ירושלם עיר קדשך. כי
העניין תקן שלמה ובית דינו והלשון כפי הזמנים יאמר.

They said: Moshe enacted *birkat ha-zan,* Joshua enacted
birkat ha-aretz, and Solomon enacted *boneh Yerushalayim.* All
of the above are not of Torah origin, but we are commanded
by the Torah to bless [God] after eating, each one according
to his understanding, in accordance with the blessing of
Binyamin Raya, who said, "Blessed be the Merciful One,
Master of this bread."[9] The prophets came and enacted an
amended version with beauty of style, and we also said, when
we were in exile ... "May the kingship of the House of David,
your anointed one, be speedily restored to its place, and may
Yerushalayim, your holy city, be rebuilt," because the matter
was enacted by Solomon and his court, and the language is
contingent on the times.[10]

The Ramban's position is that the Torah obligation of *birkat ha-mazon*
is fulfilled with the formula of Binyamin Raya: "Blessed be the Merciful
One, Master of this bread." All the other interpolations mentioned in the
Talmud that are inserted into *birkat ha-mazon* – for example, circumcision, Torah, the exodus from Egypt – are rabbinically required. The
Rambam seems to agree with the Ramban, for he articulates the Torah
obligation as one that requires a blessing after eating, while the *berachot*
themselves are rabbinic in nature. This is different from *Hilchot Tefillah,*
in which the Rambam sets forth the tripartite Torah-based obligations
of *shevah, bakashah* and *hodaah* (praise, supplication and thanksgiving),
while accentuating that the text is rabbinic in nature. The Torah dictates
no specific structure or text for *birkat ha-mazon.*

---

9 BT *Berachot* 40b.
10 Ramban, Glosses to *Sefer ha-Mitzvot,* Shoresh 1.

A second position, which the Rashba, Ritva and Tosafot ha-Rosh maintain, is that the motifs of the *berachot* are themselves of Torah origin.[11] The *Shitah Mekubetzet* seems to agree with their positions when he states that one must mention several things – his food, the bounty of Eretz Yisrael and Jerusalem – and all these ideas are of Torah import.[12]

In Tractate *Berachot, Tosafot* takes a similar position. The Talmud notes that workers who are caught up in their work may recite the first blessing of *birkat ha-mazon*, begin the second blessing and combine the theme of *boneh Yerushalayim* in *birkat ha-aretz. Tosafot* asks how this is possible when these *berachot* and their content are of Torah import. He answers on the basis of the Talmudic principle that the sages have the authority to nullify a Torah law if it infringes on the work of the employer.[13] From *Tosafot's* question it is apparent that *Tosafot* assumed that the text of these *berachot* are of *Torah* origin. This is why we must invoke the above-mentioned Talmudic principle. According to the second position of the Rashba and the Ritva, there is no need to invoke the principle, for the content is rabbinic in nature.

The Rav then proceeded to analyze these positions. The Gemara cites a *baraita*: מנין לברכת המזון מן התורה שנאמר ואכלת ושבעת וברכת את ה' א-להיך זו ברכת הזמון על הארץ זו ברכת הארץ הטובה זו בונה ירושלים – "How do we know that *birkat ha-mazon* is of Torah origin? The text states: 'You will eat and be satisfied, and you will bless.' That is *birkat ha-zan*. 'The Lord your God' is *birkat ha-zimun.* 'For the land' is *birkat ha-aretz.* 'The good land' is *boneh Yerushalayim.*" The blessing could not be perfect unless it included the sanctity of Jerusalem.

The Ramban assumes that this exegesis constitutes an *asmachta* (a rabbinic teaching which adduces a Torah source). The Torah obligation is to thank God for the food that the land has produced.

In reality, the subject of the verse is a controversy between the two

---

11 *Hiddushei ha-Rashba* on BT Berachot 48b.
12 *Shittah Mekubetzet* on BT *Berachot* 48b (הטוב והמטיב ביבנה תקנוה).
13 Tosafot on BT *Berachot* 16a, "Va-hosem."

Targumim. Targum Onkelos translates the verse as referring to thanking God for the land that he gave us.[14] Targum Yonatan ben Uziel translates the verse as a warning not to forget to thank and bless God for the fruit of the land.[15] This interpretation of Targum Yonatan ben Uziel comes from the subsequent verses, where the Torah says: השמר לך פן תשכח את ה' א־להיך – "Take care lest you forget the Lord your God ..."[16] The *Pesikta* even comments, "One who eats without a *beracha* or *tefillah* throws off the yoke of heaven: 'Take care lest you forget Hashem your God.'"[17] Targum Yonatan therefore demands both thanksgiving and blessing. According to the Ramban, the Torah obligation of *birkat ha-mazon* is filled by the recitation of Binyamin Raya, without the element of thanksgiving, but which underscores the recognition of the God's sovereignty and kingship.

Like Targum Yonatan, the Ramban's opinion is also predicated on the subsequent verses.

> השמר לך פן תשכח את ה' א־להיך ... פן תאכל ושבעת ובתים טבים תבנה וישבת. ובקרך וצאנך ירבין וכסף וזהב ירבה לך וכל אשר לך ירבה. ורם לבבך ושכחת את ה' א־להיך ... ואמרת בלבבך כחי ועצם ידי עשה לי את החיל הזה. וזכרת את ה' א־להיך כי הוא הנתן לך כח לעשות חיל ...

Take care lest you forget God ... Lest you eat and be satisfied and you build good houses and settle, your cattle and flocks increase and you increase silver and gold for yourselves and all your possessions will increase. Your heart will become haughty and you will forget God ... You may say in your heart: My strength and the might of my hand got me all this

---

14 Deuteronomy 8:10.

15 Deuteronomy 8:10.

16 Deuteronomy 8:11

17 *Pesikta Zutrata* Deuteronomy, Parashat Ekev, 13:2.

wealth. Then you shall remember the Lord your God – that
it was he who gave you strength to accumulate wealth . . ."[18]

According to the Ramban, the purpose of *birkat ha-mazon* is to
negate this kind of arrogance. The prayer expresses reverence for God
and acknowledges his sovereignty. Therefore, according to the Ramban,
birkat ha-mazon and the blessings that we recite before eating various
kinds of food contain a common element – the recognition of God's
sovereignty.

The Talmud, in Tractate *Berachot*, poses the following question:[19] We
have a source for blessing God after eating, but what is the source for
blessing him before eating? The Gemara answers with a *kal va-homer*: if
a person is obligated to bless God when his hunger has been satisfied, he
is obligated all the more so to bless Him when he is still hungry. If *Birkat
ha-mazon* is founded on the premise of thanksgiving, as suggested by
the Targum ben Uziel, then this *kal va-homer* is incomprehensible. Of
course we are obligated to give thanks after eating, but why must we do
so before we eat? Yet according to the Ramban's opinion that the major
theme is acknowledgment of God's sovereignty, then the *kal va-homer*
becomes apparent. If there is even a slight possibility that we might start
to think, after having eaten a full, delicious meal, that we alone are to
thank for our prosperity, then we must acknowledge God's sovereignty.
This applies all the more when one is hungry.

The Rambam's position parallels the Ramban's. At first, Rambam sets
forth the Torah obligation to bless God after eating, which stems from
the verse in Parashat Ekev.[20] Also in that category is the rabbinic obligation to recite various blessings over various kinds of food.[21] If *birkat
ha-mazon* is based on the principle of thanksgiving, then the rabbinic
obligation that extends this would have no connection with it. But if

---

18 Deuteronomy 8:11–14, 17–18.
19 BT *Berachot* 35a.
20 Deuteronomy 8:10.
21 *Mishneh Torah,* Hilchot Berachot 1:2.

birkat ha-mazon is based on recognition of God's sovereignty, then the Rambam's opinion is understandable. The Rambam then extrapolates from the blessing that one recites before deriving benefit from a food item to the blessing that one recites before performing a *mitzvah*. Once more, the analogy is based on the fact that God is the origin of religious law. We recognize his moral dominion and remain aware of his presence and mastery.

☙ The Heading in Mishneh Torah: His "Great and Sanctified Name"

In light of the above analysis, we understand the language of the Rambam – who, in his caption to *Hilchot Berachot*, obligates us to bless God's "great and sanctified" name. The Talmud in Tractate *Megillah* comments: "Wherever you find mention of God's greatness, you find his humility also."[22] The Gemara adduces one proof from a verse in the Torah: "For he is the God of all gods and the master of all masters."[23] In other words, greatness is identified with *adnuto* (God's sovereignty). So *birkat ha-mazon*, which expresses God's sovereignty, is directed at His great name. The word "kadosh" refers to the Ineffable Name.

☙ Finding Blessing amid Hunger and Frustration

The Rav then expounded on the Gemara in Tractate *Berachot*[24] that the Jewish people are meticulous with themselves regarding the amount of a food item – the size of an olive or of an egg – for which we are required to praise God. The Rav explained that the Torah in Parashat Ekev presents Eretz Yisrael as a land of plenty that contains streams and produces seven principal species to sustain us. Many Rishonim held that the Torah

---

22 BT *Megillah* 31a.
23 Deuteronomy 10:17.
24 Op. cit., n. 6.

obligation of *birkat ha-mazon* applies only when one is satisfied, for it is then that one praises God.

However, the *Yiddisher koah* (the strength of the Jew) is to praise God even when we are not obligated to do so. We praise God even when we have no Temple and when Yerushalayim is not in our possession. Even if we eat an amount the size of an egg, or even the size of an olive, and are not satisfied, we are still ready to give thanks to God. We find the strength to praise God even amidst suffering. In an aside, the Rav quipped that every synagogue rabbi must take some abuse, and yet he weathers it and blesses God. In the same vein, even if the Jewish nation makes mistakes, God nevertheless "shows us favor." This is because we take great care to bless God for even an egg's or an olive's worth of sustenance. This is the greatness of the Jewish people: that we experience many hardships and still praise God. It is also a sign in the Torah that even if we should falter, God will show us favor.

Re'eh: Settling the Land and Building the Temple

I N PARASHAT RE'EH, we encounter the *mitzvah* of *yerushah vi-yeshivah* – possessing and settling the Land of Israel.[1] It is well known that the Ramban criticizes the Rambam for having failed to include this *mitzvah* in his work, *Sefer ha-Mitzvot*.[2] The Ramban contends that this *mitzvah* involves several elements: possession and settlement of the land, governing the land, and demonstrating sovereignty over it. Therefore, says the Ramban, our sages emphasized the importance of the *mitzvah* of settling in the Land of Israel. Even the Rambam, who does not include it in his count of the *mitzvot*, praises those who live there.[3]

The Rambam also lists two *mitzvot* that are connected to *yerushah vi-yeshivah*. Immediately following this *mitzvah*, the Torah states the obligation to destroy all vestiges of idolatry in the Land of Israel. Rashi cites this obligation as indicated by the language of the Torah: אבד תאבדון את כל המקמות אשר עבדו שם הגוים אשר אתם ירשים אתם את אלהיהם – "You shall utterly destroy all the places where the nations that you are driving away

---

1   Deuteronomy 11:31.
2   *Sefer ha-Mitzvot*, Mitzvat Aseh 4 of the mitzvot that the Rambam forgot to count.
3   *Mishneh Torah*, Hilchot Melachim 5:10–12.

worshipped their gods."[4] This obligation to root out idolatry is only operative in the Land of Israel.

Evidently, the *mitzvah* of eradicating idolatry is an important part of the *mitzvah* of *yerushah vi-yeshivah*. In the seventh chapter of *Hilchot Avodah Zarah*, Rambam cites this *halachah* using the language of: ובארץ ישראל מצוה לרדוף אחריה עד שנאבד אותה מכל ארצנו – "In Eretz Yisroel there is an obligation to pursue and root out idolatry until we succeed in eradicating it from the entire country."[5] From Rambam's language, "from the entire country," we can infer that until the idolatry is uprooted, it is not totally considered our land. The Rambam, in *Hilchot Berachot*, writes: מקום שנעקרה ממנו עכו"ם אם בארץ ישראל הוא מברך שעקר עכו"ם מארצנו, ואם בחוץ לארץ הוא מברך שעקר עכו"ם ממקום הזה – "A place from which idolatry was uprooted – if it is in the Land of Israel, one recites the blessing: 'who uprooted idolatry from our land.' If it is outside the Land of Israel, one recites the blessing, 'who uprooted idolatry from this place.'"[6]

The Rambam saw a second connection between the *mitzvah* of *yerushah vi-yeshivah* and the building of the Temple. Indeed, he includes the *mitzvah* of building the Temple in his list of *mitzvot*. We see this from the verses that follow the *mitzvah* of *yerushah vi-yeshivah*. כי אם אל המקום אשר יבחר ה' א-להיכם מכל שבטיכם לשום את שמו שם לשכנו תדרשו ובאת שמה – "Rather, only at the place that the Lord your God shall choose from among all your tribes to place his name shall you seek out his presence and come there."[7] One might have expected this *mitzvah* of *la-shichno tidreshu*, to seek out his presence, to be found in Leviticus, adjacent to the discussion of the Temple. Instead, it was placed in *Sefer Devarim* under the rubric of *yerushah vi-yeshivah*. In a sense, it is more appropriate

---

4 Deuteronomy 12:2.
5 *Mishneh Torah,* Hilchot Avodah Zarah 7:1.
6 *Mishneh Torah,* Hilchot Berachot 10:9. In Hilchot Berachot, the Rambam writes as follows: "A place from which idolatry was uprooted – if it is in the Land of Israel, one makes a blessing over having uprooted idolatry 'from our land.' If it is outside of the Land of Israel, one makes a blessing over having uprooted idolatry 'from this place.'"
7 Deuteronomy 12:5.

to include this *mitzvah* in Deuteronomy, for this *sefer* is focused on communal issues that affect the Jewish people and on political sovereignty. The subjects of judges and a judicial system, the appointment of a king, the issue of war and its minutiae are all highlighted and come to the fore in Deuteronomy. Therefore, it is fitting to include the obligation to seek out the Land of Israel and the obligation to build the Temple in this book.

In *Hilchot Melachim*, the Rambam codifies the *mitzvah* of building a Temple upon entry into the Land of Israel. However, this obligation applies only after the fulfillment of two other *mitzvot*: appointing a king and annihilating the descendants of Amalek. The Rambam[8] adduces these obligations from a verse in Shmuel II. ויהי כי ישב המלך בביתו וה' הניח לו מסביב מכל איביו: ויאמר המלך אל נתן הנביא ראה נא אנכי יושב בבית ארזים וארון הא-להים ישב בתוך היריעה – "When the king lived in his home and the Lord had given him rest from his enemies all around, the king said to Nathan the prophet: See, now, I live in a house of cedar, while the ark of God dwells behind a curtain."[9] The obligation to build a Temple is the final step of the process of *yerushah vi-yeshivah*. The *mitzvah* of building a Tabernacle, which applied when we were in the desert, has nothing to do with *yerushah vi-yeshivah*. However, the *mitzvah* of building a Temple, which is a direct function of *yerushah vi-yeshivah*, is part of the verse that states לשכנו תדרשו – "You shall seek his presence."[10]

✃ לשכנו תדרשו – You Shall Seek His Presence

In his commentary on the verse, Ramban notes that the *mitzvah* of לשכנו תדרש is a composite of two elements: seeking God and receiving the prophet's approval.[11] At first, King David sought out the place to build

---

8 *Mishneh Torah*, Hilchot Melachim 1:2.

9 2 Samuel 7:1–2.

10 Deuteronomy 12:5.

11 Ramban on Deuteronomy 12:5.

the Temple, and then the prophet approved it. In Ekev, the Torah states: כל המקום אשר תדרך כף רגלכם בו לכם יהיה – "Everywhere that the sole of your foot treads shall belong to you."[12] This verse addresses the initial process of the conquest of the land. The next step is the political sovereignty of *yerushah vi-yeshivah*, which is described in Parashat Re'eh. This is also a prerequisite for building the Temple.

This connection between *yerushah vi-yeshivah* – sovereignty over the Land of Israel and the construction of the Temple – might explain a passage in the Book of Samuel (the *haftarah* of Parashat Shemini). When the *aron ha-kodesh* was taken to Jerusalem after twenty years during which it had had no permanent abode, King David accompanied the procession from the home of Obed-Edom to the city of David with great joy. During the procession, David danced joyfully before God. Michal, who was King Saul's daughter and David's wife, objected, feeling that it was unseemly for a king to act in such an undignified fashion. She scolded him with strong language, saying: מה נכבד היום מלך ישראל אשר נגלה היום לעיני אמהות עבדיו כהגלות נגלות אחד הרקים – "How honored was the King of Israel today, who exposed himself today in the eyes of his servants and maidservants, as one of the boors might expose himself."[13]

Michal felt that a king, the image of royalty and sovereignty, must inspire awe and reverence. Since the construction of the Temple requires absolute sovereignty, Michal told David: You are undermining the concept of kingship with your undignified behavior, as can be seen from the phrase מה נכבד היום מלך ישראל "How honored was the king of Israel today."[14] This position is based on the importance of the connection between *yerushah v-yeshivah* and the building of the Temple.

The Rambam appears to reject Michal's argument at the end of *Hilchot Lulav*, in which he describes the pageantry, majesty and joy of

---

12 Deuteronomy 11:24.
13 2 Samuel 6:20.
14 2 Samuel 6:20.

the Simhat Beit ha-Shoevah that took place on Sukkot in the Temple. He writes as follows:

מצוה להרבות בשמחה זו, ולא היו עושין אותה עמי הארץ וכל מי שירצה, אלא גדולי חכמי ישראל וראשי הישיבות והסנהדרין והחסידים והזקנים ואנשי מעשה הם שהיו מרקדין ומספקין ומנגנין ומשמחין במקדש בימי חג הסוכות, אבל כל העם האנשים והנשים כולן באין לראות ולשמוע.

It is a *mitzvah* to increase this joy, which was not demonstrated by the common folk or whoever so desired, but by the great sages of Israel, the heads of yeshivas, members of the Sanhedrin, the pious, the elders, and the people who were known for their great deeds. They danced, clapped their hands, sang and rejoiced in the Temple during Sukkot, while the masses of people, men and women, all came to see and hear.[15]

During a *simhah shel mitzvah* – a joyous occasion surrounding a *mitzvah* – the great leaders would divest themselves of any pretense, so to speak, and express their joy unabashedly. Michal disagreed strongly with this position, as we saw above. The Rambam sees King David's behavior as not only permissible but also as the paradigm for the celebration of a *simhah shel mitzvah*, in which the leader expressed joy and the commoners drew inspiration. How did the Rambam know that King David was correct and not Michal? This was shown by the verse: ולמיכל בת שאול לא היה לה ילד עד יום מותה – "Michal, daughter of Saul, had no child until the day of her death."[16] Apparently, God disapproved of her position and punished her.

Although we reject Michal's position regarding a *simhah shel mitzvah*, the principle that the Temple must be built in the context of *yerushah*

---

15 *Mishneh Torah,* Hilchot Lulav 8:14.
16 2 Samuel 6:23.

v-yeshivah – social and political sovereignty – is correct. This becomes clear from the verses in Samuel II that follow:

ויהי כי ישב המלך בביתו וה' הניח לו מסביב מכל איביו: ויאמר המלך אל נתן הנביא ראה נא אנכי יושב בבית ארזים וארון הא-להים ישב בתוך היריעה: ויאמר נתן אל המלך כל אשר בלבבך לך עשה כי ה' עמך: ויהי בלילה ההוא ויהי דבר ה' אל נתן לאמר: לך ואמרת אל עבדי אל דוד כה אמר ה' האתה תבנה לי בית לשבתי: כי לא ישבתי בבית למיום העלתי את בני ישראל ממצרים ועד היום הזה ואהיה מתהלך באהל ובמשכן: בכל אשר התהלכתי בכל בני ישראל הדבר דברתי את אחד שבטי ישראל אשר צויתי לרעות את עמי את ישראל לאמר למה לא בניתם לי בית ארזים: ועתה כה תאמר לעבדי לדוד כה אמר ה' צבא-ות אני לקחתיך מן הנוה מאחר הצאן להיות נגיד על עמי על ישראל: ואהיה עמך בכל אשר הלכת ואכרתה את כל איביך מפניך ועשתי לך שם גדול כשם הגדלים אשר בארץ: ושמתי מקום לעמי לישראל ונטעתיו ושכן תחתיו ולא ירגז עוד ולא יסיפו בני עולה לענותו כאשר בראשונה.

When the king dwelled in his home and the Lord had given him rest from his enemies all around, the king said to Nathan the prophet: See, now: I dwell in a house of cedar while the ark of God dwells within the curtain. Nathan told the king: Go and do whatever is in your heart, for the Lord is with you. That night the word of the Lord came to Nathan, saying, "Go and tell my servant David: 'Thus says the Lord: Will you build a house for me to dwell in? I have not dwelt in a house from the day I brought the children of Israel up from Egypt to this day, and I have moved about in a tent and a tabernacle. Wherever I moved about among the children of Israel, did I say a word to one of the leaders of Israel, whom I appointed to shepherd my people, saying: Why have you not built me a house of cedar? And now, say this to my servant David: So says the Lord, Master of Legions: I have taken you from the sheepfold, from following the flock, to become ruler over my people, over Israel. I was with you wherever you went, I cut down all your enemies before you and I gave you great renown, like the renown of the great men who are in the world. I dedicated a place for my people, for Israel. I planted him there and he dwelt in his place so that he might tremble no more, and that iniquitous people would no more afflict him as before.'"[17]

This is a description of complete and peaceful sovereignty in which the king's rule is firmly established. King David's statement indicates that only when he had completed his own house of cedar wood did he decide to build a house for God. Apparently, if building the Temple is a function of *yerushah vi-yeshivah*, then security is the factor that creates the obligation to build a house for God. He taught that this is how we should understand the sages' statement[18] that the Israelites were commanded to fulfill three *mitzvot* upon entering the Land of Israel – appointing a king, annihilating the descendants of Amalek and building a Temple. This idea of sovereignty is the foundation for building the Temple.

Regarding our encampments in the desert, the Torah says, ... ויסעו ויחנו ... ויסעו ... ויחנו – "They journeyed ... and they encamped ... they journeyed ... and they encamped."[19] This negates the idea of a *Beit ha-Behirah*, since the word *behirah* means a final destination. Tosafot notes, ואע"ג דשלמה בנה הבית דוד קידשה – "Even though Shlomo built the Temple, King David sanctified it."[20] Therefore, the Temple had a double sanctity, of both King David and that of King Shlomo. This constituted the fulfillment of a *Beit ha-Behira* with the requisite sovereignty.

ཚ The Guidelines for Expenditures for the Temple

A *halachah* concerning the obligation of donating money for the Temple's construction shows the connection between *yerushah vi-yeshivah* and

---

17 2 Samuel 7:1–10.

18 BT *Sanhedrin* 20b.

19 Numbers 33.

20 BT *Zevahim* 24a. ד"ה הואיל ורצפה מקדשת.

the Temple. How much money is one obligated to spend for the Temple's construction? In Hilchot Beit ha-Behirah, the Rambam writes:

ומצוה מן המובחר לחזק את הבנין ולהגביהו כפי כח הציבור ... ומפארין אותו ומייפין ... אם יכולין לטוח אותו בזהב ... ה"ז מצוה.

The best possible mitzvah is to strengthen the edifice (of the Temple) and to elevate it according to the community's means ... and we glorify it and beautify it ... if they can overlay it with gold ... it is a *mitzvah*.[21]

Moreover, the Rambam states:

היו הקהל עניים עושין אותן אפילו של בדיל ואם העשירו עושין אותן זהב.

If the community is impoverished, they can make [the Temple vessels] even of lead, and if they are wealthier, they make them of gold ...[22]

Apparently, the criteria for expenditures regarding the construction of the Temple is a function of what people can afford to spend on their own homes. If the standard of living rises and people are willing to spend more money on their own homes, then they are obligated to spend more on the *Beit ha-Mikdash*.[23] Here again we see the link between *yerushah ve-yeshivah* regarding both the personal and communal standard of living and the Temple.

✍ שכן – God as a Close Neighbor

This connection between *yerushah ve-yeshivah* and the Temple also carries a deeper philosophical message. The Rav commented on a particular phenomenon in Tanach in which idolatry is often portrayed as being על

---

21 *Mishneh Torah,* Hilchot Beit ha-Behirah 1:11.
22 *Mishneh Torah,* Hilchot Beit ha-Behirah 1:19.
23 *Mishneh Torah,* Hilchot Issurei Mizbeah 7:11

ההרים הרמים ועל הגבעות ותחת כל עץ רענן – "On high mountains and on the hills and under every verdant tree."[24] Compare this with the description of the service of God, which in Parashat Re'eh is described as לשכנו תדרשו ובאת שמה – "You shall seek out his presence and come there."[25] There is no need to climb mountains or scale cliffs. God is easily sought and found. In Judaism, God and human beings can easily become intimate friends. הרעה אתי מעודי עד היום הזה – "God who shepherds me from my inception until this day."[26]

The Torah uses the language of והתהלכתי בתוככם – "I will walk among you."[27] The use of the *binyan kal* conjugation of the verb ללכת, to walk, connotes a single occurrence of walking. However, the use of the reflexive form, התהלכתי, implies a constant walking back and forth – a total involvement. God is easily accessible to those who seek him. Compare this with the description of idol-worship. In order to create an aura of mystery and majesty, such worship takes place on high mountains or in the hills – places that are not easily accessible. But Jews may become acquainted with God simply by removing a volume of the Talmud from the bookshelf – and basking in divine illumination. The word לשכנו,[28] as in *shachen*, neighbor, implies one who lives close by, and the word *tidreshu* means investigation, study and search. Even though the area of the Temple is also described as the Mountain of the Lord,[29] this does not connote physical or emotional distance. In this context, the term *har* indicates the readiness of human beings to strive for truth. This use of the word *har* has nothing to do with mystery. Instead, it represents an initiate's indefatigable striving to learn Torah.

---

24 Deuteronomy 12:2.
25 Deuteronomy 12:5.
26 Genesis 48:15.
27 Leviticus 26:12.
28 Deuteronomy 12:5.
29 2 Isaiah 2.

Shofetim: The Mitzvah of Appointing a King

⅏ The Human Need for Social Order

KINGSHIP IS BOUND up with the human desire for companionship and coexistence. The comradeship of human beings has its
source in God's will at the moment of creation, when God said,
לא טוב היות האדם לבדו – "It is not good for human beings to be alone."[1] In
order to save Adam from loneliness, God created his helpmate, Hava.
Man's desire to overcome his loneliness impelled him to establish various types of human relationships. The human fear of loneliness and the
constant search for a social framework also led to the need for a ruling
structure.

Perfect social harmony cannot come only from the development of
social units because all human beings are different. While social cohesion
is desirable, it is a long way from perfect social integration. The paradox
of the human being is that on the one hand, he is a social creature and
does not always wish to be alone. On the other hand, he is individualis-
tic. Our sages comment, כשם שאין פרצופיהן שווין זה לזה כך אין דעתם שווין זה לזה
– just as the physiognomies of human beings are different, their world

---

1 Genesis 2:18.

views differ as well."[2] These differences may be seen both externally and spiritually. Some people prosper and become successful, while others are poor.

Judaism, which was always circumspect in this regard, felt that it was not prudent for one person to hold too much power. Preferably, power should be limited and compartmentalized. However, we must often live with the fact that power is concentrated in the hands of one individual. Individuals who are imperfect will have ruling structures that are imperfect as well. Rabbi Hanina Segan ha-Kohanim expressed this view of power as a necessary but imperfect solution when he said, הוי מתפלל בשלומה של מלכות שאלמלא מוראה איש את רעהו חיים בלעו – "Pray for the welfare of the government, for without the fear of it, people would swallow one another alive."[3] We must have some ruling framework, even if it is not ideal, in order to avoid sinking into total chaos.

The Rav remarked that whenever he read *Megillat Esther*, he was struck by how little things had changed over the generations. King Ahashverosh was impetuous in his decisions. He ordered the execution of his wife Vashti on the advice of Memuchan, one of his courtiers. Shortly thereafter, he ordered the execution of his chief adviser, Haman, immediately after Queen Esther exposed his murderous plot. Even today, we are witness to some of the attributes of Ahashverosh as the Megillah describes them. The impulsiveness of one powerful individual can still lead to conquest, war and bloodshed. It is possible that a single autocrat could press a button that would cause widespread nuclear destruction. Not much has changed from the days of Ahashverosh.

৯ Three Conditions for Appointing a King

Given Judaism's reservations regarding political power, how are we to understand and observe the commandment to appoint a king? Rav

---

2 *Midrash Tanhuma,* Pinhas 10; see also BT *Berachot* 58a and BT *Sanhedrin* 38a.
3 Mishnah *Avot* 3:2.

Moshe Soloveitchik, zt"l, explained that the *mitzvah* to appoint a king is predicated upon three conditions, which provide the historical context that legitimizes the power of royalty.

The first condition dictates that a king may be appointed only if there is an objective reason to do so for the defense of the people and the land. The famous Gemara in Tractate *Sanhedrin*[4] tells us that the Israelites were commanded to fulfill three *mitzvot* when they entered the Land of Israel: to appoint a king, to annihilate the descendants of Amalek and to build a Temple. The latter two *mitzvot* devolve upon a king. Without him, anarchy will often prevail, as described in several places in the book of Judges: בימים ההם אין מלך בישראל איש הישר בעיניו יעשה – "In those days, there was no king in Israel. Each man did what was right in his eyes."[5]

The Rambam writes, שאין ממליכין מלך תחלה אלא לעשות משפט ומלחמות – "A king is not appointed except to mete out judgment and wage wars."[6] Every king must have a specific agenda. The purpose of David's kingship was to achieve unity among the tribes of Israel, create a collective national identity, and unite the people against the country's enemies. King Solomon was able to dedicate most of his efforts towards building the Temple, the nation's spiritual center. According to our tradition, King Hizkiyahu used his kingship to disseminate Torah study.[7] According to the work *Avot de-Rebbi Natan*, King Hizkiyahu was involved in establishing the Men of the Great Assembly.[8]

The second condition is that the king be appointed at the nation's request. A king may not be imposed upon the people against their wishes. The Torah states this condition explicitly: ואמרת אשימה עלי מלך ככל הגוים אשר סביבתי: שום תשים עליך מלך – "You shall say: I will appoint a king over myself like the surrounding nations. Appoint a king over yourself."[9] The

---

4 BT *Sanhedrin* 20b.
5 Judges 21:25.
6 *Mishneh Torah*, Hilchot Melachim 4:10.
7 BT *Sanhedrin* 94b.
8 See Avot de-Rebbi Natan 1:4 and commentary of Binyan Yehoshua.
9 Deuteronomy 17:14–15.

Rambam also states this condition as follows: מאחר שהקמת מלך מצוה למה לא רצה הקב"ה כששאלו מלך משמואל לפי ששאלו בתערומות ולא שאלו לקיים המצוה אלא מפני שקצו בשמואל הנביא שנאמר כי לא אותך מאסו כי אם אותי מאסו וגו' – "Since the appointment of a king is a *mitzvah*, why didn't God consent when they [the people] asked Samuel for a king? They asked in a querulous spirit, not in order to fulfill a *mitzvah* but because they disdained the prophet Samuel, as it is written: "It was not you whom they spurned. Rather, they spurned me."[10] The obvious question is as follows: What is the connection between the request to appoint a king and the *mitzvah* to do so? According to the Rambam, it is that the people's desire and cooperation in appointing a king is a prerequisite for his viability.

❧ Third of the Three Conditions

It is clear that Judaism did not want to establish a fixed ruling structure for all generations, but linked it to historical necessity, and this is the third condition. There are three reasons why a perpetual monarchy was not desirable. First, as mentioned above, such a structure could lead to moral turpitude, deviation from a righteous path, and capricious use of authority. With the strengthening of authority in general, the personal autonomy of the authority figure also diminishes. For example, when King Saul attempted to justify having disobeyed God's order to destroy Amalek, he put the blame on the people, saying, אשר חמל העם על מיטב הצאן – "The nation had compassion on the best of the flock."[11] King Saul tried to place his own guilt upon the people. This is a classic example of a situation in which a ruler loses his own free will, becomes subordinate to the people, and cannot exercise his autonomy.

Perhaps Judaism's unwillingness to support a strong ruling structure stems from a second concern. Usually, those who are intellectually gifted are chosen to lead. Yet is that the only criterion for leadership? Judaism

---

10 *Mishneh Torah,* Hilchot Melachim 1:2.
11 1 Samuel 15:15.

never measured the axiological value of a person only by his intellectual credentials. Again and again, the emphasis is upon a person's pure heart. The Torah desires the heart, and often, God chooses the humble and modest person. However, these qualities do not do well in a political monarchy.

Finally, we say that kingship belongs exclusively to God.[12] Sometimes, God may call upon human beings to join him and follow in his ethical footsteps. This is the principle of *imitatio dei*. Yet as far as rulership and power are concerned, there is no doctrine of *imitatio dei*. Power-seeking was the source of Adam's sin, and the serpent took advantage of it. He enticed Adam and Eve with the suggestion, והייתם כא-להים – "You will be like rulers."[13] Judaism is wary of one person acquiring a great deal of political and judicial power, and maintains that such powers belong ultimately to God.

---

12 See the liturgical poem "Ha-aderet ve-ha-emunah," from the Yom Kippur liturgy, which contains the phrase "Ha-meluchah ve-ha-memshalah le-Hai Olamim."

13 Genesis 3:5, and Targum Onkelos ותהון כרברבין.

Shofetim II: The Spiritual Lessons of Kingship

Chosenness and Individual Destiny

KINGSHIP IS NOT merely a political notion associated with power and authority, but also a lofty spiritual idea. Kingship is a metaphysical notion that characterized the Jewish social covenant for millennia. ואתם תהיו לי ממלכת כהנים וגוי קדוש – "You shall be to me a kingdom of priests and a holy nation."[1]

Kingship has many facets. One of its major messages is that of chosenness – the belief that God designates a specific individual to perform a particular task, and no one else can replace that individual. In this sense, every person should feel a sense of royalty. Just as a king shoulders a heavy burden of responsibility and requires vision, each of us is born to bear a certain weight. Each one of us is born into a specific place and time, to a particular family. All of these things enable us to perform our task for God, our employer, according to our contract with him. As Job said:

אם חרוצים ימיו מספר חדשיו אתך חקיו עשית ולא יעבור: שעה מעליו ויחדל עד ירצה כשכיר יומו.

---

1   Exodus 19:6.

If his days are predetermined and the number of his months is with you, and you have made his limits which he cannot surpass, then turn away from him and let his pain be relieved, until, like a hired hand, he craves the end of his day.[2]

ᠵ Esther's Royal Mission

A person's obligation on this earth is to fulfill the mission devolving upon him. In *Megillat Esther*, we read:

ויאמר מרדכי להשיב אל אסתר אל תדמי בנפשך להמלט בית המלך מכל היהודים: כי אם החרש תחרישי בעת הזאת רוח והצלה יעמוד ליהודים ממקום אחר ואת ובית אביך תאבדו ומי יודע אם לעת כזאת הגעת למלכות.

Then Mordechai said to reply to Esther: Do not imagine that you will be able to escape in the King's palace any more than the rest of the Jews. For if you persist in keeping silent at a time like this, relief and deliverance will come to the Jews from somewhere else, while you and your father's house will perish – and who knows whether it was just for such a time that you attained the royal position?[3]

The message that Mordechai conveyed to Esther was three-fold. First, every person is charged with a particular mission. God chose Esther to intercede with the king on behalf of the Jewish people. We too must recognize our mission at the proper time. First, we must protect the physical security of each Jew wherever he or she may be – a formidable task in our own day, perhaps even more than in previous generations. In the past, the non-Jews attempted to isolate us in overcrowded ghettos, make our lives difficult and disenfranchise us. Today, as well, the enemies of the Jews in both the Diaspora and in the State of Israel threaten us

---

2 Job 14:5–6.
3 Esther 4:13–14.

with terror and war. Therefore, our foremost concern is for our people's security. We must be aware of every echo of anti-Semitism and of any threat, no matter how veiled it might be.

The second part of Mordechai's message is that the one appointed to perform the task must realize that it will ultimately be accomplished no matter what he may or may not do. He tells Esther: If you remain passive and do nothing, your task will be accomplished in some other way. On the one hand, the individual must carry out his or her mission as if it depended exclusively upon him or her. On the other hand, the individual who merited this "doctrine assignment" must realize that God's plan will ultimately be fulfilled one way or another, regardless of whether he or she succeeds or fails.

Finally, Mordechai points out a third condition: ואת ובית אביך תאבדו – "while you and your father's house perish." Mordechai warns that one who has a particular task to do and does not perform it is considered a traitor and a sinner. Just as a king realizes how great a responsibility he must carry, so each of us must appreciate the importance of our mission. If we abandon our responsibility, the result could be devastating. Although God's plan will be fulfilled nevertheless, we stand to forfeit our share in it.

ᴖ The Kabbalistic View: The Immanence of Royalty

The concept of *Shechinah* expresses God's ongoing closeness to His created beings. In our prayers, when we speak of God's existence, we stress His transcendence and distance from us. However, when we mention the *Shechinah*, we stress God's immanence and closeness to us, particularly in times of distress. ה' שמרך, ה' צלך על יד ימינך – "God is your guardian; God is your protective shade of your right hand."[4] The Hebrew words *shechinah* and *shachen*, which come from the same root, denote closeness

---

4 Psalms 121:5.

and bonding. The word *shechinah* refers to a mother's boundless love for her child, despite the child's shortcomings. A mother is forgiving even toward a rebellious child, and will never abandon the child. השכן אתם בתוך טמאתם – "that dwells with them amid their contamination."[5] The *Shechinah* not only maintains a connection with human beings, but also feels compassion for them and shares in their sorrow.

The Kabbalah compares the *Shechinah* to kingship. Jewish kings were always available to their subjects. The posture that is found in *Megillat Esther* does not apply to Jewish kings:

כל עבדי המלך ועם מדינות המלך יודעים אשר כל איש ואשה אשר יבוא אל המלך אל החצר הפנימית אשר לא יקרא אחת דתו להמית לבד מאשר יושיט לו המלך את שרביט הזהב וחיה.

All the servants of the King and the people of the King's provinces know that any man or woman who approaches the king in the inner court without having been summoned has but one law: to be put to death unless the king extends the golden scepter to him. Then, he is spared.[6]

The Tanach tells of two prostitutes who presented their case directly to King Solomon.[7] This shows us that Jewish kings had a direct connection to the common people. The protocol of Ahashverosh, in which few people could approach the king, does not accord with Judaism at all. In Judaism, every Jew may present his case before the King of Kings through the medium of prayer – directly, with no intermediary.

A king in Israel must be attentive to the needs of everyone. Even if a Jewish king is separate from the community in some respects, he is still part of the nation. He is a world unto himself, yet also deeply involved in communal life. There is no king without a constituency. A Jewish king

---

5 Leviticus 16:16.
6 Esther 4:11.
7 I Kings 3:16.

is one with the Jewish nation, which is the sum of every single Jew, good and bad, without exception.

When the Rambam speaks of a king in Israel, he uses a poignant expression: שלבו הוא לב כל קהל ישראל – "His heart is the heart of all the Jewish people."[8] In other words, not only must the king's heart be aware of his subjects, but he must behave with empathy and sensitivity towards the people. His treatment of the people must go beyond cordial relations to the true partnership that underlies *achavah* – brotherhood. In Judaism, all the concepts that relate to benevolence, *tzedakah* and *hesed* are bound up with the concept of brotherhood. In this context, the Torah does not use the words *rea* and *reut* – "friend" and "friendship" – but various forms of the Hebrew word for "brother." וכי ימוך אחיך – "If your brother is poor,"[9] or כי יהיה בך אביון מאחד אחיך – "If one of your brethren should be destitute."[10] In human relationships, the Torah does not demand understanding or familiarity, but, rather, brotherhood.

Judaism negated the idea that a king has any proprietary rights over his subjects. Only God has total ownership over the earth, for he created it.[11] Our tradition regarding kingship in terms of the Davidic dynasty, which will peak with the arrival of the Messianic king, is founded not only upon the principles of a political dynasty but on the basis of spiritual rule. Is the Messiah a political figure of great courage and strength? Not necessarily. Does he base his authority on physical prowess? No. He is a teacher and the one who will bring redemption to the world. The Rambam says the following about his personality:

מפני שאותו המלך שיעמוד מזרע דוד בעל חכמה יהיה יתר משלמה, ונביא גדול הוא קרוב למשה רבינו, ולפיכך ילמד כל העם ויורה אותם דרך ה', ויבואו כל הגוים לשומעו שנאמר והיה באחרית הימים נכון יהיה הר בית ה' בראש ההרים.

---

8 *Mishneh Torah,* Hilchot Melachim 3:6.
9 Leviticus 25:35.
10 Deuteronomy 15:7.
11 See Psalms 24:1–2.

Since the king who will arise from King David's line will be wiser than King Solomon and a great prophet approaching [the spiritual level] of Moshe Rabbenu, he will teach all the people and show them the way of God. All the non-Jews will come to hear him, as it is written: At the end of days, the mountain of the house of God will be established on the summit of the mountain.[12]

Here, the Rambam has summarized the Jewish view regarding the necessity to integrate the two functions of leader and teacher. The verse ויהי בישרון מלך – "He became king over Jeshurun"[13] also has its antecedent in Moshe Rabbenu. The greatest of the teachers and the master of the prophets in Israel was in the category of a "King in Jeshurun." Even the Talmud, when it describes King David's greatness, stresses his commitment to Torah study.[14] True Jewish kingship can only exist together with diligent study of Torah.

In addition, kingship in Israel must radiate *kedushah*. One who is striving for kingship must develop a personality filled with *kedushah* and the ability to embrace all Israel with understanding and love. A king must be able to relate to the entire Jewish people and to each individual in it.

How does the connection between kingship and sanctity express itself? What must the king do in order to demonstrate that these values are intertwined? When did the investiture of Moshe, Israel's greatest king, take place? It occurred at Mount Sinai, as we recite in the Shabbat morning prayers: כליל תפארת בראשו נתת לו בעמדו לפניך על הר סיני "You bestowed a crown of glory upon him when he stood before you on Mount Sinai." There, Moshe was crowned king of Israel. Did his coronation take place at his first or second appearance on Mount Sinai? Clearly, it took place

---

12 *Mishneh Torah,* Hilchot Teshuvah 9:2.
13 Deuteronomy 33:5.
14 BT *Berachot* 3b, JT 1:1.

when he received the second set of tablets. ושני לוחות אבנים הוריד בידו – "He brought down two stone tablets in his hand."[15] It was then that Moshe's face began to radiate light.

Why was Moshe not crowned when the Torah was first given? What happened between the first giving of the Torah (Shavuot) and the second (Yom ha-Kippurim)? The event that occurred between the two was the breaking of the tablets. One could say that if not for the breaking of the tablets, Moshe would not have been crowned as a king and would have remained in his status as a redeemer and leader, but not a king of Israel. He received kingship after the breaking of the first tablets.

In order for us to understand this, we must know that Moshe never faltered until the sin of the Golden Calf. He was successful in achieving all his goals, and the people venerated him when he brought them the news of redemption. No one doubted that redemption was imminent. But in Judaism, success and victory do not necessarily go hand in hand with the concept of kingship. In order to attain both kingship and sanctity, one must be prepared for obstacles. Only when God said, לך רד כי שחת עמך – "Go down, for your nation has become corrupt,"[16] did Moshe realize that he had faltered, as Rashi comments: לך רד מגדלתך, לא נתתי לך גדולה אלא בשבילם – "Go, descend from your greatness. I did not give you greatness except on their account." The nation was not yet ready to receive the Torah. Moshe's failure came as a terrible shock, and his descent from the mountain was painful. Therefore, he was crowned only when he received the second set of tablets.

---

15 The Shabbat morning prayers.
16 Exodus 32:7.

~ כי תצא ~

Ki Tetze: The Prohibition of Shaatnez

A MONG THE NUMEROUS commandments in Parashat Ki Tetze is
the prohibition of wearing *shaatnez*. לא תלבש שעטנז צמר ופשתים
יחדו – "Do not wear a mixture of wool and linen together."[1] The
general category of *kilayim* – mixing diverse species – includes various
prohibitions, such as mixing different species of trees, animals, and seeds.
One who mixes several items blurs boundaries that God set during the
process of creation. The Talmud says that everything grows according to
natural law[2] and that the entire world is subordinate to God, except for
those human beings who rebel. אלא עולם כמנהגו נוהג ושוטים שקלקלו עתידים
ליתן את הדין – "But the world operates according to natural law, and the
fools who corrupt it will face the consequences in the future."

Our sages comment on the verse האזינו השמים ואדברה ותשמע הארץ אמרי
פי – "Give ear, O heavens, and I will speak. May the earth hear the words
of my mouth"[3] – that we never encountered the sun setting in the east
or rising in the west. We never experienced rain that fell out of season
(in the Land of Israel). We never chanced upon a rock that fell upward.
So, too, a person must follow Divine law. One who violates the prohibi-

---

1 Deuteronomy 22:11.
2 BT Avodah Zarah 54b.
3 Deuteronomy 32:1.

430

tion against *kilayim* negates the world that was created "after its kind" according to the Ramban.[4]

⁓ איש על דגלו – Each One at His Own Banner ⁓

The principle of *kilayim* – of respecting the boundaries of unique aspects of creation – also applied to human identity and destiny. The text shows this principle regarding the Israelites' camp in the desert. In Parshiyot Bamidbar and Naso, the Torah describes how the banners of each tribe were stationed each in its own location:

וחנו בני ישראל איש על מחנהו ואיש על דגלו לצבאתם: והלוים יחנו סביב למשכן
העדת ולא יהיה קצף על עדת בני ישראל ושמרו הלוים את משמרת משכן העדות:
וידבר ה' אל משה ואל אהרן לאמר: איש על דגלו באתת לבית אבתם יחנו בני
ישראל מנגד סביב לאהל מועד יחנו.

The Children of Israel shall encamp, each man in his own camp and each man at his own banner, according to their legions. The Levites shall encamp around the Tabernacle of the Testimony so that there shall be no wrath upon the assembly of the Children of Israel, and the Levites shall safeguard the watch of the Tabernacle of the Testimony. God spoke to Moshe and Aharon, saying: "The Children of Israel shall encamp, each man by his banner according to the insignia of their father's household. They shall encamp at a distance surrounding the Tent of Meeting."[5]

In effect, the Torah is stating that each individual has his or her own characteristics and abilities. In order for the nation to live together in harmony, each person must recognize his or her unique capabilities. God wanted each person to know that he or she had a unique place. No one

---

4 See Ramban on Genesis 1:11 and Leviticus 19:19.
5 Numbers 1:52–53, 2:1–2.

person can possess every ability that exists. Only God, who is omniscient and omnipotent, can do that. The sages comment on the verse ויעבדו מצרים את בני ישראל בפרך – "The Egyptians enslaved the Children of Israel with crushing labor"[6] as meaning that the Egyptians made men and women do each other's work and made children do the work of adults, all in order to discourage and demoralize them. את כל עבודתם אשר עבדו בהם בפרך – "All the work that they did with them was crushing labor."[7] The Midrash notes, למאן דאמר בפריכה שהיו מחלפין מלאכת אנשים לנשים ומלאכת נשים לאנשים – "According to the one who said it was crushing labor, they made men and women do each other's work."[8] When an individual loses his sense of purpose, he loses all hope.

בהנחל עליון גויים – The Special Inheritance of Each Nation

This principle also applies to individual nations. Our sages understood that God gave the nations of the world unique talents. Yet a nation, like a person, must acknowledge its limitations. If it allows itself to think that it has everything, it risks descent into megalomania. Just like individuals, nations can behave in a wild manner. God not only gave each nation its geographic location on the planet, but also a unique ethos and talents.

בהנחל עליון גוים בהפרידו בני אדם יצב גבלת עמים למספר בני ישראל: כי חלק
ה' עמו יעקב חבל נחלתו.

When the Supreme One gave the nations their inheritance when he separated the children of man. He set the borders of the peoples according to the number of the Children of Israel. For God's portion is his people. Jacob is the measure of his inheritance.[9]

---

6 Exodus 1:13.
7 Exodus 1:14.
8 *Yalkut Shimoni,* Parashat Shemot 163.
9 Deuteronomy 32:8–9.

What is the unrivalled talent of the Jewish people? The answer is our uncanny ability to discover God – and, as a result, God demands that we live according to a distinctive lifestyle. The author of the *Shulhan Aruch*, Rav Yosef Caro, gave the first segment of the *Shulhan Aruch* the title *Orah Haim* (way of life) because its focus is the specifically Jewish way of life. If we succeed in achieving closeness to God, then that is a function of a particular lifestyle. If we do not develop this way of life, then all the technology in the world is worthless.

The Torah has never discouraged us from learning from non-Jews. On the contrary, our sages tell us:

מלכה ושריה בגוים אין תורה. אם יאמר לך אדם יש חכמה בגוים תאמין הדא הוא
דכתיב והאבדתי חכמים מאדום ותבונה מהר עשו (עובדיה א, ח). יש תורה בגוים
אל תאמין דכתיב מלכה ושריה בגוים אין תורה.

"Her king and her officers are among the nations; there is no Torah." Should a person tell you that there is wisdom among the nations, believe it; as it is written: "I will eradicate wise men from Edom and understanding from the mountain of Esau" (Obadia 1:8). [But if he should tell you] that there is Torah among the nations, do not believe it, as it is written: "Its king and officers are among the nations; there is no Torah."[10]

The non-Jewish world possesses no Torah, though it possesses much wisdom.

The Rambam wrote the following in *Hilchot Kiddush ha-Hodesh*:

וטעם כל אלו החשבונות ומפני מה מוסיפים מנין זה ומפני מה גורעין, והיאך נודע
כל דבר ודבר מאלו הדברים, והראיה על כל דבר ודבר, היא חכמת התקופות
והגימטריות שחברו בה חכמי יון ספרים הרבה והם הנמצאים עכשיו ביד החכמים,
אבל הספרים שחברו חכמי ישראל שהיו בימי הנביאים מבני יששכר לא הגיעו
אלינו, ומאחר שכל אלו הדברים בראיות ברורות הם שאין בהם דופי ואי אפשר

---

10 Eichah Rabbah 2:13.

לאדם להרהר אחריהם, אין חוששין למחבר בין שחברו אותו נביאים בין שחברו
אותם גוים, שכל דבר שנתגלה טעמו ונודעה אמתתו בראיות שאין בהם דופי אין
סומכין על זה האיש שאמרו או שלמדו אלא על הראייה שנתגלתה והטעם שנודע.

The reason for all these calculations, why we add to the
number and why we subtract, how we know all of these
things and the proof of each thing is the wisdom of the times
and numerology about which the Greek scholars wrote many
books and now they are found in the hands of our sages. But
the books that were authored by the Jewish scholars who
lived during the time of the prophets from the children of
Yissachar never reached us. And since all of these matters are
clear proofs that have no flaws and one cannot question their
veracity, we are not concerned over who wrote them, whether
they were prophets or from non-Jewish sources, for where
the reasoning is revealed and its truth is known from clear
proofs that cannot be refuted, we rely on the one who said
or taught it in the proof that was revealed and the reasoning
that is known.[11]

Thus, it is permitted and even necessary to learn from this wisdom
of other nations. However, there is one restriction. We must be careful
regarding what we take. We must reject any negative attributes, such
as egoism or immorality. In this sense, we must be careful to apply the
principle of *kilayim*.

⁌ Eshet Yefat Toar – Treatment of Women Prisoners of War

In light of the above discussion, we can interpret homiletically the verses
in the beginning of Ki Tetze. כי תצא למלחמה על איביך – "When you go to
war against your enemies"[12] as a reference to the spiritual war between

---

11 *Mishneh Torah*, Hilchot Kiddush Ha-Hodesh 17:24.
12 Deuteronomy 21:10.

the Jewish people and the nations of the world. וראית בשביה אשת יפת תאר וחשקת בה ולקחת לך לאשה – "and you see among its captives a woman who is beautiful of form and you desire her, you may take her as a wife."[13] Our sages say, דלא דברה תורה אלא כנגד יצר הרע – "The Torah spoke only in response to the evil inclination."[14] One may be drawn to the beauty of other nations, but one must understand the principle of *kilayim* and set appropriate boundaries.

The beauty of Japheth may be full of impurity even if its outer appearance is captivating. The Torah cautions us against being too quick to take it into our lives. והבאתה אל תוך ביתך וגלחה את ראשה ועשתה את צפרניה – "You shall bring her to your house. She shall shave her head and let her nails grow." והסירה את שמלת שביה מעליה[15] – "She shall remove the garment of her captivity . . ."[16] In other words, once we remove the outer layers, we will find cruelty and egoism. While we may learn legitimate and genuine knowledge from other cultures, we must be careful not to be taken in by the *yefat toar* – their superficiality and external trappings.

While we may learn much from the nations of the world, we must distinguish between the pure and the impure. If one takes a *yefat toar* because of her external appearance, the consequences could be disastrous. We learn this from the Torah's juxtaposition of this portion with that of the *ben sorer u-moreh* (rebellious son). The sages say that even King David did not learn from this juxtaposition, and the Talmud says: כל הנושא יפת תואר – יש לו בן סורר ומורה – "Whoever marries a *yefat toar* will have a son who is a *ben sorer u-moreh*."[17]

One may write a sefer Torah in Greek, for the Gemara says: יפיותו של יפת יהא באהלי שם – "The beauty of Yefet will be in the tents of Shem."[18] The Rambam wrote the *Guide for the Perplexed* in Arabic, and Rav

---

13 Deuteronomy 21:11.
14 BT *Kiddushin* 21b.
15 Deuteronomy 21:12.
16 Deuteronomy 21:13.
17 BT *Sanhedrin* 107a.
18 BT *Megillah* 9b.

Saadya Gaon wrote *Emunot ve-deot* in Arabic. However, Rav Yehuda Halevi writes that one must be able to distinguish between the flowers and the fruit of Greek wisdom.[19] Unfortunately, many failed. They transgressed the prohibition against *kilayim*, not knowing how to integrate them, and thus became the parents of rebellious children. In America, we venerate politicians who often lie, and we admire powerful people even though they may be cruel. We do not learn the "beauty of Yefet" from them. Instead, we absorb all that is negative about them. In other words, we have assimilated the fingernails and the garment of captivity of the *yefat toar*.

The "beauty of Yefet" could not be brought into the Temple proper. The Torah says:

כי יכרית ה' א-להיך את הגוים אשר אתה בא שמה לרשת אותם מפניך וירשת
אתם וישבת בארצם: השמר לך פן תנקש אחריהם אחרי השמדם מפניך ופן
תדרש לא-להיהם לאמר איכה יעבדו הגוים האלה את אלהיהם ואעשה כן גם אני:
לא תעשה כן לה' א-להיך כי כל תועבת ה' אשר שנא עשו לאלהיהם כי גם את
בניהם ואת בנתיהם ישרפו באש לאלהיהם.

When the Lord your God cuts down the nations where you will be arriving, driving them away from before you, and you have driven them away and settled on their land, take care lest you be drawn after them after they have been destroyed from before you, and lest you seek out their gods saying, "How did these nations worship their gods? I will do the same." You shall not do this to the Lord your God, for they worshipped their gods by doing everything that God abominates, even burning their sons and daughters in the fire for their gods.[20]

---

19 From the poem by Yehuda Halevi:
ואל תשיאך חכמת יונית, אשר אין לה פרי, כי אם פרחים, ופריה: כי אדמה לא רקועה וכי לא אהלי שחק מתוחים, ואין
ראשית לכל מעשה בראשית ואין אחרית לחידוש הירחים. שמע דברי נבונה נבוכים, בנויים על יסוד תהו וטוחים – ותשוב
לך בלב ריקם ונעור ופה מלא ברב שיגים ושיחים. ולמה זה אבקש לי ארחות עקלקלות ואעזוב אם ארחים.
20 Deuteronomy 12:29–31.

Rashi learns that these verses refer to Jews who might be led astray into idolatry after seeing the practice of the land's previous inhabitants.[21] The Ramban provides a different interpretation: ועתה בפרשה הזאת הזהיר – לא תעשה כן לה' א-להיך לעבדו במקדשו בעבודות שלהם – "In this section, it enjoins us: You shall not do so to the Lord your God, to worship him in the Temple with their types of worship."[22] The more sanctified one is, the more cautious he must be. Therefore, the Torah tells us at great length about the arrangement of the tribal camps and the fact that they were closely supervised by Aharon, the High Priest.

Over the course of the year, on new moons and festivals, they brought goats as sin-offerings in order to atone for the Temple and its sanctity. On Yom ha-Kippurim, they brought the *se'ir la-Azazel,* which atoned for everything. Therefore, the Torah insisted on clearly defined boundaries. Without such boundaries, the quest for sanctity can be completely undermined.

---

21 Deuteronomy 12:30.
22 Ramban on Deuteronomy 12:30.

~~ כי תבא ~~

Ki Tavo: The Convenant of Arvot Moav

IN PARASHAT KI Tavo, the Torah describes entering into a covenant with God:

 וידבר משה והכהנים הלוים אל כל ישראל לאמר הסכת ושמע ישראל היום הזה נהיית לעם לה' א־להיך: ושמעת בקול ה' א־להיך ועשית את מצותו ואת חקיו אשר אנכי מצוך היום.

Moshe, the Kohanim and the Levites spoke to all Israel, saying: Be attentive and hear, Israel. This day you have become a nation of the Lord your God. You shall hearken to the voice of the Lord your God, and you shall perform all his commandments and his decrees that I command you today.[1]

What is striking is the emphasis of the present tense – היום – meaning "this very day." This passage bears some similarity to the opening of the second section of *keriat Shema*:

והיה אם שמע תשמעו אל מצותי אשר אנכי מצוה אתכם היום לאהבה את ה' א־להיכם ולעבדו בכל לבבכם ובכל נפשכם.

---

1 Deuteronomy 27:9–10.

It shall come to pass that if you hearken to my commandments that I command you today: to love the Lord your God and to serve him with all your heart and with all your soul . . .[2]

Commenting on the use of the present tense, Rashi quotes the sages: שיהיו עליכם חדשים, כאלו שמעתם בו ביום – "The commandments should be as new to you as if you had received them today."[3]

⹂ Two Distinct Covenants

God made two different covenants with the children of Israel. The first is described in Parashat Behukotai: אלה החקים והמשפטים והתורת אשר נתן ה' בינו ובין בני ישראל בהר סיני ביד משה – "These are the decrees, ordinances and teachings that the Lord gave between Himself and the Children of Israel, at Mount Sinai through Moshe."[4] This is the covenant at Mount Sinai. The second covenant took place in Arvot Moab, as described in Parashat Ki Tavo. אלה דברי הברית אשר צוה ה' את משה לכרת את בני ישראל בארץ מואב מלבד הברית אשר כרת אתם בחרב – "These are the words of the covenant that Hashem commanded Moshe to seal with the Children of Israel in the land of Moab besides the covenant that he sealed with them in Horeb."[5] This second covenant may be called the *brit* of Arvot Moav.

There is a need for two separate covenants because each one had a specific purpose and was tailored to a specific stage of development of the Jewish people. The first, the covenant of Mount Sinai, was a treaty with the Israelites who left Egypt. In the second, which took place in Arvot Moav at the end of the forty years, God formed a covenant with the new generation. God forced us to accept the covenant at Mount

---

2 Deuteronomy 11:13.
3 Rashi on Deuteronomy 11:13.
4 Leviticus 26:46.
5 Deuteronomy 28:69.

Sinai,[6] which applied to the Jewish people in every geographic location, according to the verse:

אתם ראיתם אשר עשיתי למצרים ואשא אתכם על כנפי נשרים ואבא אתכם אלי:
ועתה אם שמוע תשמעו בקלי ושמרתם את בריתי והייתם לי סגלה מכל העמים
כי לי כל הארץ.

"You have seen what I did to Egypt, and that I have borne you on the wings of eagles and brought you to me. Now, if you hearken well to me and keep my covenant, you shall be the most beloved treasure of all peoples to me, for the entire world is mine."[7]

God made the covenant at Mount Sinai, when the Torah was given, with that particular generation. There is no reference to future generations. In contrast, the covenant of Arvot Moab relates to the new generation about to enter the Land of Israel and to the future generations, and focuses specifically upon that land. In this sense, it is similar to the *brit Avot* as elucidated by the Ramban.[8]

ࣾ Rebuke with Consolation vs. Rebuke without Consolation

There is another difference between the covenant of Sinai and that of Arvot Moab. The covenant of Mount Sinai is ensconced within the rebuke of Parashat Behukotai, while this rebuke is accompanied by words of consolation:

והתודו את עונם ואת עון אבתם במעלם אשר מעלו בי ואף אשר הלכו עמי בקרי:
אף אני אלך עמם בקרי והבאתי אתם בארץ איביהם או אז יכנע לבבם הערל
ואז ירצו את עונם: וזכרתי את בריתי יעקוב ואף את בריתי יצחק ואף את בריתי
אברהם אזכר והארץ אזכר... אף גם זאת בהיותם בארץ איביהם לא מאסתים ולא

---

6 BT *Shabbat* 88a.
7 Exodus 19:4–5.
8 Ramban on Genesis 15:18.

גְּעַלְתִּים לְכַלֹּתָם לְהָפֵר בְּרִיתִי אִתָּם כִּי אֲנִי ה' אֱ־לֹהֵיהֶם: וְזָכַרְתִּי לָהֶם בְּרִית רִאשֹׁנִים אֲשֶׁר הוֹצֵאתִי אֹתָם מֵאֶרֶץ מִצְרַיִם לְעֵינֵי הַגּוֹיִם לִהְיֹת לָהֶם לֵא־לֹהִים אֲנִי ה'.

Then they will confess their sin and the sin of their forefathers, the treachery with which they betrayed me, and also their disregard of me. I, too, shall behave towards them with disregard, and I will bring them into the land of their enemies. Perhaps then, their unfeeling heart will be humbled and then they will expiate their sin. I will remember my covenant with Jacob and also my covenant with Isaac and also my covenant with Abraham will I remember, and I will remember the land . . . But despite all this, while they are in the land of their enemies, I will not be revolted by them nor will I reject them to the point of obliterating them in order to annul my covenant with them, for I am the Lord their God. I will remember to their merit the covenant of the ancients, those whom I took out of the land of Egypt before the eyes of the nations, to be their God. I am the Lord.[9]

Unlike the *Tochaha* of Behukotai, this *Tochaha* of Arvot Moab concludes abruptly, with no words of consolation or support. וְהֵשִׁיבְךָ ה' מִצְרַיִם בָּאֳנִיּוֹת בַּדֶּרֶךְ אֲשֶׁר אָמַרְתִּי לְךָ לֹא תֹסִיף עוֹד לִרְאֹתָהּ וְהִתְמַכַּרְתֶּם שָׁם לְאֹיְבֶיךָ לַעֲבָדִים וְלִשְׁפָחוֹת וְאֵין קֹנֶה – "The Lord will return you to Egypt in ships, on the road that I told you that you would never see again. There you will offer yourselves for sale to your enemies as slaves and maidservants, but there will be no buyer."[10]

There are Rishonim [11] who felt that Parashat Nitzavim was an exten-

---

9 Leviticus 26:40–42, 44–45.
10 Deuteronomy 28:68.
11 See Tosafot on BT *Megillah* 31b, ד"ה הקללות שבתורת כהנים, in the name of Rav Nissim Gaon. See also *Midrash Tanaaim* on *Devarim Mechilta*: (דברים כט:טו) אתם נצבים היום כלכם וגו' טפכם נשיכם וגו' מפני מה לעברך בברית ה' אלקיך וגו'. איזה הוא הברית שכרת עמהן בערבות מואב שנאמר

sion of the covenant of Arvot Moab. There, the Torah explains the nature of this covenant:

לעברך בברית ה' א-להיך ובאלתו אשר ה' א-להיך כרת עמך היום: למען הקים
אתך היום לו לעם והוא יהיה לך לא-להים כאשר דבר לך וכאשר נשבע לאבתיך
לאברהם ליצחק וליעקב: ולא אתכם לבדכם אנכי כרת את הברית הזאת ואת
האלה הזאת: כי את אשר ישנו פה עמנו עמד היום לפני ה' א-להינו ואת אשר איננו
פה עמנו היום.

For you to pass into the covenant of the Lord your God and into his imprecation that the Lord your God seals with you today. In order to establish you today as a people to him and that he be a God to you as he spoke to you and as he swore to your forefathers, to Abraham, to Isaac and to Jacob. Not with you alone do I seal this covenant and this imprecation but with whomever is here standing with us today before the Lord our God and with whoever is not here with us today.[12]

Here in Nitzavim, we encounter words of consolation:

והיה כי יבאו עליך כל הדברים האלה הברכה והקללה אשר נתתי לפניך והשבת
אל לבבך בכל הגוים אשר הדיחך ה' א-להיך שמה: ושבת עד ה' א-להיך ושמעת
בקלו ככל אשר אנכי מצוך היום אתה ובניך בכל לבבך ובכל נפשך: ושב ה' א-להיך
את שבותך ורחמך ושב וקבצך מכל העמים אשר הפיצך ה' א-להיך שמה: אם
יהיה נדחך בקצה השמים משם יקבצך ה' א-להיך ומשם יקחך: והביאך ה' א-להיך
אל הארץ אשר ירשו אבתיך וירשתה והיטבך והרבך מאבתיך: ומל ה' א-להיך את
לבבך ואת לבב זרעך לאהבה את ה' א-להיך בכל לבבך ובכל נפשך למען חייך.

It shall be when all these things come upon you – the blessing and the curse that I have presented before you – then you will take it to your heart among all the nations where the Lord your God has dispersed you; and you will return to the Lord your God and listen to his voice, according to everything that

12 Deuteronomy 29:11–14.

I command you today, you and your children, with all your heart and soul. Then the Lord your God will bring back your captivity and have mercy upon you, and he will gather you in from all the nations to which the Lord your God scattered you. If your dispersed will be at the ends of heaven, from there the Lord your God will gather you in, and from there he will take you. The Lord your God will bring you to the land that your forefathers possessed and you shall possess it; he will treat you well and make you more numerous than your ancestors. The Lord your God will circumcise your heart and the heart of your offspring to love the Lord your God with all your heart, and with all your soul, that you may live.[13]

The Behag (*Baal Halachot Gedolot*) enumerated in his *Sefer ha-Mitzvot* the *berachot* and *kelalot* of Mount Gerizim and Mount Eval as a *mitzvah* for posterity. Rambam critiques this position for he contends that the *mitzvah* was only of provisional duration. In response to this critique, the Rambam notes:

ומנה פרשת ברכות וקללות שהיא קבלה שקבלו אבותינו עליהם ועל זרעם לדורות התורה כולה בפרט וכלל וקבלו אותה באלה ובשבועה.

He (the Behag) counted the Parashah of Berachot and Kelalot, which is a tradition that our forefathers accepted the Torah in its entirety, specifically and generally upon themselves and their descendants and accepted it with an imprecation and an oath.[14]

In other words, this covenant is binding on all future generations. Rashi on the verse הנסתרת לה' א-להינו והנגלת לנו ולבנינו עד עולם לעשות את כל דברי התורה הזאת – "The hidden sins are for the Lord our God, but the revealed sins are for us and our children forever to carry out all the words of this Torah"[15] – makes the following comment:

ואם תאמרו מה בידינו לעשות, אתה מעניש את הרבים על הרהורי היחיד שנאמר,
פן יש בכם איש או אשה או משפחה או שבט וגו', ואחר כך וראו את מכות הארץ
ההיא, והלא אין אדם יודע במטמוניו של חברו.

And if you say, "What can we do? You are punishing the many for the sinful thoughts of the individual, as it says: 'Perhaps there is among you a man or a woman or a family or tribe,' and afterwards it says, 'When they see the plagues of that land [indicating suffering of the multitude],' is it not true that a person does not know the hidden thoughts of his friend?"[16]

Rashi explains, citing the sages,[17] that once we crossed the Jordan, we became *arevim*, guarantors, for each other. Therefore, we are held accountable for the sinful thoughts of another individual.

↝ The Transgression of Korah vs. the Sin of Achan

There is a remarkable proof to this idea. When Korah rebelled, God wanted to destroy all of his followers.[18] Moshe and Aharon pleaded on their behalf, offering the following argument. ויפלו על פניהם ויאמרו אל א-להי הרוחת לכל בשר האיש אחד יחטא ועל כל העדה תקצף – "They fell on their faces and said: God of the spirits of all flesh, shall one man sin and you be angry with the entire assembly?"[19] In other words, should the multitude be responsible for Korah's plots? God accepted this argument. Why? God did so because this event occurred before we crossed the Jordan; the doctrine of *arevut*, of being guarantors for one another, did not

---

15 Deuteronomy 29:28.
16 Rashi on Deuteronomy 29:28.
17 BT *Sanhedrin* 43b.
18 Numbers 16:21.
19 Numbers 16:22.

apply at the time. However, once we crossed the Jordan, this argument became irrelevant.

The principle of *arevut* following the crossing of the Jordan is demonstrated in the story of the trespassing against the consecrated property on the part of *Achan* in the book of Joshua. There, the verse says, וימעלו בני ישראל מעל בחרם – "The Children of Israel trespassed against the consecrated property."[20] Later, when God points a finger, he accuses the entire Jewish people. חטא ישראל וגם עברו את בריתי אשר צויתי אותם וגם לקחו מן ההרם וגם גנבו וגם כחשו וגם שמו בכליהם –"Israel has sinned. They have also violated my covenant that I commanded them. They have also taken from the consecrated property. They have stolen and also denied. They have also placed it in their baggage."[21] The entire community had to bear the responsibility because the doctrine of *arevut* went into effect once the Israelites crossed the Jordan.

שמע ישראל of the Singular and of the Plural

This idea is embedded in the verse in Parashat Ki Tavo: וידבר משה והכהנים הלוים אל כל ישראל לאמר הסכת ושמע ישראל היום הזה נהיית לעם לה' א-להיך – "Moshe, the Kohanim and the Levites spoke to all Israel, saying: Be attentive and hear, O Israel: this day, you have become a people to the Lord your God."[22] This *shema Yisrael* differs from the one that occurs in Parashat Vaethanan, which is addressed to the individual. The one in Parashat Ki Tavo emphasized the idea of *arevut*. The Rambam was asked why the *viddui* is recited in the plural. Why should a member of the congregation confess to sins that he or she did not commit? The Rambam felt that this was founded upon the verse והתודו את עונם ואת עון אבתם – "Then they will confess their sin and the sin of their ances-

---

20 Joshua 7:1.
21 Joshua 7:11.
22 Deuteronomy 27:9.

tors . . ."[23] Why must we include our ancestors' sins? The reason for this is that the doctrine of *arevut* binds us all together as one. הסכת ושמע ישראל היום הזה נהיית לעם לה' א-להיך – "Be attentive and hear, O Israel: this day you have become a nation to the Lord your God."[24] A new covenant had been struck that differed from the initial Decalogue, which had been formulated in the singular. Here, the doctrine of *arevut* had been given, rendering the plural form for *viddui* as the best one possible.

The concepts of *hillul ha-Shem* (desecration of God's name) and *kiddush ha-Shem* (sanctification of God's name) are founded upon the view that the non-Jewish world sees and judges us as a single entity, for good or ill. Among all the anti-Jewish decrees that the Romans issued, they never included the field of private Torah study. They outlawed only public Torah study. If Jews were still able to learn Torah privately, then why did Rabbi Akiva and so many others see fit to give up their lives for the sake of public Torah study? The answer, lies in the doctrine of *arevut*, which mandates that one teach Torah to others even if it became a matter of *yehareg ve-al ya'avor* (be killed rather than violate the commandment). The covenant at Sinai, which was consummated with דם הברית – "the blood of the covenant"[25] – was connected with our acceptance of the *mitzvot* and our willingness to lay down our lives for them if need be. However, in Ki Tavo we were commanded to be prepared to give our lives for the principle of *arevut* – for the sake of public Torah study.

This idea was also present in the sages' interpretation of Deuteronomy 27:9: הסכת ושמע ישראל – כתתו עצמכם על דברי תורה . . . שאין דברי תורה מתקיימין אלא במי שממית עצמו עליה – "Be attentive and hear, O Israel, Cut yourself on the words of Torah . . . Divrei Torah endure only for one who is ready to die for them"[26] – not only for one's own private Torah study but also for the sake of others' learning. We should note another exegetical com-

---

23 Leviticus 26:40.
24 Deuteronomy 27:9.
25 Exodus 24:8.
26 BT *Berachot* 63b.

ment by the sages on the word *hasket*. "Form groups – *kitot* – to engage in the study of Torah."[27] This idea differs from the first *shema Yisrael* of Parashat Vaethanan, which states: "These matters that I command you today shall be upon your heart."[28] This indicates an obligation that devolves upon the individual rather than upon the masses.

We could learn important things from this *parashah*. First, we should not focus only on ourselves when it comes to Torah study. The sages tell us that a prophet who suppresses the prophecy that he is supposed to deliver is liable to the death penalty imposed by heaven.[29] The Rambam, in his *Guide for the Perplexed*,[30] explains as follows. If the prophet had understood and believed the prophecy that he had received, it would be impossible for him not to deliver it, for it is impossible to fill up a cup of water continuously without the water overflowing. This aptly describes the role of the prophet, as Jeremiah states, "I said I would not mention him, nor would I speak in his name any more. His word would be like a burning fire in my heart, stored in my bones, and though I might struggle to contain it, I could not."[31] Similarly, one who learns by himself without feeling the need to transmit his learning to others lacks the capacity of *mesirut nefesh* for the Torah. In effect, this principle is comparable to the *mitzvah* of *tzedakah*, which is intended to help us to grow spiritually. The prohibition of לא תאמץ את לבבך ולא תקפץ את ידך מאחיך האביון – "You shall not harden your heart or close your hand against your destitute brother"[32] applies to the teaching of Torah as well.

The Gemara in Tractate *Makkot*[33] discusses a verse in Jeremiah. The prophet states, חרב אל הבדים ונאלו – "A sword against the sorcerers – let

---

27 BT *Berachot* 63b.
28 Deuteronomy 6:6.
29 Mishnah *Sanhedrin* 11:5.
30 *Guide for the Perplexed*, part 2, chapter 37.
31 Jeremiah 20:9.
32 Deuteronomy 15:7.
33 BT *Makkot* 10a.

them be shown to be fools."[34] The context is the fall of the Babylonian empire. Yet the Gemara extrapolates from there and applies the verse to Torah study. "A sword against the enemies of Torah scholars [euphemistically expressed] who study Torah privately – not only that, but they will also be shown to be fools." What do curses against Babylonia, which is on the verge of destruction in any case, have to do with Torah study? The Babylonian and Egyptian sorcerers practiced idolatry and were versed in the secrets of nature. But they were selfish and unwilling to share that knowledge with the general public. The sages were referring to the sorcerers who hoarded their knowledge so that they could bask in their pride, and who were punished for their arrogance.

If this teaching can apply to idolatry, how much more does it apply to the study of Torah, which is the authentic divine truth. We are commanded to spread it. Furthermore, Torah scholars should not fear that they will lose their status to their students, who may surpass them. This is a narrow-minded and self-centered stance, for the Torah is not an exclusive treasure reserved for individuals. Without collegial involvement or students to whom they impart the Torah and its secrets, no Torah scholar will succeed in his learning – as is demonstrated by the well-known Gemara in Tractate *Makkot*: מתלמידי יותר מכולן – "From my students I have learned more than anyone else."[35] *Arevut* is therefore the most important principle in Parashat Ki Tavo and the covenant of Arvot Moab.

----

34 Jeremiah 50:36.
35 BT *Makkot* 10a.

❧ נצבים ❧

Nitzavim: Two Levels of Mehilah

THERE IS A dispute among those *rishonim* who compiled lists of the *taryag* (613) *mitzvot* regarding the source of the mitzvah of *teshuvah*. The סמ"ק derives the *mitzvah* from the statement in Parashat Nitzavim,

ושבת עד ה' א־להיך – "You shall return to the Lord your God."[1] Other *rishonim* understand this verse as a promise about the future rather than a command.[2] Regardless of whether the verse is a commandment or a promise, the idea of *teshuvah* permeates Parashat Nitzavim.

The *Mishnah* at the end of Tractate *Yoma*[3] says that Yom Kippur atones only for transgressions between man and God. If a person sins against his friend, Yom Kippur does not atone. Rather, he must make amends to the one whom he wronged. Rav Elazar Ben Azarya in the *Mishnah* exegetically derived this from the verse כי ביום הזה יכפר עליכם לטהר אתכם מכל חטאתיכם לפני ה' תטהרו – "On this day he shall provide atonement for you to cleanse you; of all your sins before the Lord shall you be cleansed."[4] The verse, as he reads it, indicates that Yom Kippur provides cleansing

---

1 Deuteronomy 30:2.
2 See Ramban on Deuteronomy 30:2.
3 BT *Yoma* 85b.
4 Leviticus 16:30.

only for sins before the Lord, meaning between human beings and God. On the other hand, Rabbi Akiva in the *Mishnah* interprets a verse in Ezekiel[5] as telling us that God will cleanse us of all of our sins, including those that take place within human relationships.

The *Mishnah* at the end of *perek ha-hovel* in Tractate *Bava Kamma*[6] tells us that a person who strikes someone and pays off his obligation for all five categories of payment[7] remains unforgiven until he asks for pardon. The *Mishnah* adduces a proof from Avimelech, who was not pardoned for having taken Sarah to his palace until he asked Abraham to pardon him and pray for him. We may ask why there is a need for two seemingly duplicate *mishnayot*, one that speaks of the need for appeasement (*Yoma*) and one that mentions the need for pardon (*Bava Kamma*). After all, the ideas that they express are identical.

The author of the *Sefer Havot Yair* suggests a novel interpretation. The *Mishnah* in *Bava Kamma* speaks of the obligation to ask pardon for a transgression between human beings. The *Mishnah* in *Yoma* tells us that if one does not appease the aggrieved party, then Yom Kippur does not atone for even transgressions between human beings and God. The lack of appeasement between the perpetrator and the one wronged prevents the former from receiving atonement in both situations.

In two different places, the Rambam cites the *Mishnah* both of Tractate *Yoma* and of *Bava Kama*. In *Hilchot Teshuvah*, the Rambam codifies the *Mishnah* in *Yoma*:

אין התשובה ולא יום הכפורים מכפרין אלא על עבירות שבין אדם למקום כגון מי שאכל דבר אסור או בעל בעילה אסורה וכיוצא בהן, אבל עבירות שבין אדם לחבירו כגון החובל את חבירו או המקלל חבירו או גוזלו וכיוצא בהן אינו נמחל לו לעולם עד שיתן לחבירו מה שהוא חייב לו וירצהו, אע"פ שהחזיר לו ממון שהוא חייב לו צריך לרצותו ולשאול ממנו שימחול לו.

---

5   Ezekiel 36:25.
6   BT *Bava Kamma* 92a.
7   BT *Bava Kamma* 83b.

Neither *teshuvah* nor Yom Kippur atones except for transgressions between man and God – for example, eating forbidden food or engaging in forbidden sexual activity and the like. But transgressions between human beings – for example, one who strikes, curses or steals from his friend – will never be pardoned until he gives his friend that which he is obligated to give and appeases him. Even if he returned the money that he owes him, he must appease him and ask him for forgiveness . . .[8]

In *Hilchot Hovel u-Mazik*, the Rambam codifies the *Mishnah* in *Bava Kamma*.

אינו דומה מזיק חבירו בגופו למזיק ממונו, שהמזיק ממון חבירו כיון ששלם מה שהוא חייב לשלם נתכפר לו אבל חובל בחבירו אע"פ שנתן לו חמשה דברים אין מתכפר לו ואפילו הקריב כל אילי נביות אין מתכפר לו ולא נמחל עונו עד שיבקש מן הנחבל וימחול לו.

One cannot compare one who damages his friend's property to one who harms his person. One who damages his property receives atonement once he pays compensation for the damage. But one who strikes his fellow human being, even if he compensates him with the five payments, does not receive atonement. Even if he brings all the sacrifices in the world, he does not receive atonement, nor is his sin pardoned until he asks for forgiveness from the injured party, and he pardons him.[9]

There are four questions one can pose regarding the Rambam:

1. Why did the Rambam find it necessary to reformulate a *halachah* in *Hilchot Hovel u-Mazik* that he already codified in *Hilchot Teshuvah*?

2. In *Hilchot Hovel u-Mazik*, the Rambam uses the terminology of

---

8   *Mishneh Torah,* Hilchot Teshuvah 2:9.
9   *Mishneh Torah,* Hilchot Hovel u-Mazik 5:9.

the *Mishnah* in *Bava Kama*. His language is terse. He speaks constantly of *mehilah*. In Hilchot Teshuvah, he is much more elaborate. After stating the basic *halachah*, he goes on to explain:

אפילו לא הקניט את חבירו אלא בדברים צריך לפייסו ולפגע בו עד שימחול לו, לא רצה חבירו למחול לו מביא לו שורה של שלשה בני אדם מריעיו ופוגעין בו ומבקשין ממנו, לא נתרצה להן מביא לו שניה ושלישית לא רצה מניחו והולך לו וזה שלא מחל הוא החוטא, ואם היה רבו הולך ובא אפילו אלף פעמים עד שימחול לו.

Even if he annoyed his friend only verbally, he must appease him and entreat him until he forgives him. If his friend does not wish to forgive him, he brings a group of three of his friends who entreat him and ask him. If he is unwilling to respond to their overtures, he brings them a second and a third time. If he is still unwilling, he leaves him, and the aggrieved party that would not grant forgiveness is the transgressor. If it is his teacher, he is obligated to importune him a thousand times until he grants him forgiveness.[10]

The Rambam continues to expound on this law, telling us that one should not be stubborn and should allow himself to be appeased, for that is the Torah's approach, unlike the non-Jewish system, which maintains an eternal grudge.[11] The Rambam concludes the chapter with a fascinating *halachah*:

החוטא לחבירו ומת חבירו קודם שיבקש מחילה מביא עשרה בני אדם ומעמידן על קברו ויאמר בפניהם חטאתי לה׳ א־להי ישראל ולפלוני זה שכך וכך עשיתי לו.

If the aggrieved party died before granting forgiveness, the perpetrator must bring ten people to the grave and say aloud:

---

10 *Mishneh Torah,* Hilchot Teshuvah 2:9.
11 *Mishneh Torah,* Hilchot Teshuvah 2:10.

"I sinned against the Lord, the God of Israel, and against So-
and-so [the aggrieved party] by doing such-and-such to him."[12]

In *Hilchot Teshuvah*, the Rambam employs various terms to describe
the process that the person who committed the verbal offense must
undergo in order to obtain forgiveness. Why is the procedure here more
complex than the one in *Hilchot Hovel u-Mazik*?

3. In *Hilchot Hovel u-Mazik*, the Rambam implies that if the injured
party did not pardon the offender, then even if the latter were to offer all
the sacrifices in the world, he would never attain forgiveness. In *Hilchot
Teshuvah*, the Rambam said that if the offender takes three friends with
him and asks for pardon three times and the wronged party still refuses,
he is off the hook, so to speak. Why is there a difference between the two
sets of *halachot*?

4. Why only in *Hilchot Teshuvah* does the *Rambam* discuss the
importance of the offender seeking out ten people and bringing them to
the grave of the aggrieved party if he is deceased?

The Maharshal notes that the declaration before the deceased begins
with the statement, "I transgressed against God[13] and against So-and-so."
Why begin by mentioning a sin against God? Again, the order almost
suggests the position of the Havot Yair that a sin against one's fellow
human being affects not only one's relationship with that particular
person but also – and primarily – one's relationship with God.

✺ Pardon vs. Reconciliation and Appeasement

In order to resolve these questions, we need to distinguish semantically,
and thereby conceptually, between the two *mishnayot* and between
Hilchot Teshuvah and *Hilchot Hovel u-Mazik*. The term *mehilah* – pardon – is a formal, legal term that relates to the waiving of a debt. This

---

12 *Mishneh Torah*, Hilchot Teshuvah 2:11.
13 Maharshal, *Yam shel Shlomo*, Bava Kamma 8:49.

idea occurs many times in the writings of the sages. Two examples are the phrase *mehilat hov* (waiving a debt) and the following principle: המוכר שטר חוב לחברו וחזר ומחלו מחול – "If one sells a promissory note to his fellow man and then waives the debt, the debt is indeed forgiven."[14] The term *mehilah* also refers to *mehilat avonot* (pardon of transgressions), as occurs in Tractate *Shabbat*: שמחל לו הקב"ה על אותו עון – "who forgave him [King David] for that sin."[15]

Unlike *mehilah, piyus* or *ritzui* – appeasing the injured party – requires psychological preparation. One must first devise a strategy and look for an opportune moment. Doing so requires a thorough, painstaking endeavor. The sages speak of *hagasha la-piyus* as requiring a great amount of psychic energy. This is because *piyus* involves not only the *mefayes* (the one who must appease) but also the *mitpayes* (the one to be appeased). The Gemara in Tractate *Niddah* speaks of *mekabel piyusin* (one who receives appeasement).[16] *Piyus* is a deeper overture, fraught with tension and anguish.

Ritzui, too, is no mere gesture but an act of propitiation that requires profound prayer and comes from the heart.[17] It involves reconciliation, rapproachment and intimacy. *Ritzui* and *piyus* can bring about a metamorphosis in a relationship that has gone awry, transforming an enemy into a friend.

‎ﬗ Mundane vs. Metaphysical Reparation

In *Hilchot Hovel u-Mazik*, the Rambam focuses on the act of injuring someone and the need to rectify the situation. Not only must the offender provide compensation for financial loss, but must also assuage his fellow man's emotional hurt via the medium of *mehilah*. The

---

14 BT *Bava Batra* 147b.
15 BT *Shabbat* 30a.
16 BT *Niddah* 31b.
17 See Targum Onkelos and Ramban on Genesis 33:10.

Rambam codifies that one cannot obtain full atonement until he pays compensation and asks for *mehilah*. Here, the Rambam is quite clear that regarding a sin between human beings, *mehilah* is indispensable for the atonement.

In the first two chapters of *Hilchot Teshuvah*, the Rambam focuses not on the injury and need for restitution, but rather on the *mitzvah* of *teshuvah*. Here, what must be rectified is the relationship between the human being and God, which has been damaged by the sin of one human being against another. From this perspective, the Rambam tells us that although a pro forma act of *mehilah* may win atonement, it is not enough for *teshuvah*. Here, we require that the guilty party seek out the injured party with words of *piyus* and *ritzui;* that he entreat him to once again become a friend. If necessary, he must even bring a group of friends with him. The sages surely designed this cathartic act of *ritzui* and *piyus* to purge the individual guilty of verbal assault.

The conclusion of the foregoing analysis is that there are two different concepts that the Rambam chose to include under two different headings – one in the category of *Hoshen Mishpat*, of torts and damages, while the other is part of *Hilchot Teshuvah*. One is a formal legal procedure that is necessary for atonement, while the other is a profound emotional process of personal reconstruction of one's character and transforming a foe into a friend.

✺ Piyus and Ritzui on Yom Kippur Eve

The Rav noted another intriguing phenomenon. The Gemara in *Yoma*[18] relates several anecdotes about *ritzui* and *piyus* that took place on the eve of Yom Kippur. The concept of *mehilah* is not limited in terms of time, but can and should take place any time that a grievance exists. Yet the more profound concept of appeasement seems to have particular

---

18 BT *Yoma* 87a–87b.

relevance on Erev Yom ha-Kippurim. The author of the *Shulhan Aruch*, Rav Yosef Karo, gives Section 606 of *Orah Hayyim* the following title: "That a person should appease his friend on erev Yom Kippur." Why does the obligation of *piyus* come so much into focus on erev Yom ha-Kippurim?

✣ Achieving the Goal of Kapparat ha-Tzibbur

The Rosh in Tractate *Yoma* writes:

וישים אדם אל לבו ערב יום הכפורים לפייס כל אדם שנוטר לו איבה... כדי שיהא
לב כל ישראל שלם עם חברו כדאיתא בפרקי דרבי אליעזר. ראה סמאל שלא
מצא חטא בישראל ביום הכפורים ואמר רבון העולם יש לך עם אחד כמלאכי
השרת... מה מלאכי השרת שימת שלום ביניהם אף ישראל ביום הכפורים כן.

On erev Yom ha-Kippurim, a person should make an effort to appease every person who bears a grudge against him ... so that the heart of every Jew shall be at peace with his friend, as it says in *Pirkei de-Rabbi Eliezer*:[19] "Samael, seeing that the Jewish people were free of sin on Yom ha-Kippurim, said: 'Master of the World, there is one nation that is likened to the ministering angels ... Just as angels live in peace and harmony, the Jewish people also live in peace and harmony on Yom ha-Kippurim.'"[20]

There are two kinds of *kapparah*: *kapparat ha-yahid* (individual atonement) and *kapparat ha-tzibbur* (communal atonement). A community is more than a collection of individuals. It is a single entity united in the love and friendship among the many people who comprise it. The Rosh indicates that we are striving for *kapparat ha-tzibbur* on Yom Kippur. This can occur only if each one of us is willing to

---

19 See Pirkei de-Rabbi Eliezer 46.
20 Rosh on BT *Yoma* 8:24.

overlook our petty grievances and quarrels and find in our hearts the ability to forgive. *Mehilah* can be accomplished all year, but *piyus* and *ritzui* are intended to reunite the Jewish people into a single unit so that they may achieve the *kapparat ha-tzibbur* that is necessary on erev Yom Kippur. It seeks more than forgiveness for a particular transgression, but to repair a fractured relationship and to transform an enemy into a friend.

The words of the *piyyut* following the *Avodah* from the Yom Kippur liturgy, which describes Yom Kippur as "A day of implanting love and friendship, a day of forsaking jealousy and competition" are especially apt. This ambience is a function of the *piyus* and *ritzui* of erev Yom Kippur and one must use every possible method, including the presence of close friends, to achieve this *kapparat ha-tzibbur*.

In his commentary to *Mishnayot*, the Rambam speaks of *tzom Kippur*.[21] Why is Yom Kippur referred to as a *tzom* when all other fast days are called *taanit*? The word *tzom* is related to the verse in *Shir ha-Shirim*: הנך יפה רעיתי הנך יפה עיניך יונים מבעד לצמתך – "Behold, you are beautiful, my beloved. Behold, you are beautiful; your eyes are dovelike behind your braids."[22] When individual strands of hair are gathered together and plaited into a single entity, the result is a braid.

The Gemara in Tractate *Keritut* states: כל תענית שאין בה מפושעי ישראל אינה תענית – "any fast day that does not include the transgressors of Israel is no legitimate fast day."[23] Therefore, on Kol Nidrei night, we recite, "We sanction holding prayer services together with the transgressors." On Yom Kippur, the entire Jewish community must join together in love and friendship. This will be possible only if, in addition to asking *mehilah* for ourselves, we take part in *piyus* and *ritzui* as well. Therefore, the term *tzom* is appropriate here, for it reflects the effort that we must

---

21 Rambam's commentary on MIshnah Yoma 8:7.
22 Songs of Songs 4:1.
23 BT *Keritut* 6b.

make in order to integrate all the various strands of *Klal Yisrael* and achieve *kapparat ha-tzibbur*.

In short, there are two ways of making up with our neighbor: *mehilah*, which is based on *Hoshen Mishpat*, and *ritzui* and *piyus*, which are based on *Hilchot Teshuvah*, and that they reach their peak during the *teshuvah* process on Yom ha-Kippurim.

‏וילך‏

Vayelech: The Dual Nature of Torah Study

IN PARASHAT VAYELECH, the Torah sets forth the *mitzvah* of *hakhel* as follows:

ויצו משה אותם לאמר מקץ שבע שנים במעד שנת השמטה בחג הסכות: בבוא כל ישראל לראות את פני ה' א־להיך במקום אשר יבחר תקרא את התורה הזאת נגד כל ישראל באזניהם: הקהל את העם האנשים והנשים והטף וגרך אשר בשעריך למען ישמעו ולמען ילמדו ויראו את ה' א־להיכם ושמרו לעשות את כל דברי התורה הזאת: ובניהם אשר לא ידעו ישמעו ולמדו ליראה את ה' א־להיכם כל הימים אשר אתם חיים על האדמה אשר אתם עברים את הירדן שמה לרשתה.

Moshe commanded them saying: At the end of seven years, at the time of the Sabbatical year during the Sukkot festival, when all Israel comes to appear before the Lord your God in the place that he shall choose, you shall read the Torah aloud before all Israel. Gather together the people – the men, the women, and the small children, and your stranger who is in your cities – so that they may hear, and learn and fear the Lord your God, and be careful to perform all the words of this Torah. Their children, who do not know – they shall hear and learn to fear the Lord your God all the days that you live on the land to which you are crossing the Jordan in order to possess it.[1]

Rav Elazar Ben Azarya in Tractate *Hagigah* expounds on the verse about the gathering of men, women and children: אם אנשים באים ללמוד, נשים באות לשמוע, טף למה באין? כדי ליתן שכר למביאיהן – "If the men come to learn and women come to listen, why do the small children come? To give a reward to those who bring them."[2] It is evident that there are two main components of the *mitzvah* of *hakhel*: to learn, which implies understanding, and to hear, even if one does not understand. This duality is also reminiscent of *keriat ha-Torah* and the *mitzvah* of *Talmud Torah*. One kind of *keriah*, which is an aspect of learning Torah, is based on a profound understanding of the text and involves knowledge of the Written and Oral Torah, *midrash, halachot* and *aggadot.* The second kind of *keriah* is the public proclamation of God's word – an independent *mitzvah* whose source is the verse in Parashat Vaethanan:

הקהל לי את העם ואשמעם את דברי אשר ילמדון ליראה אתי כל הימים אשר הם חיים על האדמה ואת בניהם ילמדון.

Gather the people to me and I shall let them hear my words so that they shall learn to fear me all the days that they live on the earth and they shall teach their children.[3]

This *mitzvah* is connected primarily to the Written Law because the Oral Law is more connected to understanding. The *mitzvah* of hearing concerns only the Written Law, which does not necessarily involve understanding. Therefore, the section concerning *hakhel* meshes well with the *mitzvah* of *keriat ha-Torah* because both have the requirement of hearing.

The Rambam's language in *Hilchot Hagigah* reflects this idea as well:

---

1 Deuteronomy 31:10–13.
2 BT *Hagigah* 3a.
3 Deuteronomy 4:10.

וגרים שאינן מכירין חייבין להכין לבם ולהקשיב אזנם לשמוע באימה ויראה וגילה
ברעדה כיום שניתנה בו בסיני.

Proselytes who are not familiar [with the law] are obligated
to prepare their hearts and open their ears to listen with
trepidation, awe, and joy, in trembling, like the day that the
Torah was given on Mount Sinai.[4]

The requirement of hearing that is associated with *hakhel* applies only
to the Written Torah because in the Oral Torah, there is no fulfillment
without comprehension. Proof that comprehension is essential for תורה
שבעל פה (the Oral Law) can be adduced from the Gemara in *Berachot*
that says אגרא דפרקא – רהטא – "The reward for learning is the running."[5]
Rashi explains:

עיקר קבול שכר הבריות הרצים לשמוע דרשה מפי חכם – היא שכר המרוצה,
שהרי רובם אינם מבינים להעמיד גרסא ולומר שמועה מפי רבן לאחר זמן שיקבלו
שכר למוד.

The main reward that people receive for running to hear
the *derashah* from a *hacham* is the reward for running. Most
of them do not have the proper understanding to establish
the authenticity of the text and repeat the lecture in their
teacher's name after some time has passed in order to receive
the reward of learning.[6]

Here, Rashi states that the *mitzvah* of learning the Written Torah
depends not only upon understanding the words at the moment of the
shiur, but remembering and using them afterwards, which presupposes
understanding and comprehension. The distinction between the Written
Law and the Oral Law is further demonstrated by Rashi in Tractate
Berachot that says, תורה] זה מקרא. חומש שמצוה לקרות בתורה: [והמצוה] זו משנה]
שיתעסקו במשנה "[Torah] is *mikra. Humash,* for it is a *mitzvah* to read

---

4 *Mishneh Torah,* Hilchot Hagigah 3:6.
5 BT *Berachot* 6b.
6 Rashi on BT *Berachot* 6b.

from the Torah [and the *mitzvah*] is Mishnah that one should occupy oneself with Mishnah."[7] The Written Torah lends itself to reading, while the Oral Torah demands intellectual involvement and understanding.

The study of the Written Torah contains two levels: reading and understanding. The proof comes from the verse in Vayelech:

ועתה כתבו לכם את השירה הזאת ולמדה את בני ישראל שימה בפיהם למען

תהיה לי השירה הזאת לעד בבני ישראל . . . והיה כי תמצאן אתו רעות רבות

וצרות וענתה השירה הזאת לפניו לעד כי לא תשכח מפי זרעו.

So now, write this song for yourselves and teach it to the Children of Israel. Place it in their mouth so that this song shall be a witness for me against the Children of Israel . . . It shall be that when many evils and distresses come upon them, then this song shall speak up before them as a witness, for it shall not be forgotten from the mouth of their offspring . . .[8]

These verses speak of a double fulfillment of reading the Written Law. The phrase "Place it in their mouth" implies an external reading of the text itself. The phrase "This song shall speak up before them as a witness" connotes teaching it to the Jewish people so that they understand it well. It is impossible to conceive of the *shirah* as a witness if our relationship to it is only a mechanical, rote reading of the text. If we do not understand it properly, how can it serve as a witness? Only profound analysis and comprehension can render the *shirah* an effective witness.

A cursory reading of the text relates only to the Written Law and has nothing to do with the Oral Law at all. However, the *mitzvah* of the *shirah* becoming a witness by means of deep understanding merges the Written Law with the Oral Law. This merging is the ideal situation. However, even a superficial reading can be enough to elevate the soul. Merely reading a sacred text can purify and sanctify one's character and personality.

---

7   Rashi on BT *Berachot* 5a.
8   Deuteronomy 31:19, 21.

462

Haazinu: Sefer Devarim as Mishneh Torah

IN EXPLAINING THE terminology of Sefer Devarim, we should note the Ramban's preamble to Sefer Devarim, in which he writes, "This *sefer*, which is *mishneh Torah*, has known content. Moshe Rabbenu explained most of the *mitzvot* of the Torah that the Israelites required to the generation that entered the Land of Israel."

We encounter the term *mishneh Torah* in the section that discusses the laws concerning a king.

והיה כשבתו על כסא ממלכתו וכתב לו את משנה התורה הזאת על ספר מלפני הכהנים הלוים: והיתה עמו וקרא בו כל ימי חייו.

It shall be that when he sits on the throne of his kingdom, he shall write this *mishneh Torah* [two copies of the Torah] for himself in a book before the Kohanim and the Levites. It shall be with him and he shall read from it all the days of his life . . .[1]

Rashi comments on the verse:

---

1 Deuteronomy 17:18–19.

שתי ספרי תורה. אחת שהיא מונחת בבית גנזיו ואחת שנכנסת ויוצאת עמו. ואונקלוס תרגם פתשגן, פתר משנה לשון שנון ודבור.

Two Torah scrolls: one to be placed in his treasury and one that enters and goes forth with him. Onkelos rendered the word *mishneh* as *patshegen* – account. He interpreted the word *mishneh* as referring to learning and speaking.[2]

Rashi's explanation arises prima facie from the *mitzvah* of writing a Torah scroll, which a king is commanded to do.

כותב ספר תורה לשמו ... אמר [רבה] אף על פי שהניחו לו אבותיו לו אבותיו ספר תורה – מצוה לכתוב משלו, שנאמר ועתה כתבו לכם את השירה ולמדה את בני ישראל שימה בפיהם.

He writes a Torah scroll for its own sake ... Rabba says: Even if the person's forbears left him a Torah scroll, the *mitzvah* is to write his own, as it is written: "So now, write this song for yourselves ..."[3]

The conclusion of the Gemara is that a king is doubly obligated in the *mitzvah* of writing a Torah scroll. He is obligated first as a Jew, as we see from the verse in Parashat Haazinu, ועתה כתבו לכם את השירה הזאת – "So now write this song,"[4] and also as a king, who must write a Torah scroll for its own sake.

The Rambam writes in *Hilchot Melachim*: בעת שישב המלך על כסא מלכותו, כותב לו ספר תורה לעצמו יתר על הספר שהניחו לו אבותיו – "When a king sits on the throne of his kingship he writes a Torah scroll for himself in addition to the one that his forebears left him."[5] In *Hilchot Sefer Torah*, he writes:

---

2 Rashi on Deuteronomy 17:18.
3 BT *Sanhedrin* 21b.
4 Deuteronomy 31:19.
5 *Mishneh Torah,* Hilchot Melachim 3:1.

והמלך מצוה עליו לכתוב ספר תורה אחד לעצמו לשם המלך יתר על ספר שיהיה
לו כשהוא הדיוט, שנאמר והיה כשבתו על כסא ממלכתו וכתב לו וגו׳.

The king is obligated to write a Torah scroll – one for himself, for the sake of the king, in addition to the scroll that he would have as a commoner, as it is written: "It shall be that when he sits on the throne of his kingdom, he shall write for himself . . ."[6]

Based on this *halachah* that devolves on the king, it is readily apparent that Rashi understood the term *mishneh Torah* as meaning two Torah scrolls. However, Rashi himself was quite aware that the sages often used the term *mishneh Torah* to refer to *Sefer Devarim*.

The section in Parashat *Vayelech* that begins ועתה כתבו לכם את השירה הזאת – "So now write this song for yourselves"[7] is perhaps the most distinctive section in the *Humash*. The sages comment on the greatness of this *shirah*, which encompasses the past, present and future, this world and the next.[8] The transmission of *Haazinu* differs from that of all the other sections of the Torah. In those sections, God spoke to Moshe, who conveyed God's message to the Israelites and then wrote it down. Yet regarding *Haazinu*, God instructed Moshe first to write it down to complete the Torah, and then teach it from a written text, similar to the way in which *keriat ha-Torah* is done in our day.

This is explicitly inferred from the text itself:

ועתה כתבו לכם את השירה הזאת ולמדה את בני ישראל שימה בפיהם למען
תהיה לי השירה הזאת לעד בבני ישראל . . . ויכתב משה את השירה הזאת ביום
ההוא וילמדה את בני ישראל . . . ויהי ככלות משה לכתב את דברי התורה הזאת
על ספר עד תמם: ויצו משה את הלוים . . . לקח את ספר התורה הזה . . . הקהילו
אלי את כל זקני שבטיכם ושטריכם ואדברה באזניהם את הדברים האלה . . .

---

6   *Mishneh Torah*, Hilchot Sefer Torah 7:2.
7   Deuteronomy 31:19.
8   See *Sifrei*, Haazinu 333 (cited by Ramban on Deuteronomy 32:40).

וידבר משה באזני כל קהל ישראל את דברי השירה הזאת עד תמם... ויבא משה
וידבר את כל דברי השירה הזאת באזני העם הוא והושע בן נון.

So now write this song for yourselves and teach it to the
Children of Israel, place it in their mouth so that this song shall
be for Me a witness against the Children of Israel ... Moshe
wrote this song on that day and he taught it to the Children
of Israel ... So it was that when Moshe finished writing the
words of this Torah in a book, until their conclusion. Moshe
commanded the Levites ... Take this book of the Torah ...
Gather to me all the elders of your tribes and your officers and
I shall speak these words in their ears .... Moshe spoke the
words of this song into the ears of the entire Congregation of
Israel until their conclusion ... Moshe came and spoke all the
words of this song in the ears of the people, he and Hoshea,
son of Nun.[9]

～ The Mitzvah of Writing a Sefer Torah

The Rambam wrote about the mitzvah incumbent upon each Jew to
write a *sefer Torah*, which is the last mitzvah of the *taryag mitzvot*, as
follows: "It is incumbent upon each Jew to write a *sefer Torah* himself, as
it is written: "So now write this song."[10] The actual *mitzvah* is to write
the *shirah* itself, but since the *shirah* is part of the Torah, which cannot
be divided into segments, we must write the entire *sefer Torah*. Only then
does the *shirah* of *Haazinu* acquire the sanctity of the Written Torah.

In this context, we can understand the question of the *Shaagat Aryeh*
regarding this *mitzvah*.[11] Is the *mitzvah* that every Jew must write the
shirah of Moshe Rabbenu on parchment – but since the Torah cannot

---

9 Deuteronomy 31:19, 22, 24–26, 28, 30 and 32:44.
10 *Mishneh Torah,* Hilchot Sefer Torah 7:1.
11 See Shaagat Aryeh 34.

be written in segments, he must write the entire Torah? Or is the intent of the *mitzvah* that we must write not only this *shirah* but the entire *sefer Torah* without omitting even a single letter? The *Shaagat Aryeh* cites proof for both positions, and Rav Soloveitchik said in either the name of his father or grandfather that both sides of the inquiry are well-founded even though they constitute an oxymoron. In short, the element that precipitates the *mitzvah* is the obligation to write the *shirah*, but the *mitzvah* is accomplished only by writing an entire *sefer Torah*.

In conclusion, one may say that in *mishneh Torah,* we encounter the final speech of Moshe Rabbenu, which God allowed him to change from the oral expression to the written idiom. A paradigm in the reverse direction is the *shirah* recited by Moshe Rabbenu, which was written down at first and spoken only afterwards (see Parashat Vayelech in this volume).

וזאת הברכה

Ve-Zot ha-Berachah: Erusin vs. Nissuin in the Study of Torah

IN THE BEGINNING of Parashat Ve-Zot ha-Berachah, we read:

תורה צוה לנו משה מורשה קהלת יעקב.

The Torah that Moshe commanded us is the heritage of the congregation of Jacob.[1]

The Talmud tells us, אל תקרי מורשה אלא מאורשה – "Do not read '*morasha*' but rather '*me'orasa*'"[2] ("Do not read 'heritage' but rather 'betrothed'"). The intimate connection between a Torah scholar and his learning is compared to a betrothal. The explanation that Rashi and others provide for Proverbs 5:18 is quite different:

יהי מקורך ברוך ושמח מאשת נעוריך. אילת אהבים ויעלת חן...באהבתה תשגה תמיד.

Your source will be blessed and you will rejoice over the wife of your youth. A beloved hind inspiring favor ... you will always be intoxicated with her love.[3]

---

1 Deuteronomy 33:4.
2 BT *Berachot* 57a.
3 Proverbs 5:18–19.

Based on the Gemara in Tractate *Ketubbot*,[4] we see that these verses refer to the profound bonding of Torah scholars with their Torah and its ability to protect them. Here, the scholar's relationship to Torah study is compared not to *erusin* – betrothal – but to *nissuin* – marriage.

Erusin and *nissuin* are two stages in the marriage ceremony. They represent two forms of bonding between a married couple. *Erusin*, which is based on *Hoshen Mishpat*, takes place by means of the legal act of *kinyan* (a legal acquisition). Thus, the connection of *erusin* is begun by a legal act of free will and a decision to enter into this contractual relationship. The legal effect of this process is that the bride becomes forbidden to the entire world and designated solely for her husband. By rabbinic law, she remains forbidden to her husband-to-be, and metaphysically they are still two independent, autonomous beings. Their tie is a formal, external one.

Nissuin, which takes place during the *huppah* ceremony, contains no elements from the *Hoshen Mishpat*. Rather, it is an existential bonding of the man and woman whose lives now intertwine and whose destinies merge. It is the consummation of a *brit* – a metaphysical covenant. Each resonates to the other's heartbeat. Two personalities converge (here the Rav paraphrased Rav Shlomo ibn Gabirol) as each partner sees his or her essence as an integral part of the other. It is fascinating that the sages interpreted the verse כי אם לשארו הקרוב אליו – "to his relative, who is the closest to him of his family"[5] – as referring to his wife.[6]

Although *erusin* establishes a tie between the couple, it does not include the full rights and duties of marriage. The husband-to-be does not yet have the halachic obligation to provide food and clothing for his wife. If her husband-to-be is a kohen, he is not yet obligated to incur *tumah* by caring for her corpse if she should die.[7] In the Rav's Yiddish,

---

4 BT *Ketubbot* 77b.
5 Leviticus 21:2.
6 See Rashi on BT *Bava Metzia* 18a; *Yevamot* 29b, *Sanhedrin* 28b.
7 Rashi on BT *Bava Metzia* 18a.

it is not yet one *shizgal* (destiny), but merely a declaration of intention and impending commitment. A husband-to-be does not go through the process of mourning as set down by *halachah* if his fiancée should die. The connection is not strong enough yet. At this point, the relationship is one of *tenaim* (conditions) and legal exclusivity without the full application of the laws of *baalut* or *ishut*.

The husband's commitments to his wife begin with *nissuin*, the solidification of their relationship. The language of the Torah in Genesis also reflects this change in status.

ויבן ה' א-להים את הצלע אשר לקח מן האדם לאשה ויבאה אל האדם: ויאמר האדם זאת הפעם עצם מעצמי ובשר מבשרי לזאת יקרא אשה כי מאיש לקחה זאת.

The Lord God built the rib that he had taken from the man into a woman, and he brought her to the man. The man said, "This time it is bone of my bones and flesh of my flesh. She shall be called woman, for from man she was taken."[8]

The *Midrash Rabbah* states: הוא תני לה בשם ר' שמעון בן יוחי קישטה ככלה והביאה לו – "He learned in the name of Rav Shimon ben Yohai: He [God] adorned Eve as a bride and brought her to him."[9] Two personalities have merged into one. על כן יעזב איש את אביו ואת אמו ודבק באשתו והיו לבשר אחד – "Therefore, a man shall leave his father and his mother and cleave to his wife and they shall become one flesh."[10] Rashi comments that this oneness is actualized with the birth of a child: הולד נוצר על ידי שניהם, ושם נעשה בשרם אחד – "The child is formed by both the man and the woman, and there in the child, their flesh becomes one."[11] This is a union that unites them forever.

Our connection to the Torah is also of a dual nature. A Jew can merit

---

8 Genesis 2:22–23.
9 Genesis Rabbah 18:1.
10 Genesis 2:24.
11 Rashi on Genesis 2:24.

the acquisition of Torah the way a person acquires property or betroths a woman – by means of money or a deed. He acquires spiritual assets – the knowledge and keen understanding of Torah – through toil in the Talmud and its commentaries. As he acquires knowledge in Torah, the Torah becomes legally his. The Talmud in Tractate *Kiddushin*[12] states: תורה דיליה היא, דכתיב: ובתורתו יהגה יומם ולילה – "The Torah becomes his own, as it is written, 'He meditates upon his Torah day and night.'"[13] Rashi there explains: בתחילה היא נקראת תורת השם ומשלמדה וגרסה היא נקראת תורתו – "At first, it is deemed God's Torah, but when he learns it and formulates it, it is called his Torah."[14] In short, one who is betrothed to the Torah has the ability to rise to heights of Torah scholarship, to write Torah works and to grow from this relationship.

However, there is a level that transcends that of *erusin* with the Torah: the level of *nissuin*. In the relationship of *nissuin*, he absorbs the Torah into his very being and acquires a *neshamah* of Torah from which flows a wellspring of blessing. When the gap between the Torah and a human being vanishes completely, the forty-nine gates of halachic sensitivity open before him. His personality, purified by his study, combines with sanctified inspiration, resulting in logical halachic thinking. A mysterious intuition becomes the source of creativity and halachic productivity. The *ish ha-halachah* who is wedded to the Torah senses halachic ideas. He not only exists inside the framework of the *halachah*, but he also lives and breathes the *halachah* itself. His Torah begins from the wellsprings of his heart and concludes with his mind and intellect.[15]

---

12 BT *Kiddushin* 32b.

13 Psalms 1:2.

14 Rashi on BT *Kiddushin* 32b.

15 See Rav Soloveitchik's eulogy for his uncle, Rav Velvel Soloveitchik zt"l, entitled מה דודך מדוד, in which he expands on the difference between *erusin* and *nissuin*.

❧ Written Torah and Oral Torah

The *erusin* of the Israelites to God occurred at Mount Sinai, when God compelled us to accept the Torah. Immediately after this betrothal, the Israelites committed the sin of the Golden Calf. However, the *nissuin* of the Jewish people is linked inextricably with the Oral Law. While we complete the annual reading cycle of the Written Torah every Simhat Torah, the Oral Torah is a limitless expanse.

Although the Christians got their sense of the importance of the Written Torah from the Jews, the Written Torah is worthless without the Oral Torah. *Le-havdil*, it's like having the Constitution of the United States without the decisions of the Supreme Court. The importance that the Karaites attributed to the Written Torah also came from us – and they are practically extinct. One who is not only betrothed to the Torah but wedded to it is indissolubly bound up with the Oral law. We derive the idea that Sukkot is the Yom Tov of the Oral Law from its details: the identity of the *pri etz hadar* that we are supposed to take in honor of the holiday, the dimensions of the sukkah, and so on. The holiday of Shemini Atzeret symbolizes the *yihud* and total commitment to the ideals of the Oral Law and to the *nissuin* of God and the Jewish people.

Rav Soloveitchik fondly remembered his father and grandfather, who stayed awake the entire night of Yom Kippur and remained in prayer for the entire day, until the end of Neilah. In our day, he said, he was asked by a wealthy Jew in New York whether he could take a sleeping pill on Kol Nidrei night because he suffered from insomnia. The Rav answered that Tisha be-Av is too bitter for sleep and Yom Kippur is too sweet for sleep. This is the way that a Jew should feel when he is not only betrothed to the Torah but bound up with it in marriage, when the *Torah she-bi-chtav* and the *Torah she'beal peh* are indelibly engraved upon his heart.